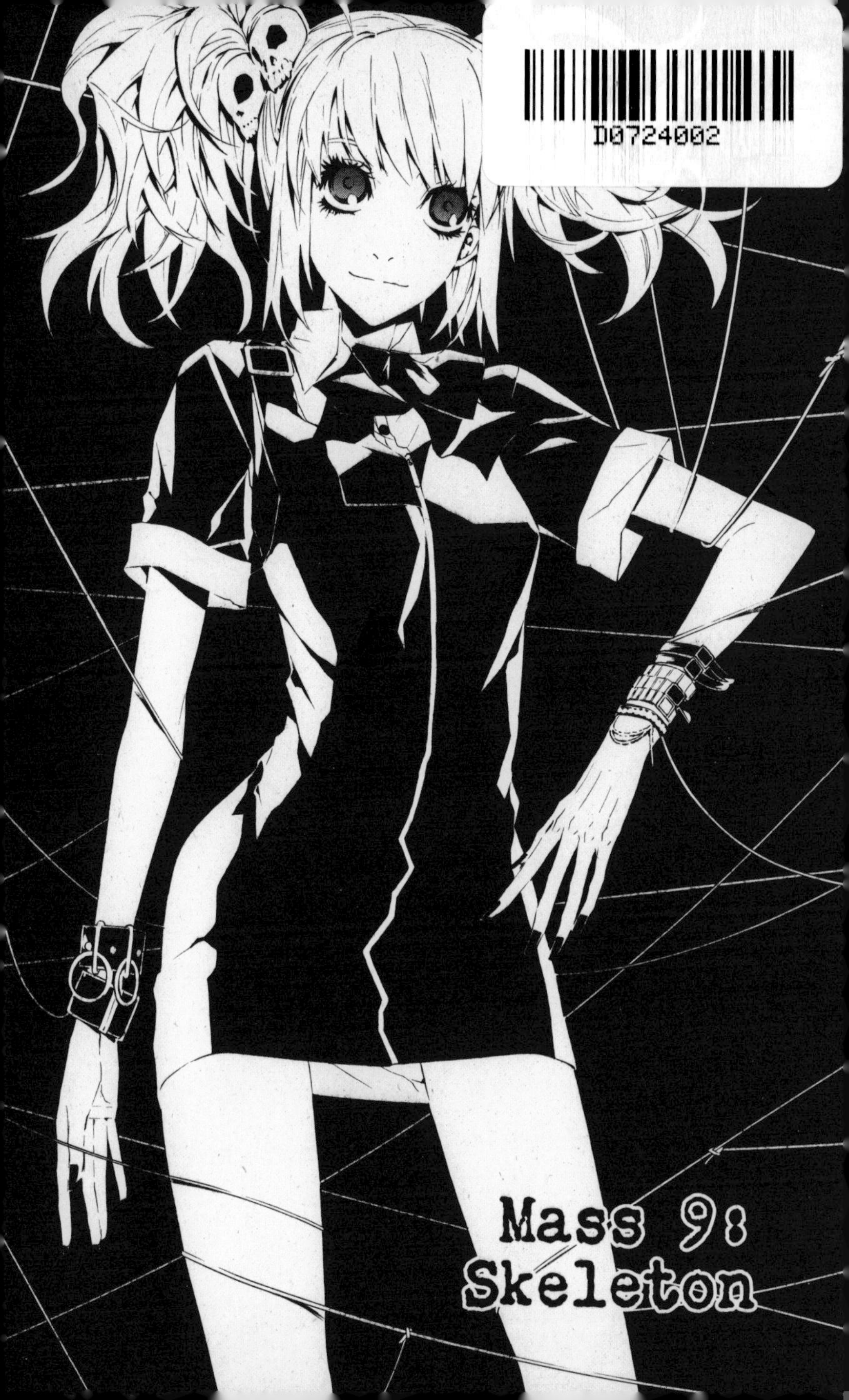
Mass 9:
Skeleton

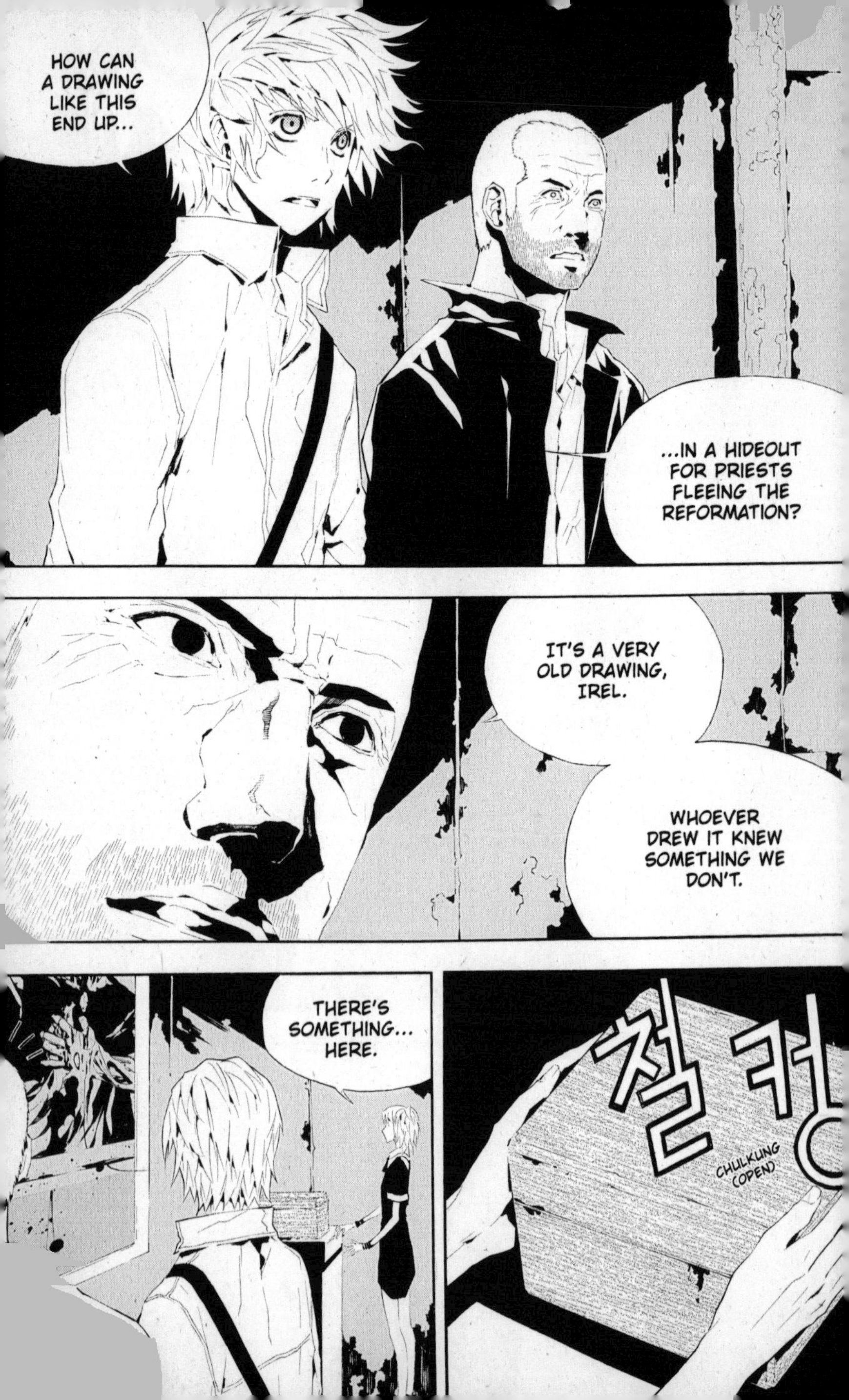
HOW CAN A DRAWING LIKE THIS END UP...
...IN A HIDEOUT FOR PRIESTS FLEEING THE REFORMATION?
IT'S A VERY OLD DRAWING, IREL.
WHOEVER DREW IT KNEW SOMETHING WE DON'T.
THERE'S SOMETHING... HERE.
철컹
CHULKUNG (OPEN)

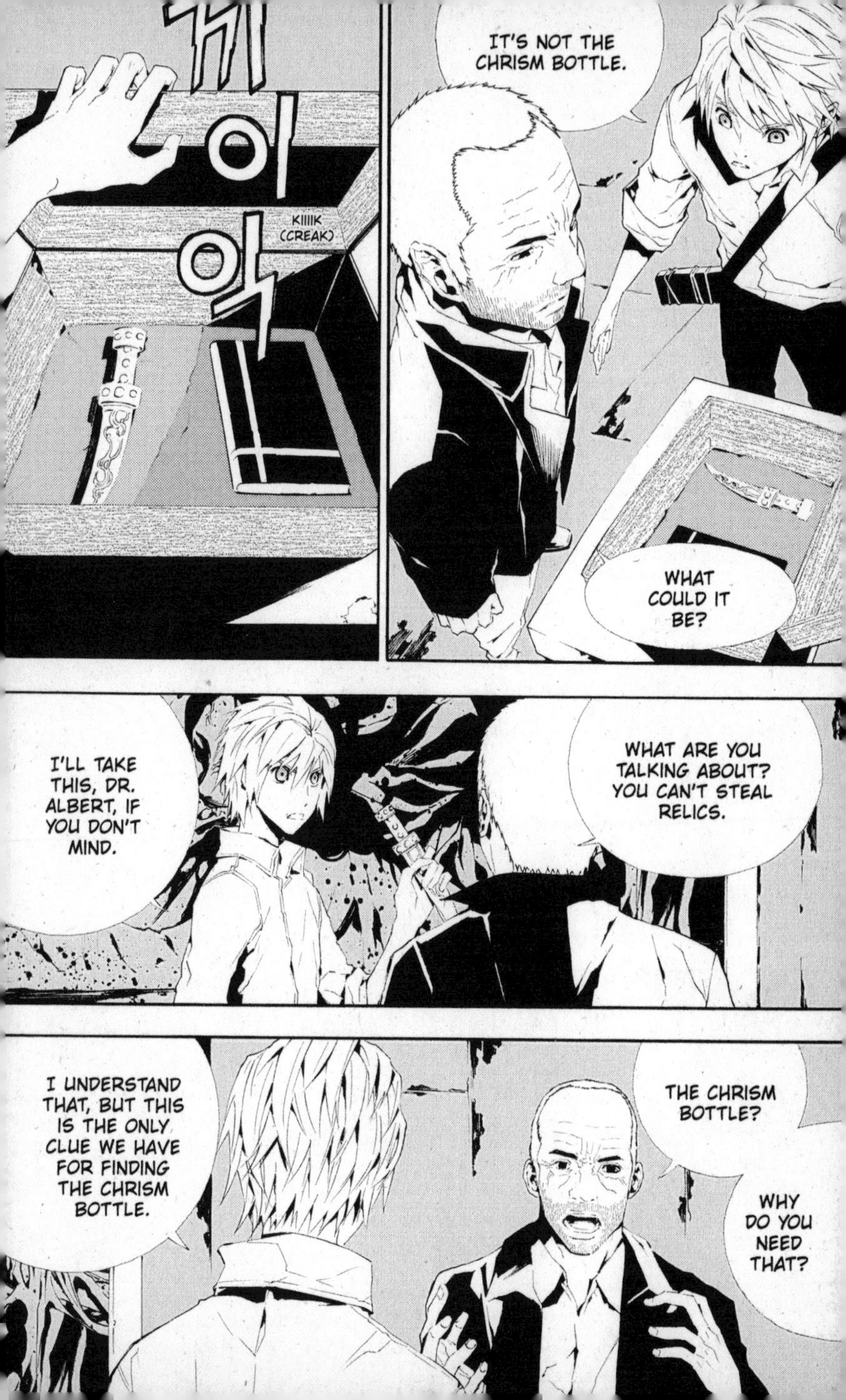
KIIIK (CREAK)
IT'S NOT THE CHRISM BOTTLE.
WHAT COULD IT BE?
I'LL TAKE THIS, DR. ALBERT, IF YOU DON'T MIND.
WHAT ARE YOU TALKING ABOUT? YOU CAN'T STEAL RELICS.
I UNDERSTAND THAT, BUT THIS IS THE ONLY CLUE WE HAVE FOR FINDING THE CHRISM BOTTLE.
THE CHRISM BOTTLE?
WHY DO YOU NEED THAT?

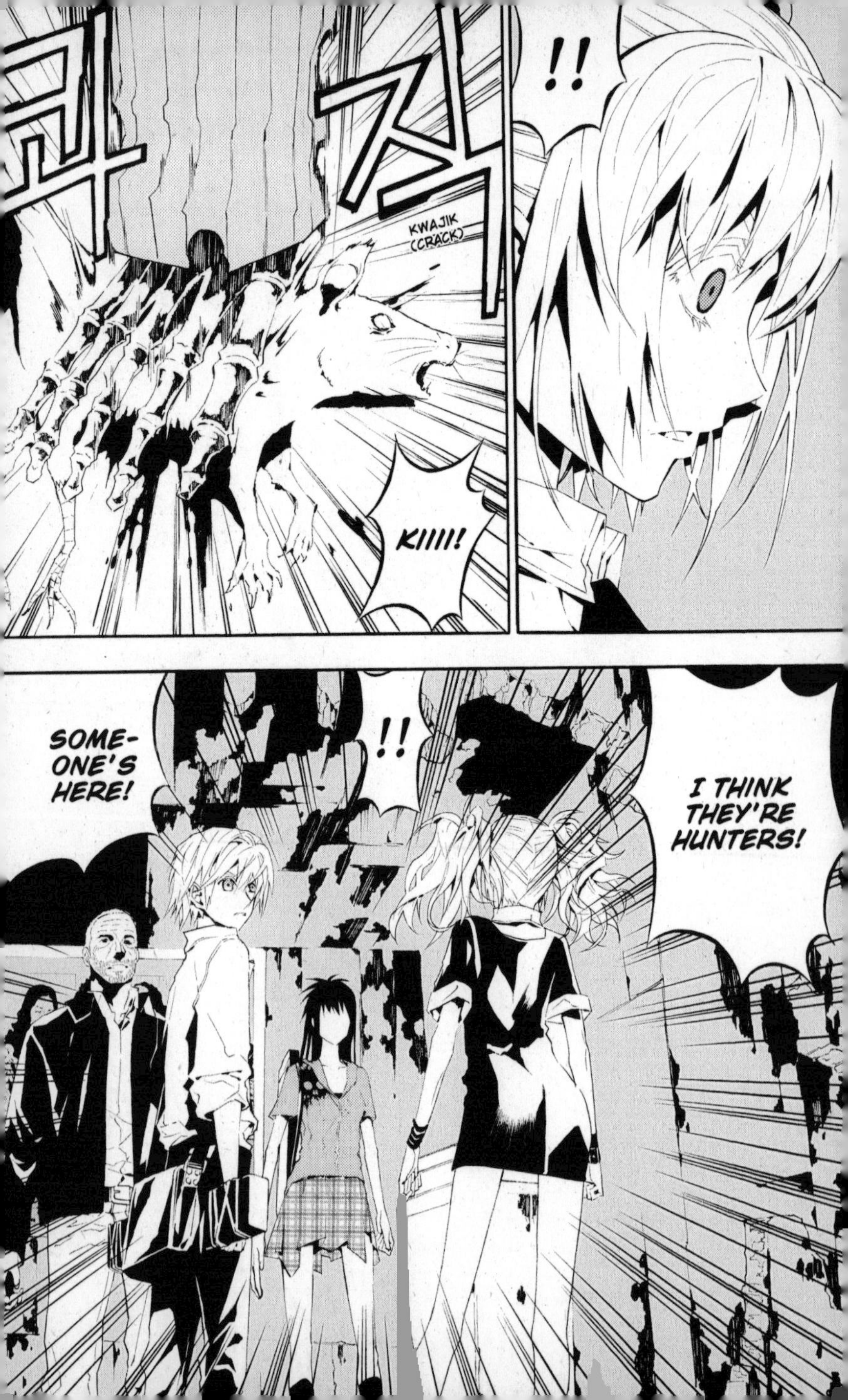

콰직
KWAJIK (CRACK)
KIIII!
!!
SOME-ONE'S HERE!
!!
I THINK THEY'RE HUNTERS!

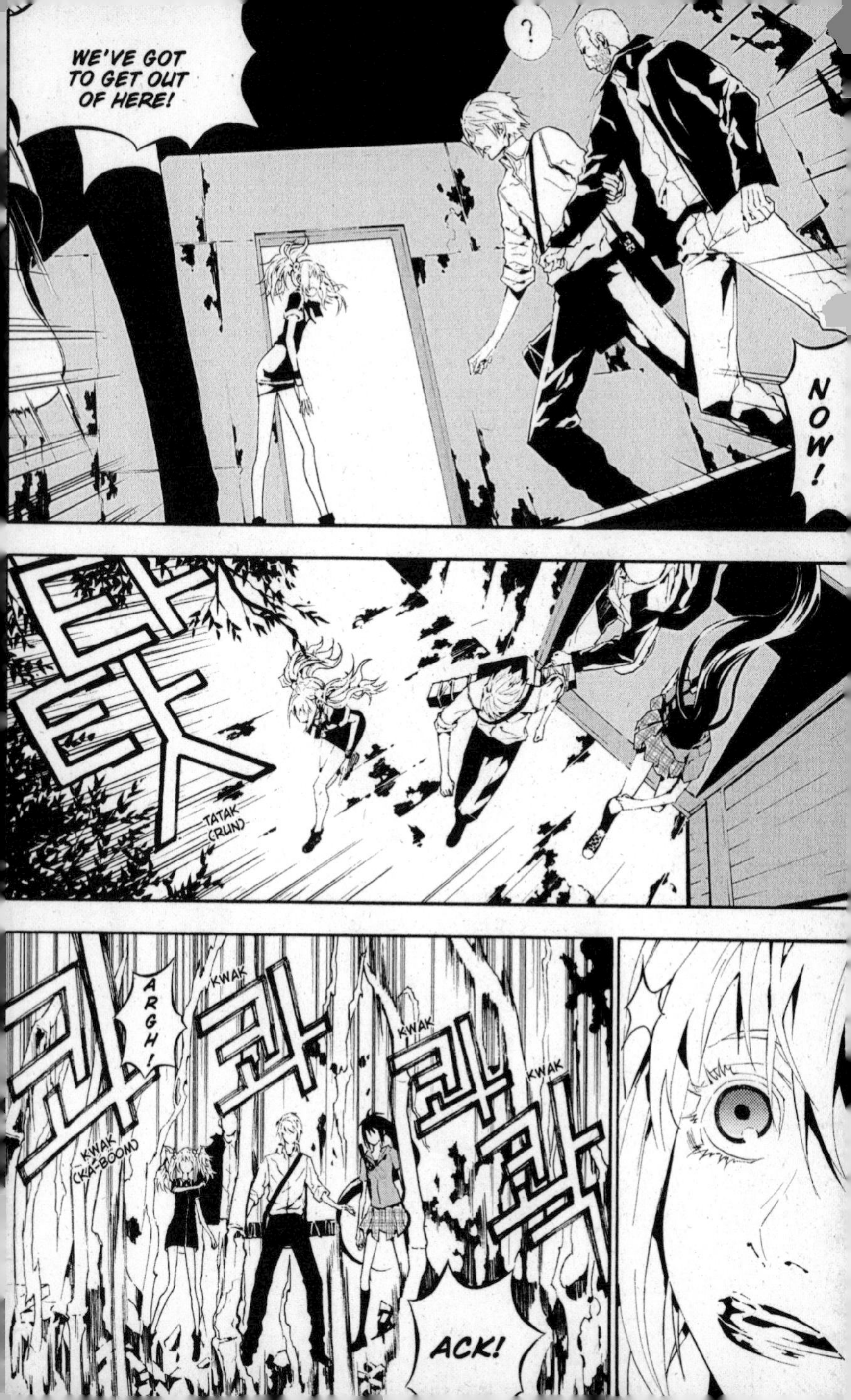
WE'VE GOT TO GET OUT OF HERE!
?
NOW!
TATAK (RUN)
ARGH!
KWAK
KWAK (KA-BOOM)
KWAK
KWAK
ACK!

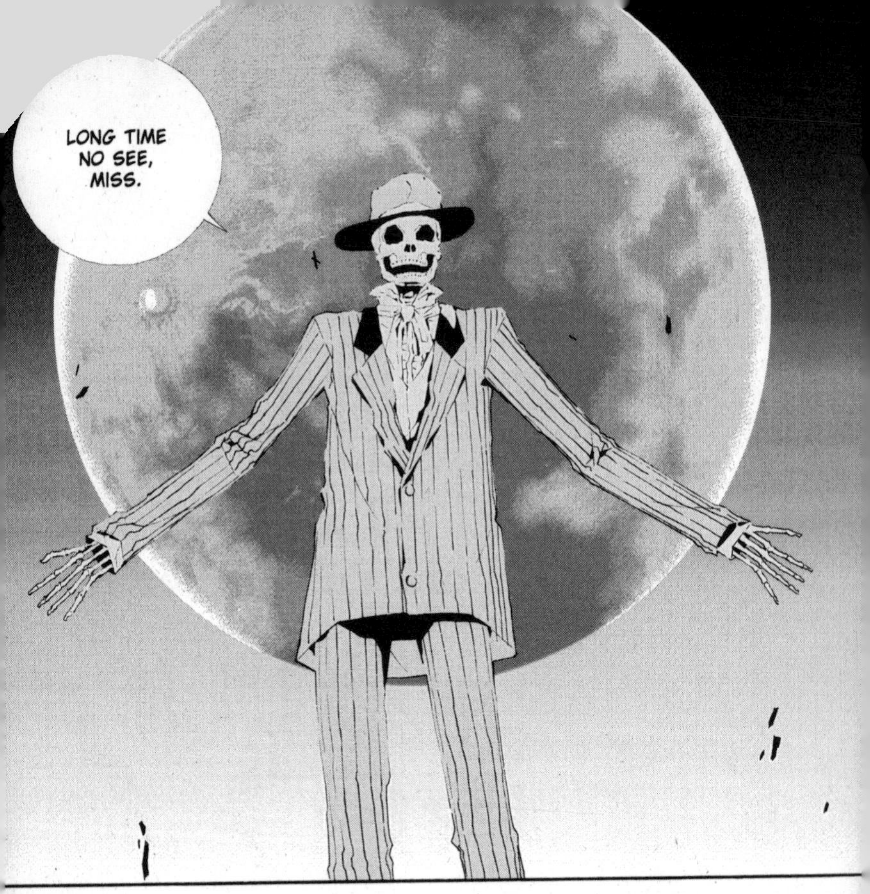
LONG TIME NO SEE, MISS.
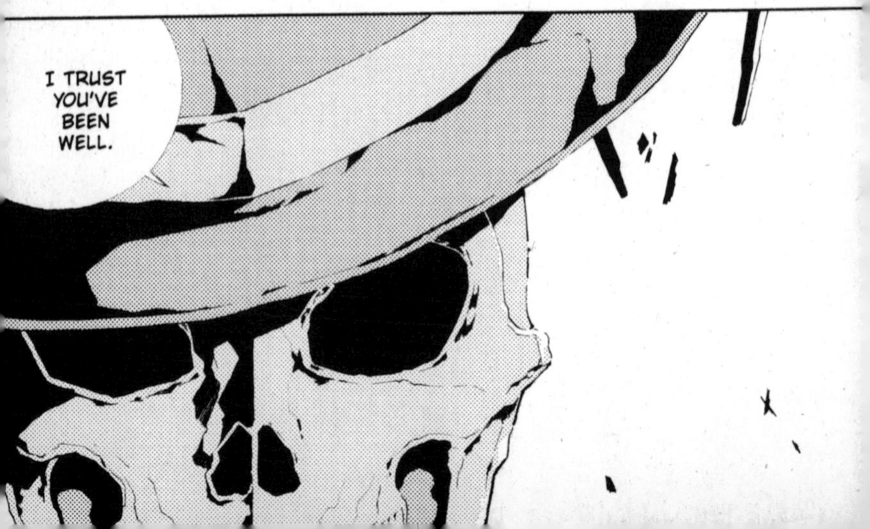
I TRUST YOU'VE BEEN WELL.

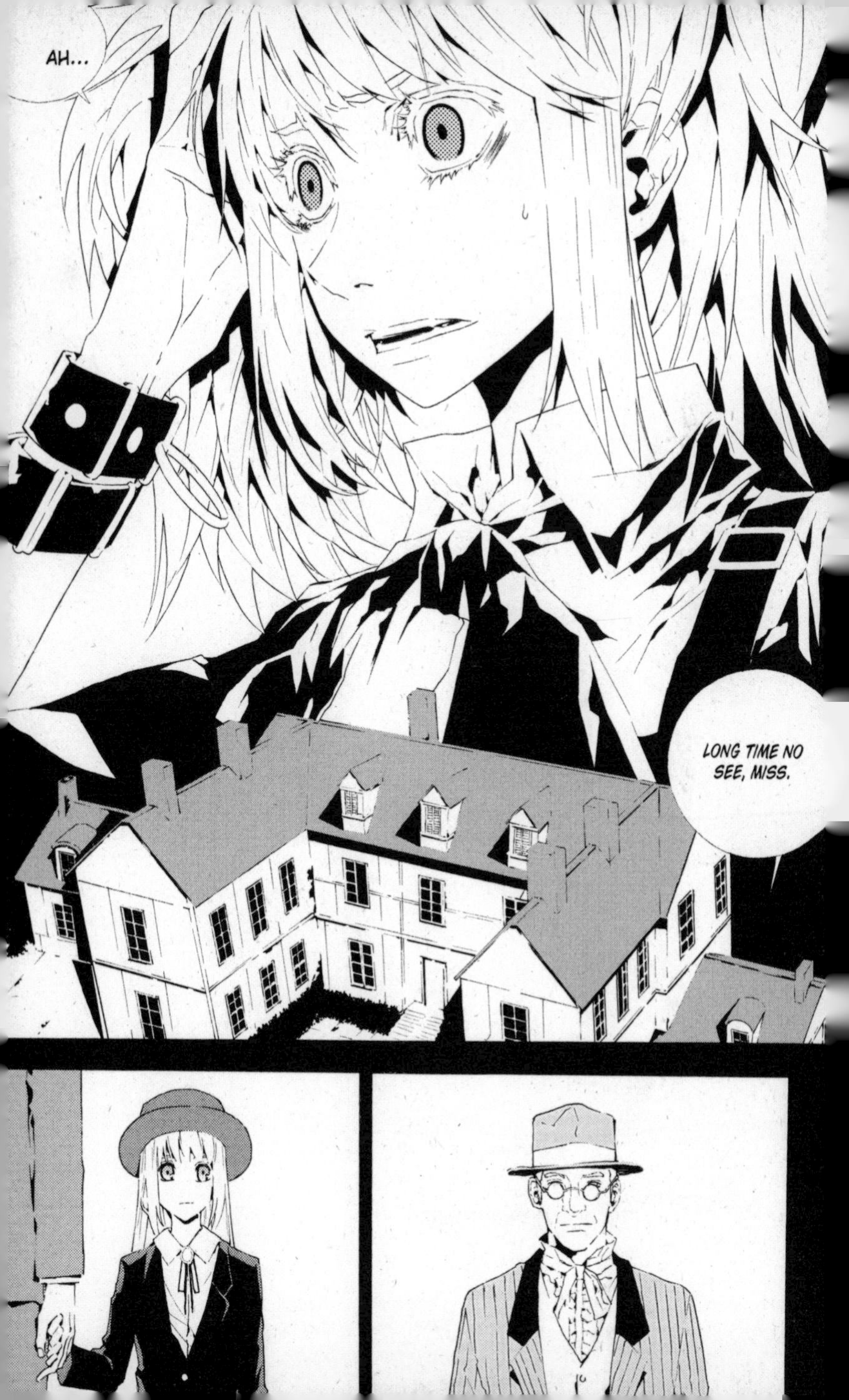
AH...
LONG TIME NO SEE, MISS.

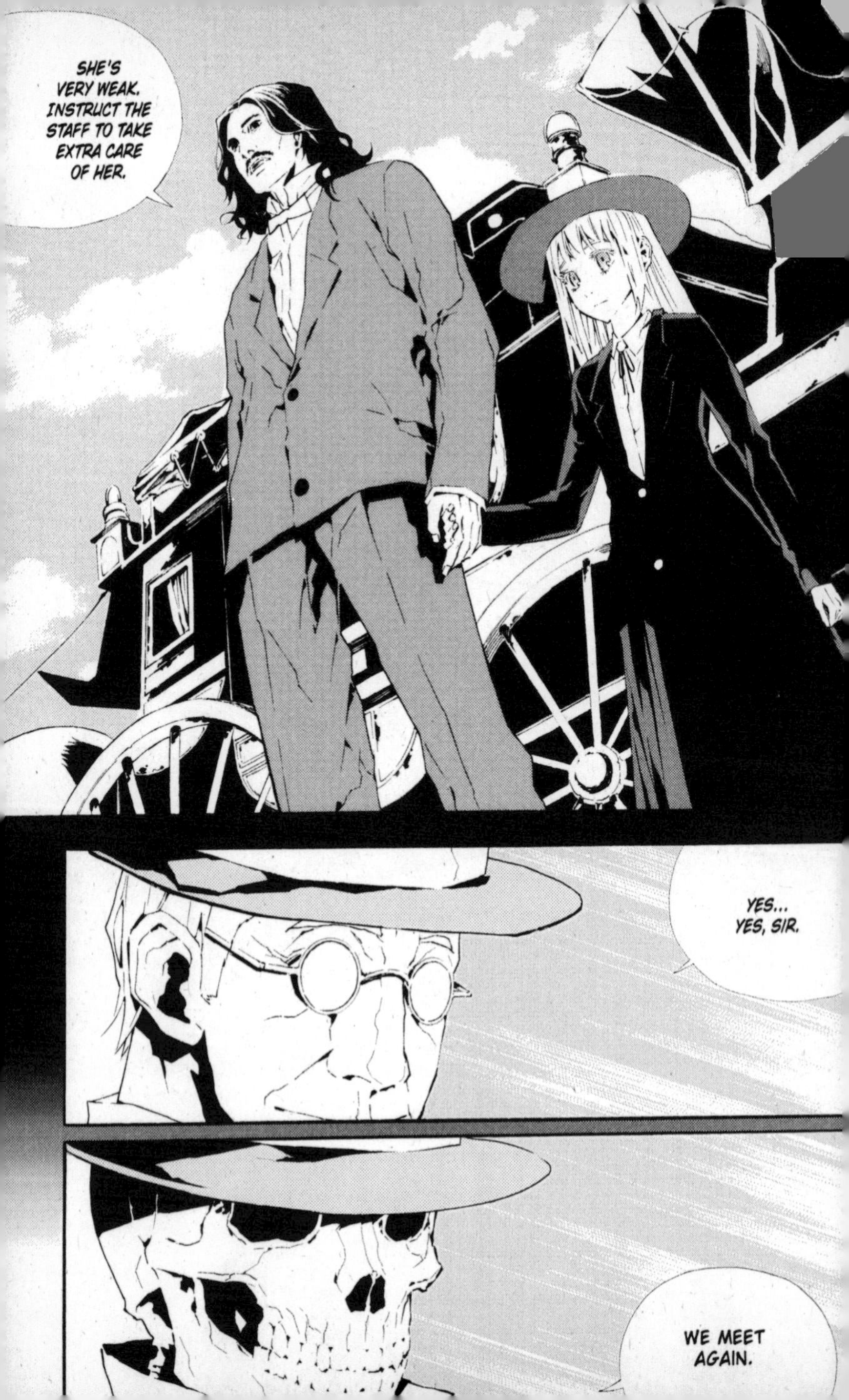
SHE'S VERY WEAK. INSTRUCT THE STAFF TO TAKE EXTRA CARE OF HER.
YES... YES, SIR.
WE MEET AGAIN.

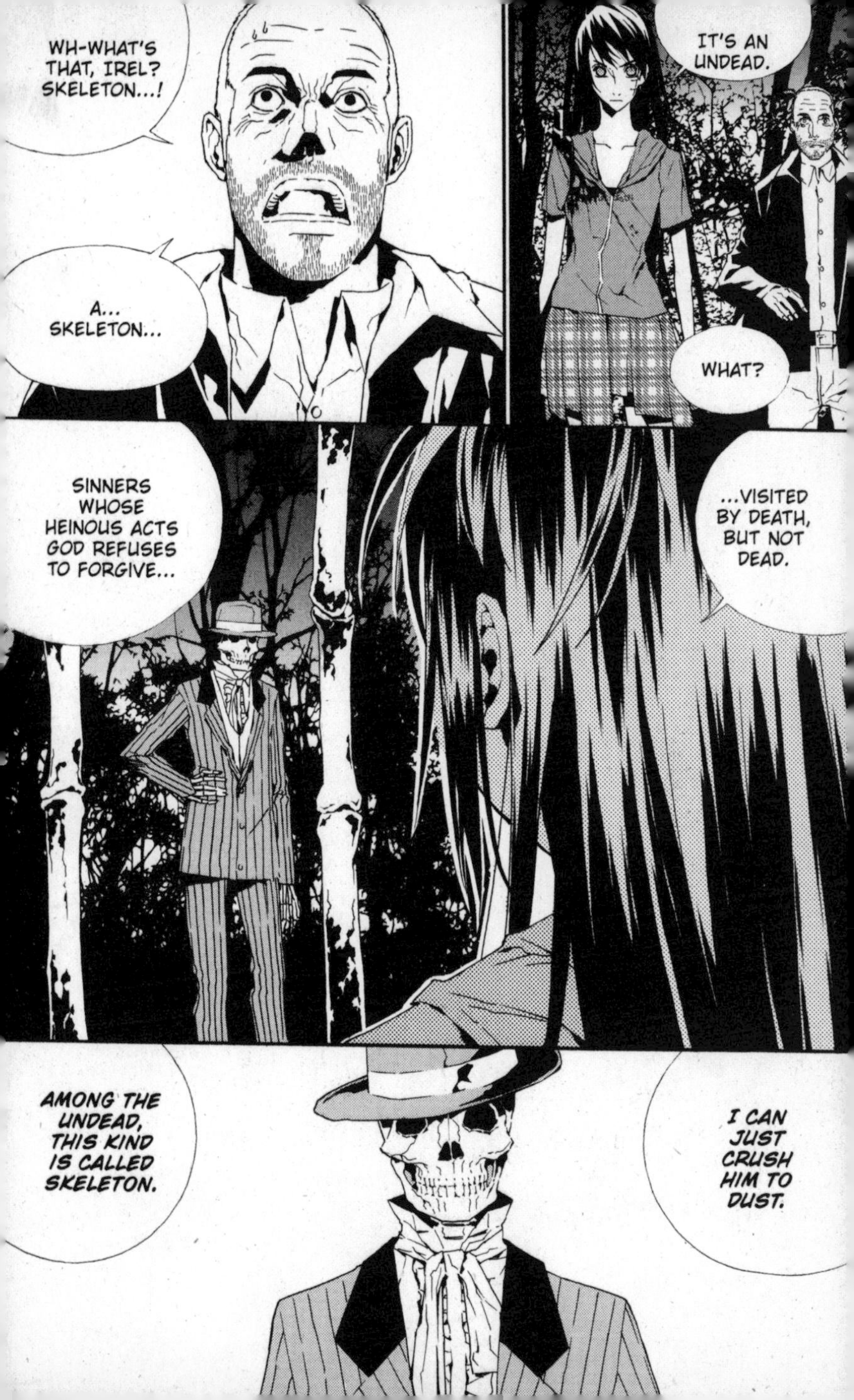
WH-WHAT'S THAT, IREL? SKELETON...!
A... SKELETON...
IT'S AN UNDEAD.
WHAT?
SINNERS WHOSE HEINOUS ACTS GOD REFUSES TO FORGIVE...
...VISITED BY DEATH, BUT NOT DEAD.
AMONG THE UNDEAD, THIS KIND IS CALLED SKELETON.
I CAN JUST CRUSH HIM TO DUST.

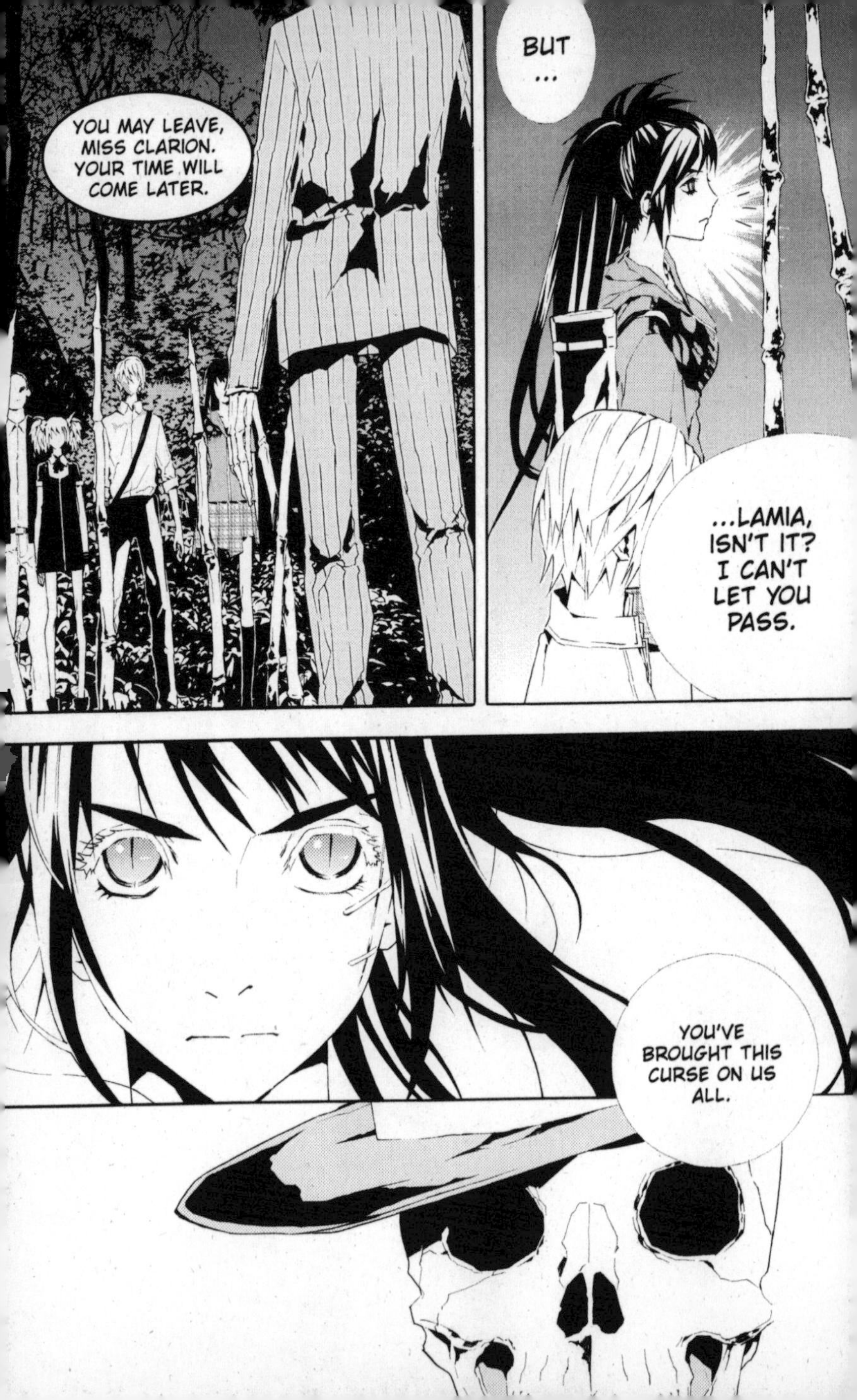
YOU MAY LEAVE, MISS CLARION. YOUR TIME WILL COME LATER.
BUT ...
...LAMIA, ISN'T IT? I CAN'T LET YOU PASS.
YOU'VE BROUGHT THIS CURSE ON US ALL.

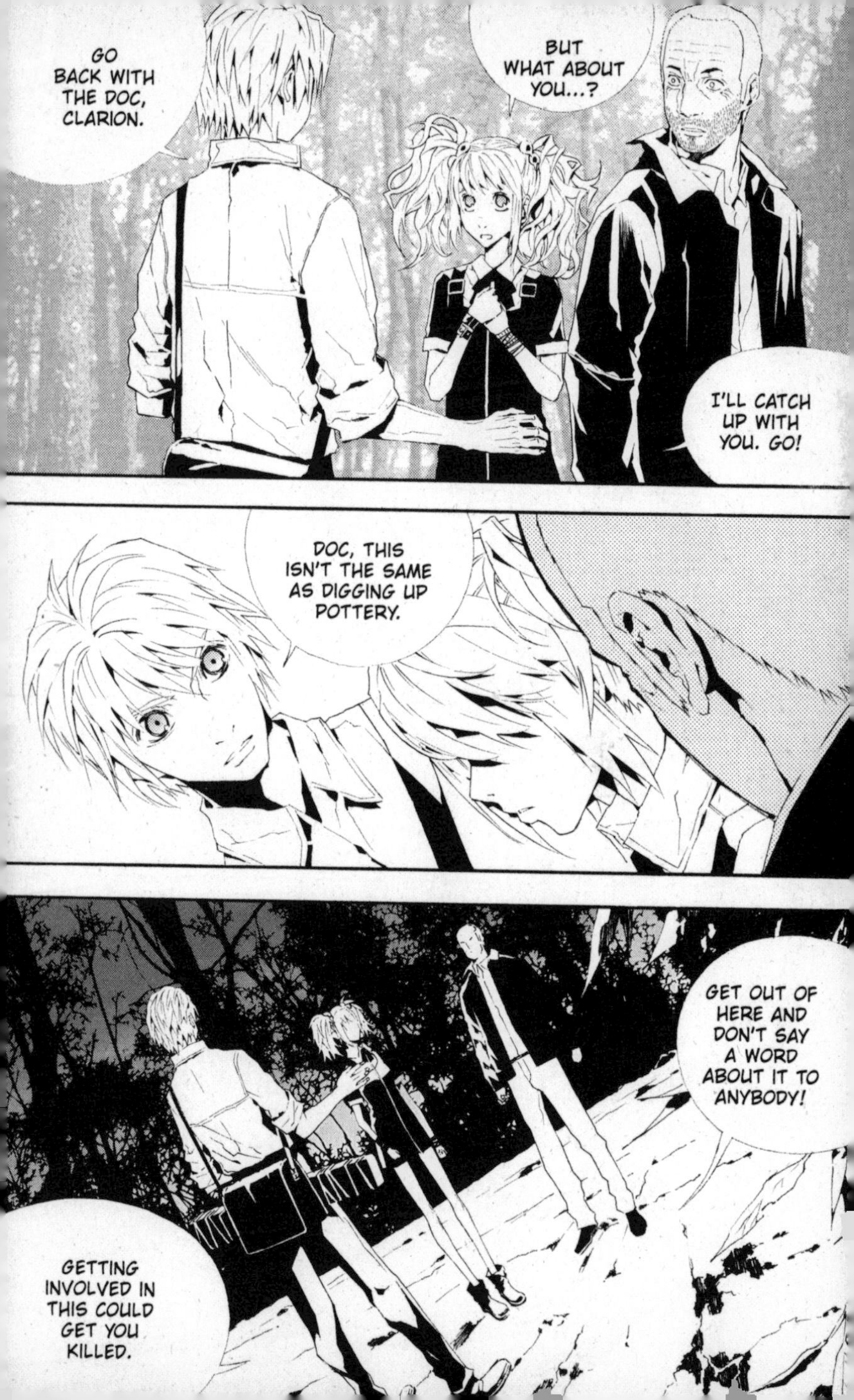
GO BACK WITH THE DOC, CLARION.
BUT WHAT ABOUT YOU...?
I'LL CATCH UP WITH YOU. GO!
DOC, THIS ISN'T THE SAME AS DIGGING UP POTTERY.
GETTING INVOLVED IN THIS COULD GET YOU KILLED.
GET OUT OF HERE AND DON'T SAY A WORD ABOUT IT TO ANYBODY!

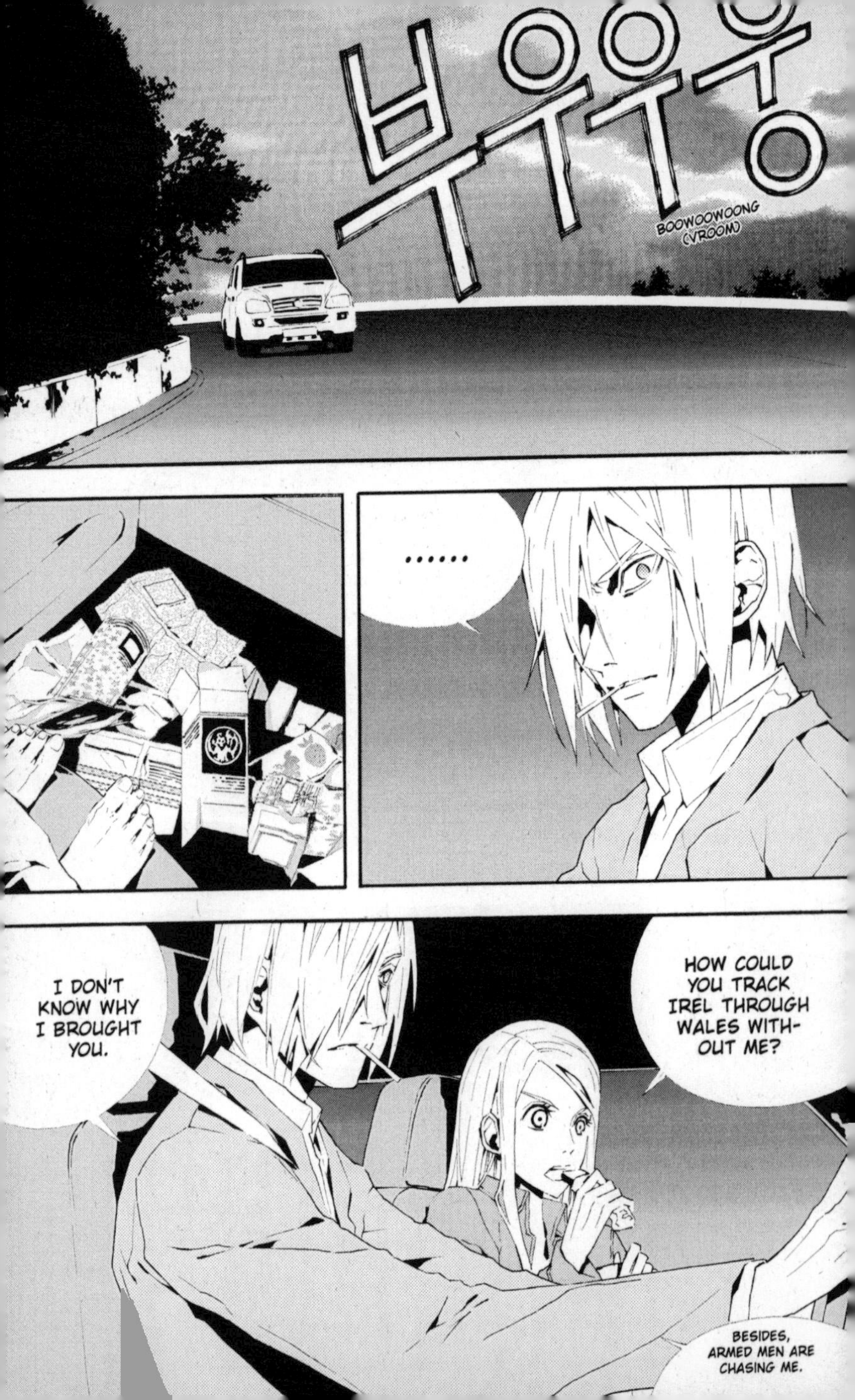
부우우웅
BOOWOOWOONG
(VROOM)
......
I DON'T KNOW WHY I BROUGHT YOU.
HOW COULD YOU TRACK IREL THROUGH WALES WITH-OUT ME?
BESIDES, ARMED MEN ARE CHASING ME.

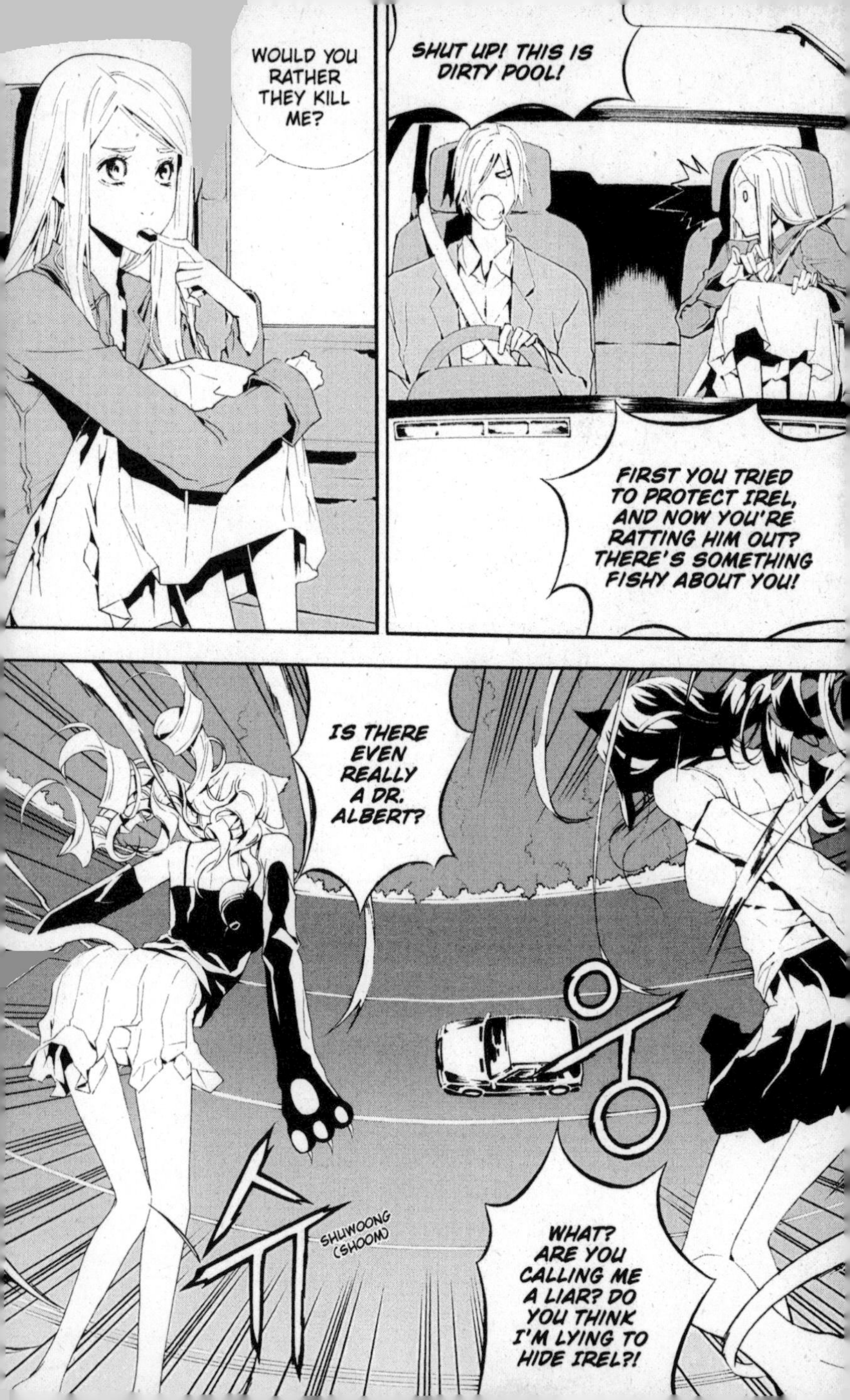
WOULD YOU RATHER THEY KILL ME?
SHUT UP! THIS IS DIRTY POOL!
FIRST YOU TRIED TO PROTECT IREL, AND NOW YOU'RE RATTING HIM OUT? THERE'S SOMETHING FISHY ABOUT YOU!
IS THERE EVEN REALLY A DR. ALBERT?
SHUWOONG (SHOOM)
WHAT? ARE YOU CALLING ME A LIAR? DO YOU THINK I'M LYING TO HIDE IREL?!

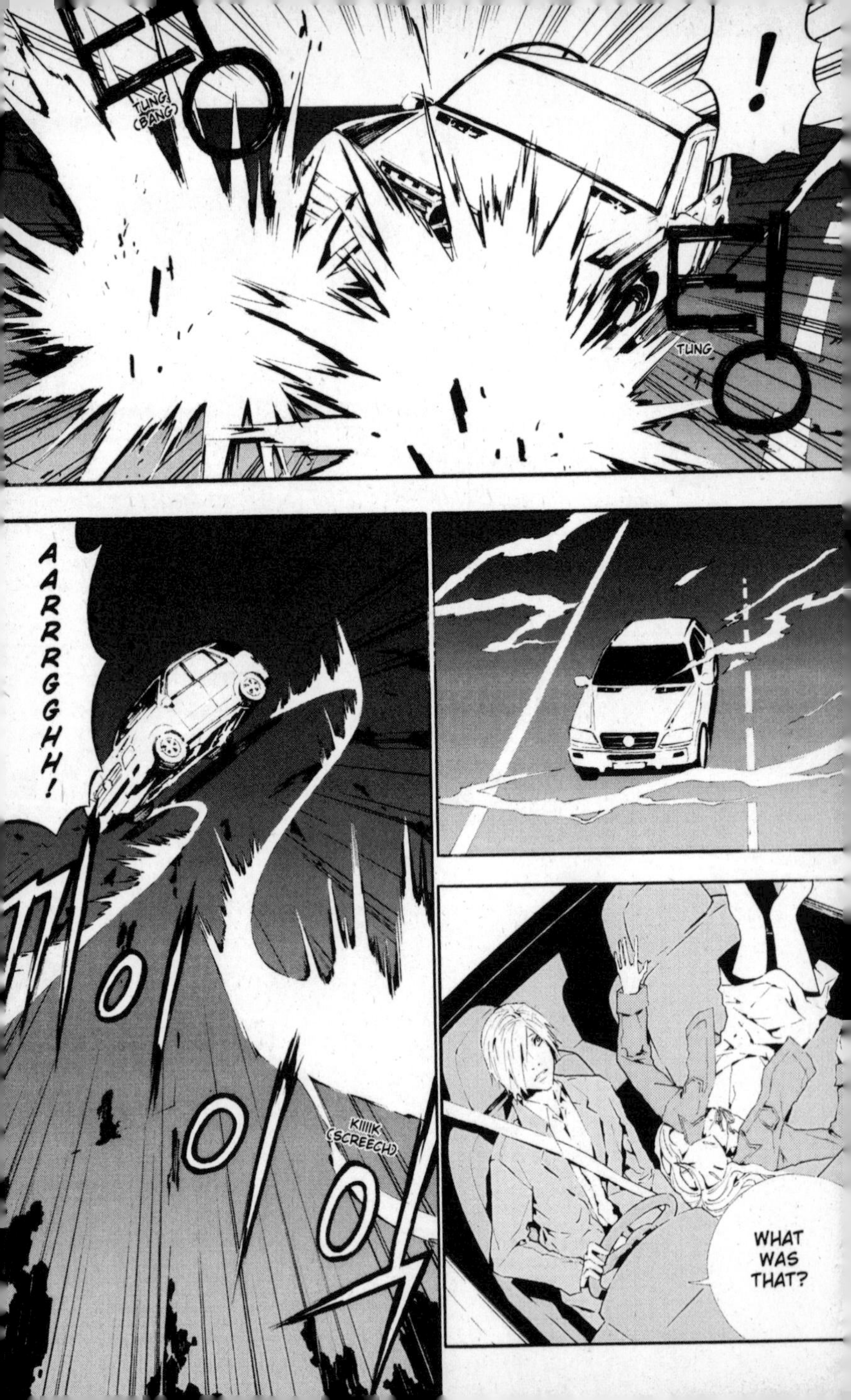
TUNG! (BANG)
!
TUNG
AARRRGGHH!
KIIIIK (SCREECH)
WHAT WAS THAT?

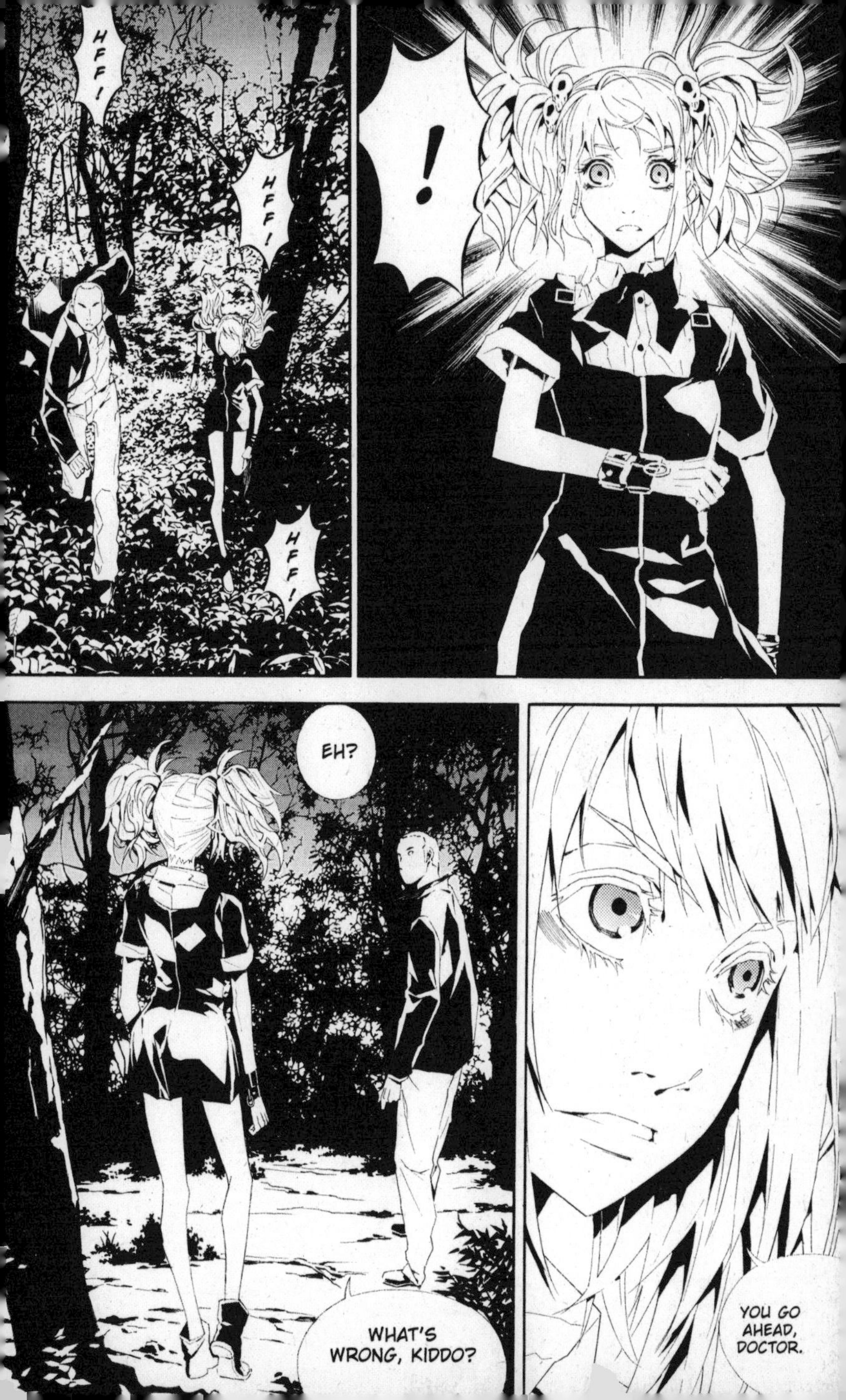
HFF!
HFF!
HFF!
!
EH?
WHAT'S WRONG, KIDDO?
YOU GO AHEAD, DOCTOR.

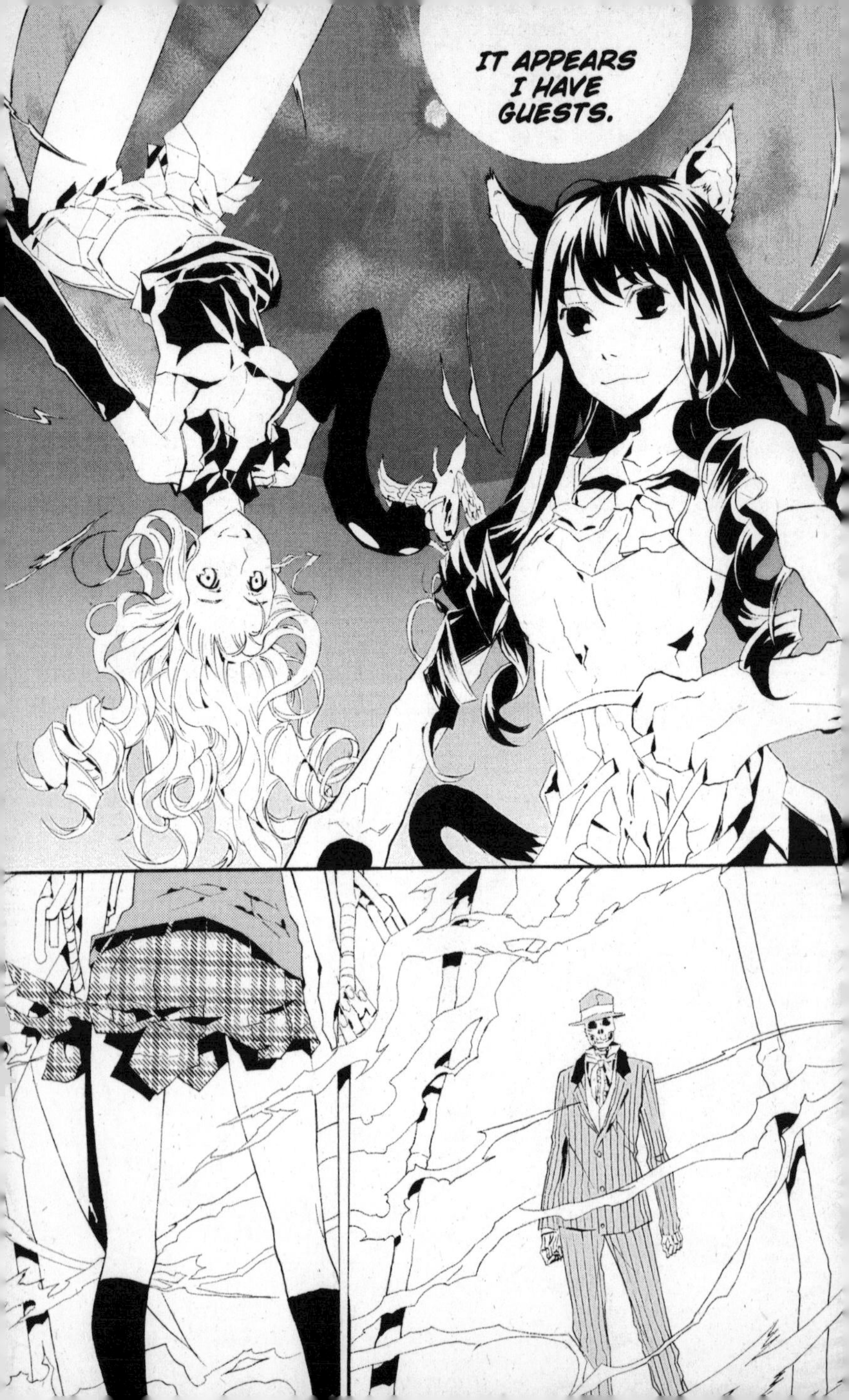
IT APPEARS I HAVE GUESTS.

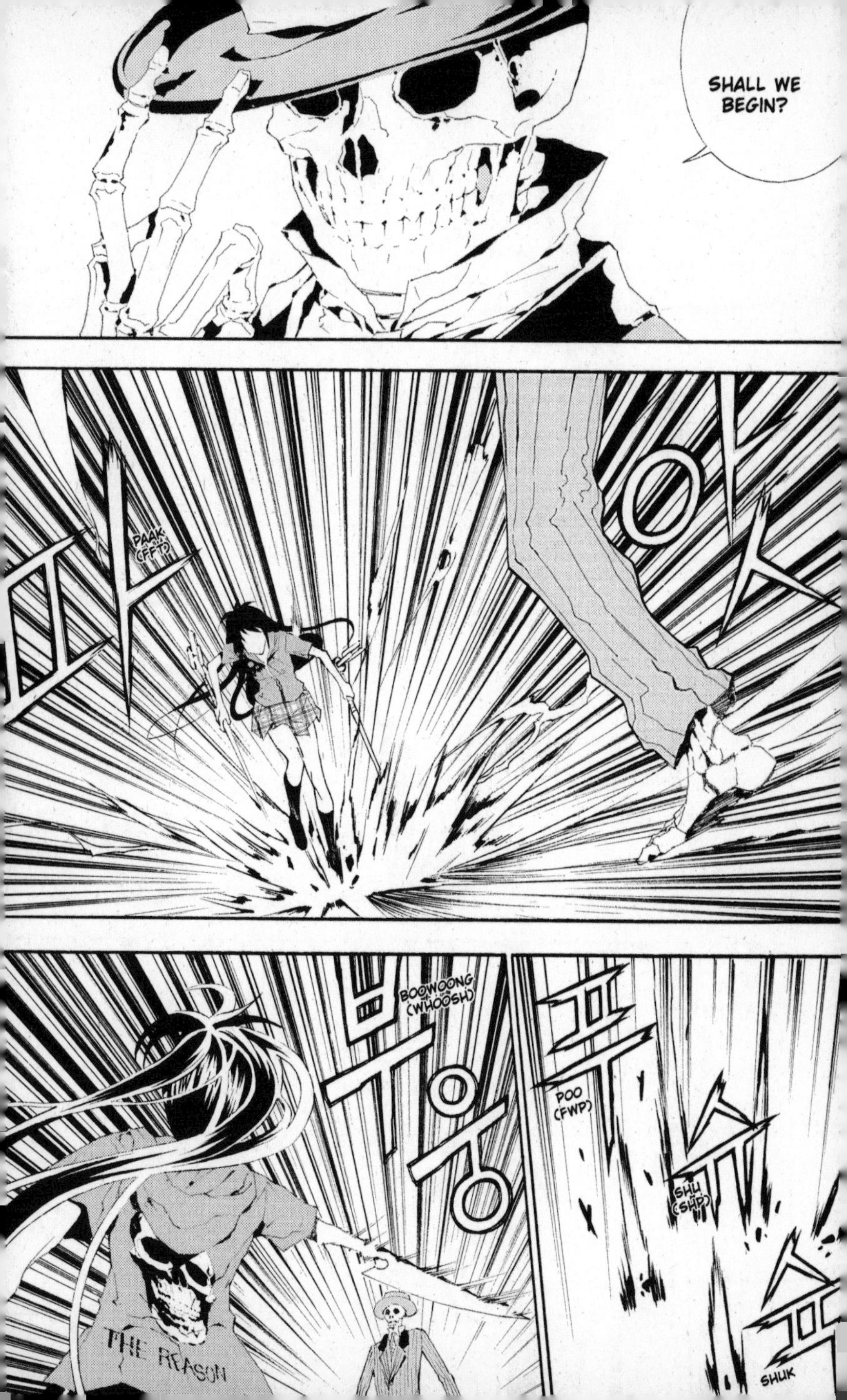
SHALL WE BEGIN?
PAAK (FFT)
BOOWOONG (WHOOSH)
THE REASON
POO (FWP)
SHU (SHP)
SHUK

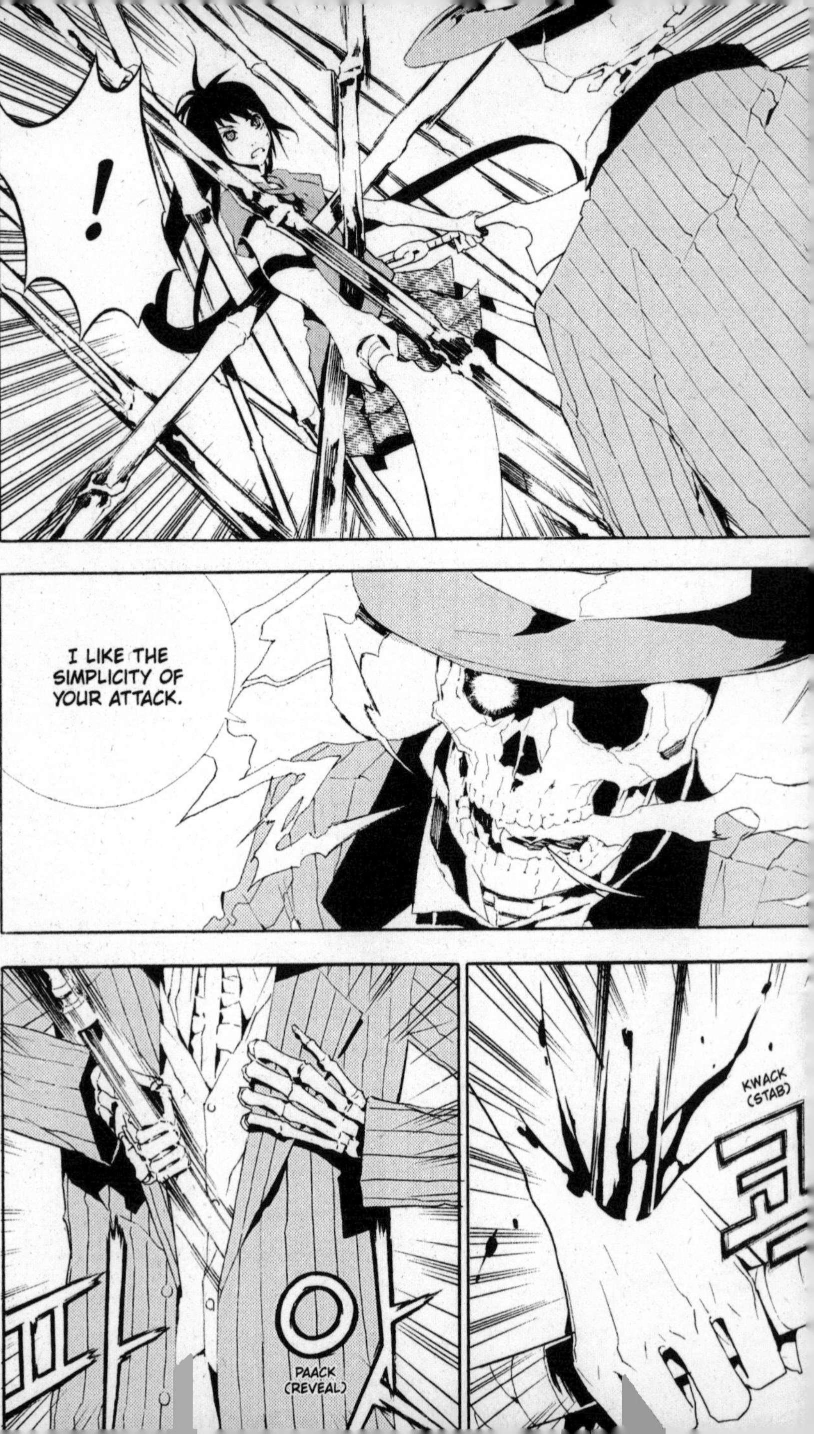
!
I LIKE THE SIMPLICITY OF YOUR ATTACK.
PAACK (REVEAL)
KWACK (STAB)

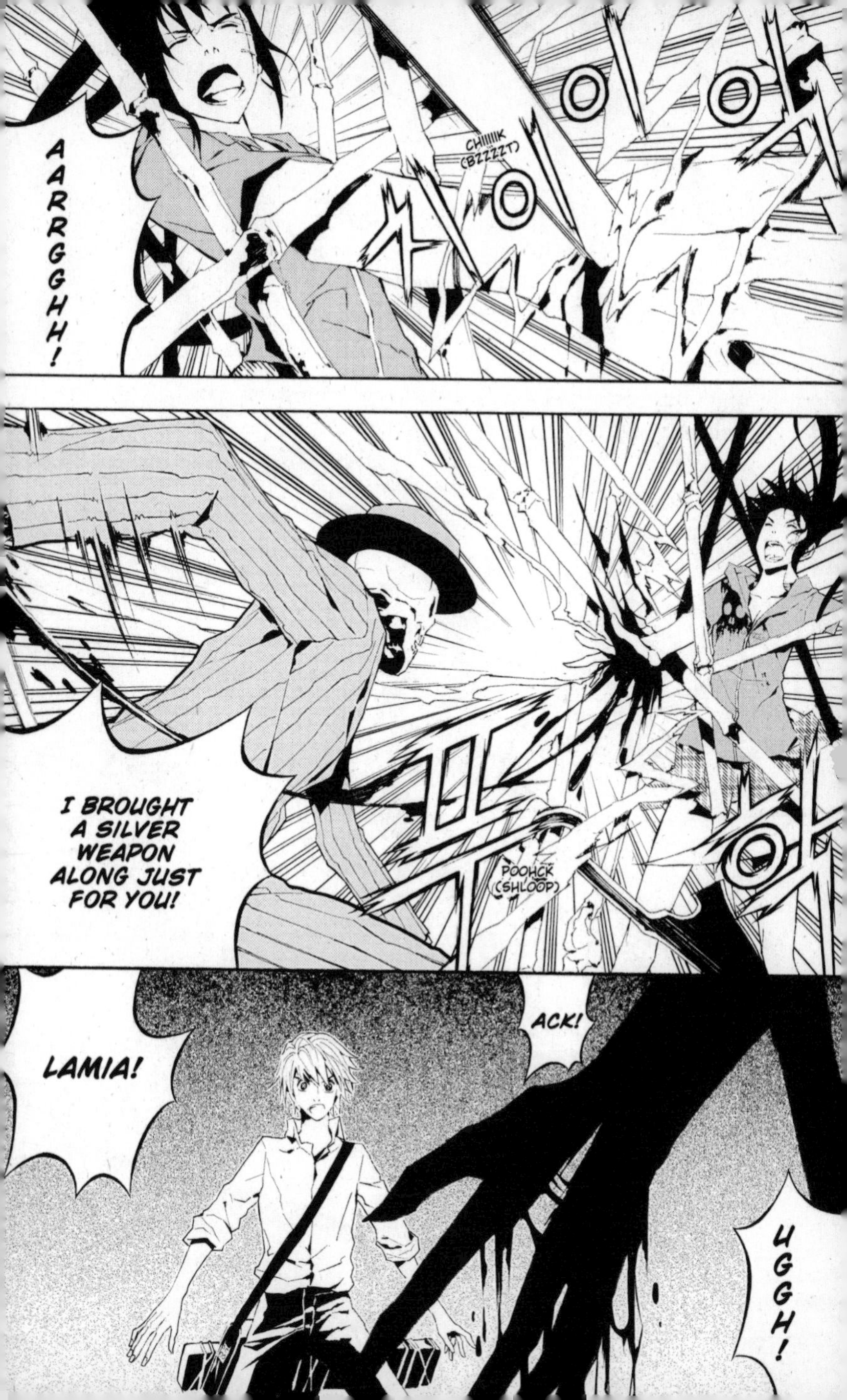
AARRGGHH!
CHIIIIK (BZZZZT)
I BROUGHT A SILVER WEAPON ALONG JUST FOR YOU!
POOHCK (SHLOOP)
LAMIA!
ACK!
UGGH!

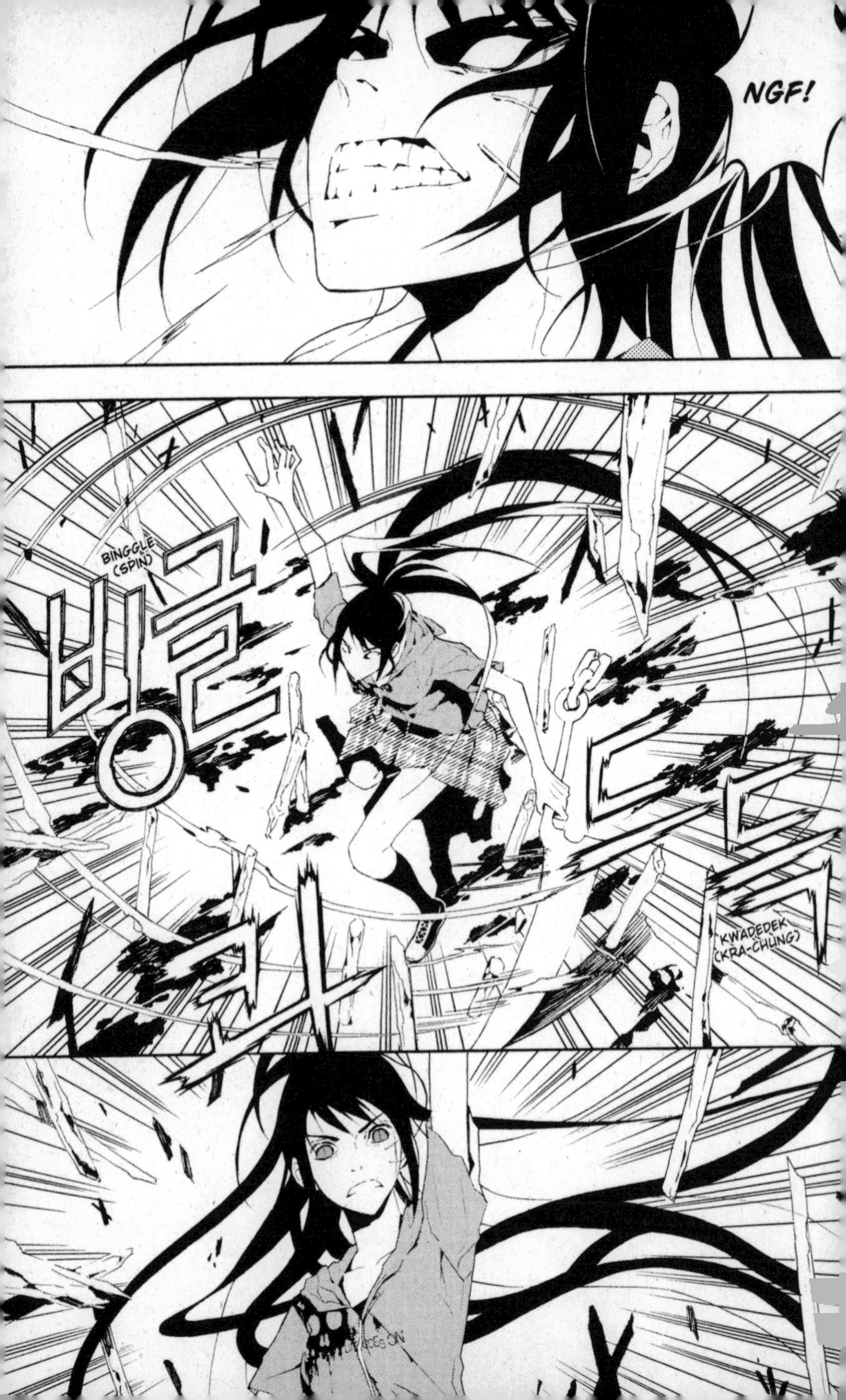
NGF!
BINGGLE (SPIN)
빙글
KWADEDEK (KRA-CHUNG)

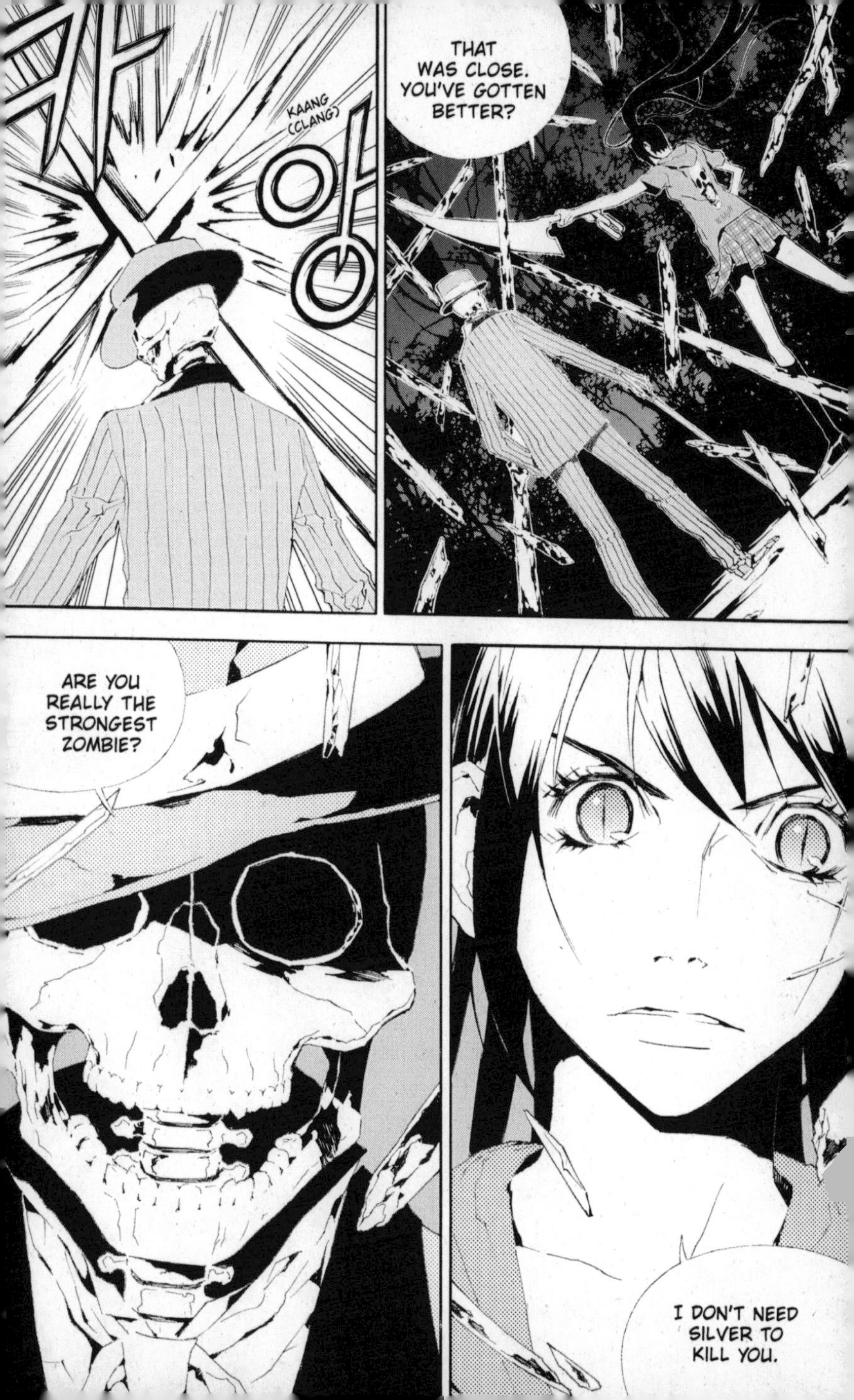
KAANG (CLANG)
THAT WAS CLOSE. YOU'VE GOTTEN BETTER?
ARE YOU REALLY THE STRONGEST ZOMBIE?
I DON'T NEED SILVER TO KILL YOU.

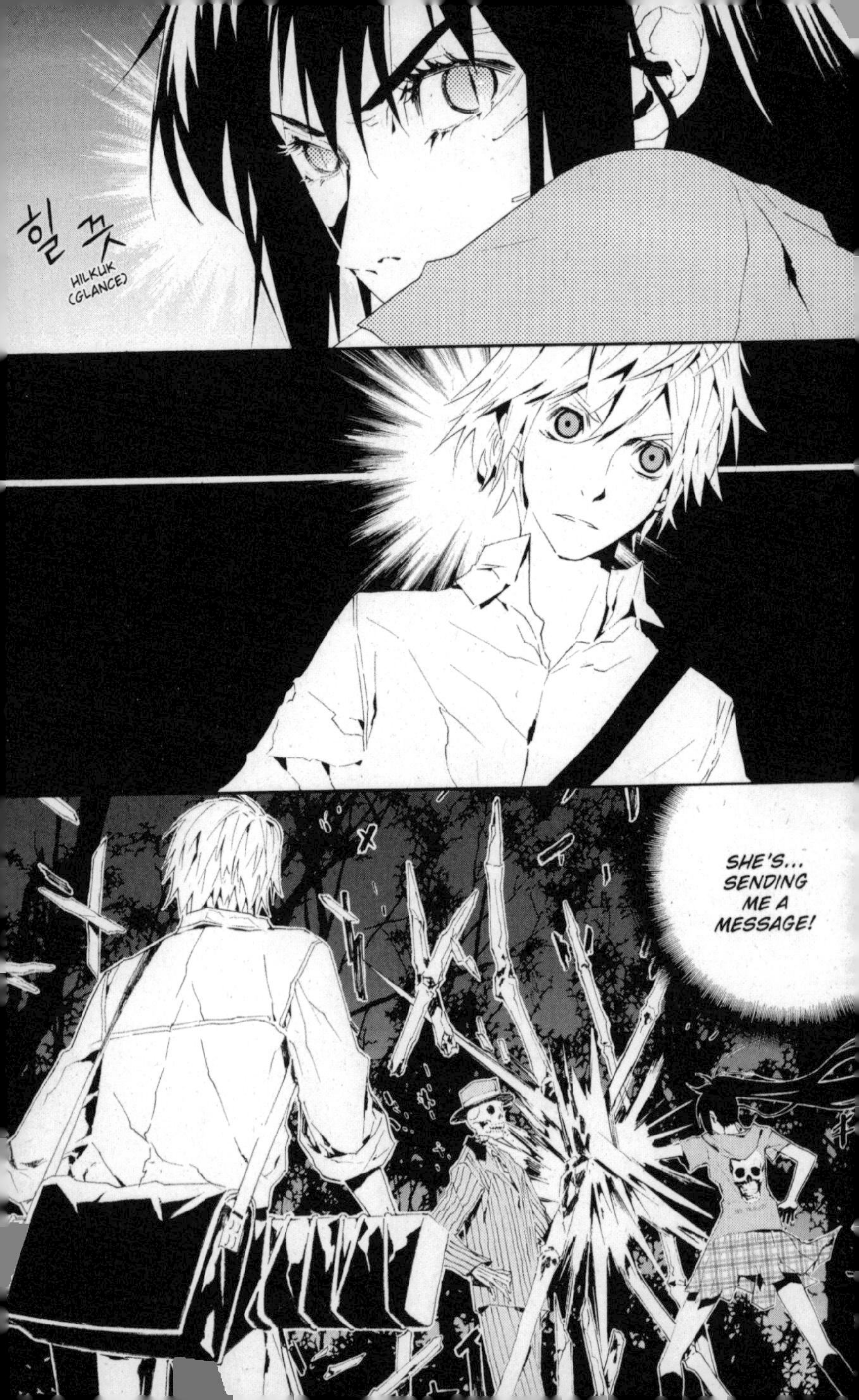
힐끗
HILKUK (GLANCE)
SHE'S... SENDING ME A MESSAGE!

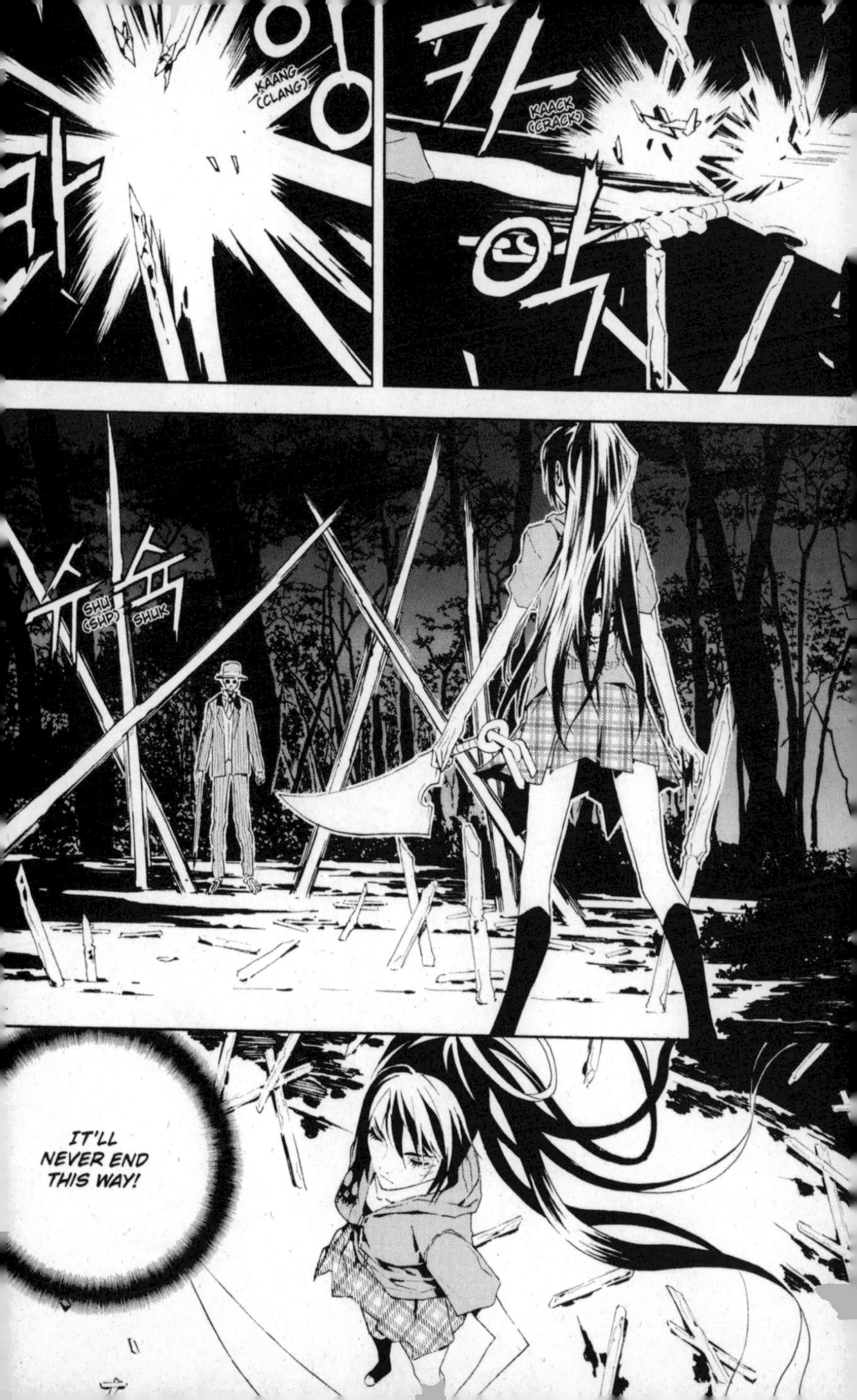
캉
KAANG (CLANG)
카앙
KAACK (CRACK)
슈 슉
SHU (SHP) SHUK
IT'LL NEVER END THIS WAY!

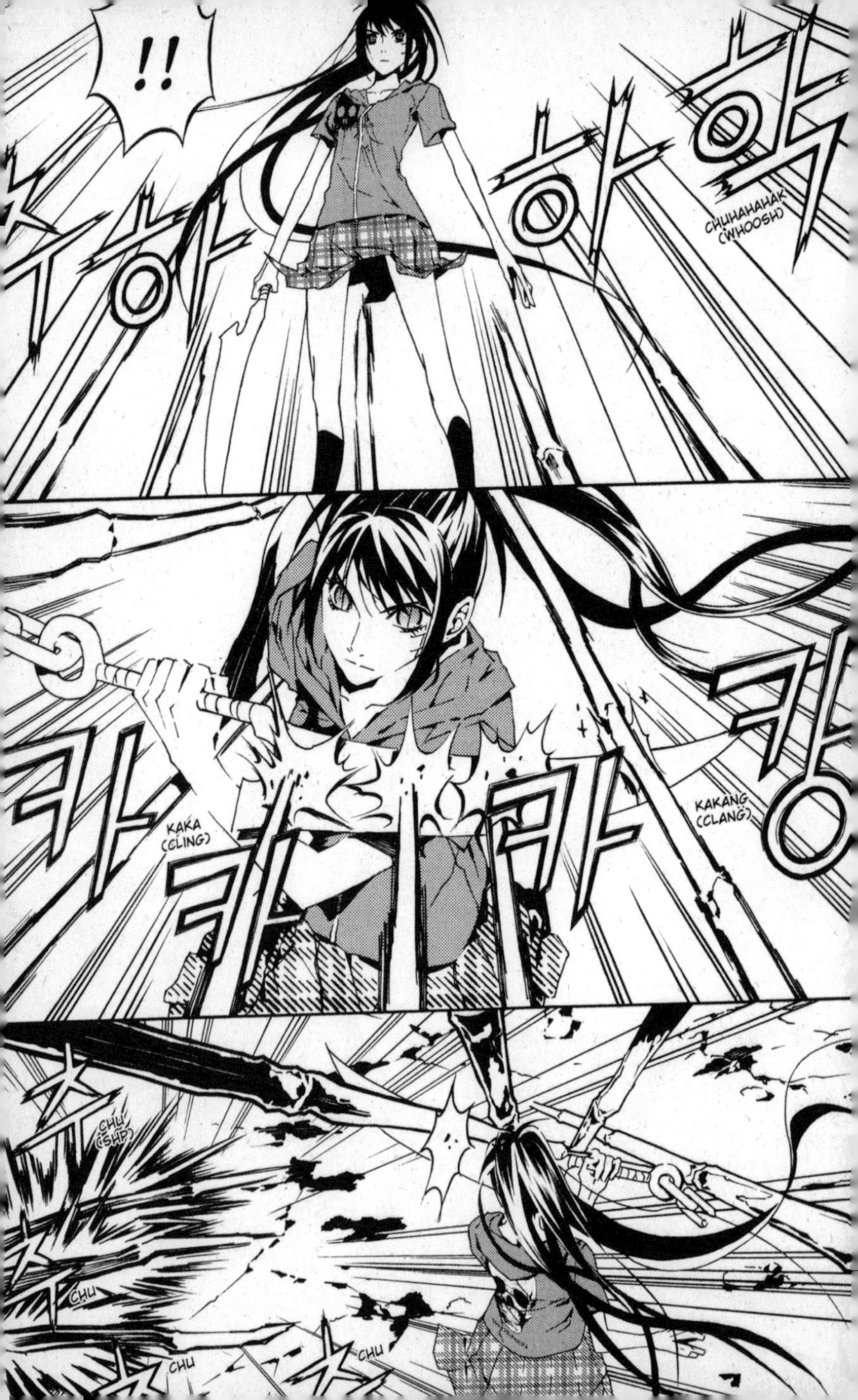
!!
CHUHAHAHAK (WHOOSH)
KAKA (CLING)
KAKANG (CLANG)
CHU (SHP)
CHU
CHU
CHU

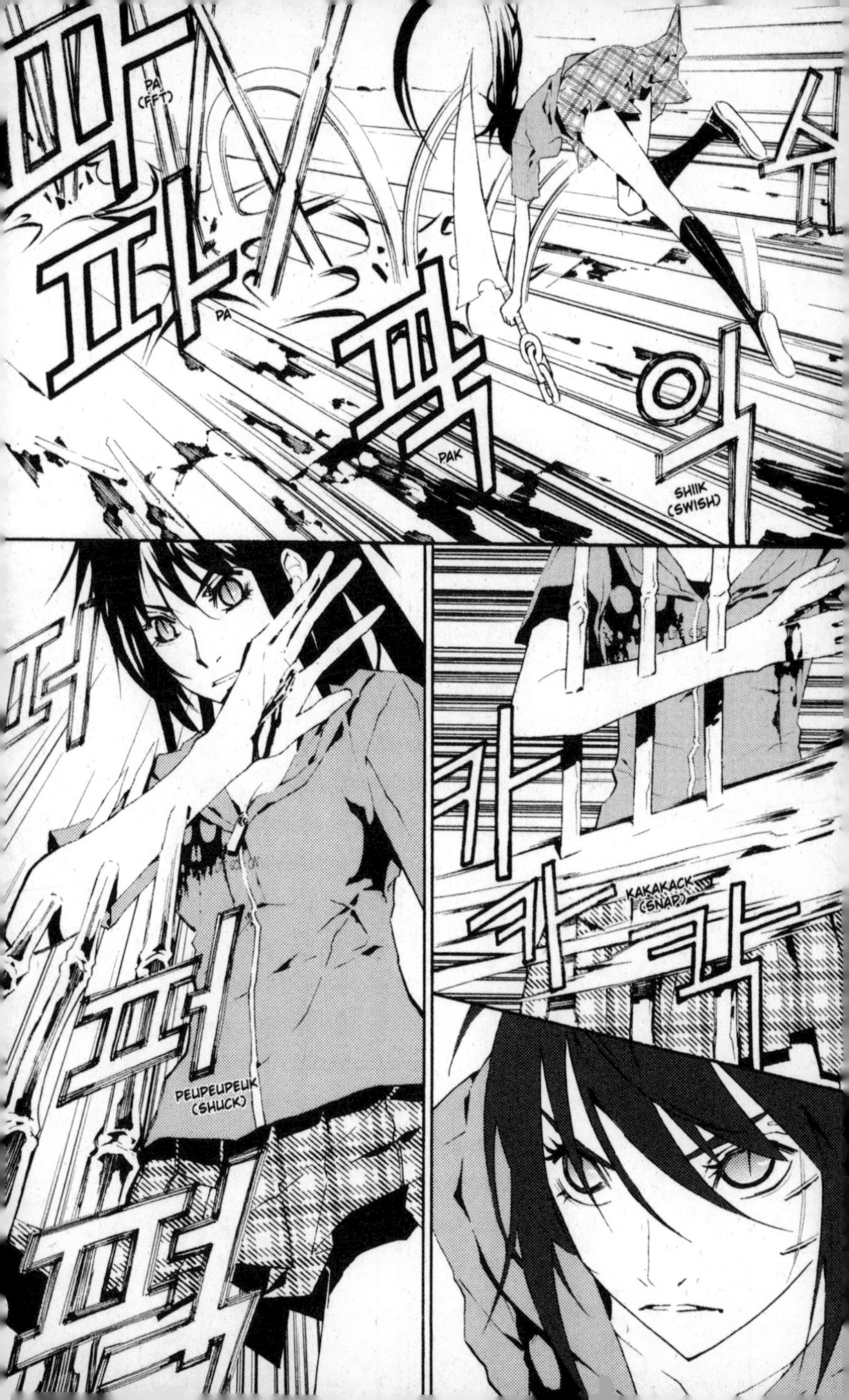
PA (FFT)
PA
PAK
SHIIK (SWISH)
PEUPEUPEUK (SHUCK)
KAKACK (SNAP)

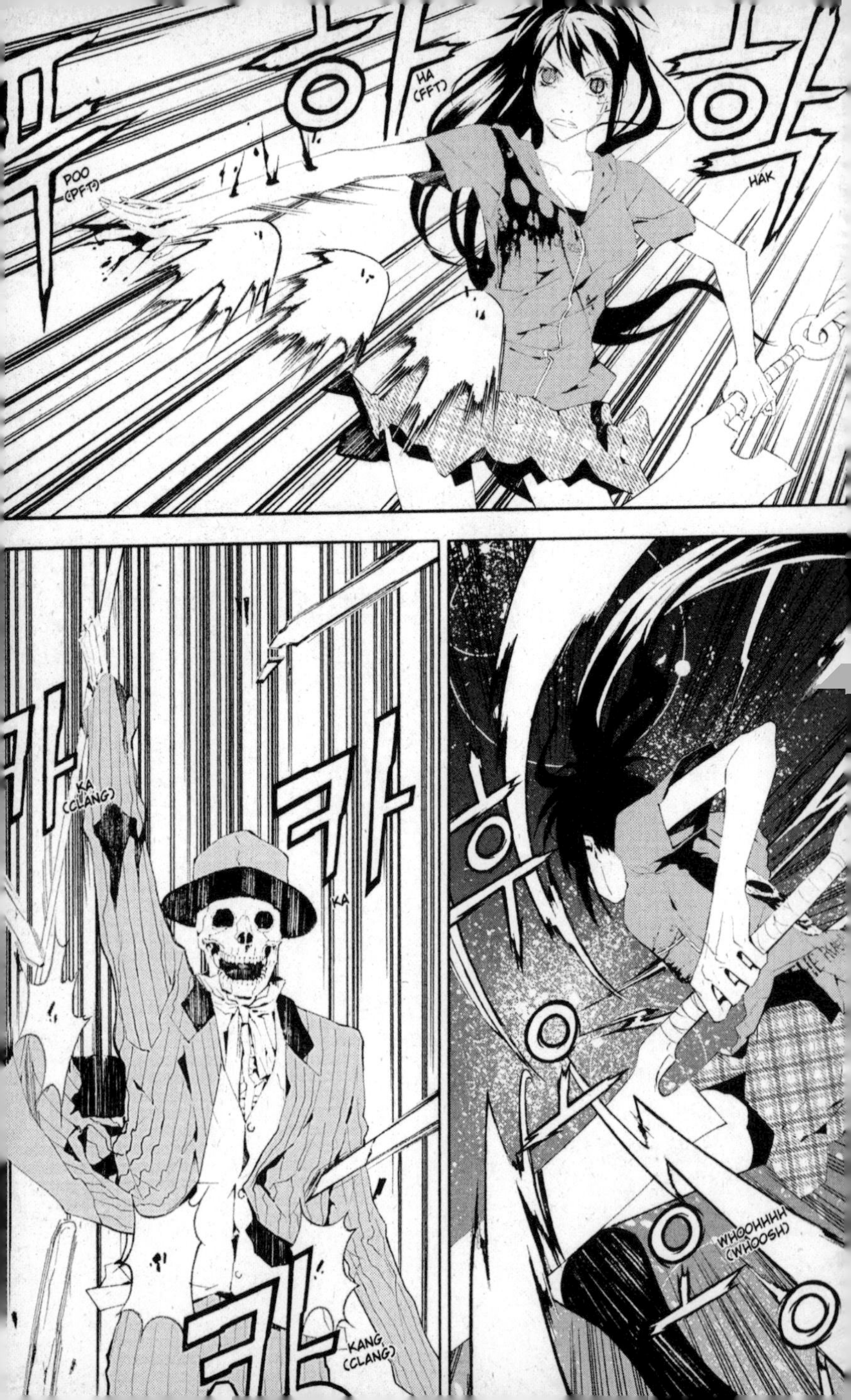
POO (PFFT)
HA (FFT)
HAK
KA (CLANG)
KA
KANG (CLANG)
WHOOHHHH (WHOOSH)

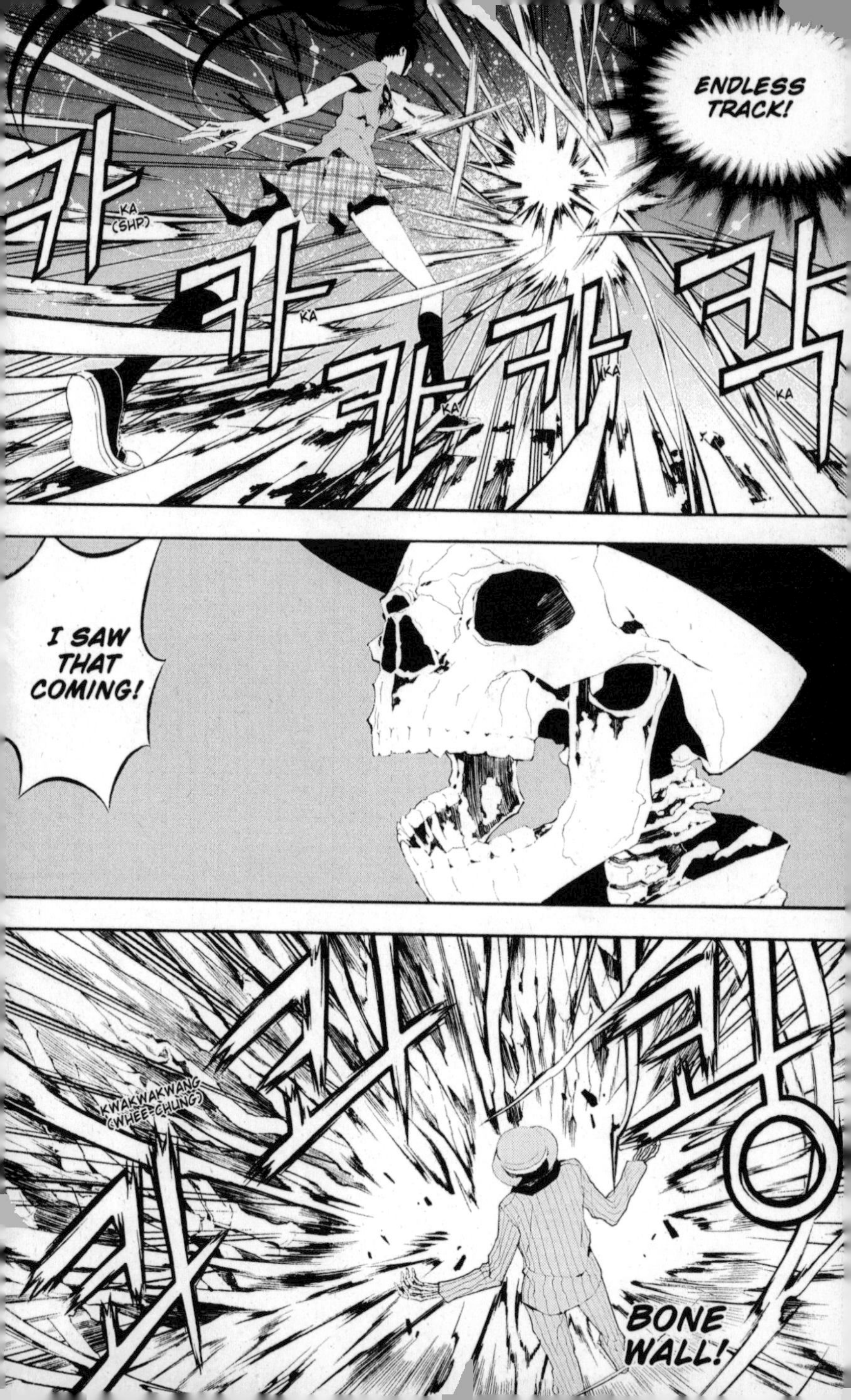
KA (SHP)
KA
KA
KA
KA
ENDLESS TRACK!
I SAW THAT COMING!
KWAKWAKWANG (WHEE-CHUNG)
BONE WALL!

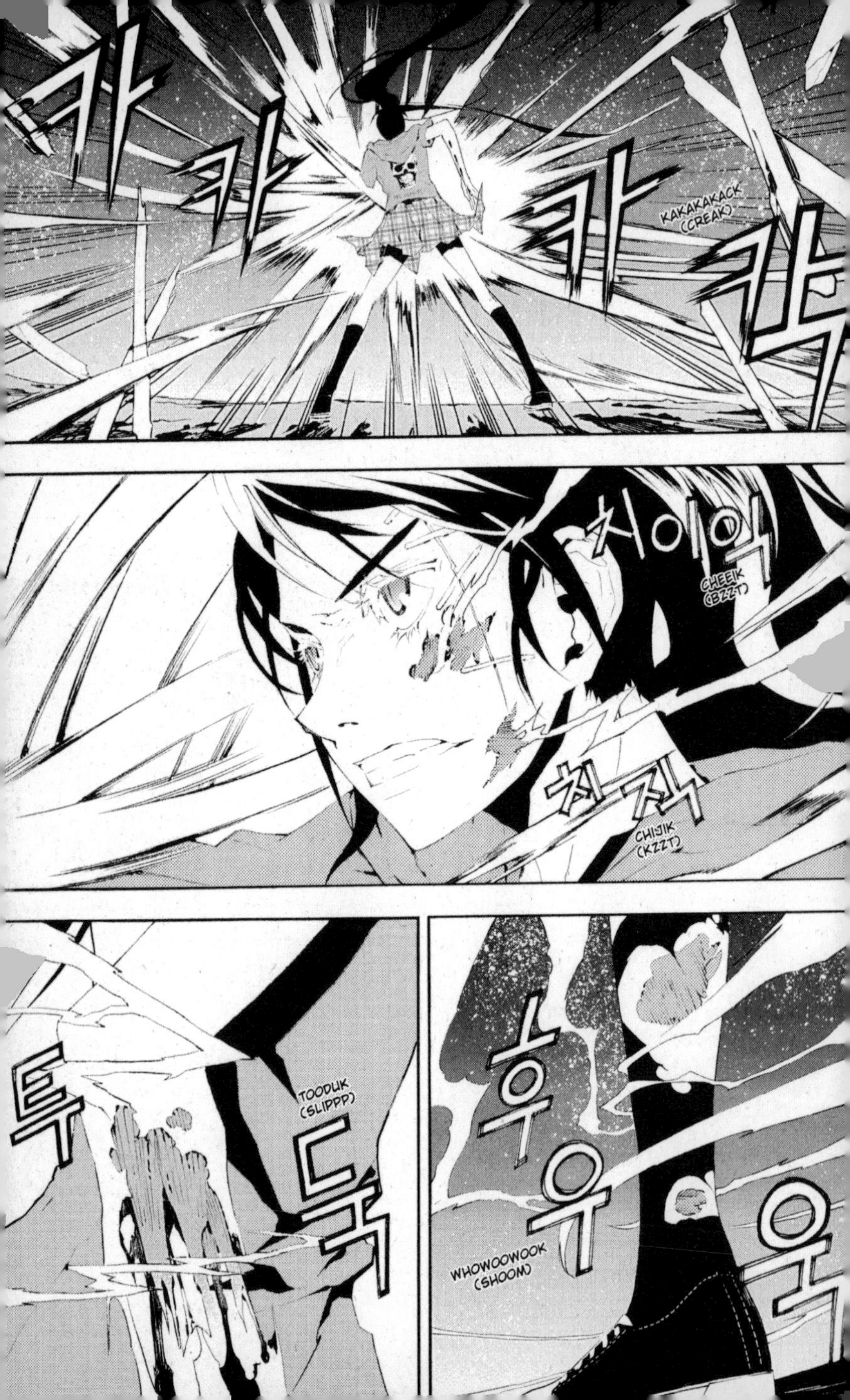
카카카칵
KAKAKAKACK
(CREAK)
치이이익
CHEEIK
(BZZT)
치직
CHIJIK
(KZZT)
투둑
TOODUK
(SLIPPP)
후우욱
WHOWOOWOOK
(SHOOM)

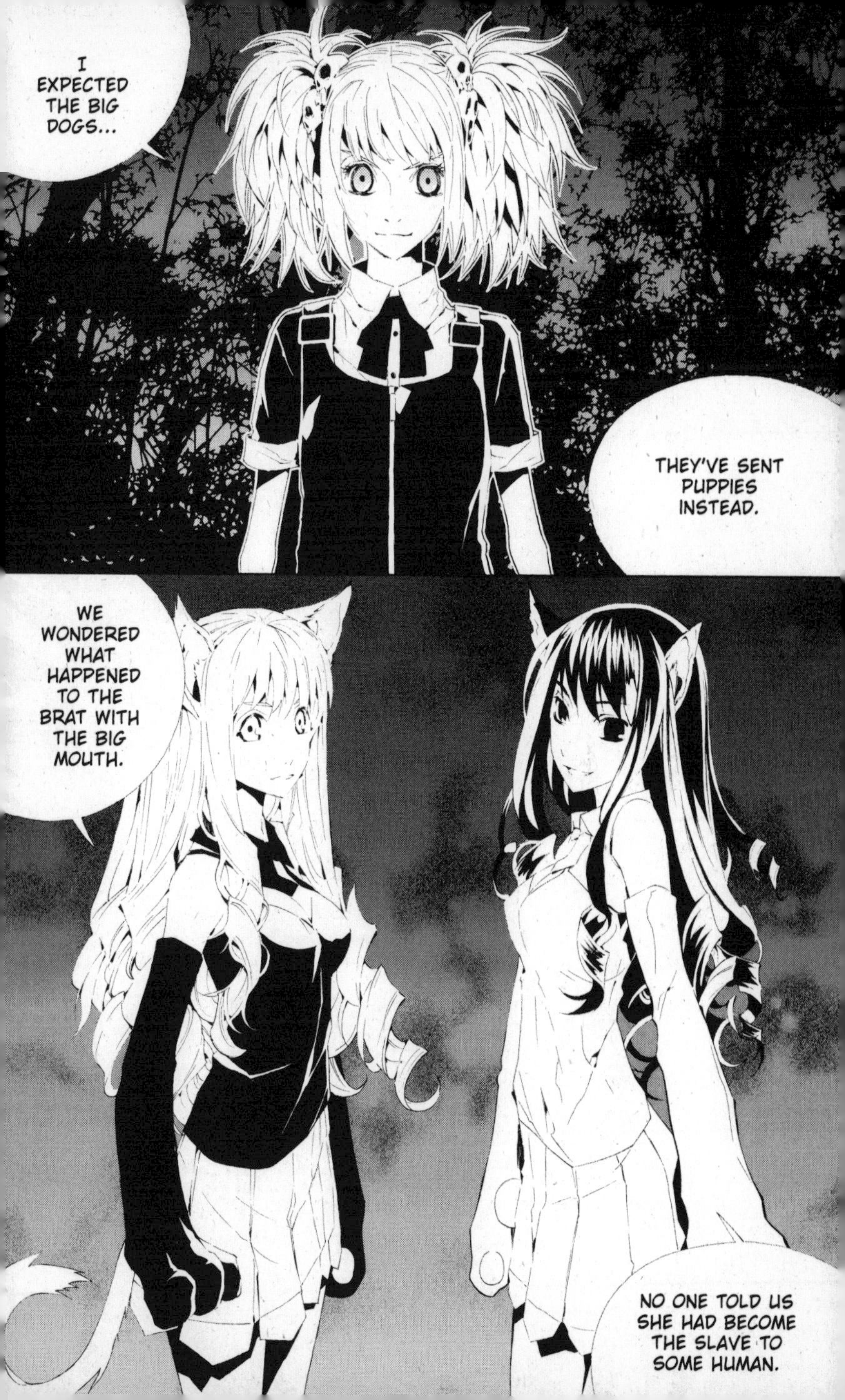
I EXPECTED THE BIG DOGS...
THEY'VE SENT PUPPIES INSTEAD.
WE WONDERED WHAT HAPPENED TO THE BRAT WITH THE BIG MOUTH.
NO ONE TOLD US SHE HAD BECOME THE SLAVE TO SOME HUMAN.

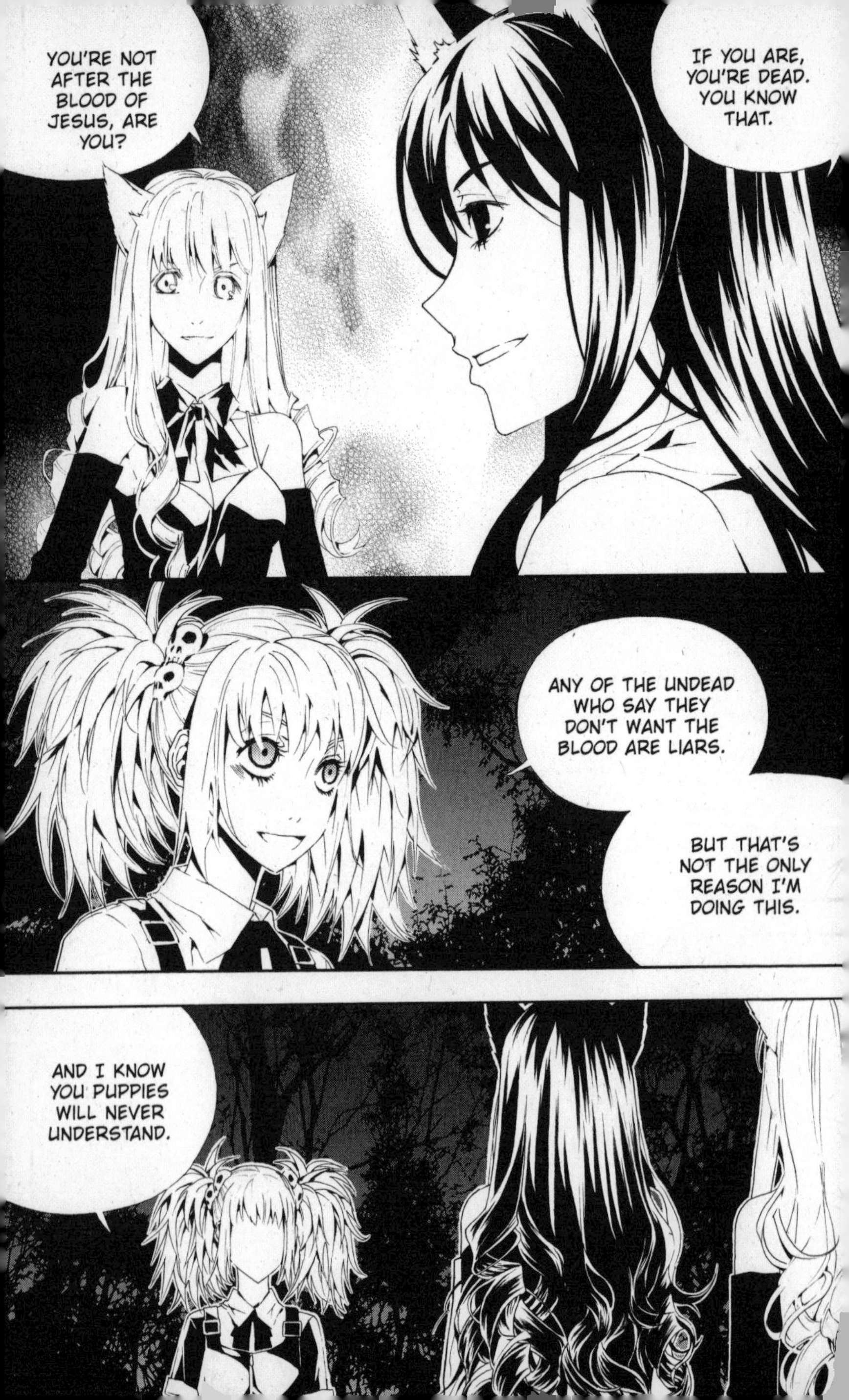
YOU'RE NOT AFTER THE BLOOD OF JESUS, ARE YOU?
IF YOU ARE, YOU'RE DEAD. YOU KNOW THAT.
ANY OF THE UNDEAD WHO SAY THEY DON'T WANT THE BLOOD ARE LIARS.
BUT THAT'S NOT THE ONLY REASON I'M DOING THIS.
AND I KNOW YOU PUPPIES WILL NEVER UNDERSTAND.

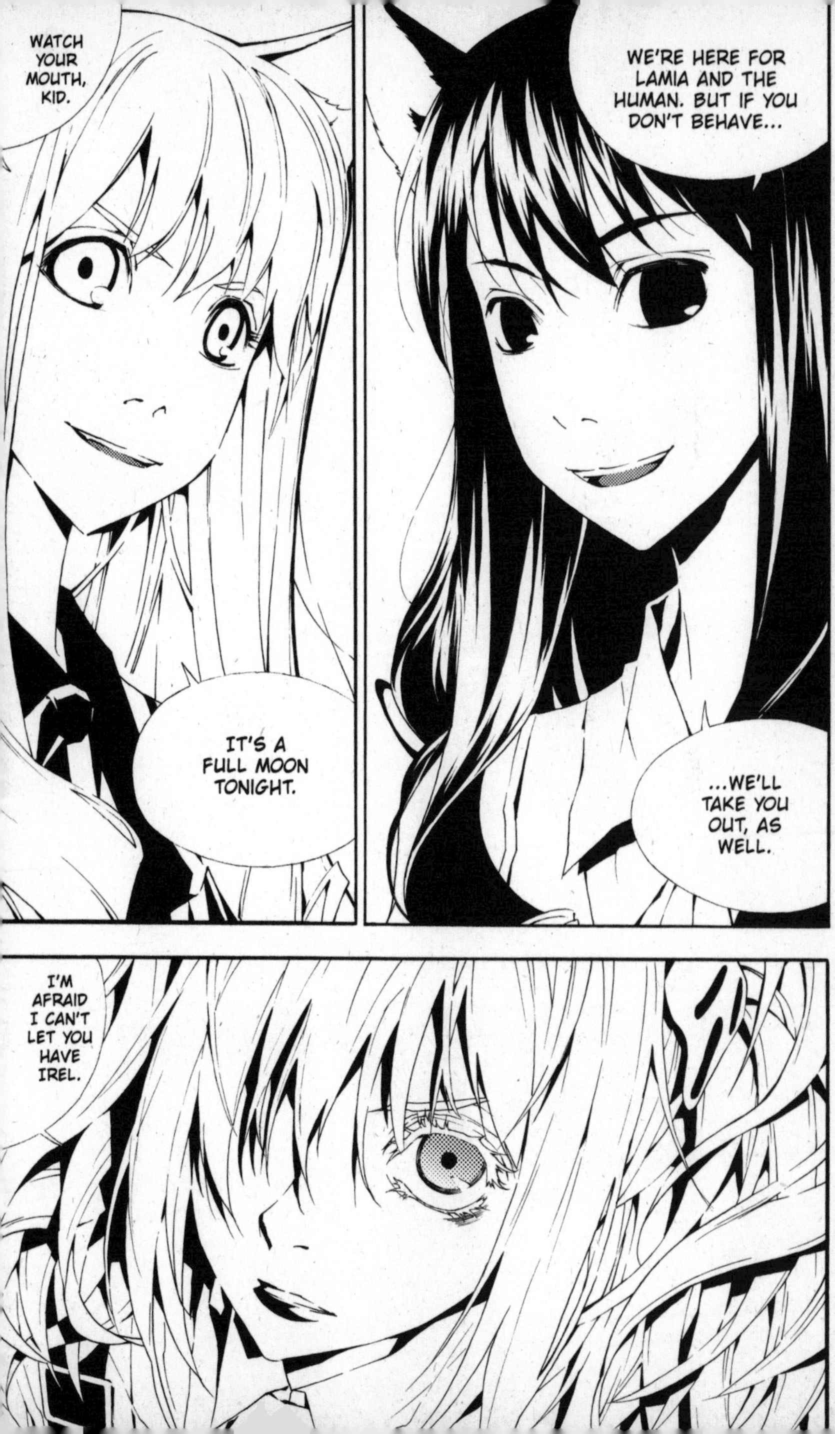
WATCH YOUR MOUTH, KID.
IT'S A FULL MOON TONIGHT.
WE'RE HERE FOR LAMIA AND THE HUMAN. BUT IF YOU DON'T BEHAVE...
...WE'LL TAKE YOU OUT, AS WELL.
I'M AFRAID I CAN'T LET YOU HAVE IREL.

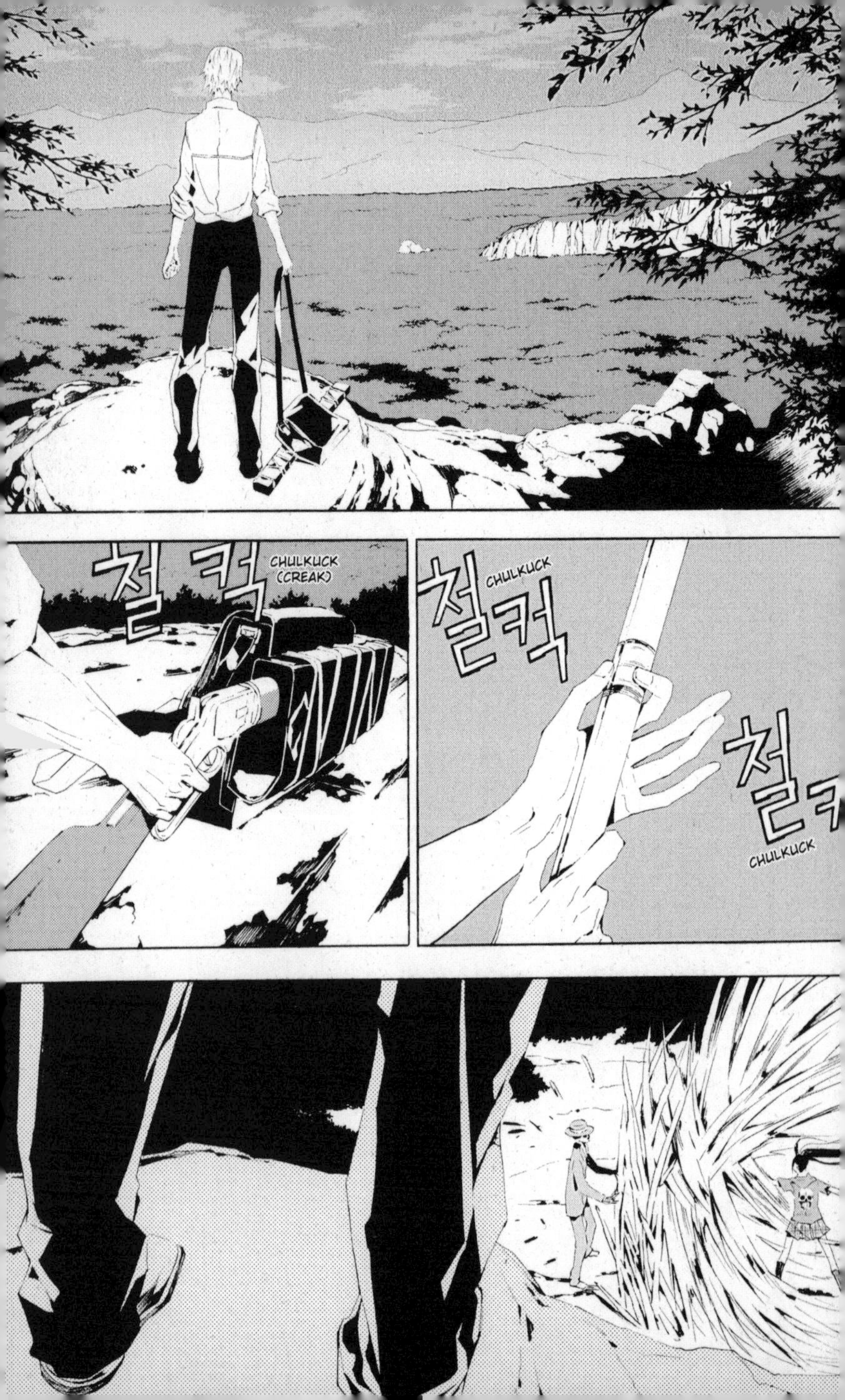
철컥
CHULKUCK
(CREAK)
철컥
CHULKUCK
CHULKUCK

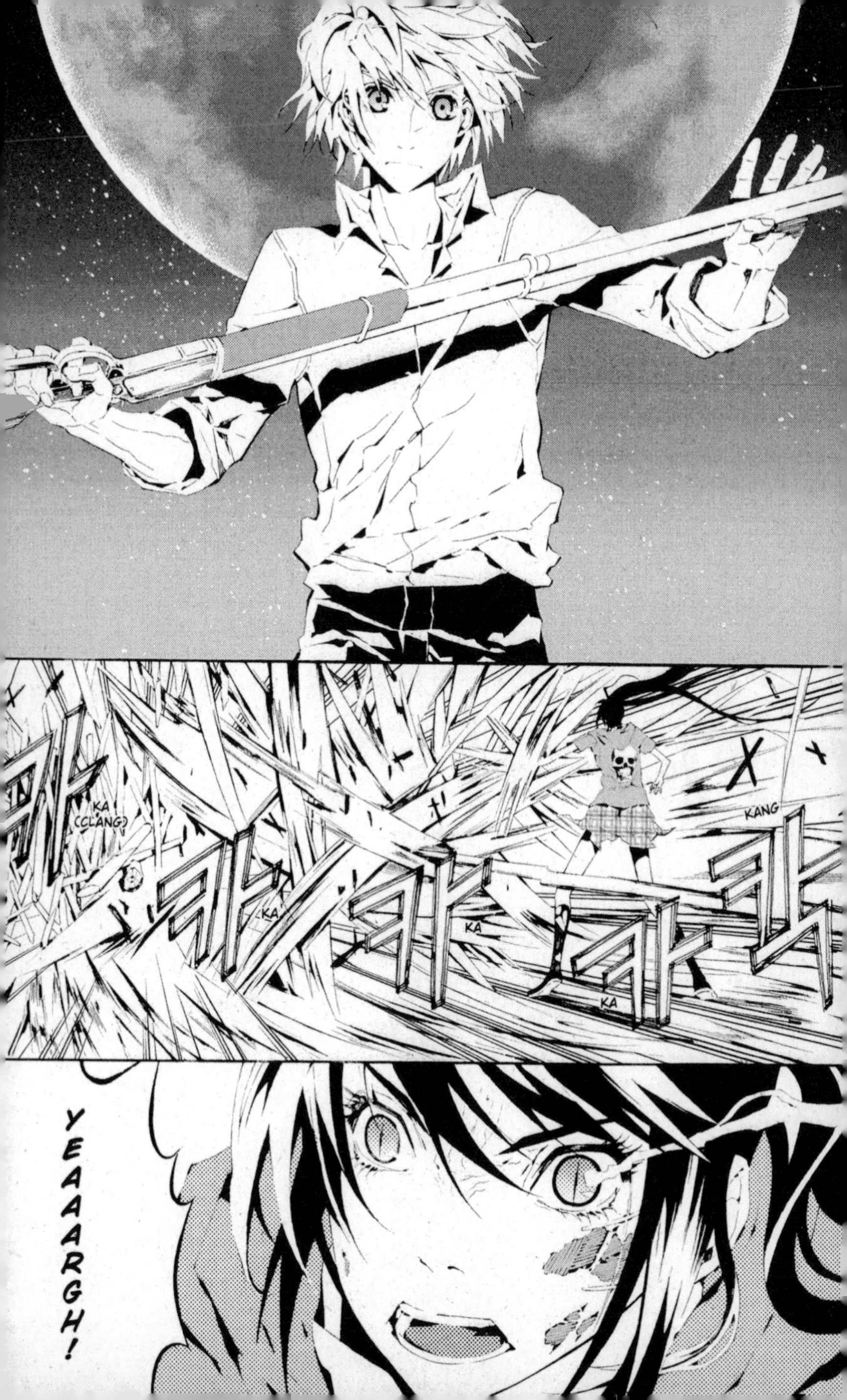
KA (CLANG)
KA
KA
KA
KANG
YEAAAARGH!

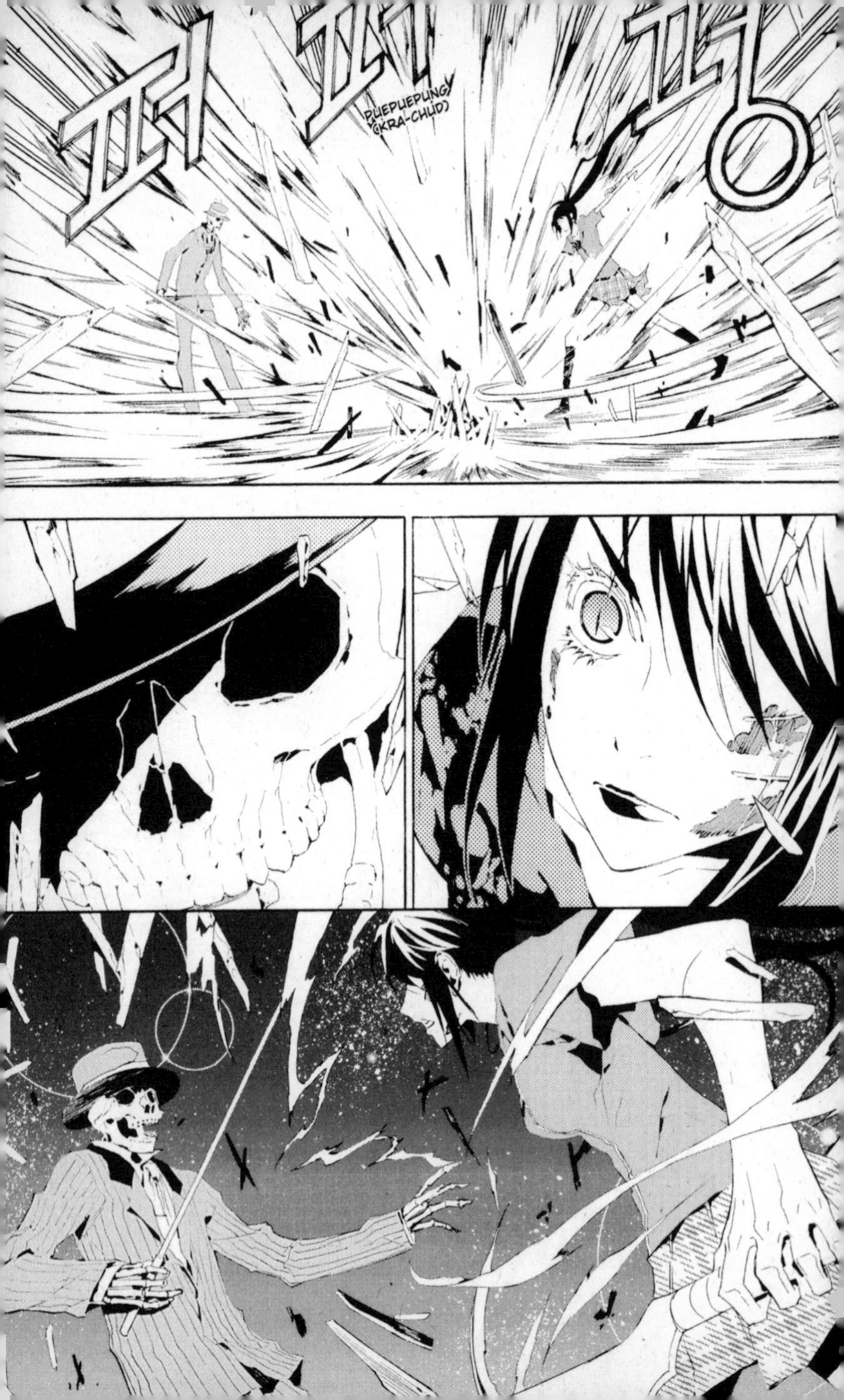
퍼퍼펑
PUEPUEPUNG (KRA-CHUD)

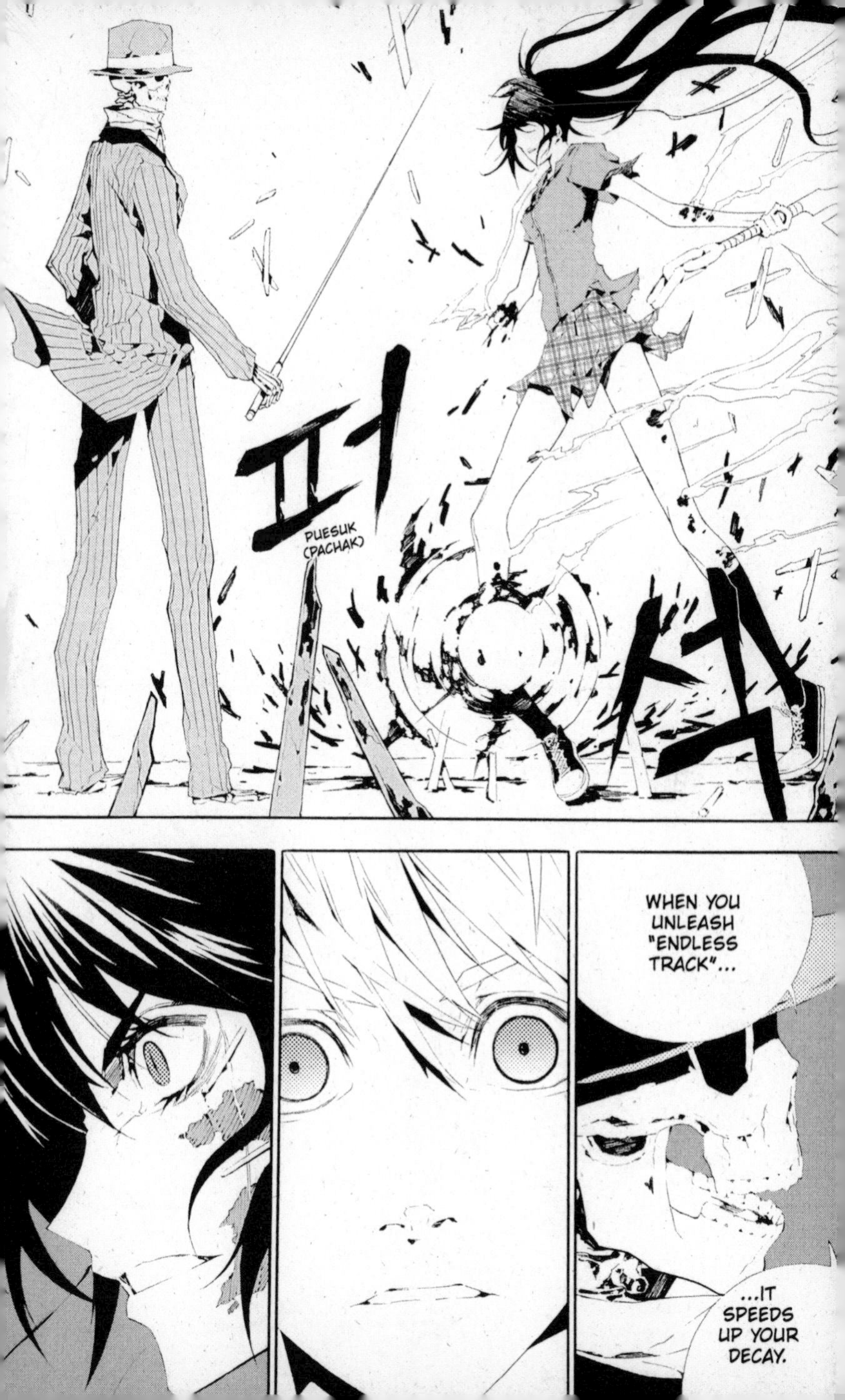
PUESUK
(PACHAK)
WHEN YOU UNLEASH "ENDLESS TRACK"...
...IT SPEEDS UP YOUR DECAY.

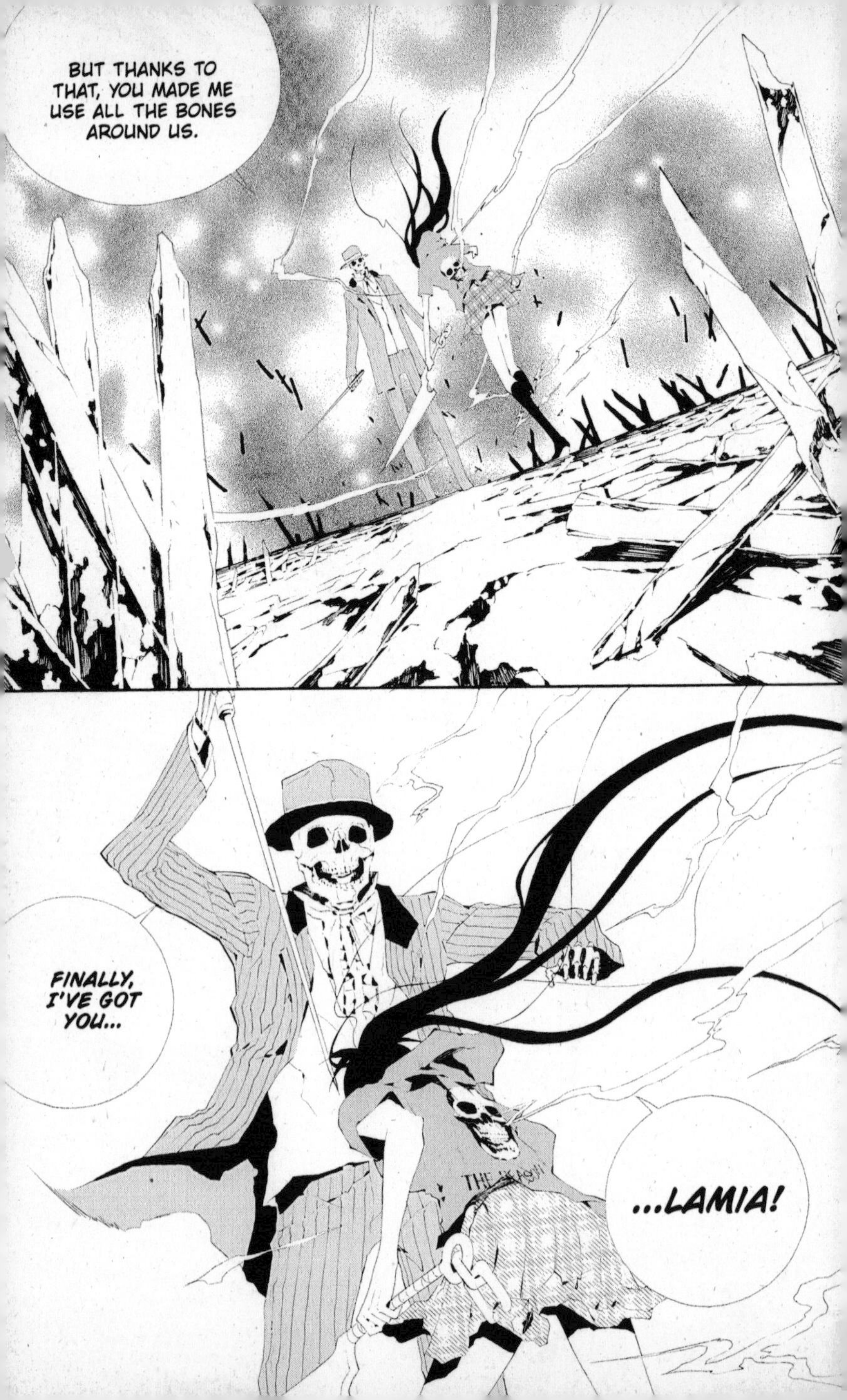
BUT THANKS TO THAT, YOU MADE ME USE ALL THE BONES AROUND US.
FINALLY, I'VE GOT YOU...
...LAMIA!

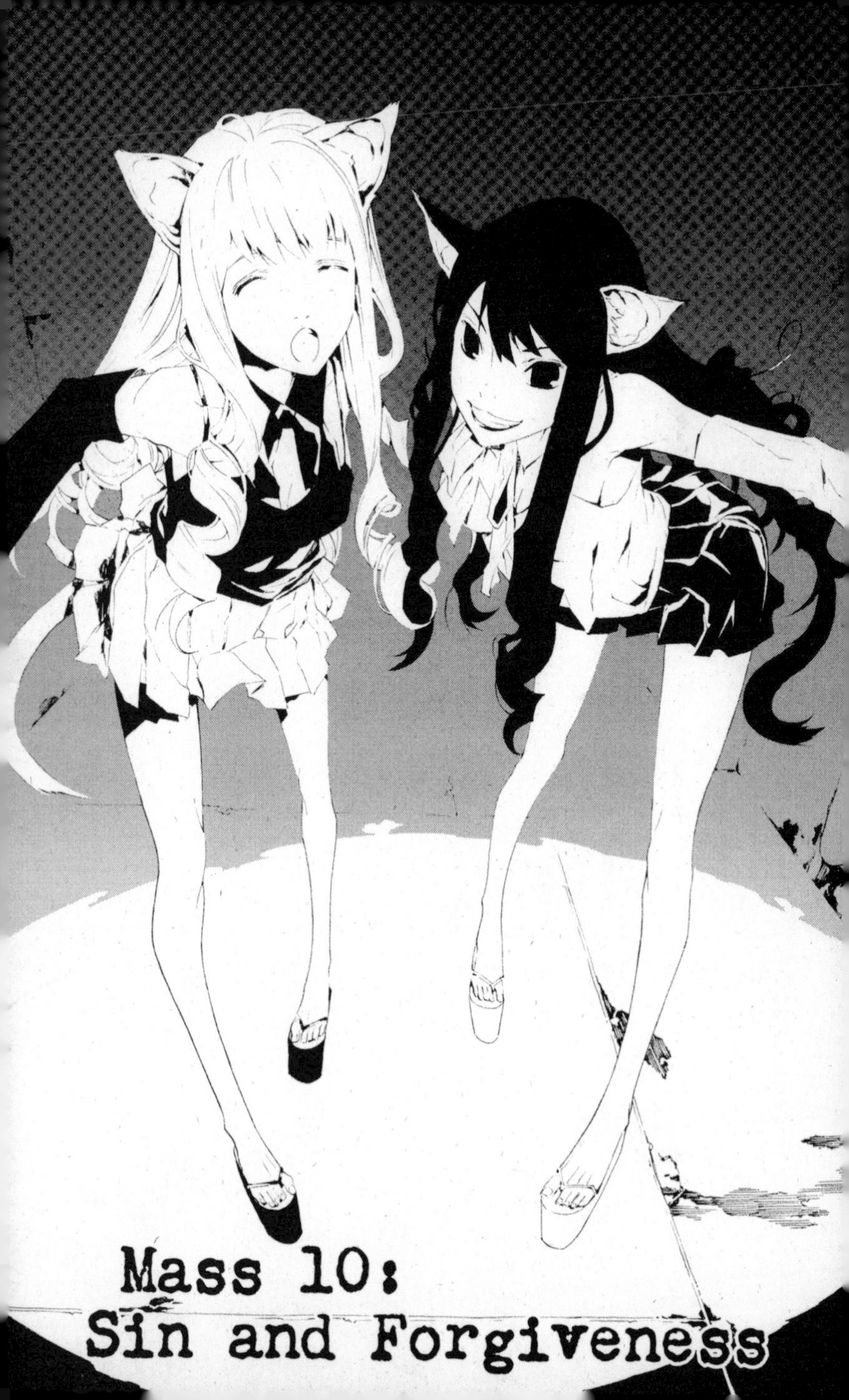

Mass 10: Sin and Forgiveness

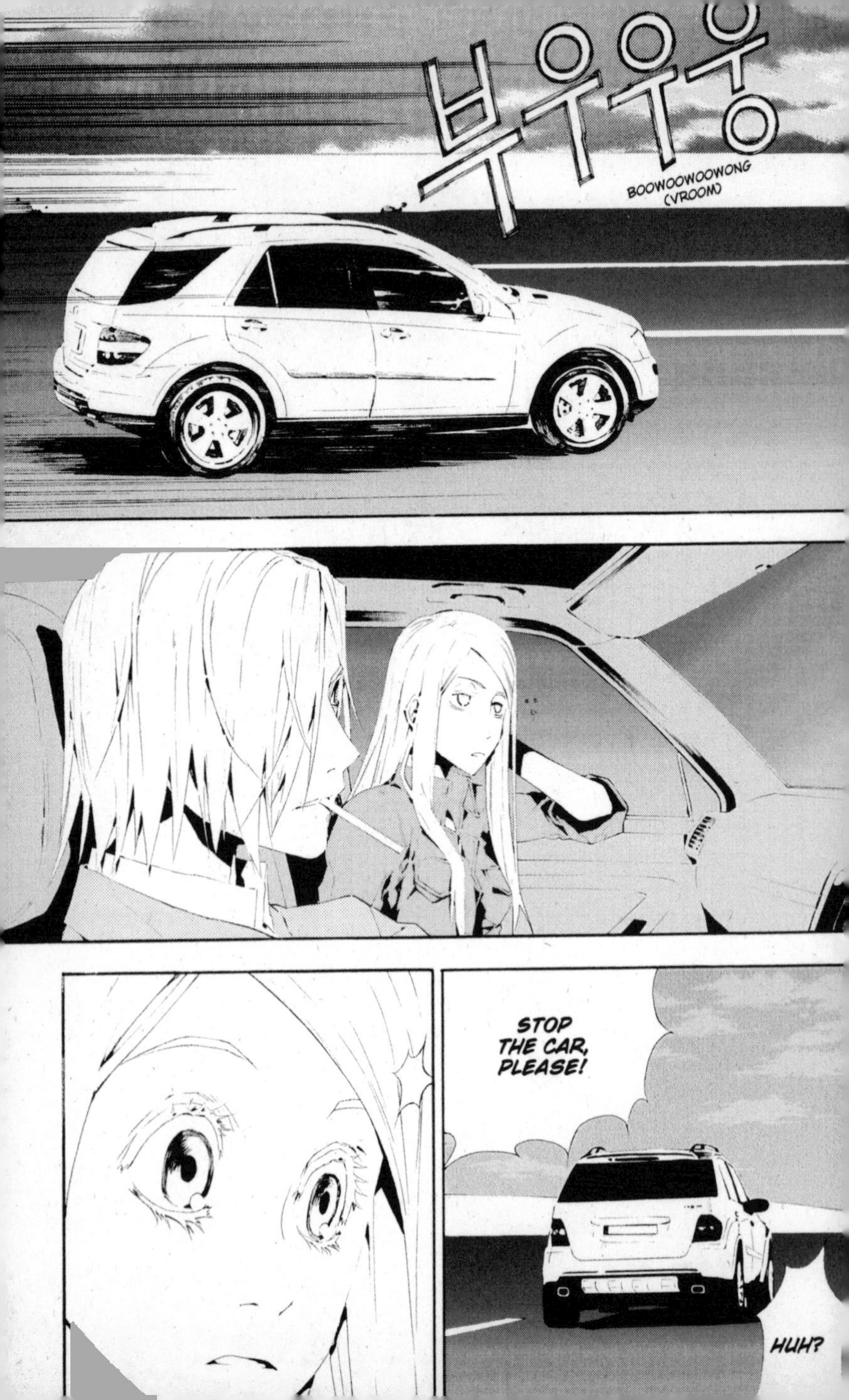
부우우웅
BOOWOOWOOWONG (VROOM)
STOP THE CAR, PLEASE!
HUH?

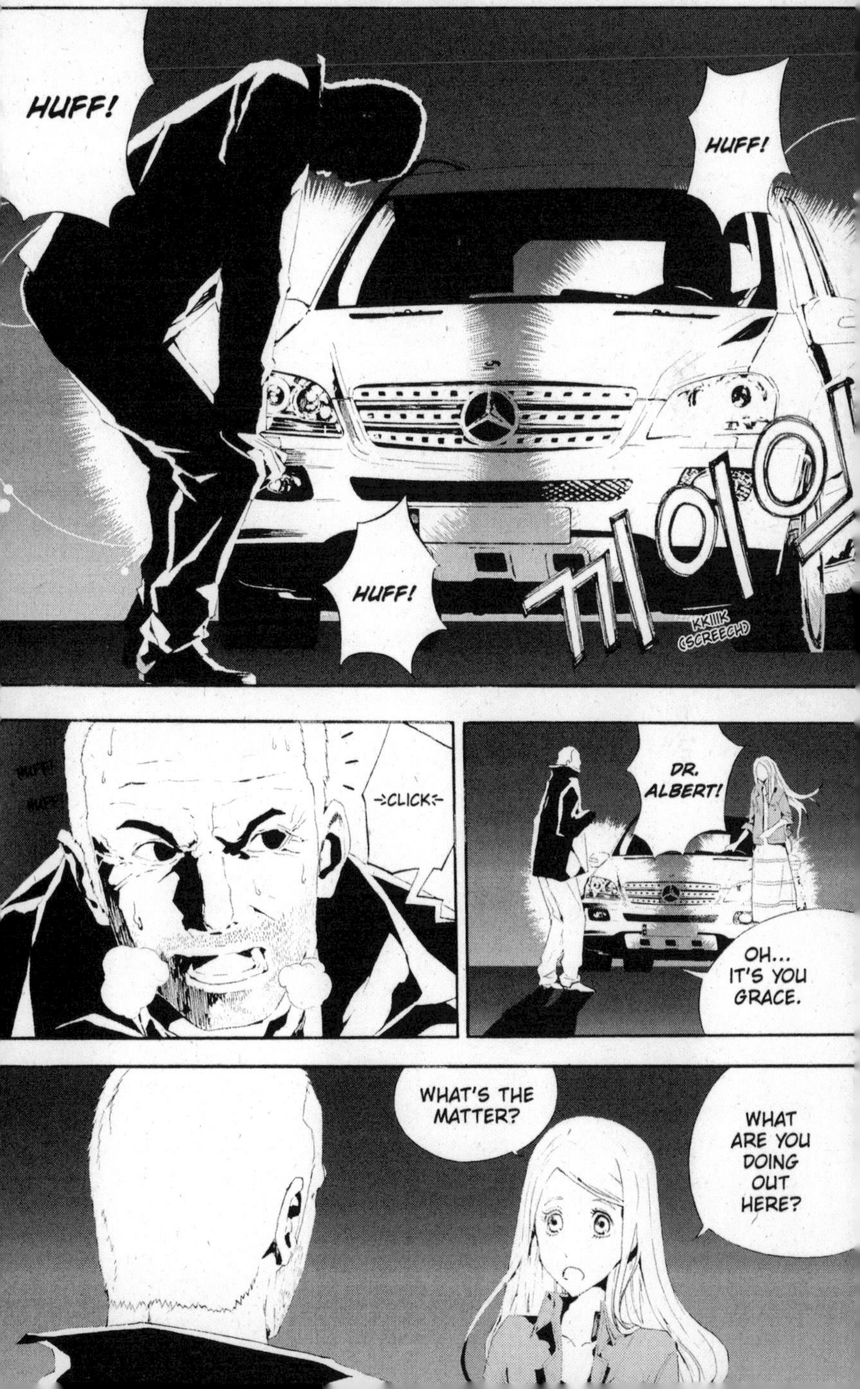
HUFF!
HUFF!
HUFF!
끼이익
KKIIIK (SCREECH)
CLICK
DR. ALBERT!
OH... IT'S YOU GRACE.
WHAT'S THE MATTER?
WHAT ARE YOU DOING OUT HERE?

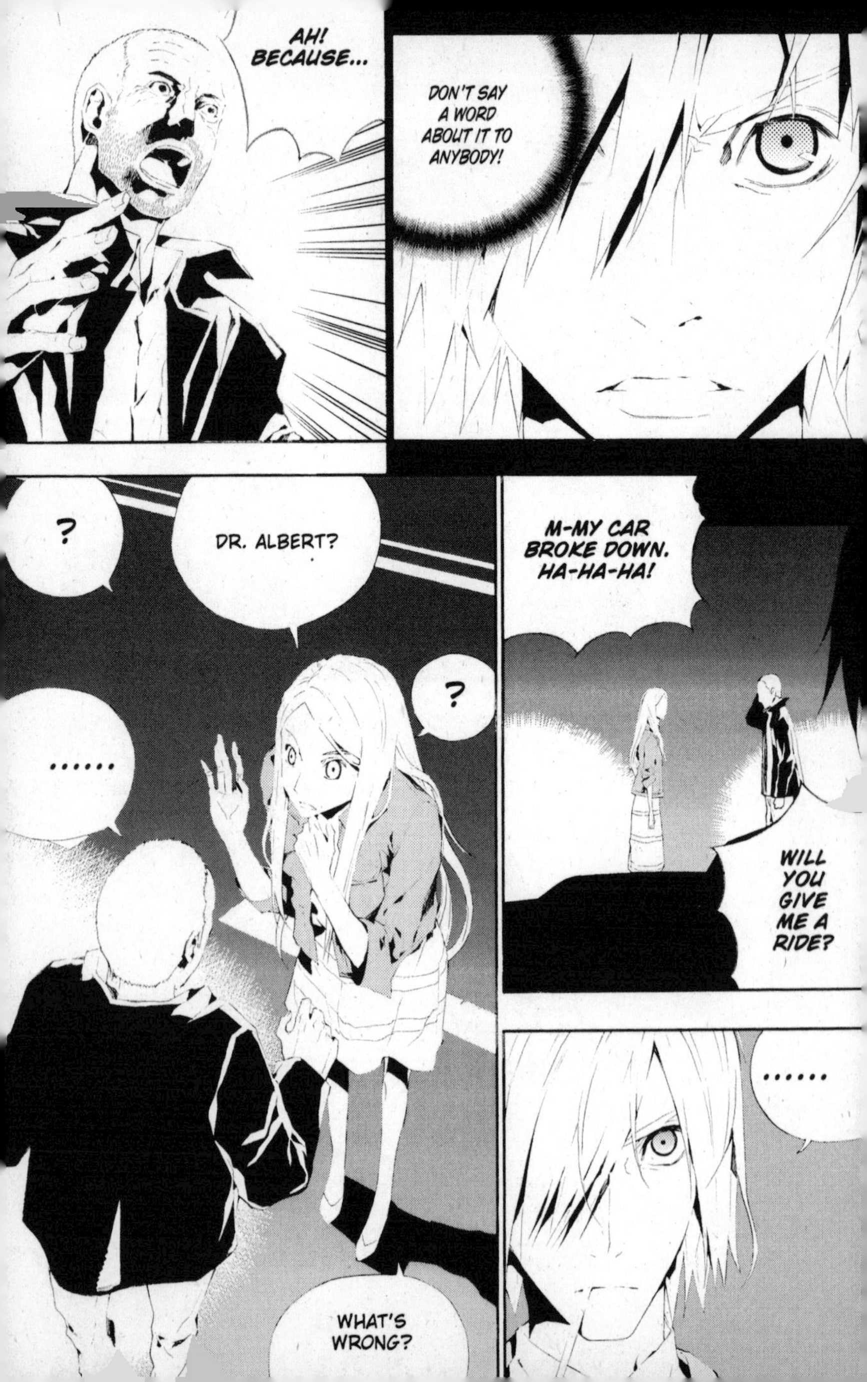
AH! BECAUSE...
DON'T SAY A WORD ABOUT IT TO ANYBODY!
?
DR. ALBERT?
?
......
WHAT'S WRONG?
M-MY CAR BROKE DOWN. HA-HA-HA!
WILL YOU GIVE ME A RIDE?
......

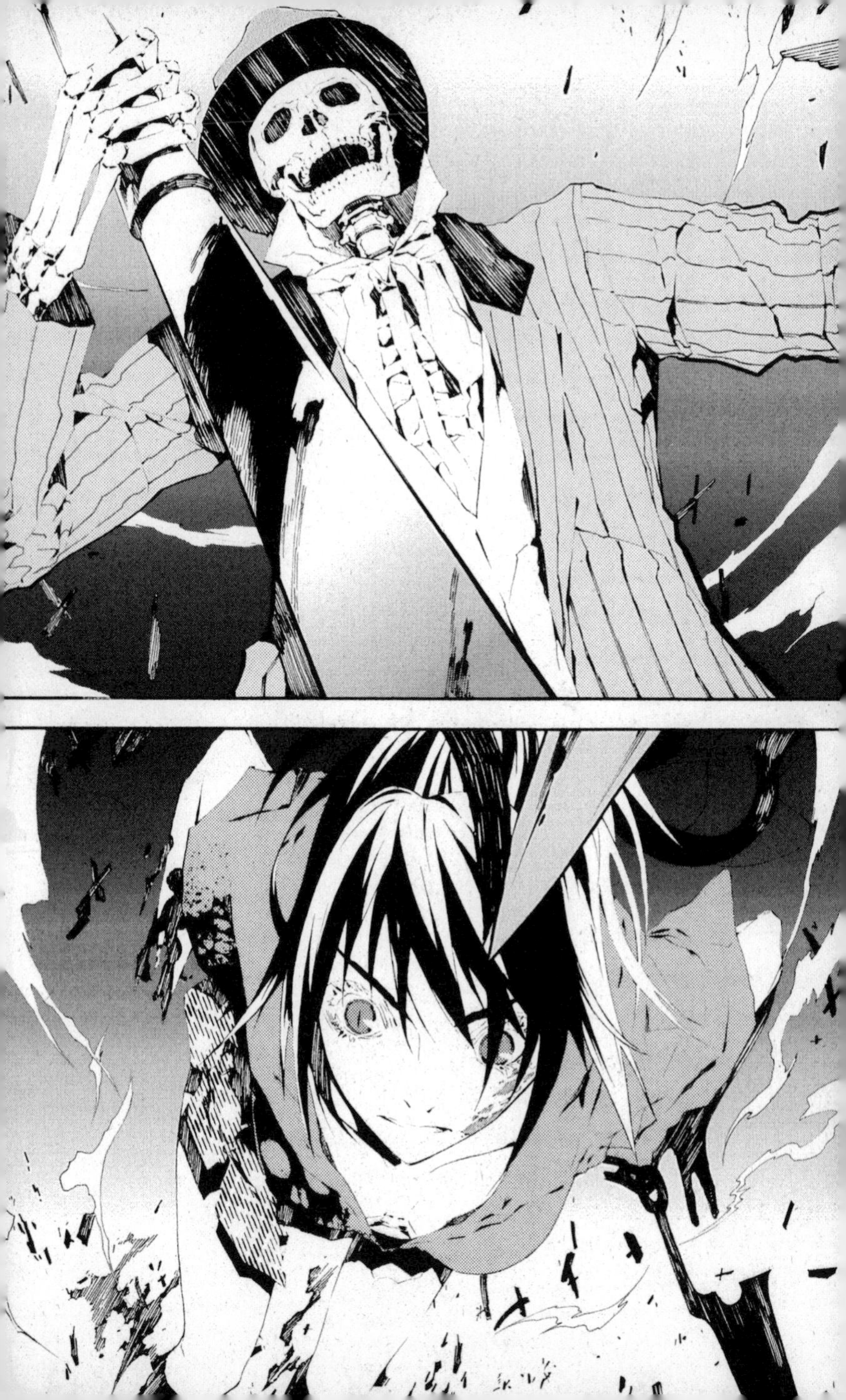

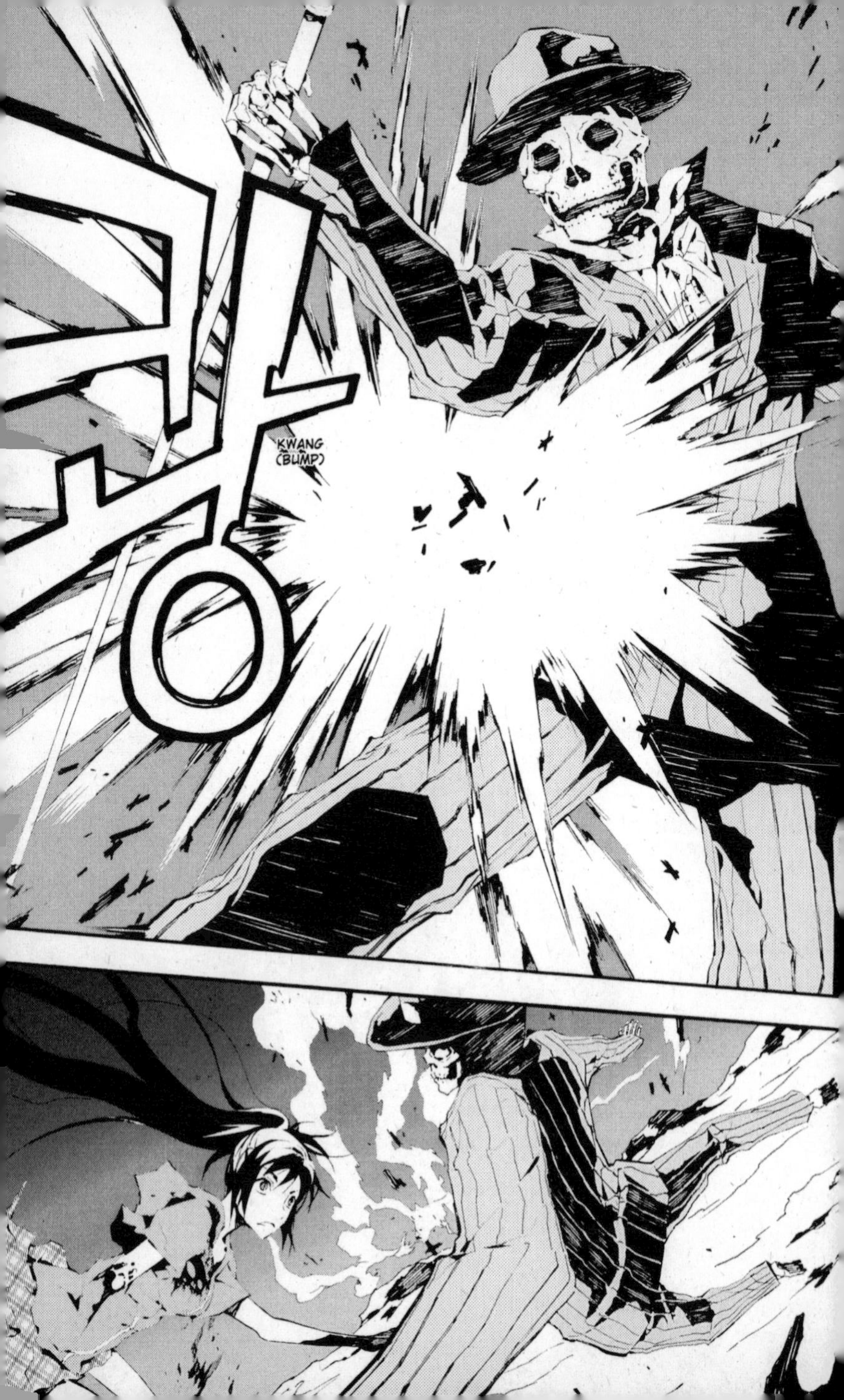
KWANG
(BUMP)

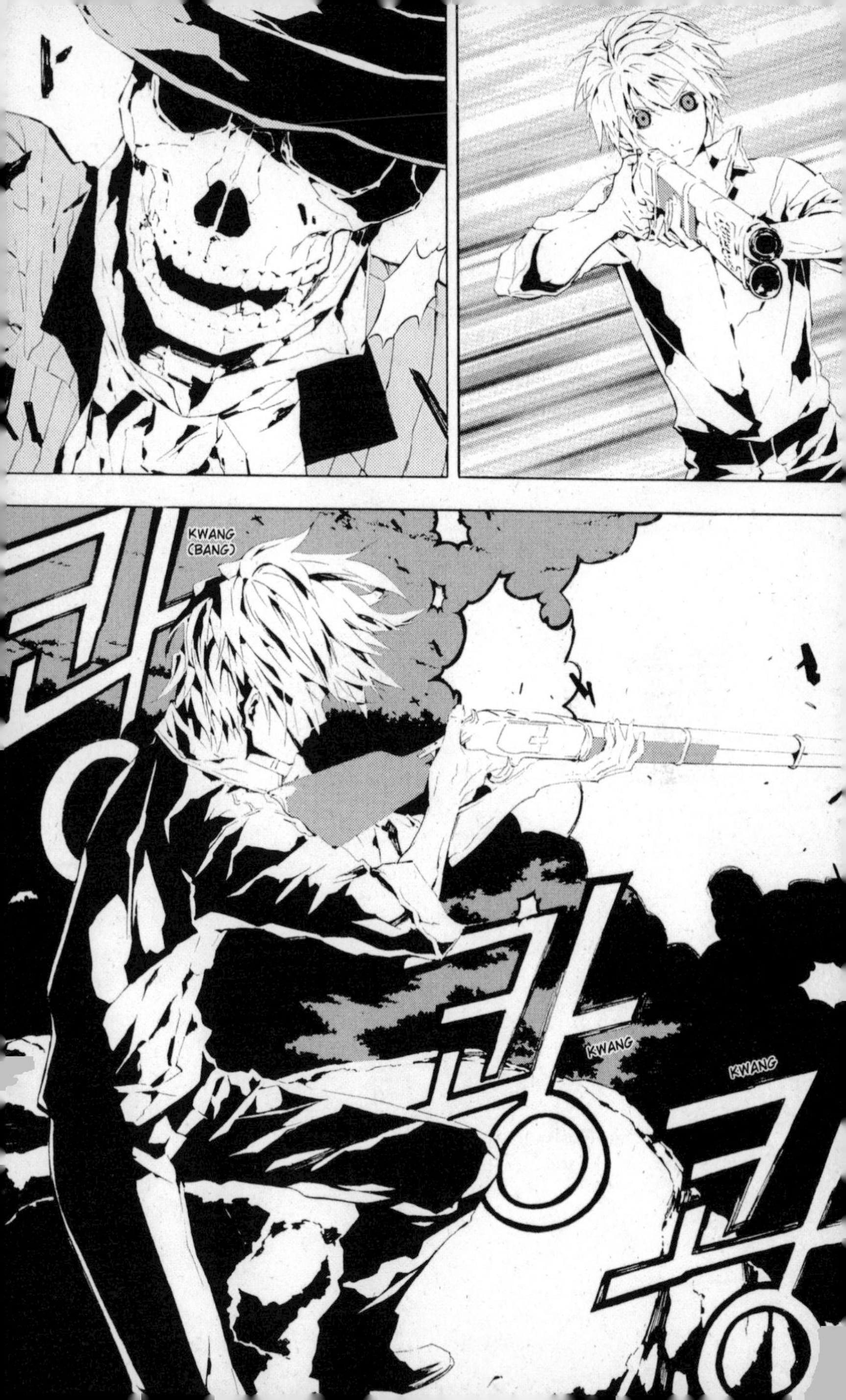
KWANG
(BANG)
KWANG
KWANG

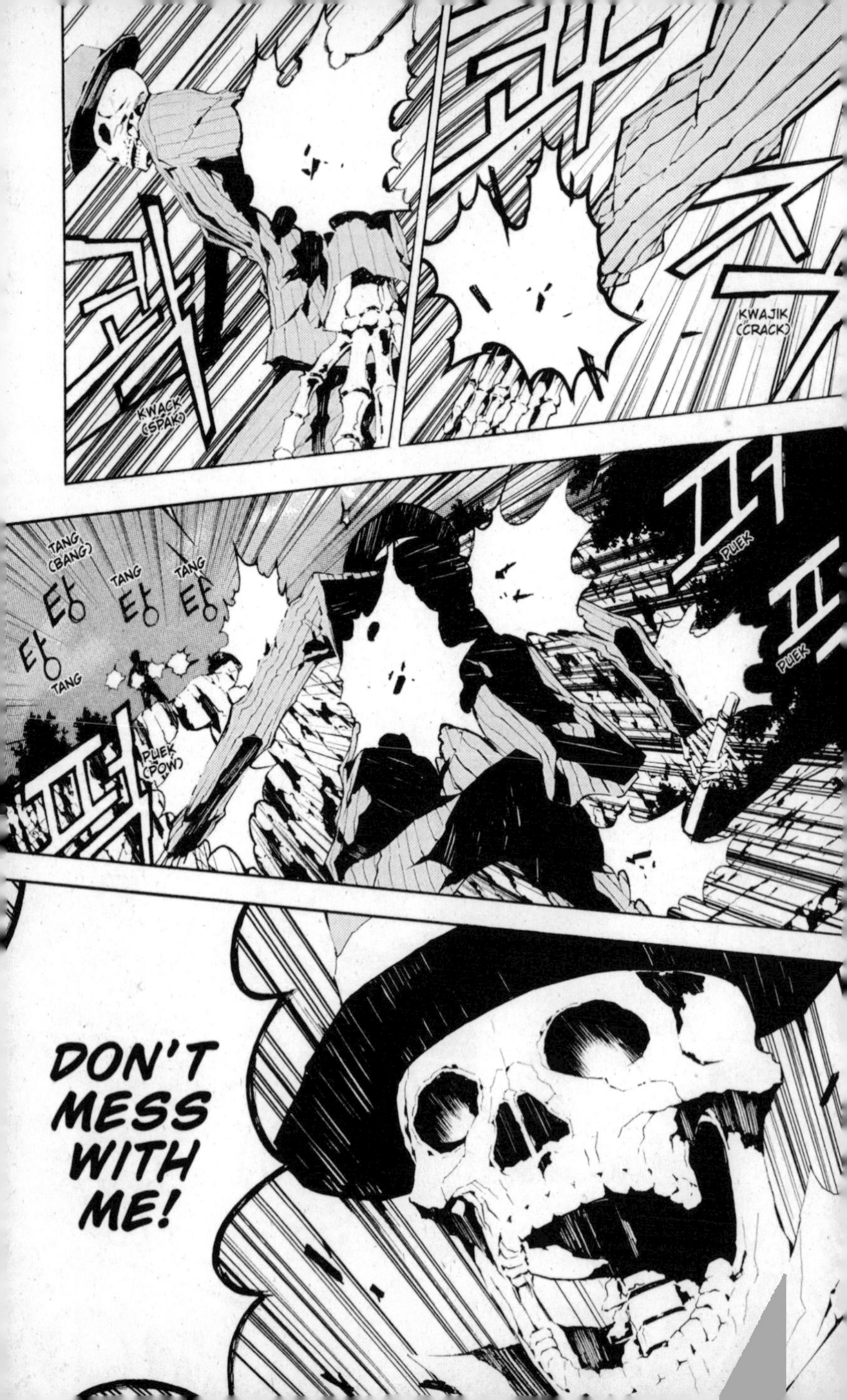
KWACK (SPAK)
KWAJIK (CRACK)
탕
TANG (BANG)
탕
TANG
탕
TANG
탕
TANG
PUEK
PUEK
PUEK (POW)
DON'T MESS WITH ME!

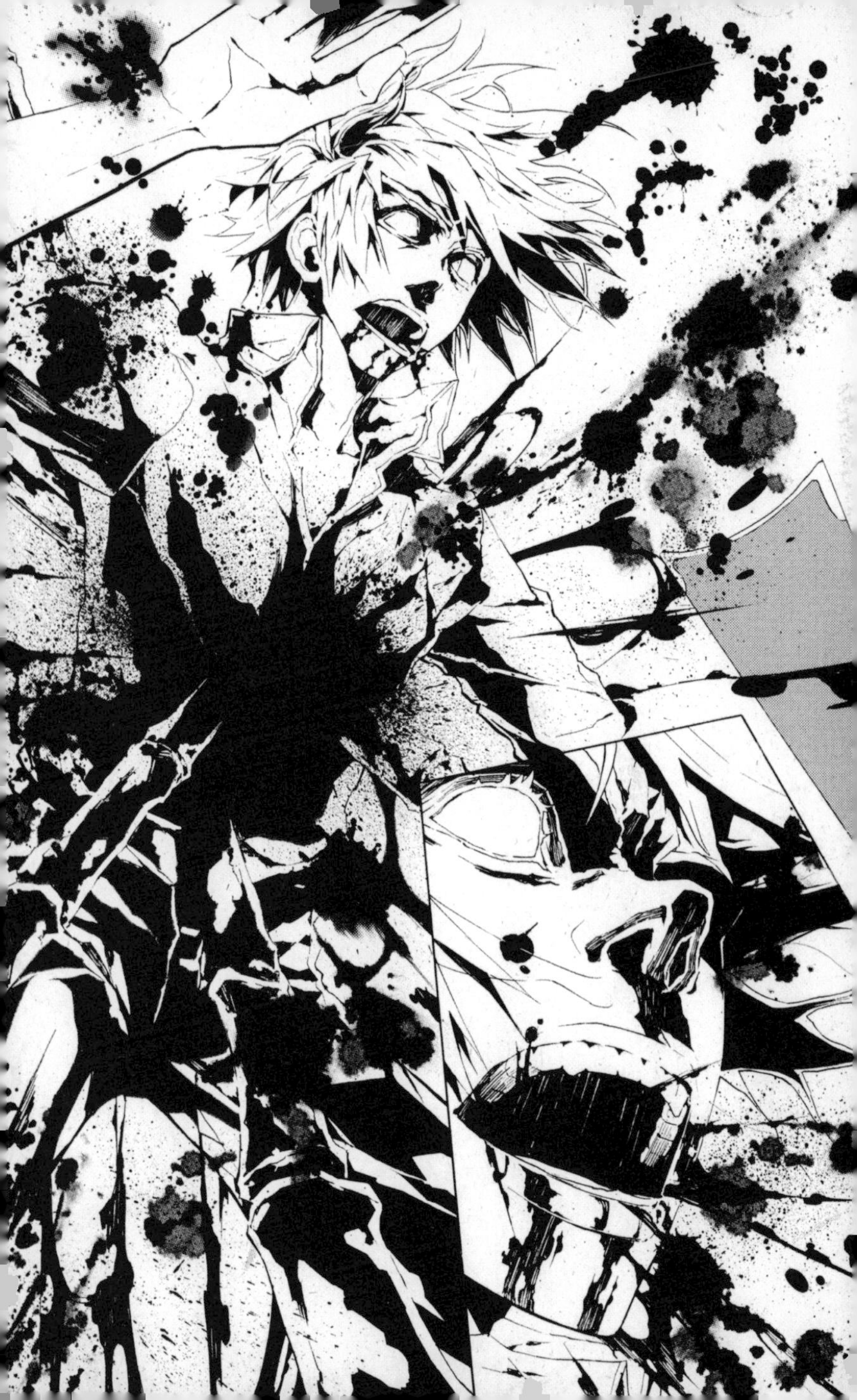

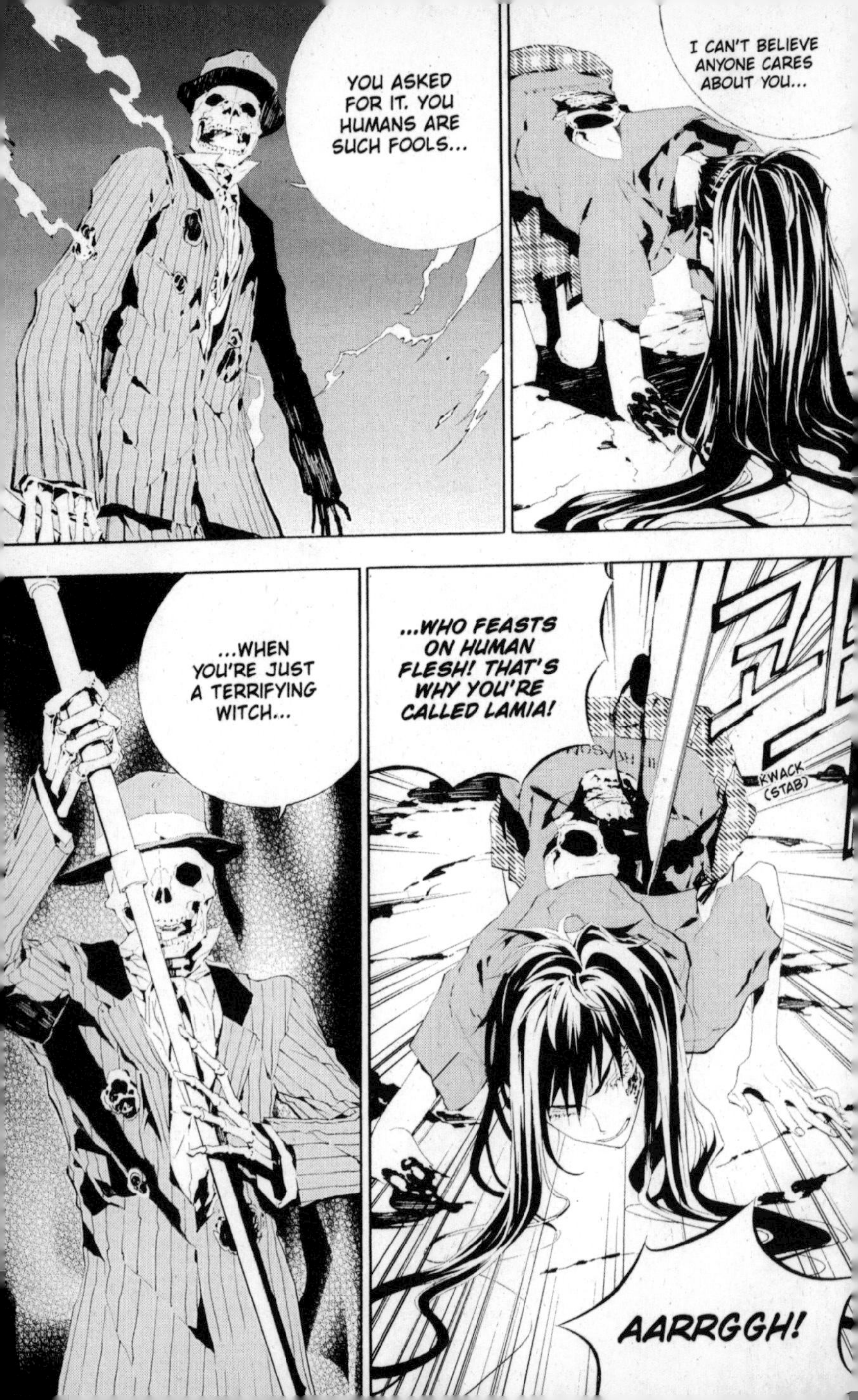
YOU ASKED FOR IT. YOU HUMANS ARE SUCH FOOLS...
I CAN'T BELIEVE ANYONE CARES ABOUT YOU...
...WHEN YOU'RE JUST A TERRIFYING WITCH...
...WHO FEASTS ON HUMAN FLESH! THAT'S WHY YOU'RE CALLED LAMIA!
KWACK (STAB)
AARRGGH!

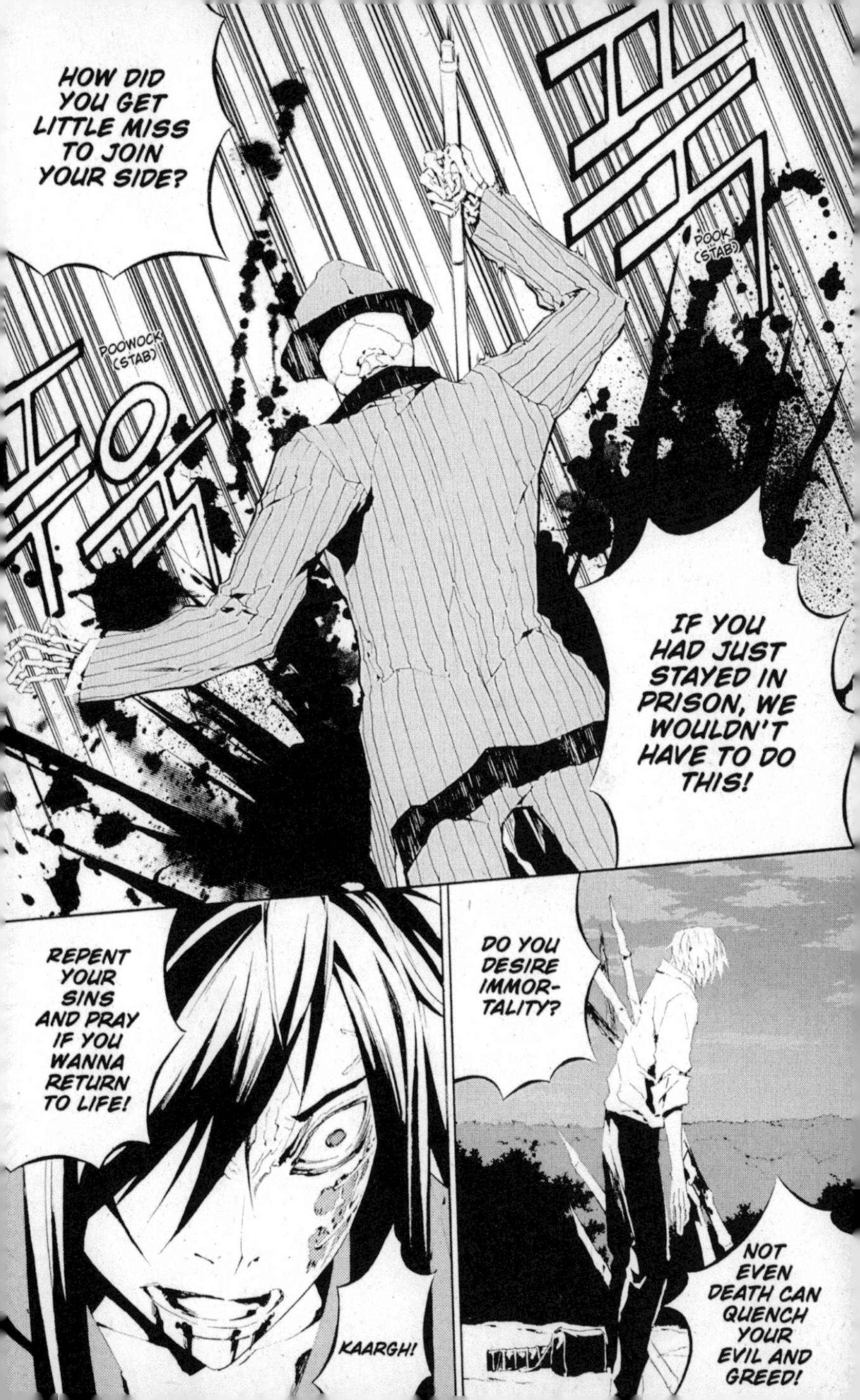
HOW DID YOU GET LITTLE MISS TO JOIN YOUR SIDE?
POOK (STAB)
POOWOCK (STAB)
IF YOU HAD JUST STAYED IN PRISON, WE WOULDN'T HAVE TO DO THIS!
REPENT YOUR SINS AND PRAY IF YOU WANNA RETURN TO LIFE!
KAARGH!
DO YOU DESIRE IMMORTALITY?
NOT EVEN DEATH CAN QUENCH YOUR EVIL AND GREED!

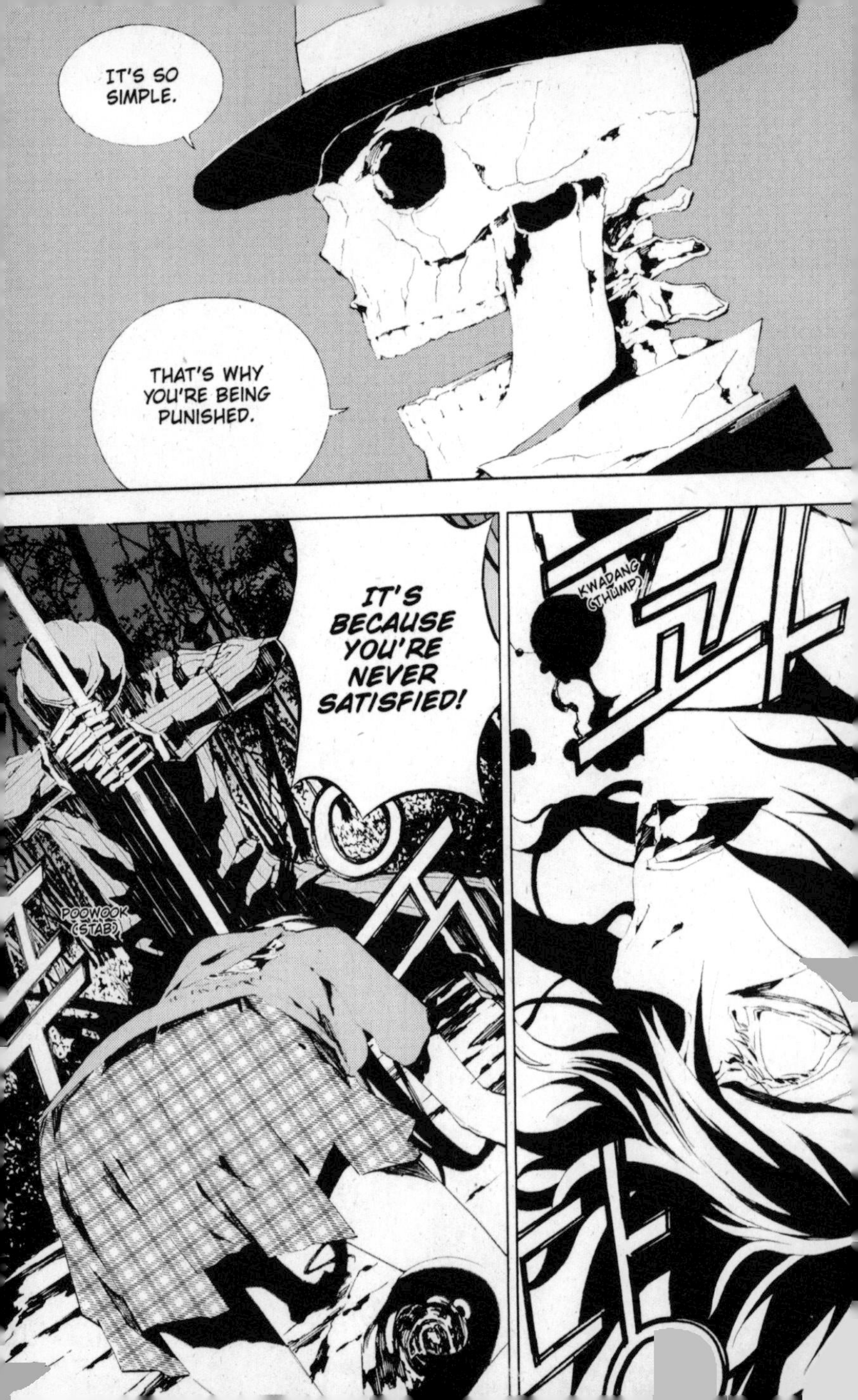
IT'S SO SIMPLE.
THAT'S WHY YOU'RE BEING PUNISHED.
IT'S BECAUSE YOU'RE NEVER SATISFIED!
POOWOOK (STAB)
KWADANG (THUMP)

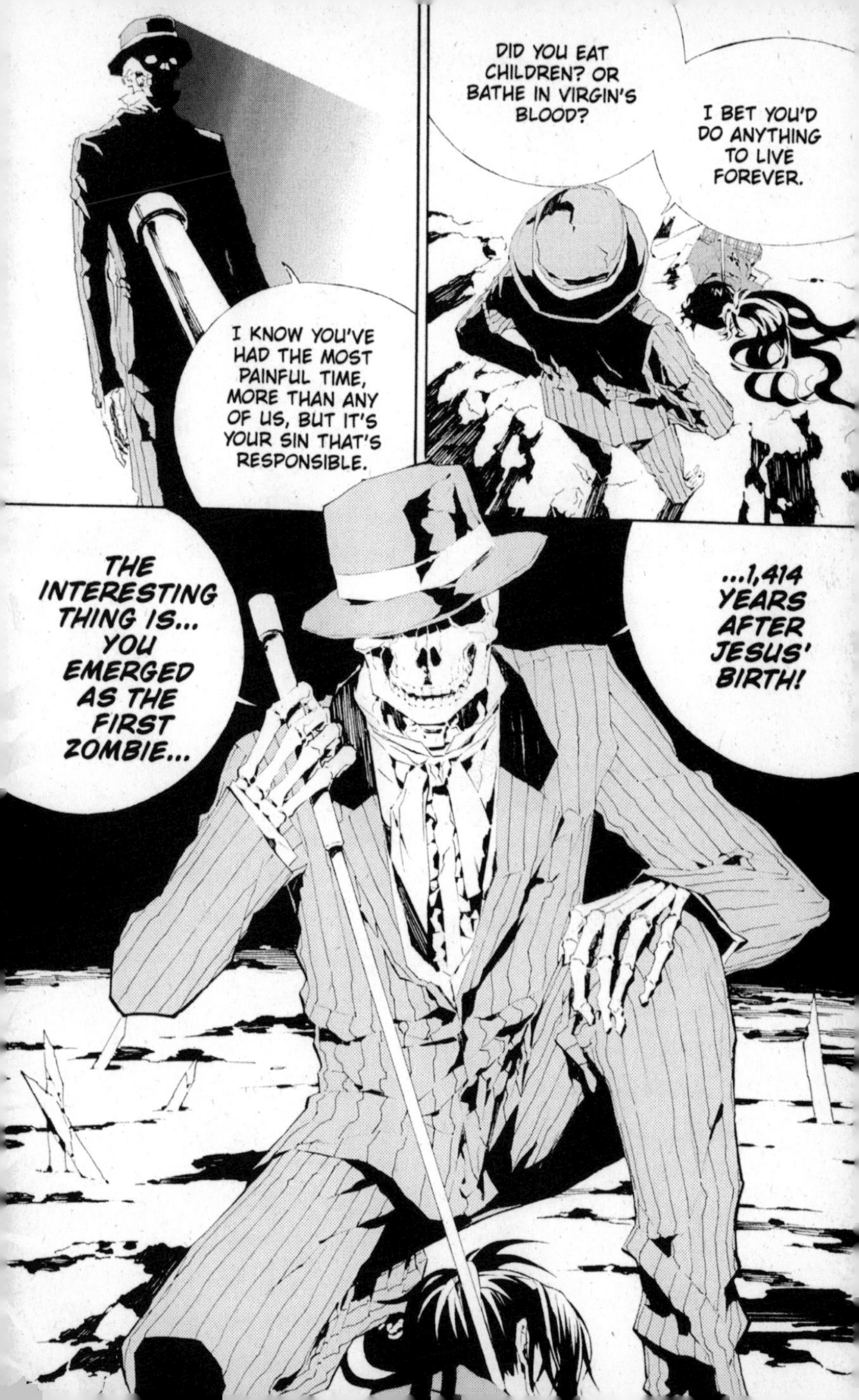
I KNOW YOU'VE HAD THE MOST PAINFUL TIME, MORE THAN ANY OF US, BUT IT'S YOUR SIN THAT'S RESPONSIBLE.
DID YOU EAT CHILDREN? OR BATHE IN VIRGIN'S BLOOD?
I BET YOU'D DO ANYTHING TO LIVE FOREVER.
THE INTERESTING THING IS... YOU EMERGED AS THE FIRST ZOMBIE...
...1,414 YEARS AFTER JESUS' BIRTH!

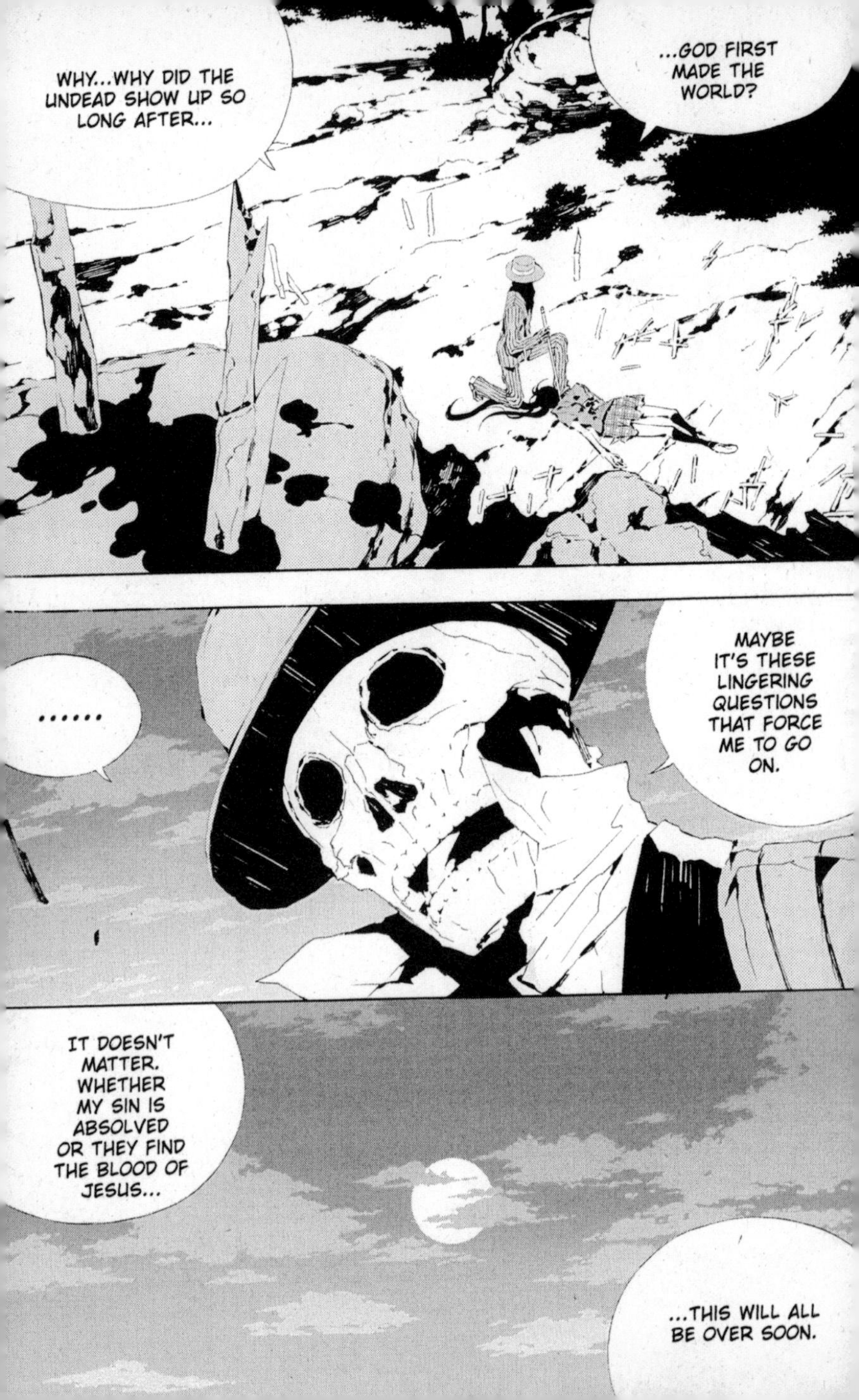
WHY...WHY DID THE UNDEAD SHOW UP SO LONG AFTER...
...GOD FIRST MADE THE WORLD?
......
MAYBE IT'S THESE LINGERING QUESTIONS THAT FORCE ME TO GO ON.
IT DOESN'T MATTER. WHETHER MY SIN IS ABSOLVED OR THEY FIND THE BLOOD OF JESUS...
...THIS WILL ALL BE OVER SOON.

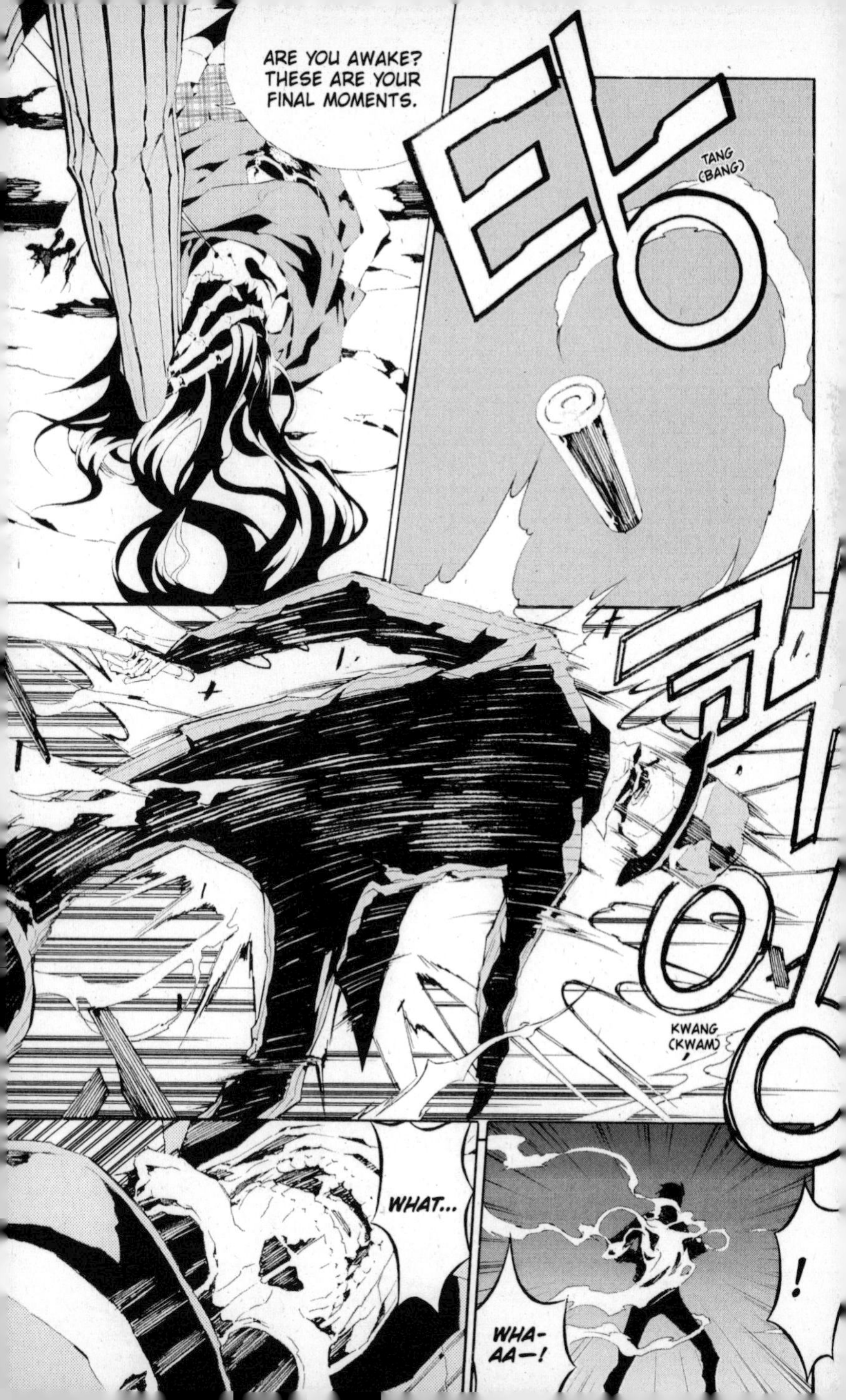
ARE YOU AWAKE? THESE ARE YOUR FINAL MOMENTS.
탕
TANG (BANG)
KWANG (KWAM)
WHAT...
WHA-AA—!
!

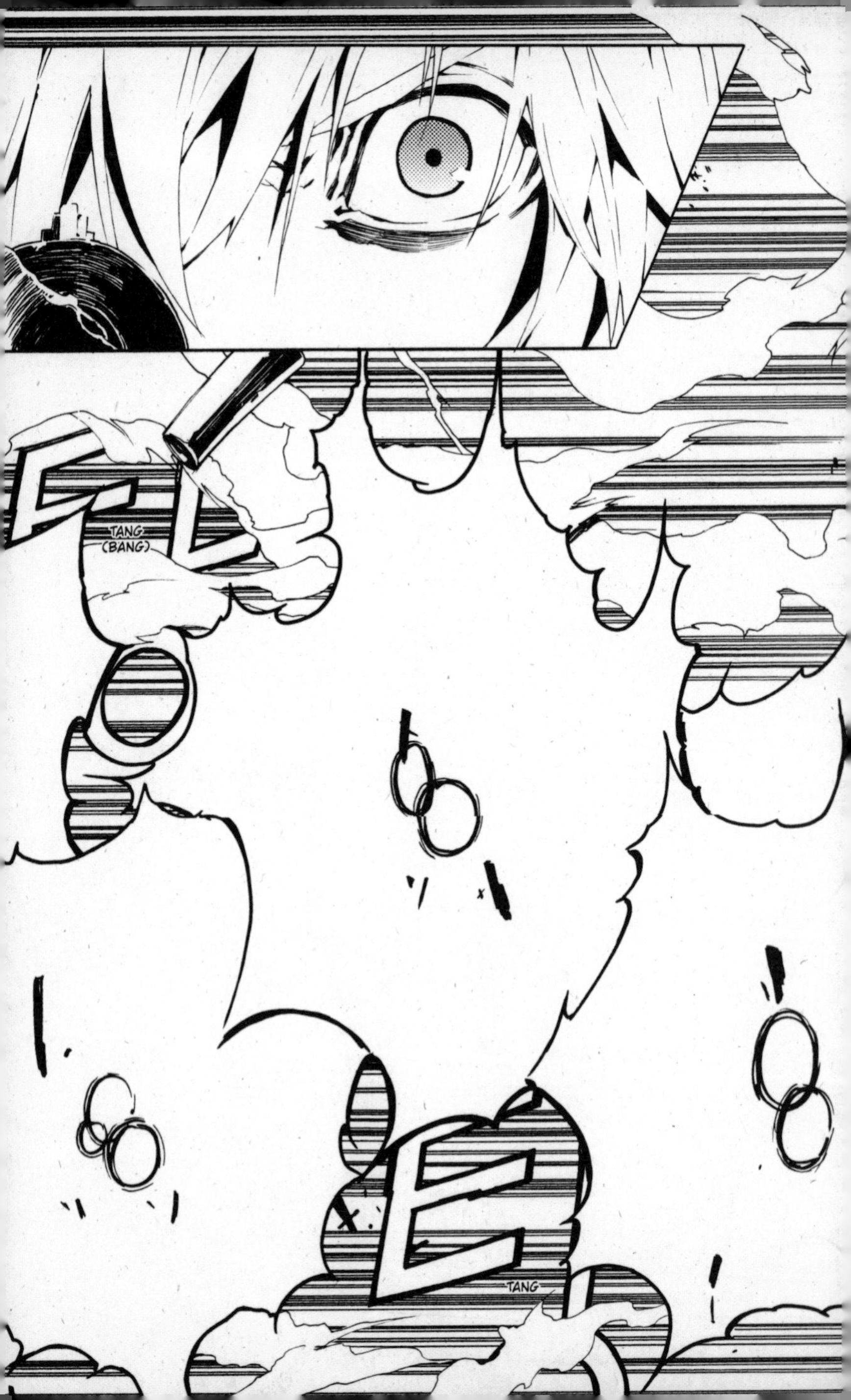
TANG
(BANG)
TANG

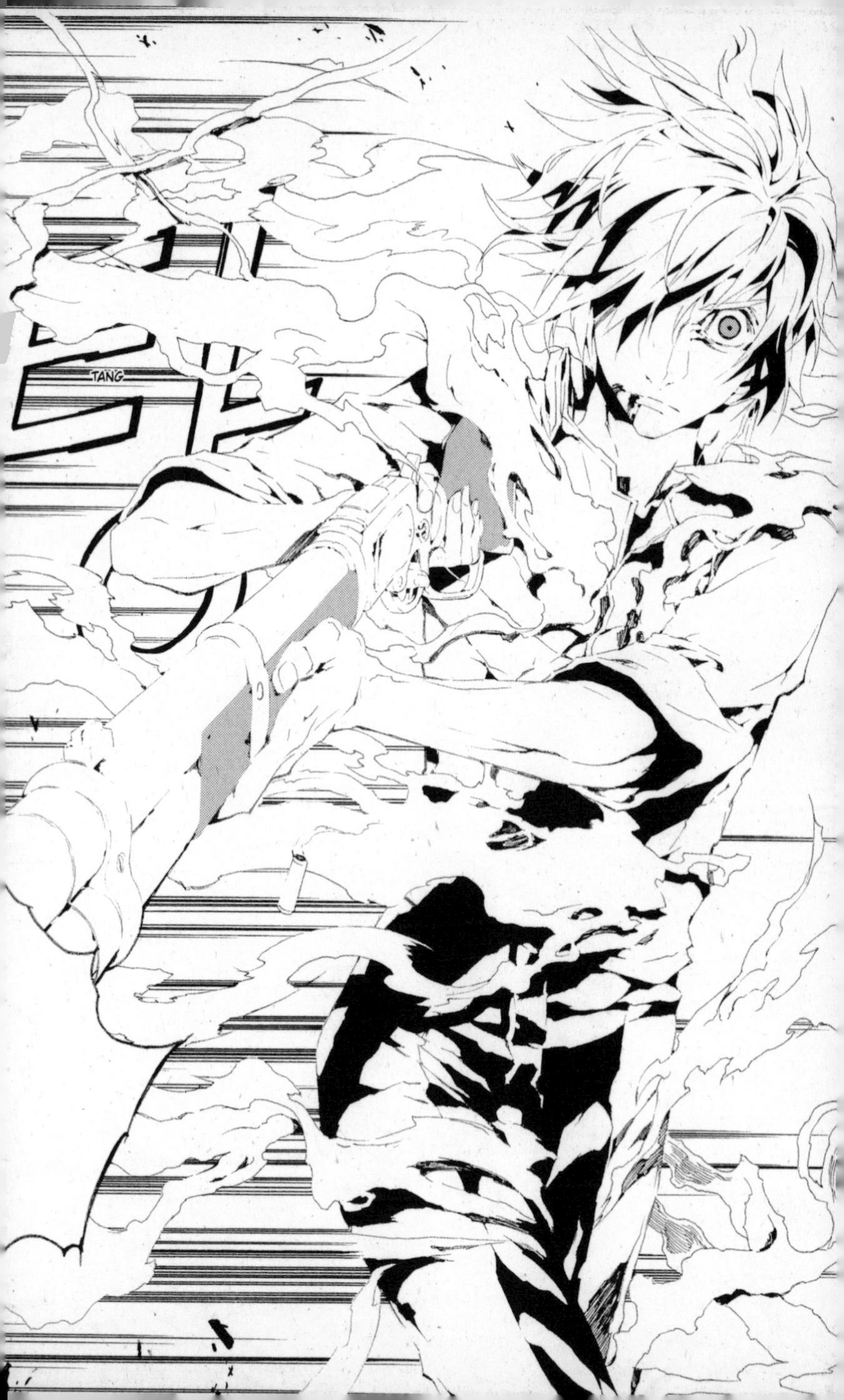
TANG

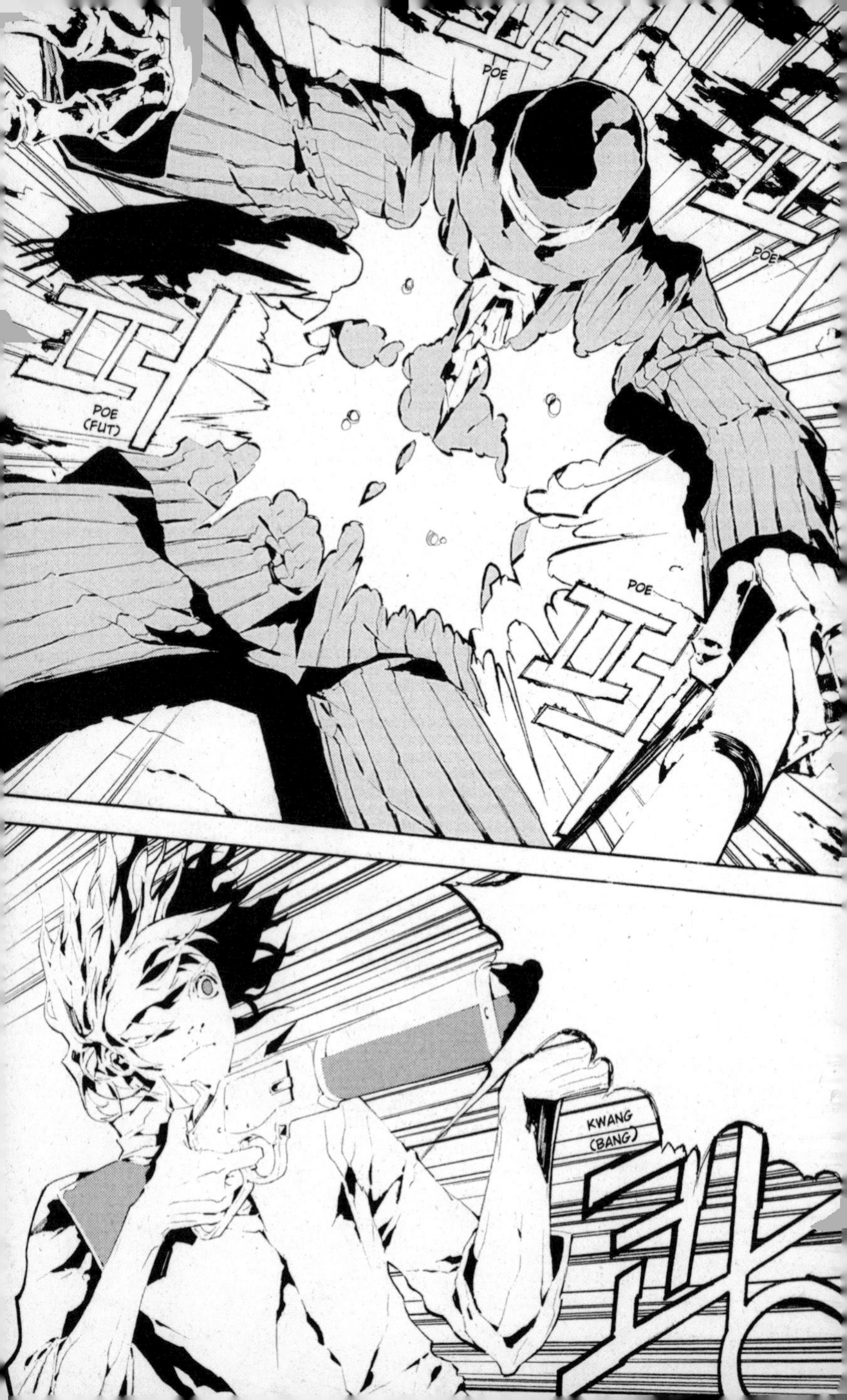
POE
POE
POE
(FUT)
POE
KWANG
(BANG)

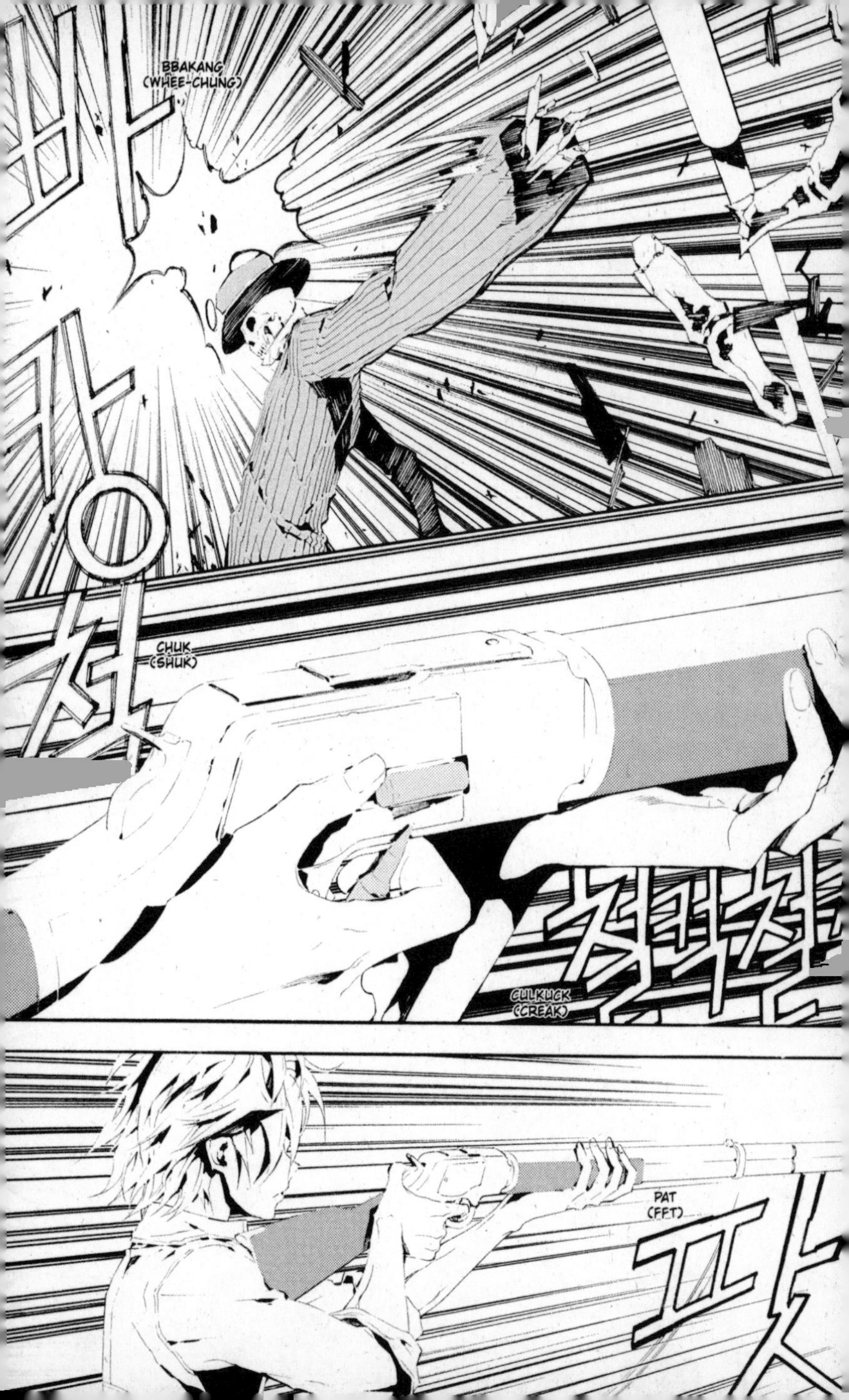

BBAKANG (WHEE-CHUNG)
CHUK (SHUK)
CULKUCK (CREAK)
PAT (FFT)

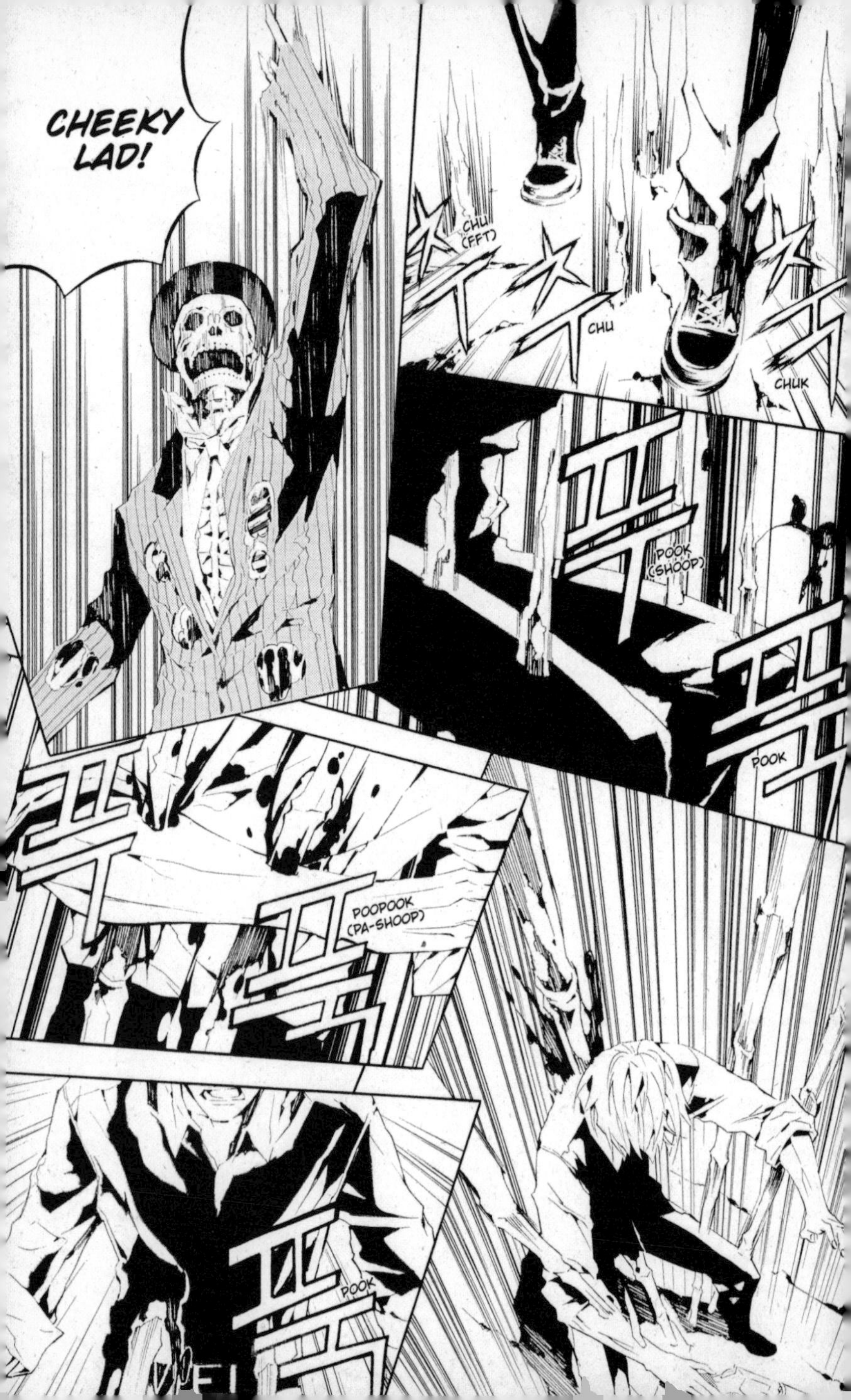
CHEEKY LAD!
CHU (FFT)
CHU
CHUK
POOK (SHOOP)
POOK
POOPOOK (PA-SHOOP)
POOK

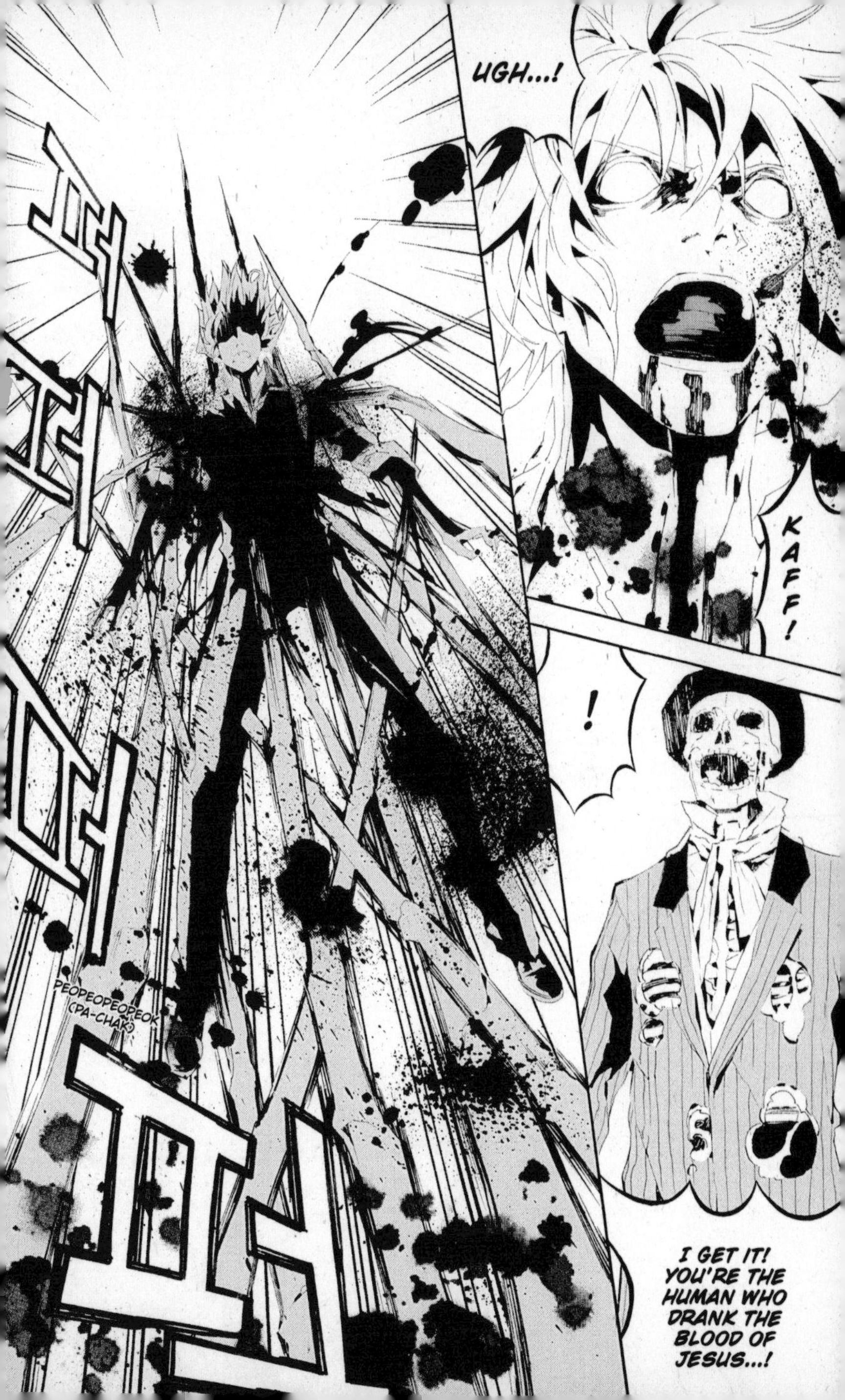
PEOPEOPEOPEOK
(PA-CHAK)
UGH...!
KAFF!
!
I GET IT! YOU'RE THE HUMAN WHO DRANK THE BLOOD OF JESUS...!

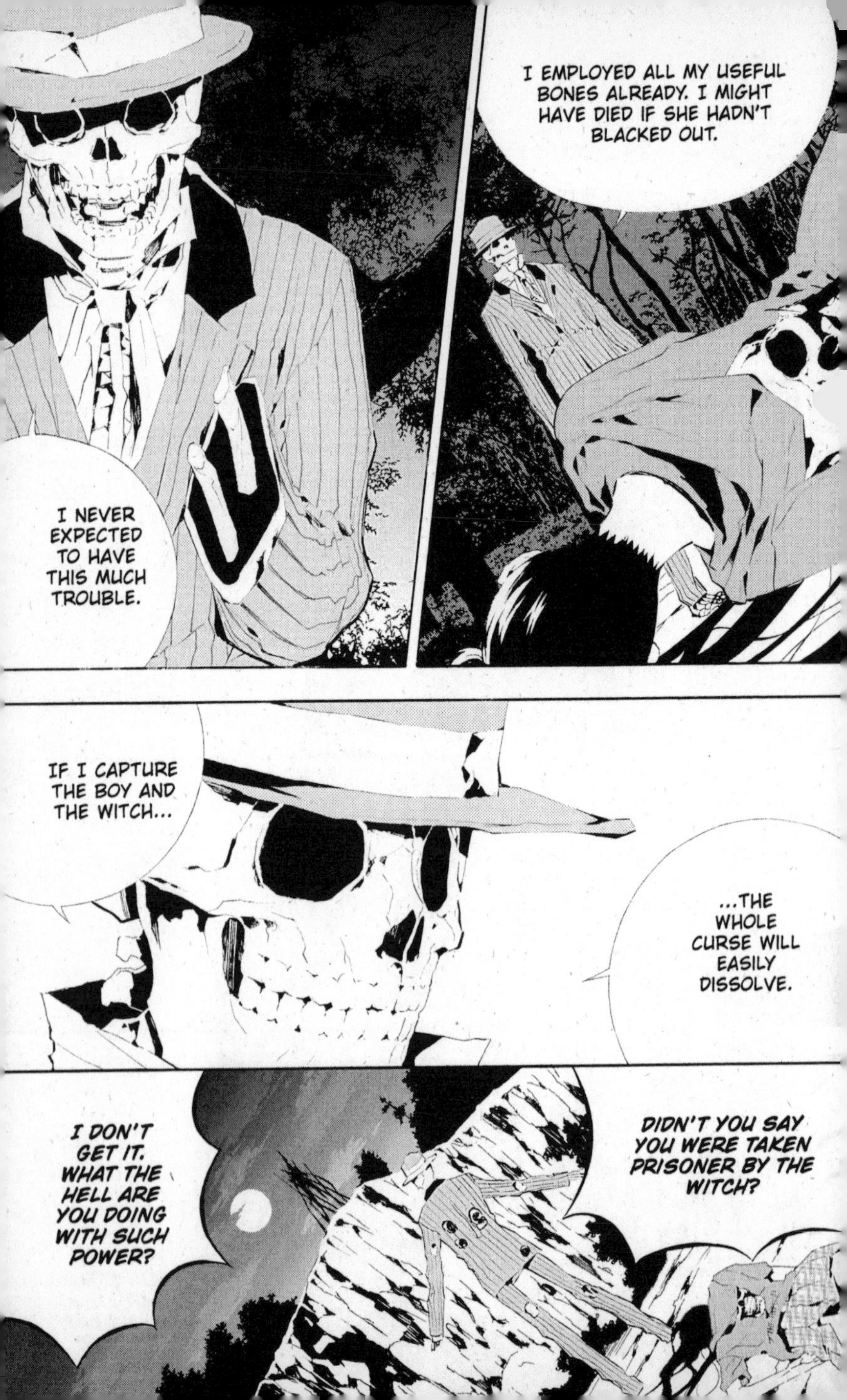
I NEVER EXPECTED TO HAVE THIS MUCH TROUBLE.
I EMPLOYED ALL MY USEFUL BONES ALREADY. I MIGHT HAVE DIED IF SHE HADN'T BLACKED OUT.
IF I CAPTURE THE BOY AND THE WITCH...
...THE WHOLE CURSE WILL EASILY DISSOLVE.
I DON'T GET IT. WHAT THE HELL ARE YOU DOING WITH SUCH POWER?
DIDN'T YOU SAY YOU WERE TAKEN PRISONER BY THE WITCH?

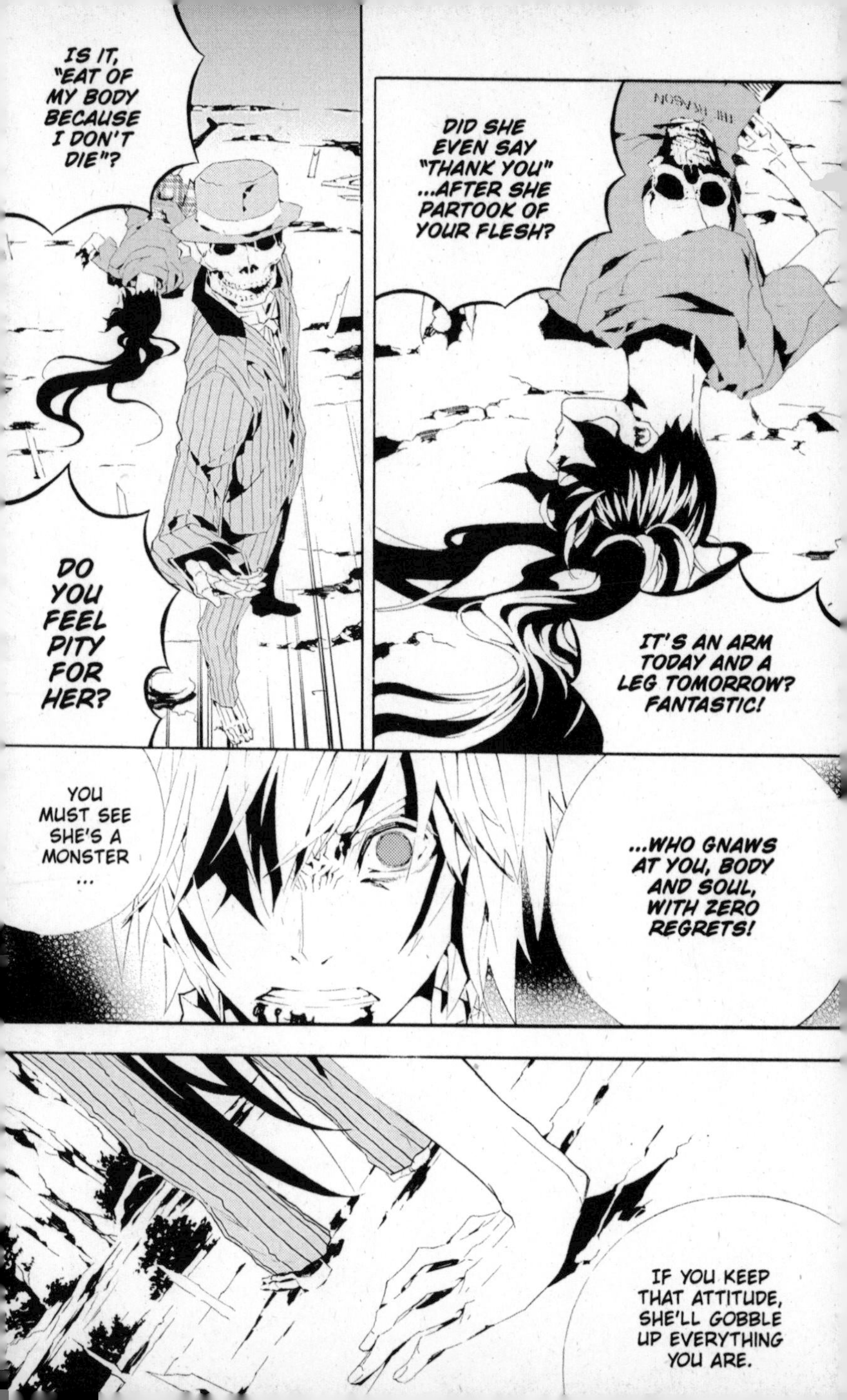
IS IT, "EAT OF MY BODY BECAUSE I DON'T DIE"?
DO YOU FEEL PITY FOR HER?
DID SHE EVEN SAY "THANK YOU" ...AFTER SHE PARTOOK OF YOUR FLESH?
IT'S AN ARM TODAY AND A LEG TOMORROW? FANTASTIC!
YOU MUST SEE SHE'S A MONSTER ...
...WHO GNAWS AT YOU, BODY AND SOUL, WITH ZERO REGRETS!
IF YOU KEEP THAT ATTITUDE, SHE'LL GOBBLE UP EVERYTHING YOU ARE.

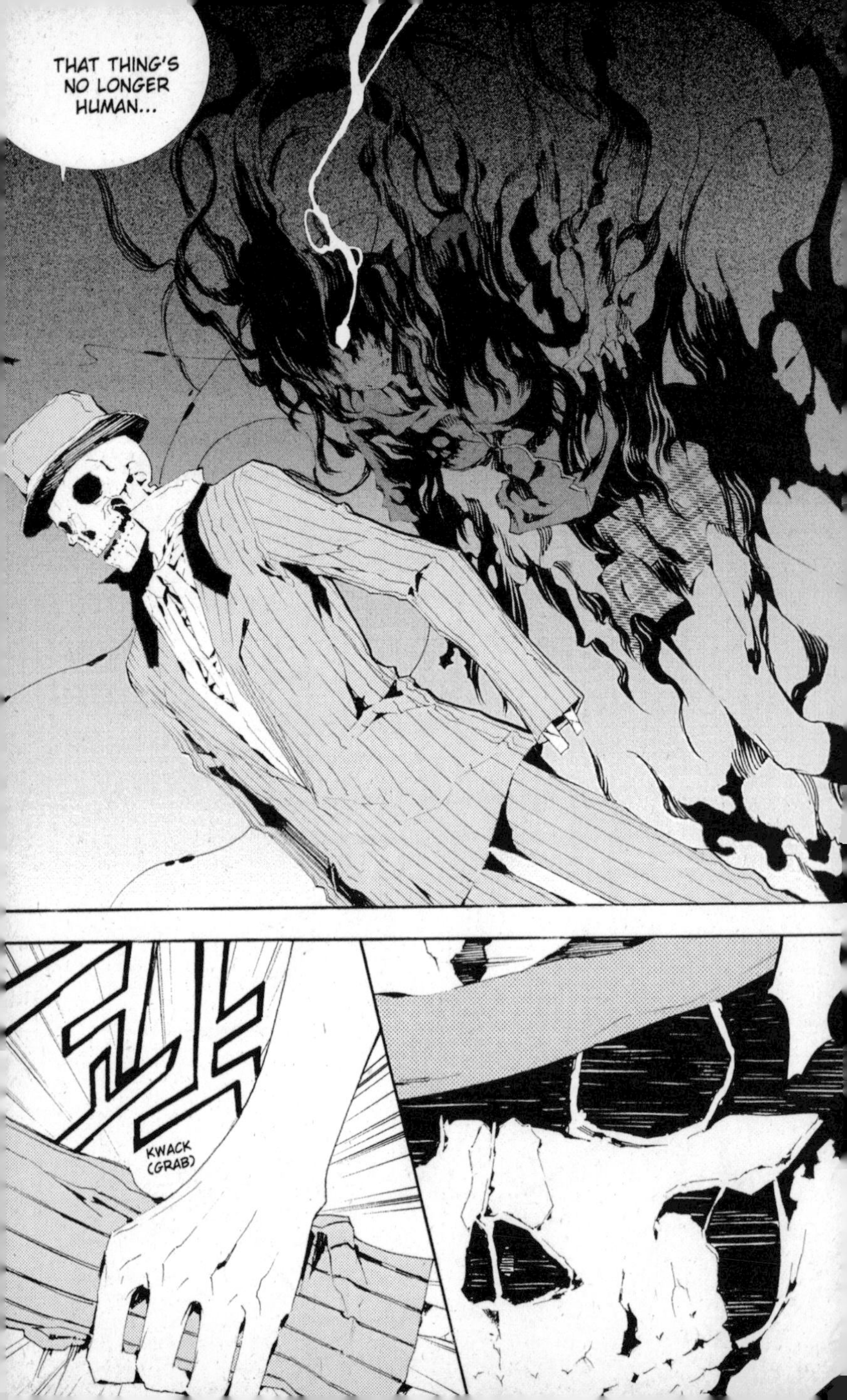
THAT THING'S NO LONGER HUMAN...
KWACK (GRAB)

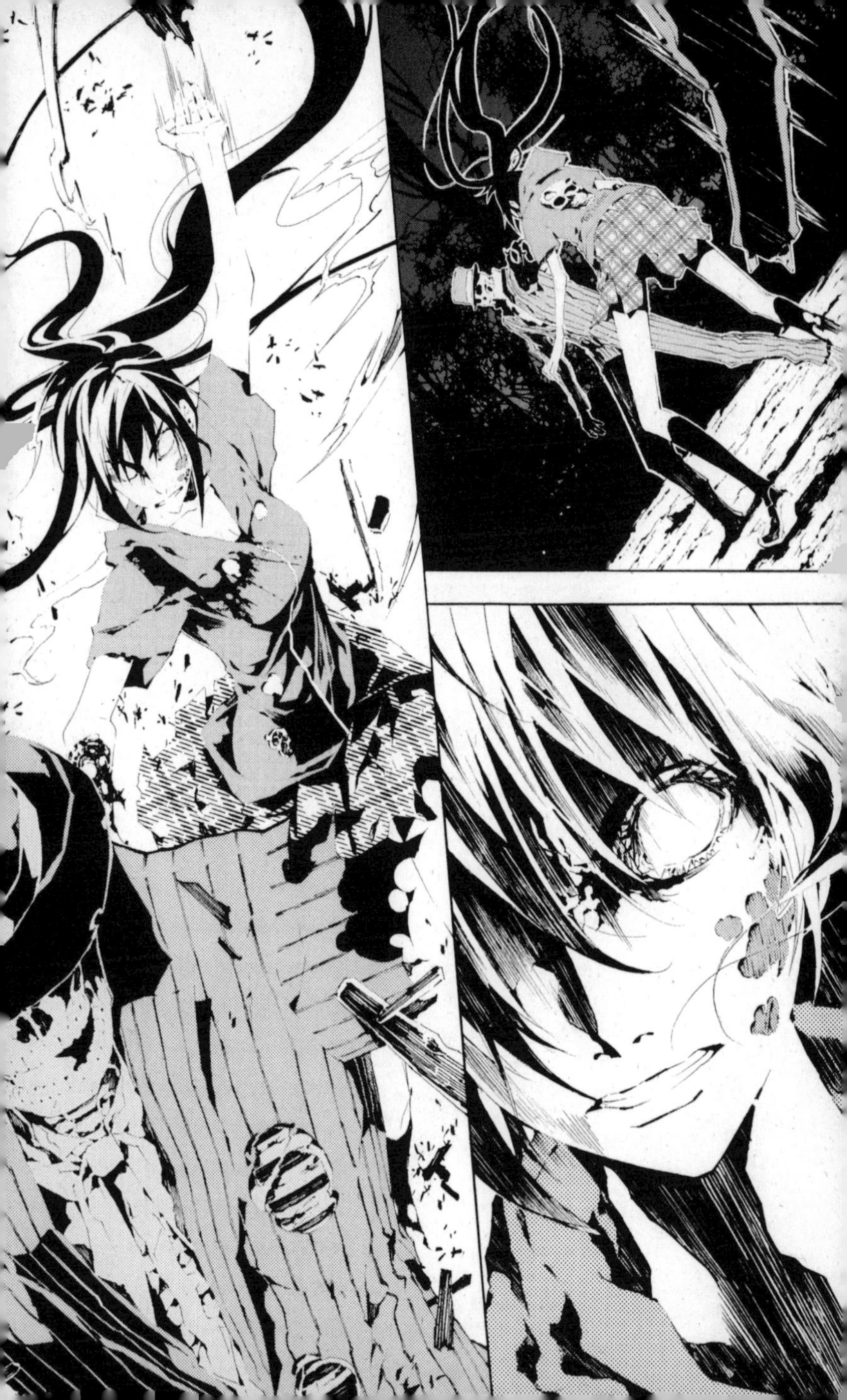

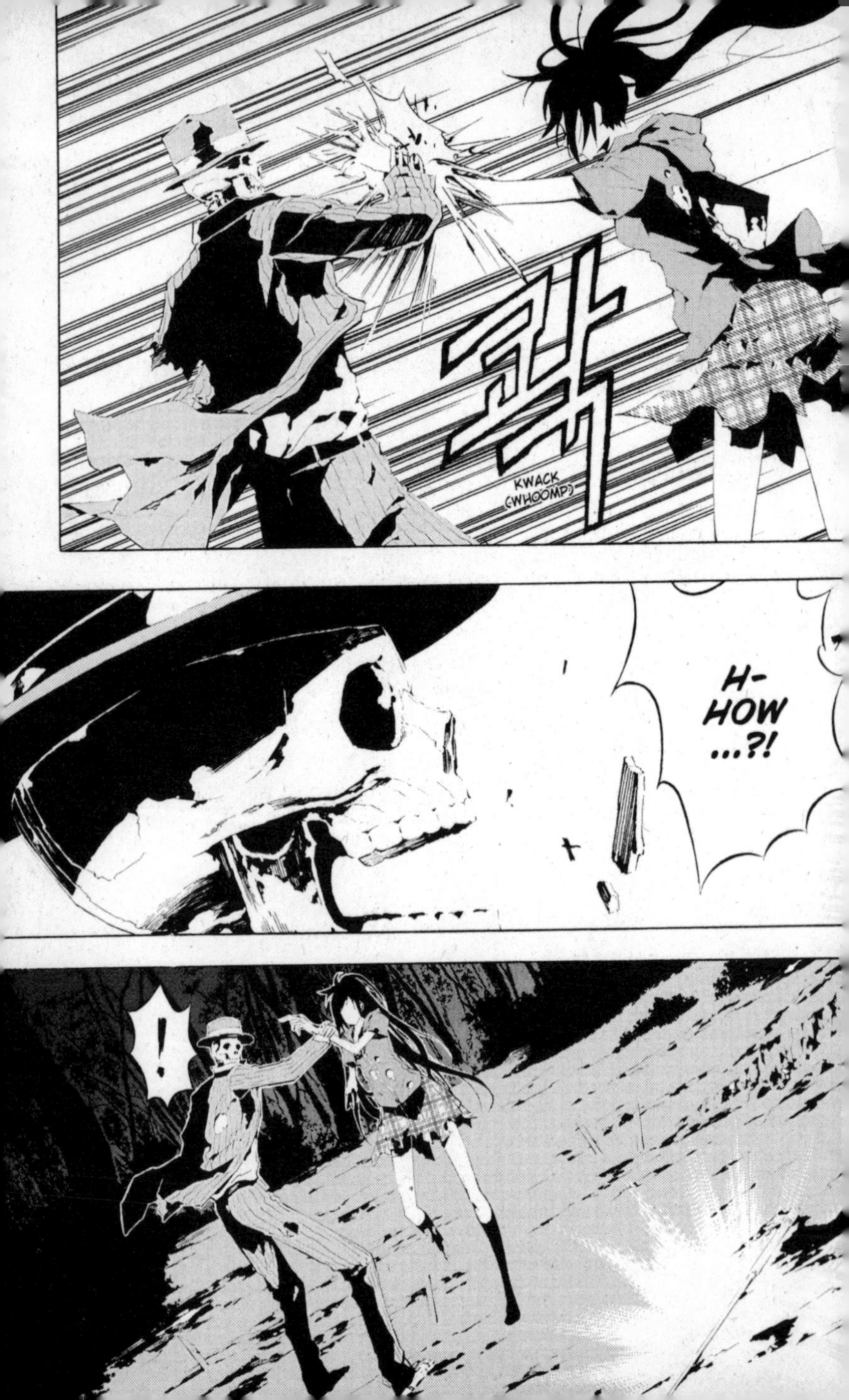

KWACK
(WHOOMP)
H-HOW...?!
!

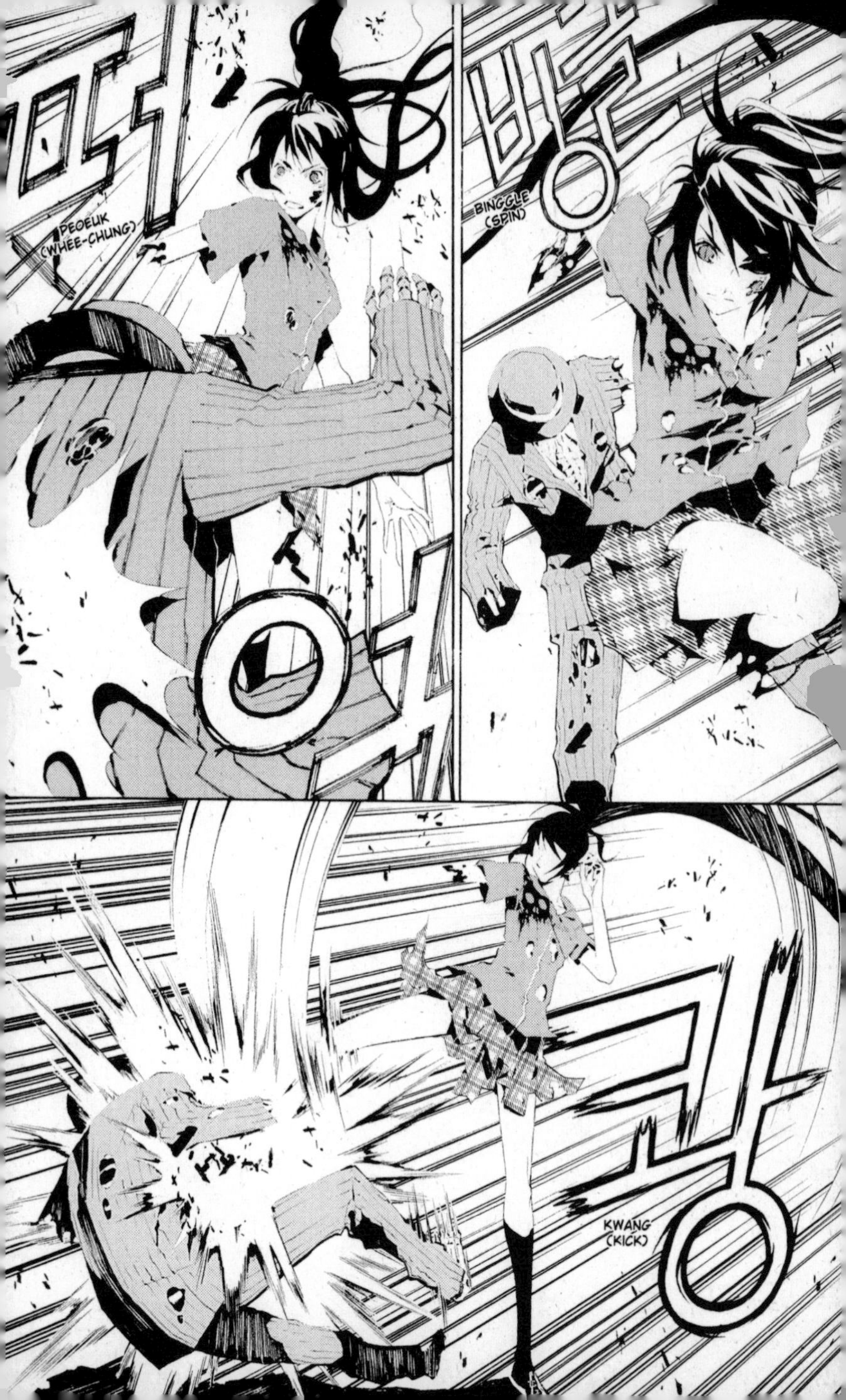
PEOEUK
(WHEE-CHUNG)
BINGGLE
(SPIN)
KWANG
(KICK)

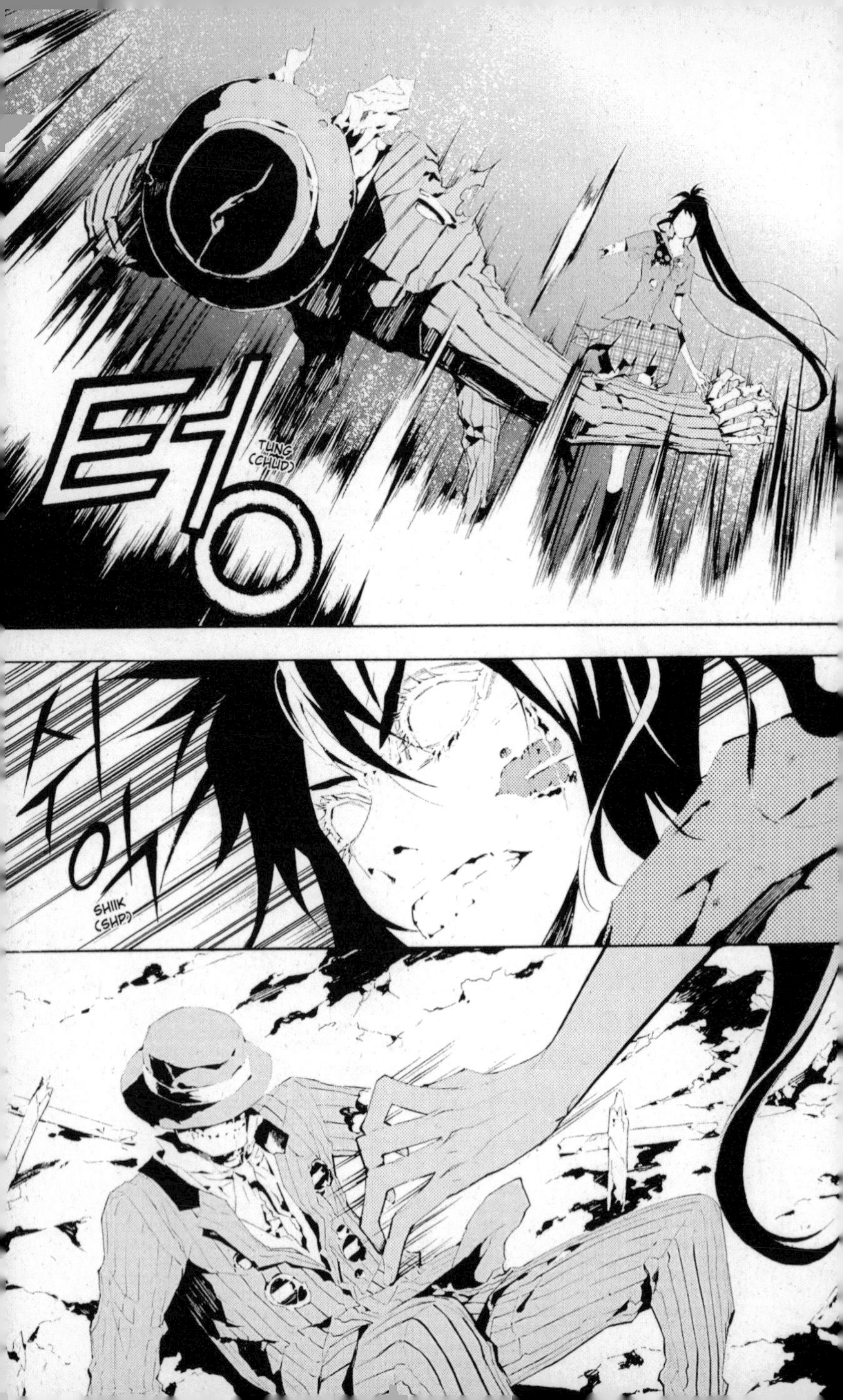
텅
TUNG (CHUD)
SHIIK (SHP)

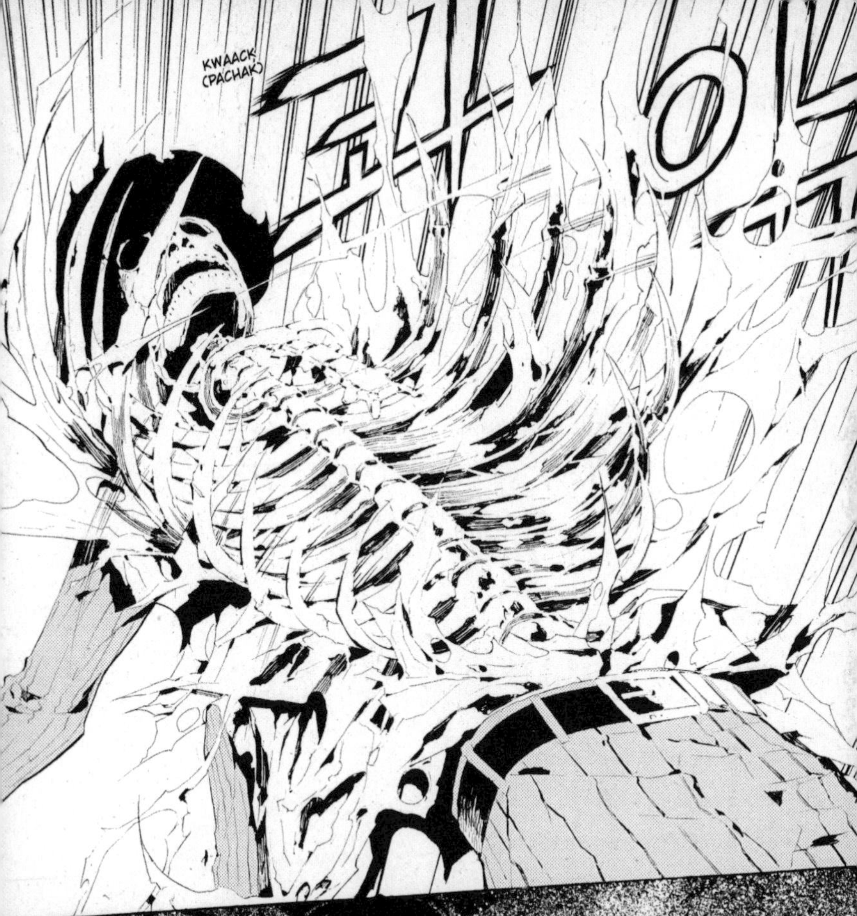
KWAACK
(PACHAK)
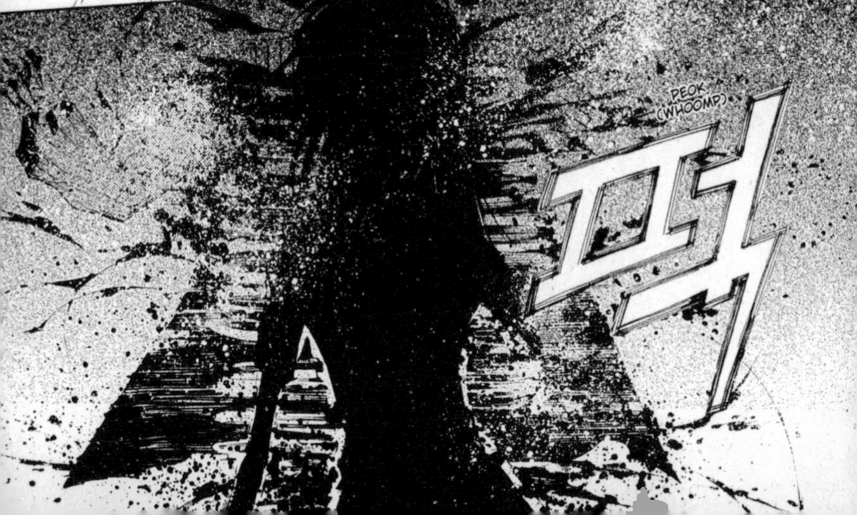
PEOK
(WHOOMP)

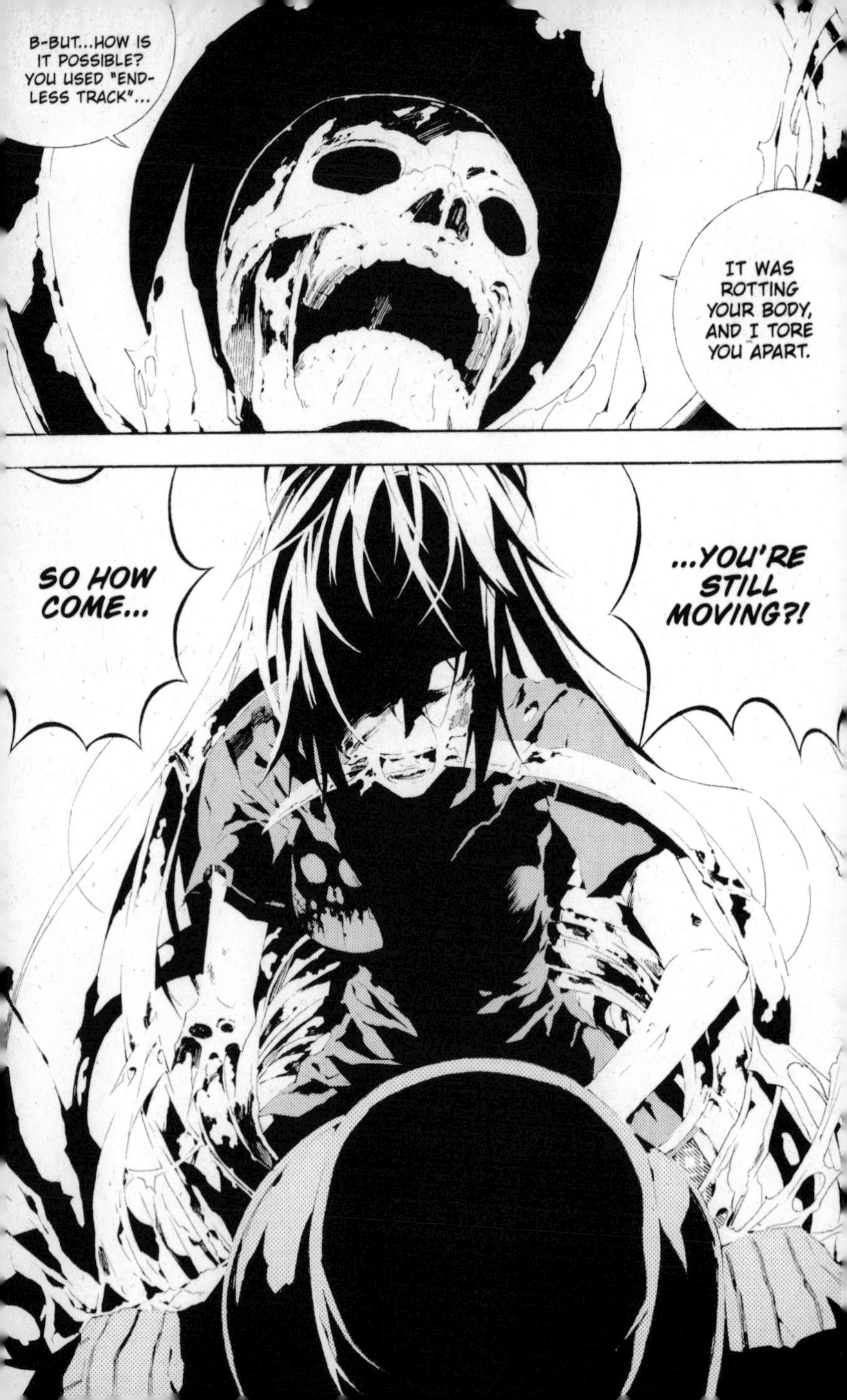
B-BUT...HOW IS IT POSSIBLE? YOU USED "END-LESS TRACK"...
IT WAS ROTTING YOUR BODY, AND I TORE YOU APART.
SO HOW COME...
...YOU'RE STILL MOVING?!

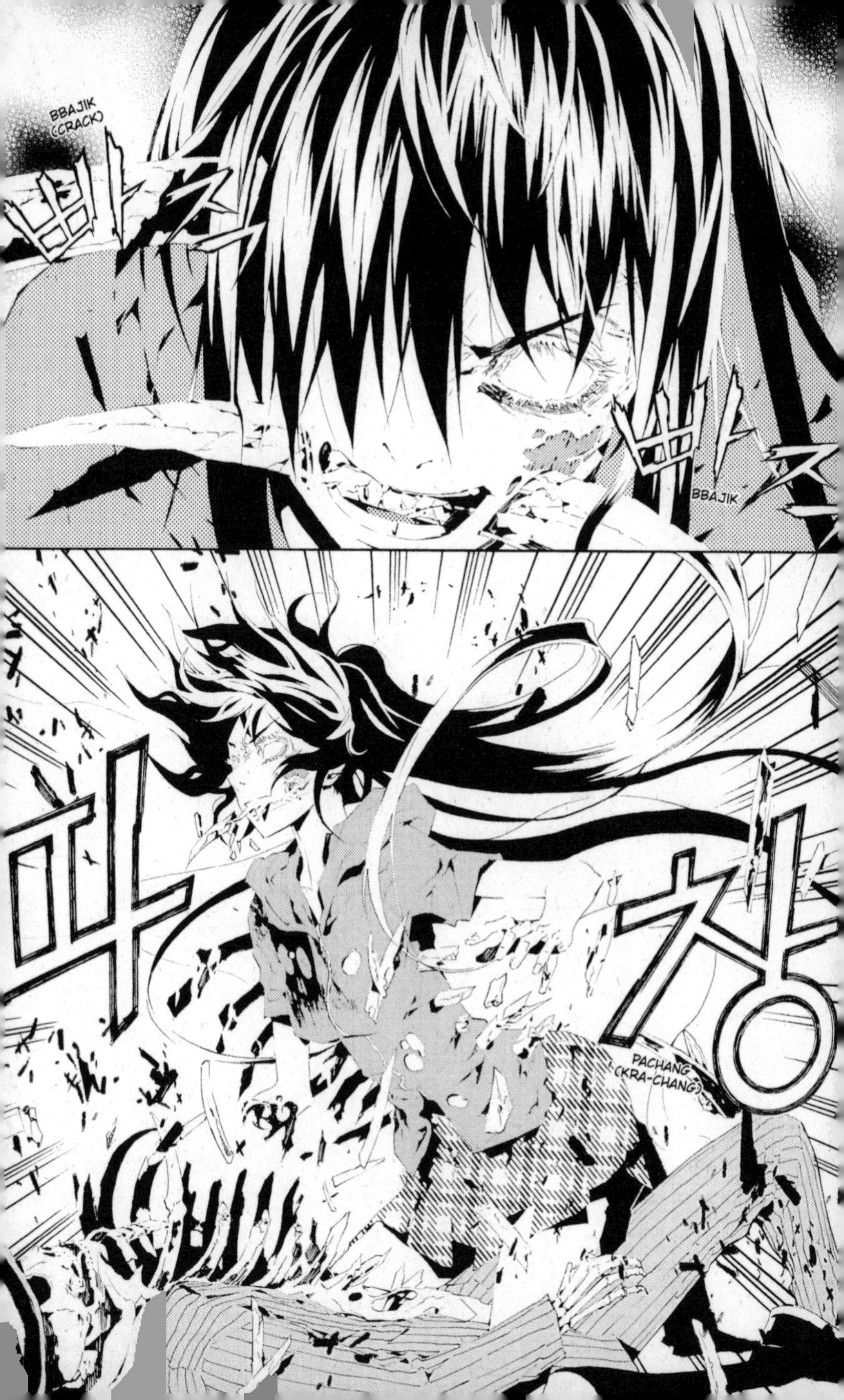

빠직
BBAJIK (CRACK)
빠직
BBAJIK
파창
PACHANG (KRA-CHANG)

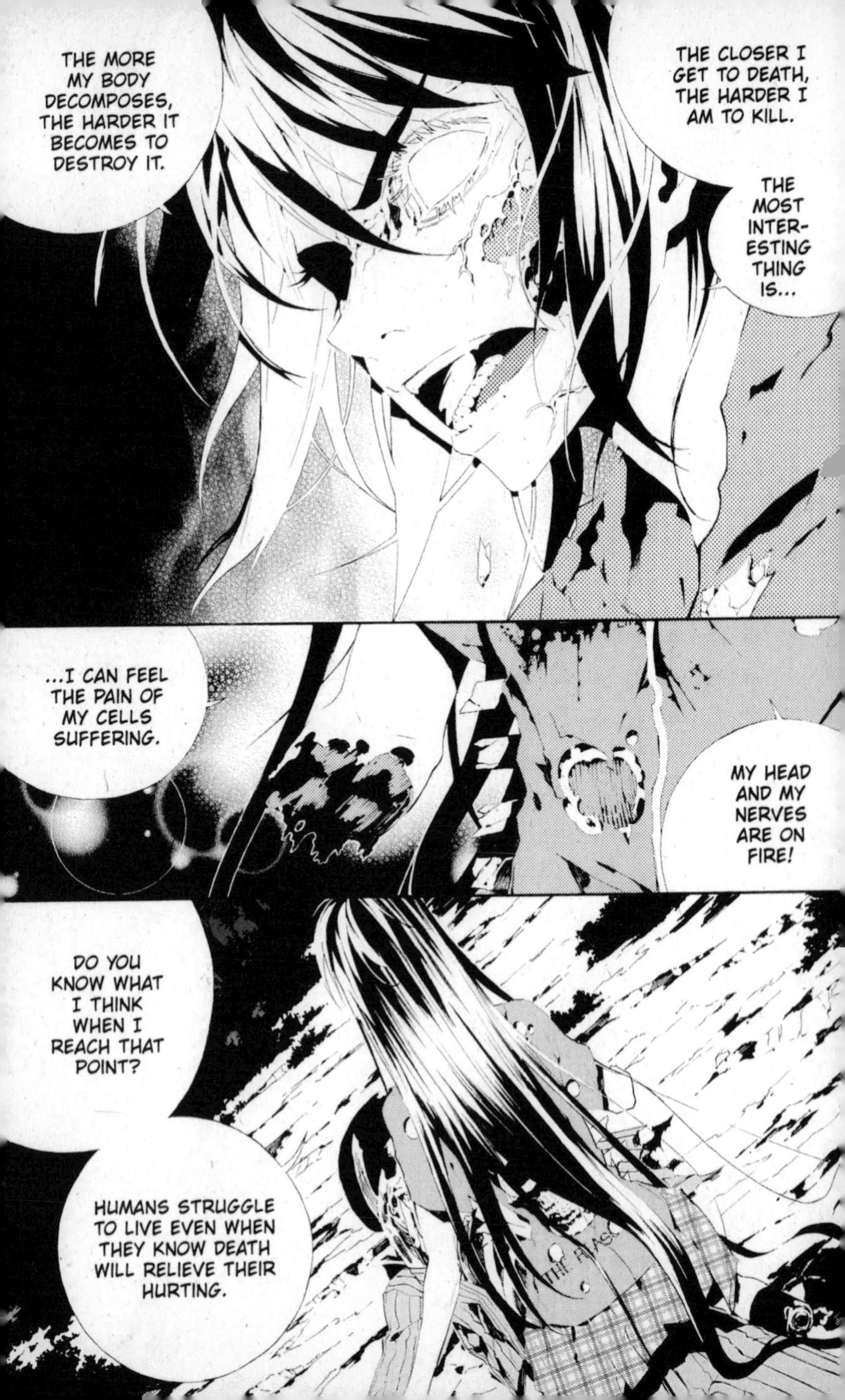
THE CLOSER I GET TO DEATH, THE HARDER I AM TO KILL.
THE MORE MY BODY DECOMPOSES, THE HARDER IT BECOMES TO DESTROY IT.
THE MOST INTER-ESTING THING IS...
MY HEAD AND MY NERVES ARE ON FIRE!
...I CAN FEEL THE PAIN OF MY CELLS SUFFERING.
DO YOU KNOW WHAT I THINK WHEN I REACH THAT POINT?
HUMANS STRUGGLE TO LIVE EVEN WHEN THEY KNOW DEATH WILL RELIEVE THEIR HURTING.

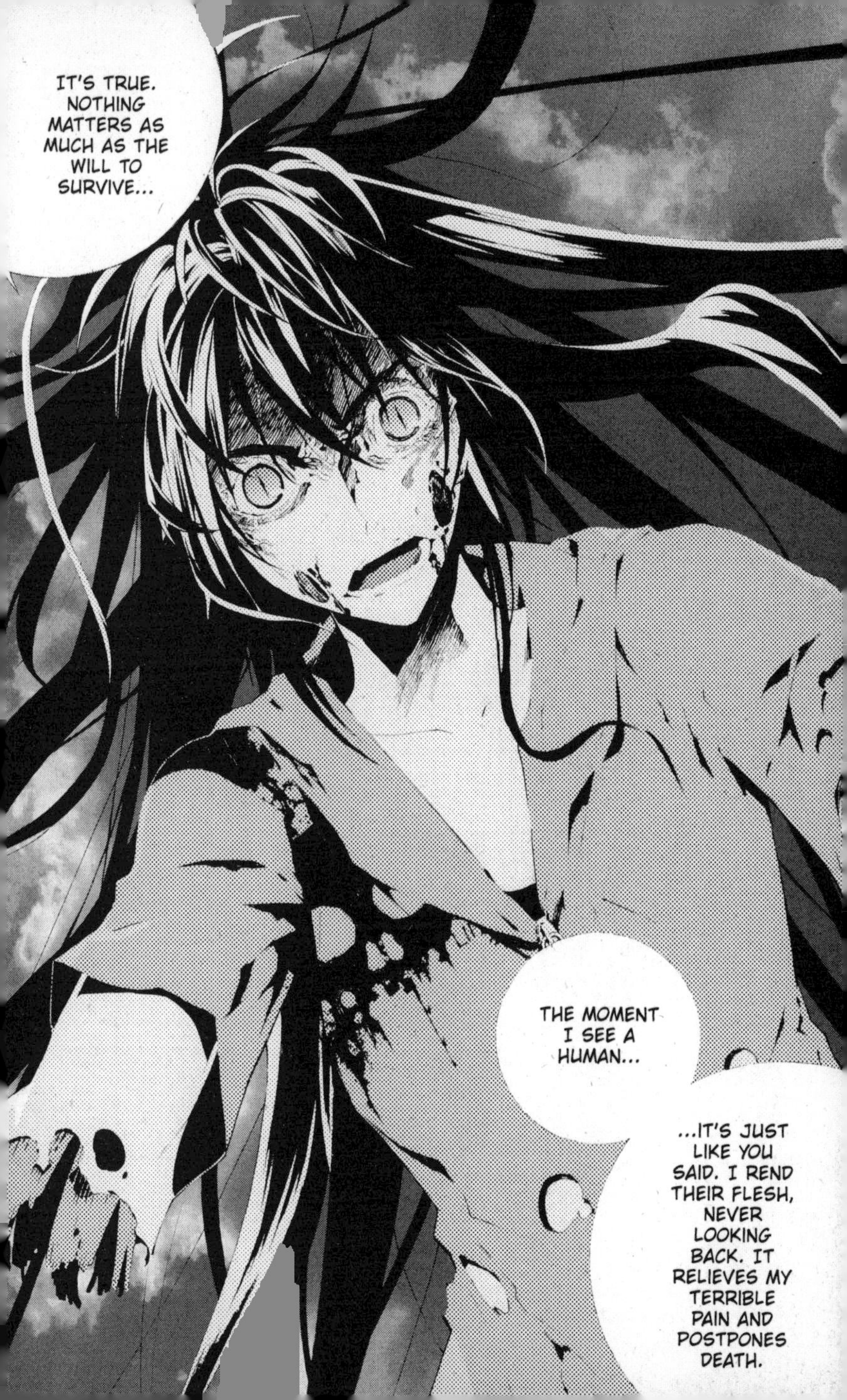
IT'S TRUE. NOTHING MATTERS AS MUCH AS THE WILL TO SURVIVE...
THE MOMENT I SEE A HUMAN...
...IT'S JUST LIKE YOU SAID. I REND THEIR FLESH, NEVER LOOKING BACK. IT RELIEVES MY TERRIBLE PAIN AND POSTPONES DEATH.

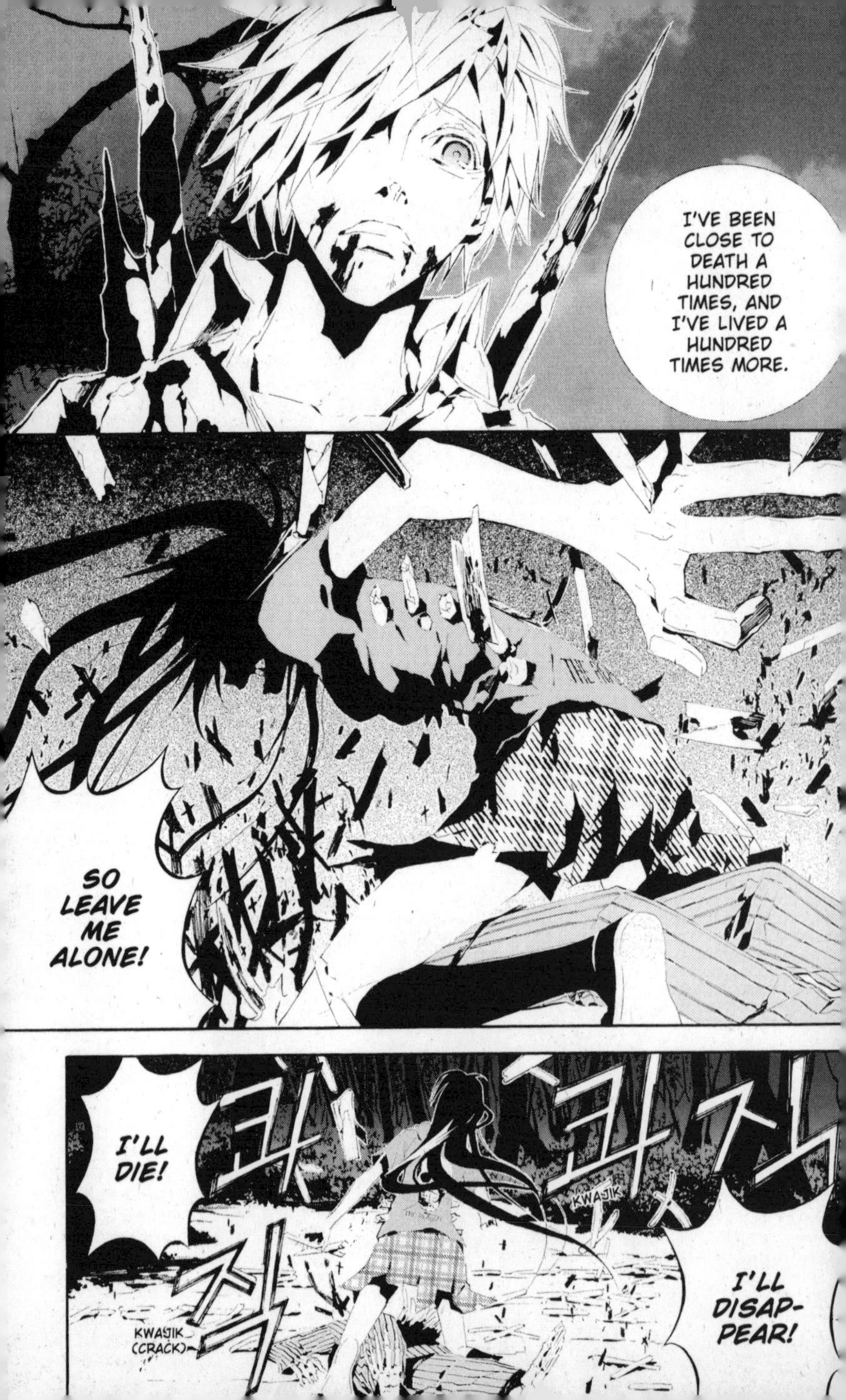
I'VE BEEN CLOSE TO DEATH A HUNDRED TIMES, AND I'VE LIVED A HUNDRED TIMES MORE.
SO LEAVE ME ALONE!
I'LL DIE!
KWAJIK
I'LL DISAP-PEAR!
KWAJIK (CRACK)

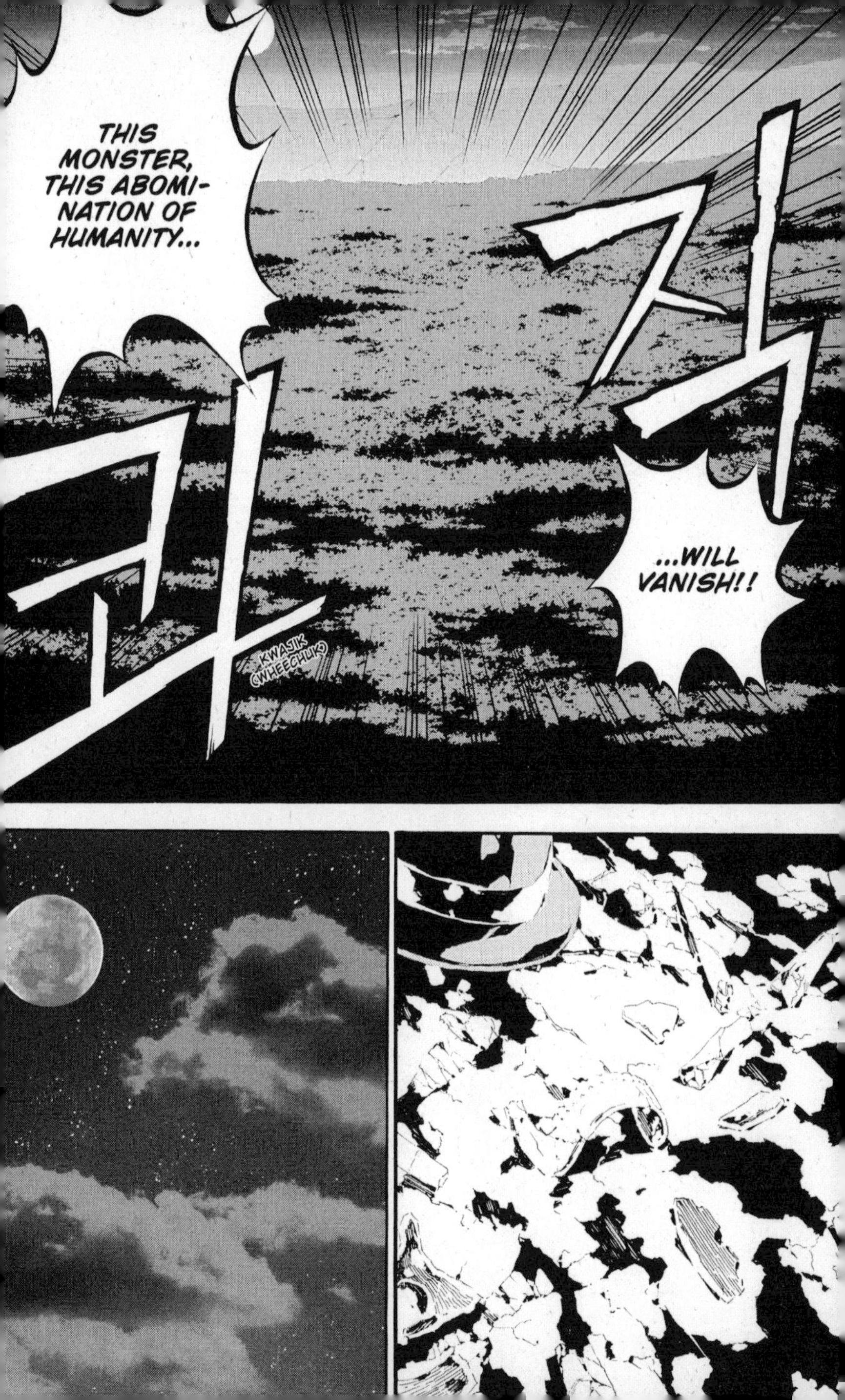
THIS MONSTER, THIS ABOMINATION OF HUMANITY...
KWAJIK (WHEECHUK)
...WILL VANISH!!

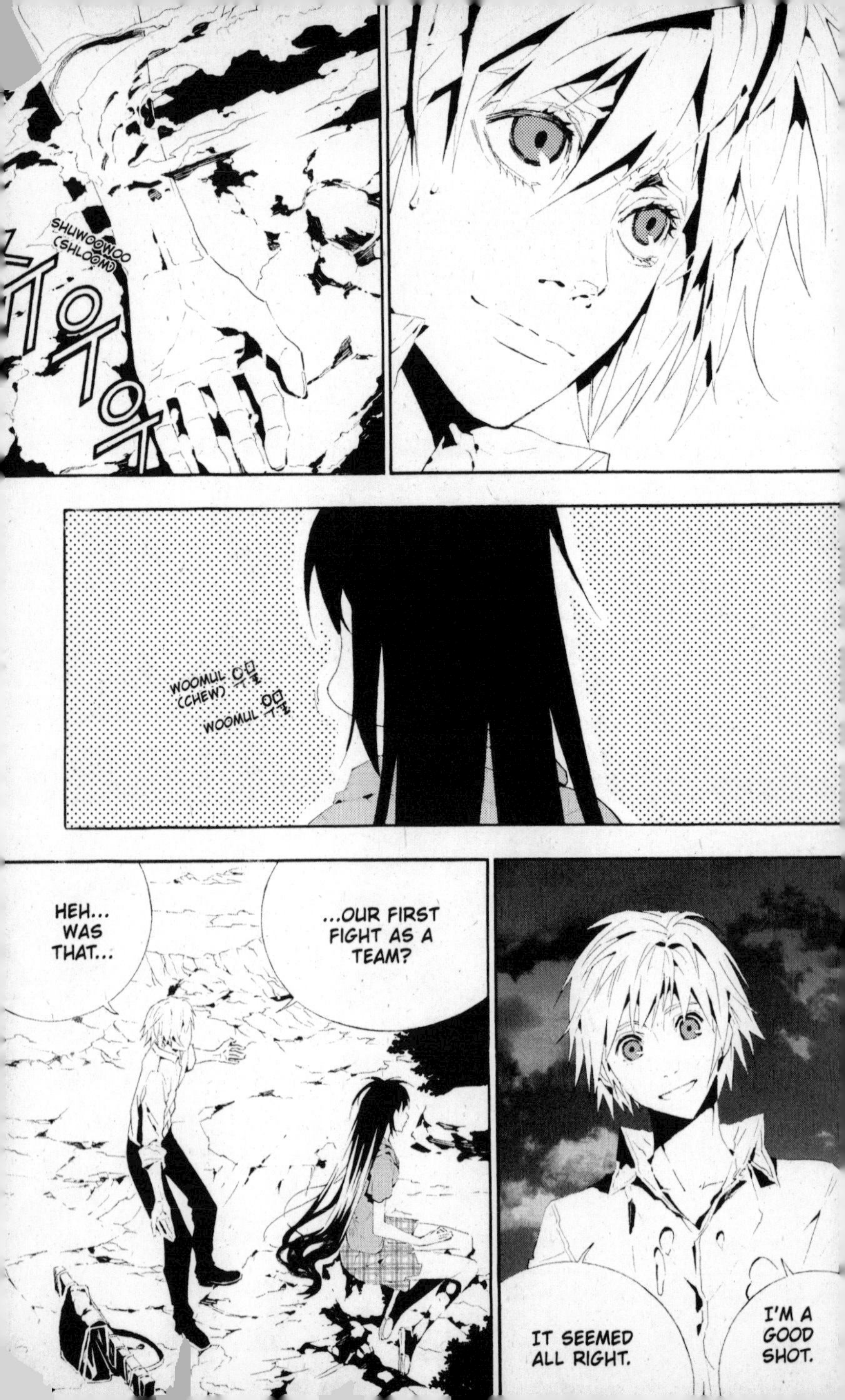

SHUWOOWOO (SHLOOM)
슈아아아
WOOMUL (CHEW) 우물
WOOMUL 우물
HEH... WAS THAT...
...OUR FIRST FIGHT AS A TEAM?
IT SEEMED ALL RIGHT.
I'M A GOOD SHOT.

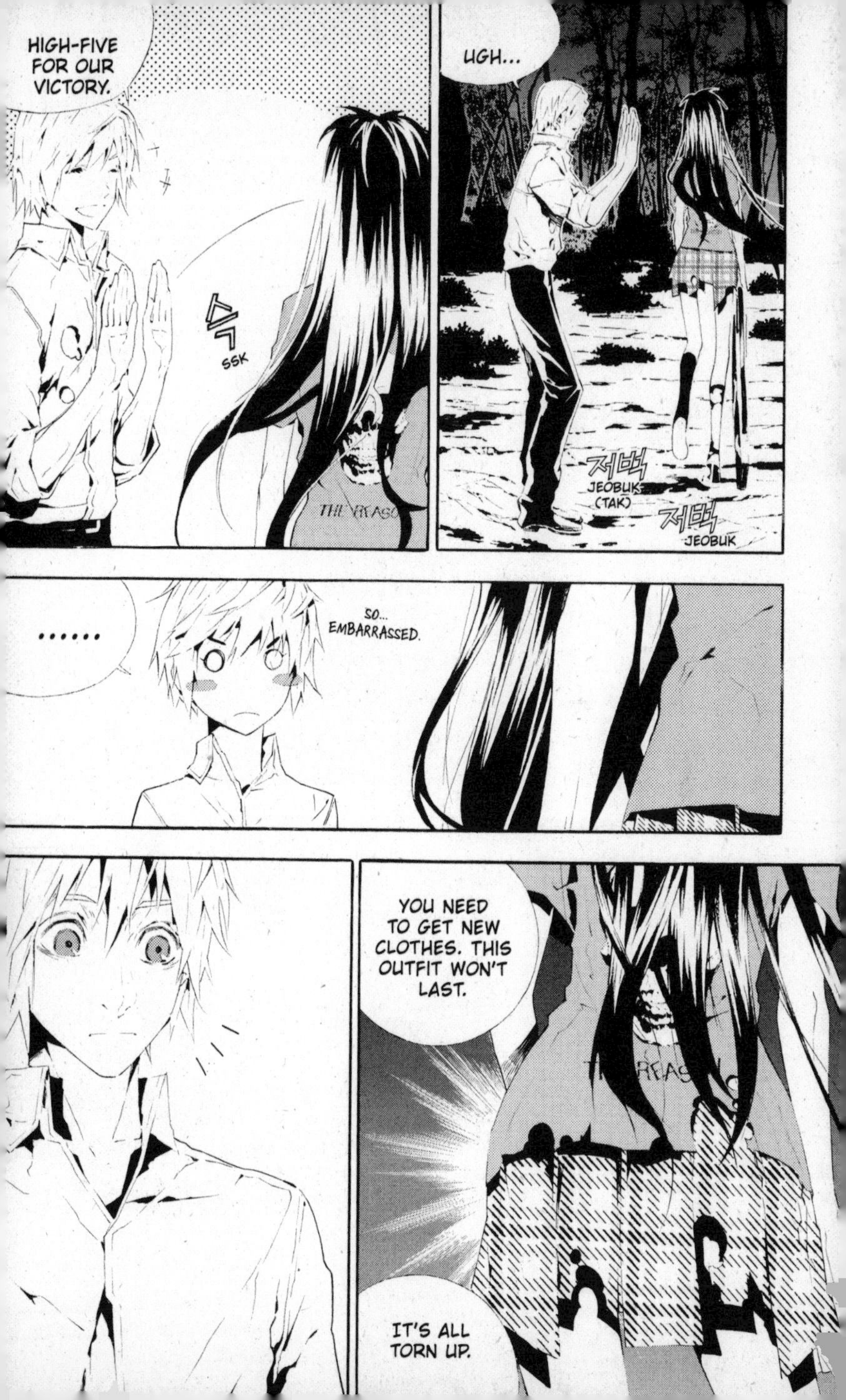
HIGH-FIVE FOR OUR VICTORY.
슥
SSK
UGH...
저벅
JEOBUK (TAK)
저벅
JEOBUK
......
SO... EMBARRASSED.
YOU NEED TO GET NEW CLOTHES. THIS OUTFIT WON'T LAST.
IT'S ALL TORN UP.

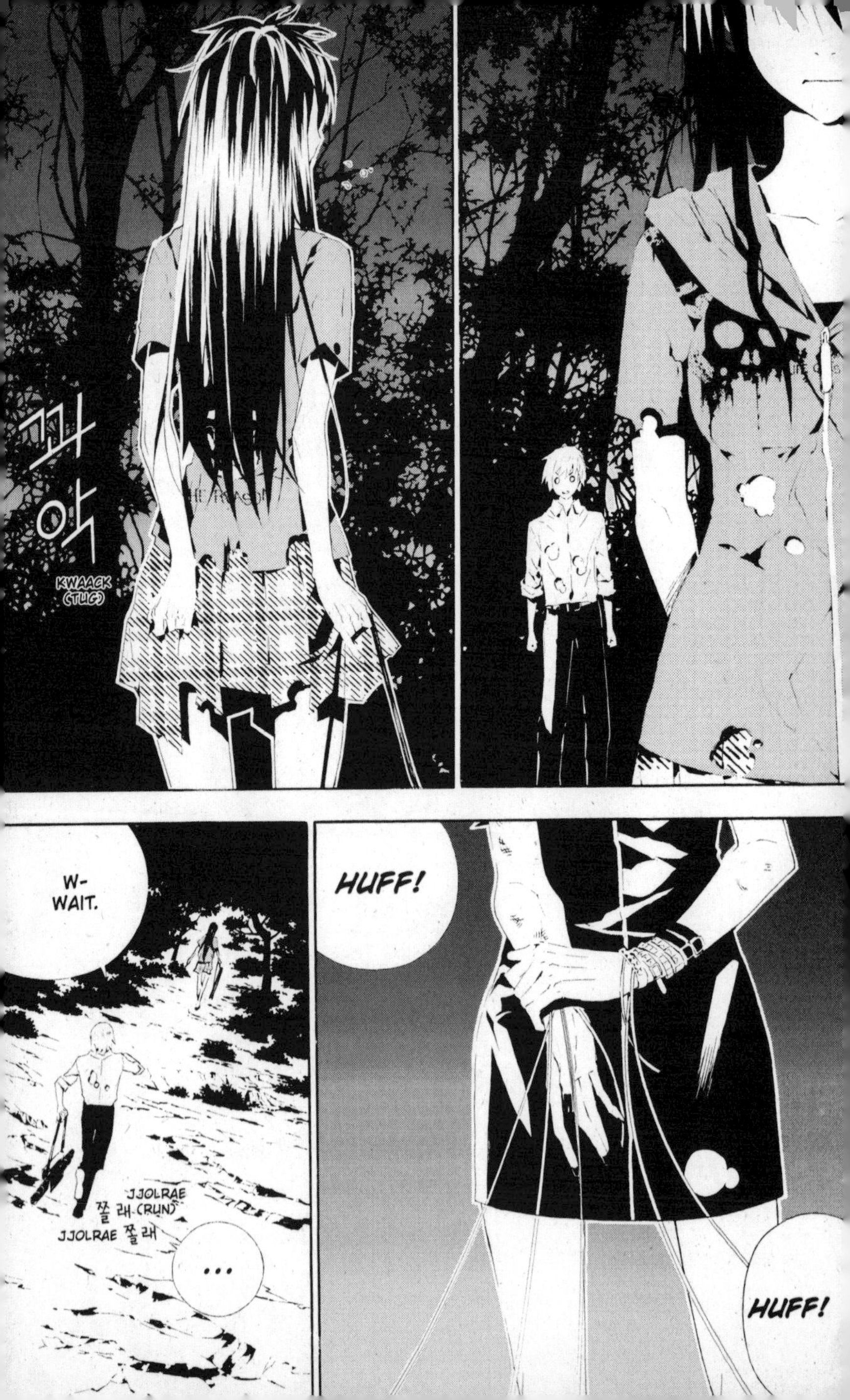

꽈악
KWAACK (TUG)
W-WAIT.
JJOLRAE 쫄래 (RUN)
JJOLRAE 쫄래
...
HUFF!
HUFF!

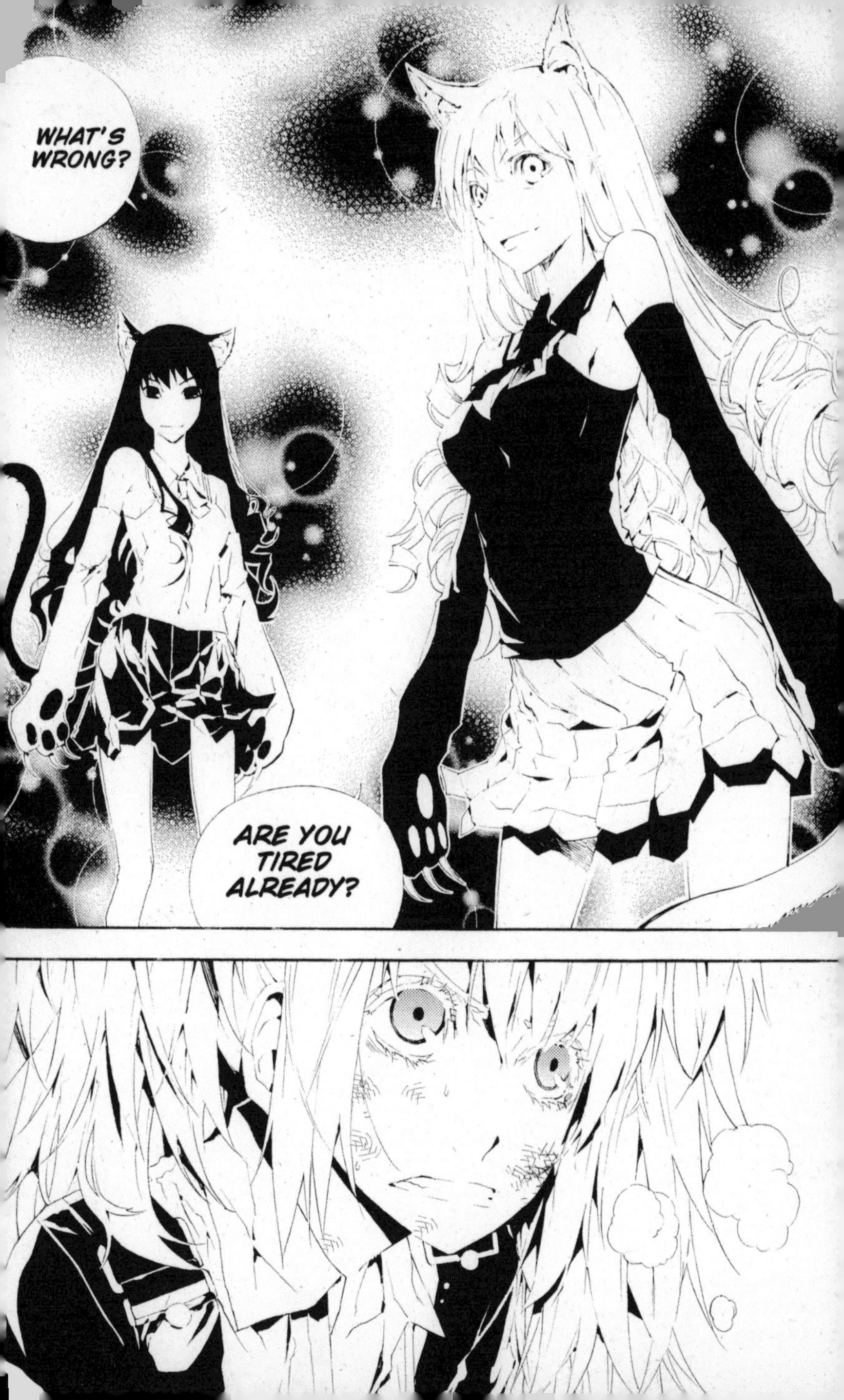
WHAT'S WRONG?
ARE YOU TIRED ALREADY?

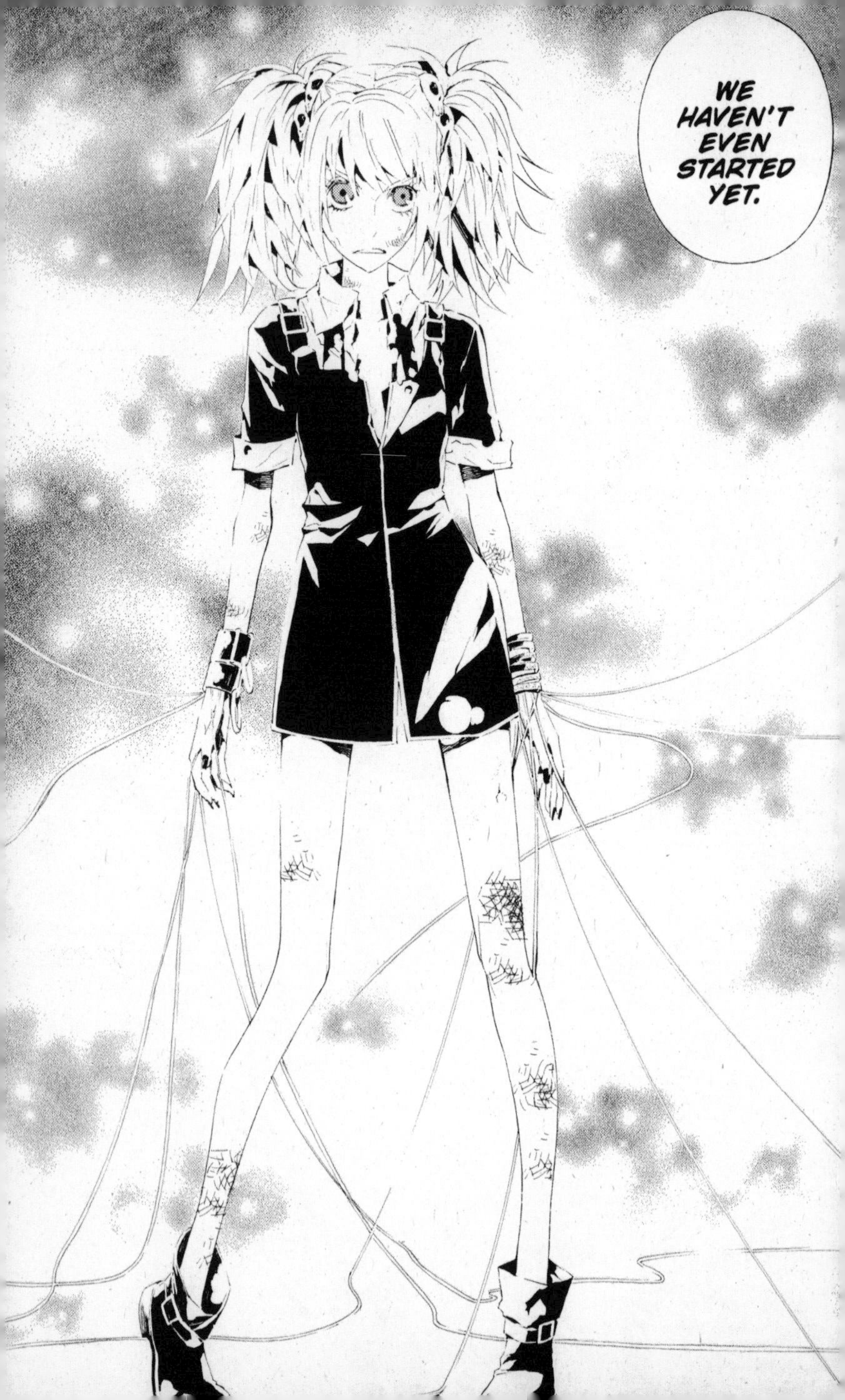
WE HAVEN'T EVEN STARTED YET.

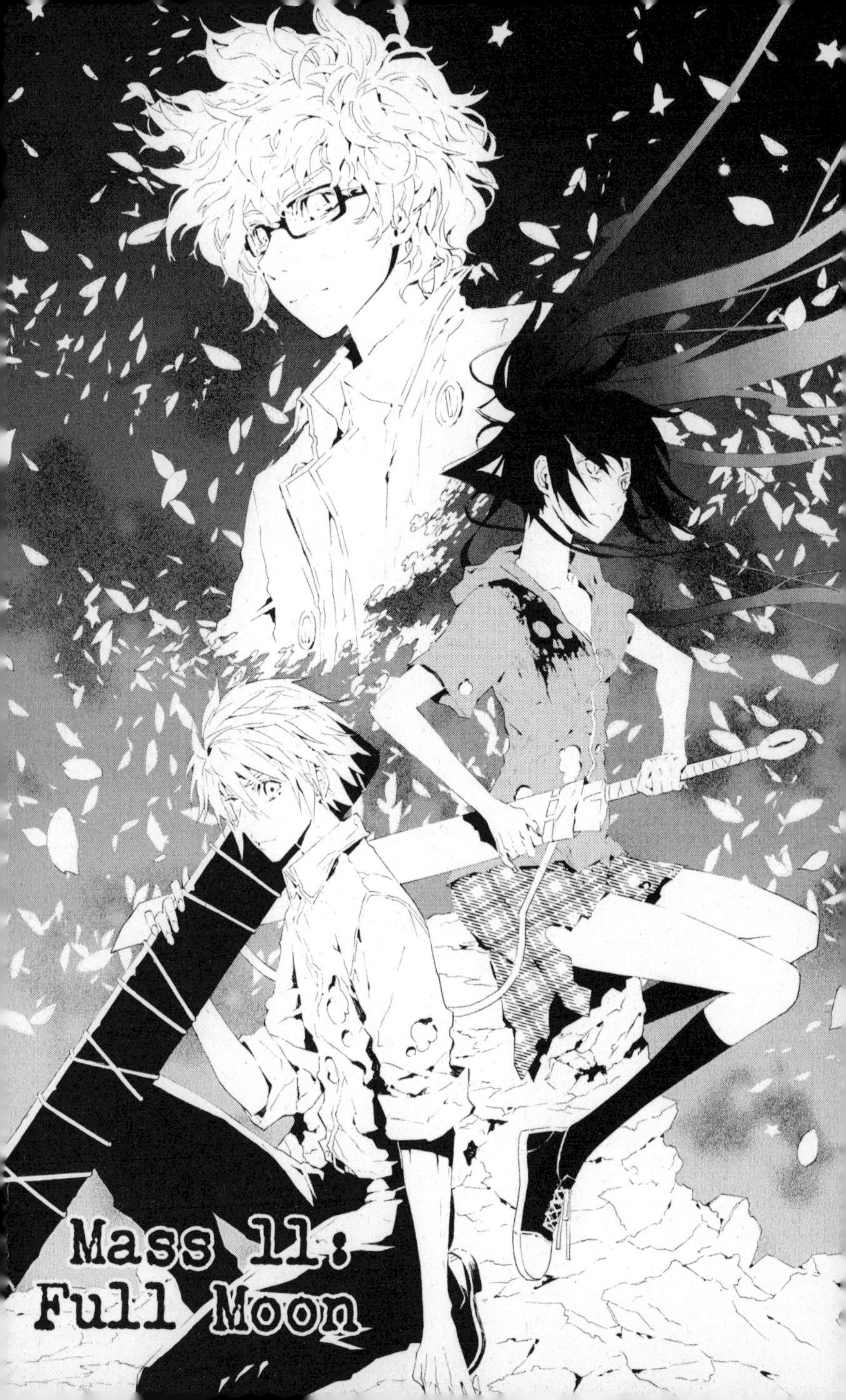
Mass 11:
Full Moon

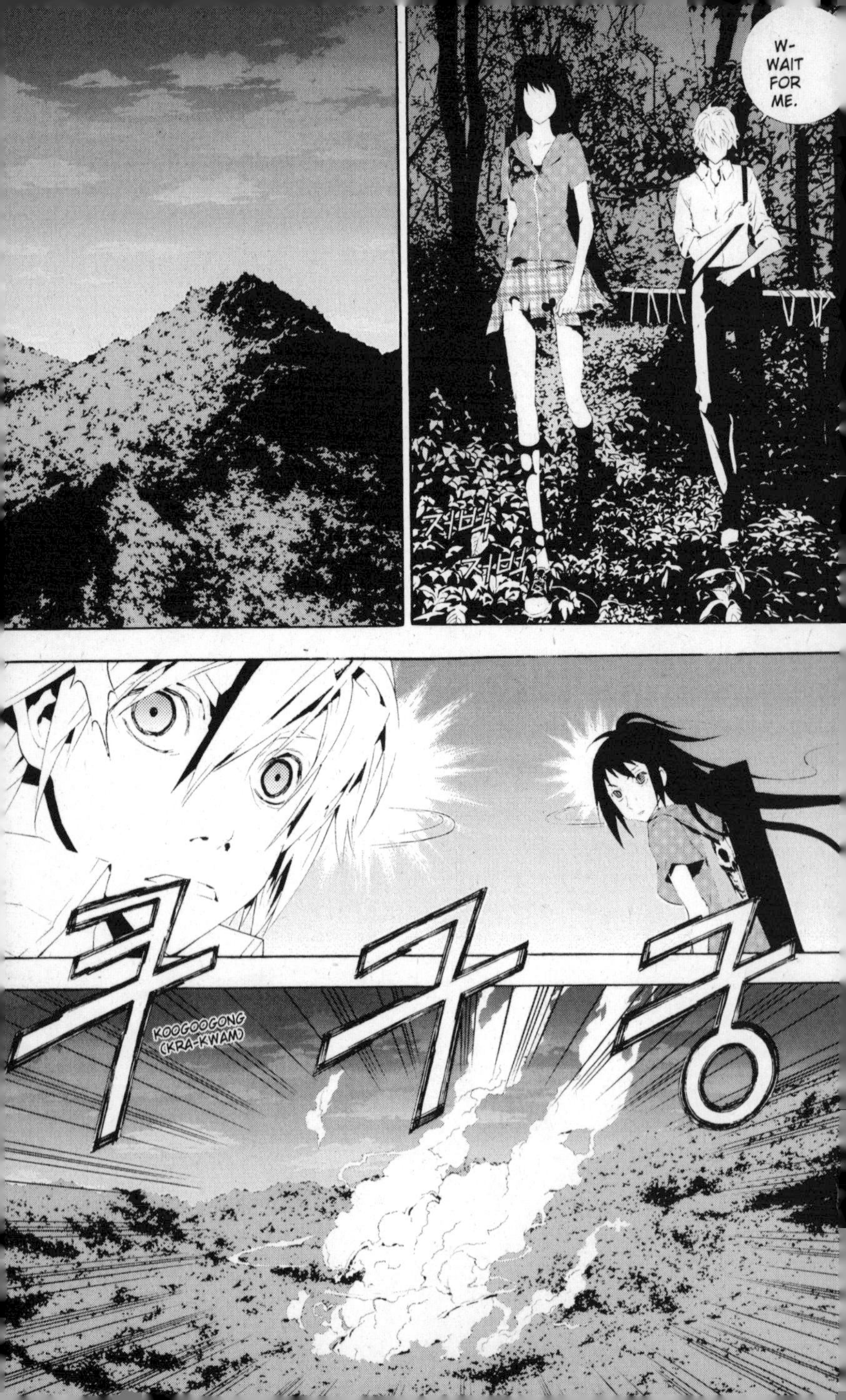
W-
WAIT
FOR
ME.
KOOGOOGONG
(KRA-KWAM)

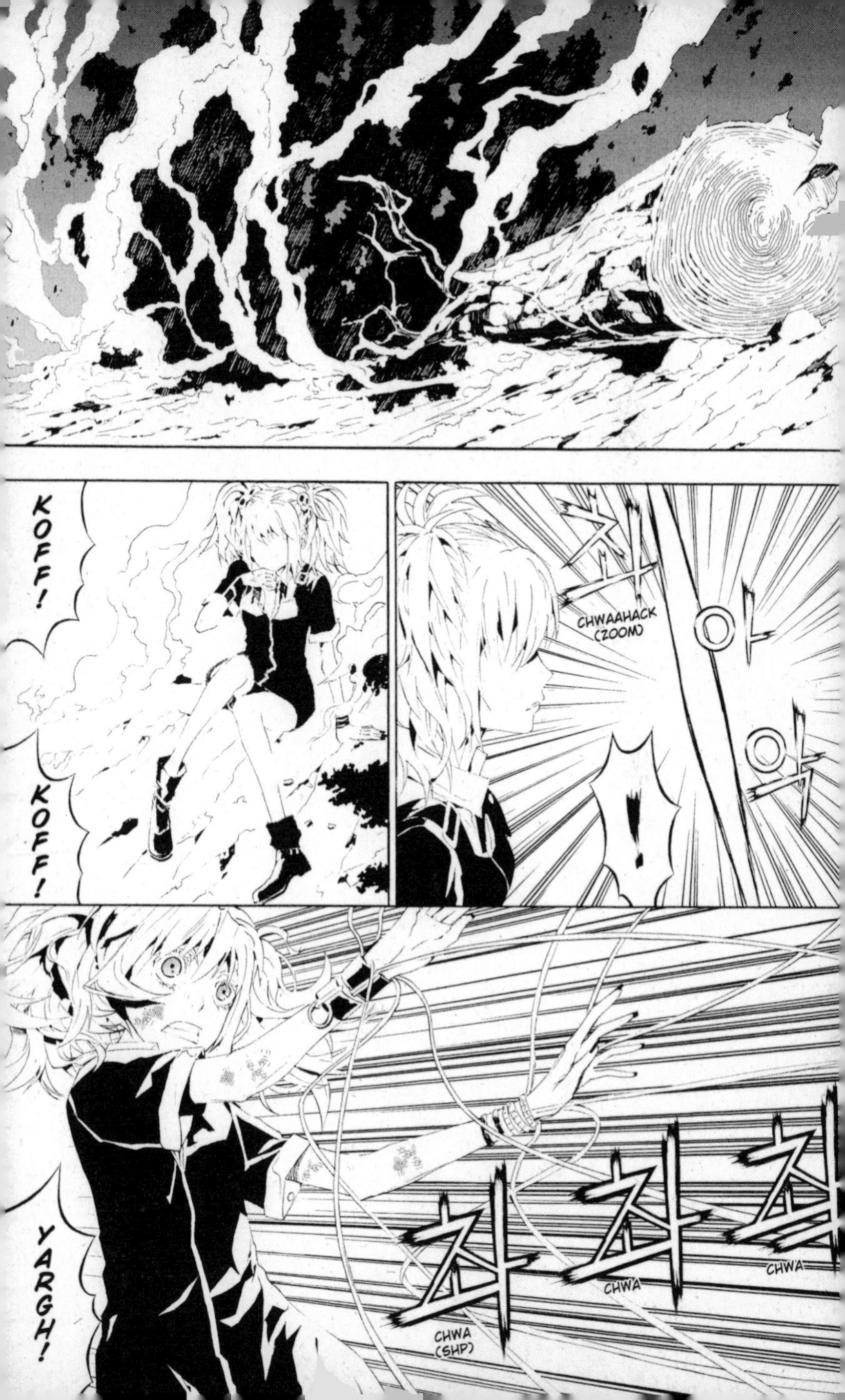
KOFF! KOFF!
CHWAAHACK (ZOOM)
YARGH!
CHWA (SHP)
CHWA
CHWA

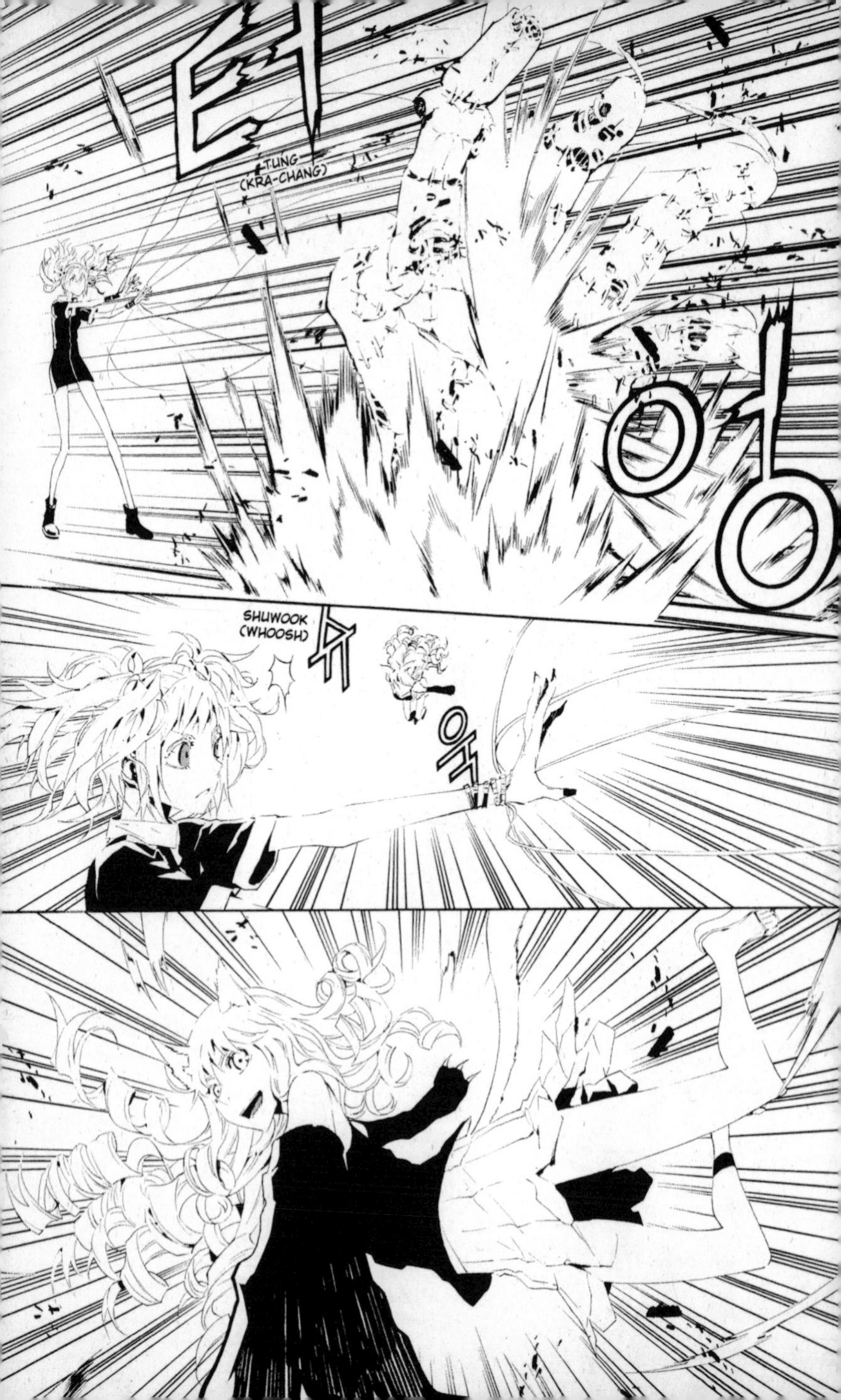

TUNG
(KRA-CHANG)
SHUWOOK
(WHOOSH)

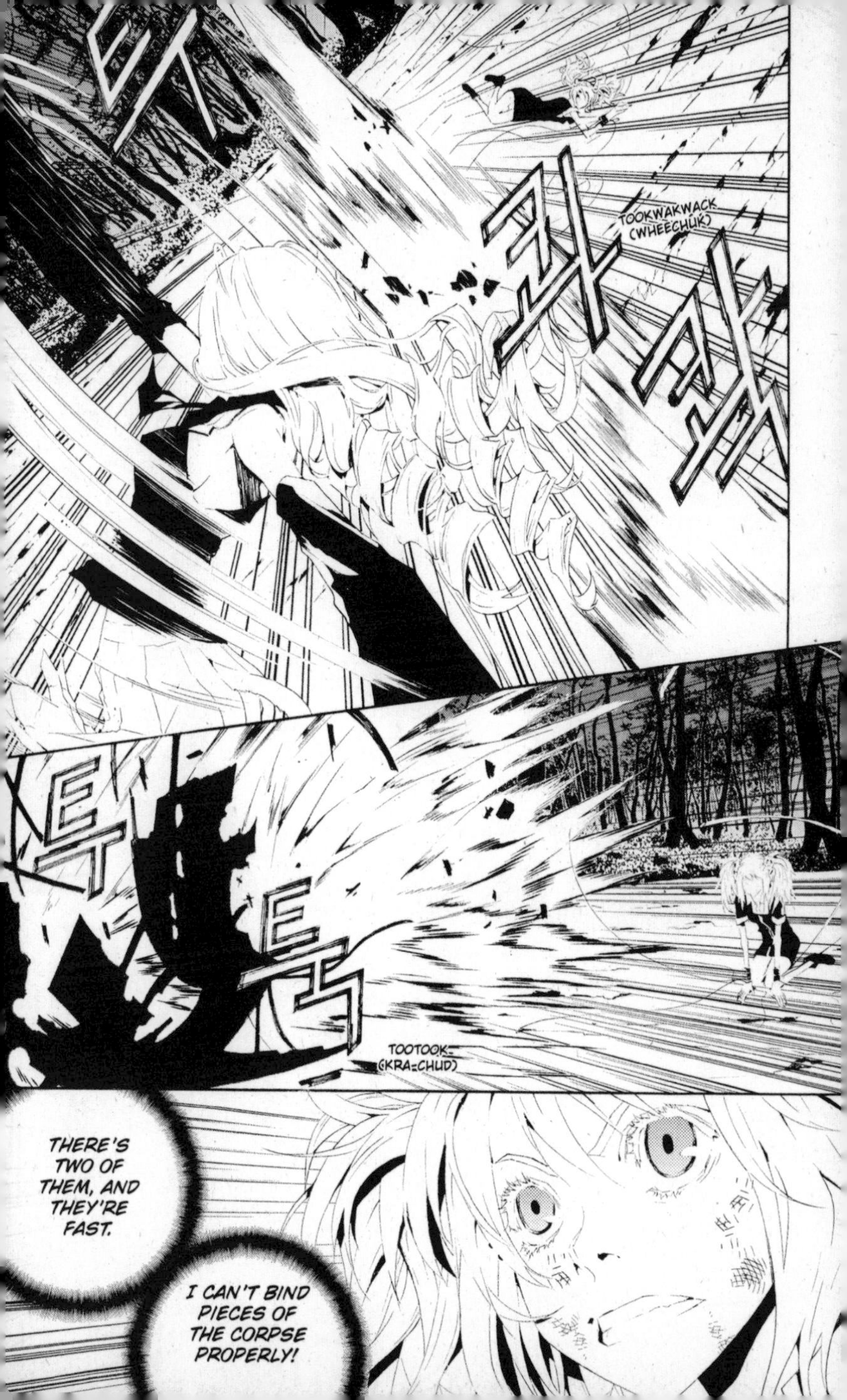
TOOKWAKWACK (WHEECHUK)
TOOTOOK (KRA-CHUD)
THERE'S TWO OF THEM, AND THEY'RE FAST.
I CAN'T BIND PIECES OF THE CORPSE PROPERLY!

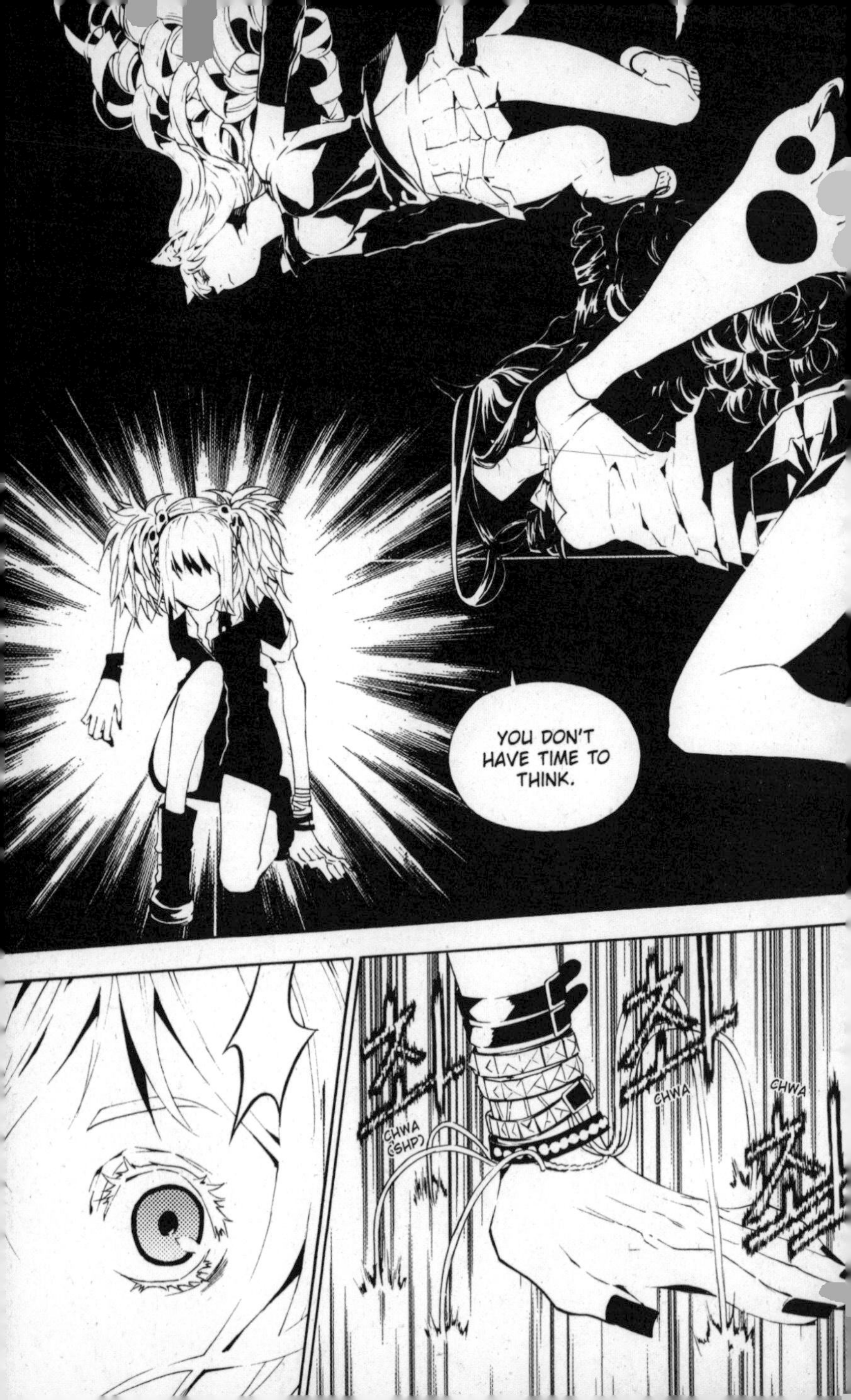
YOU DON'T HAVE TIME TO THINK.
CHWA (SHP)
CHWA
CHWA

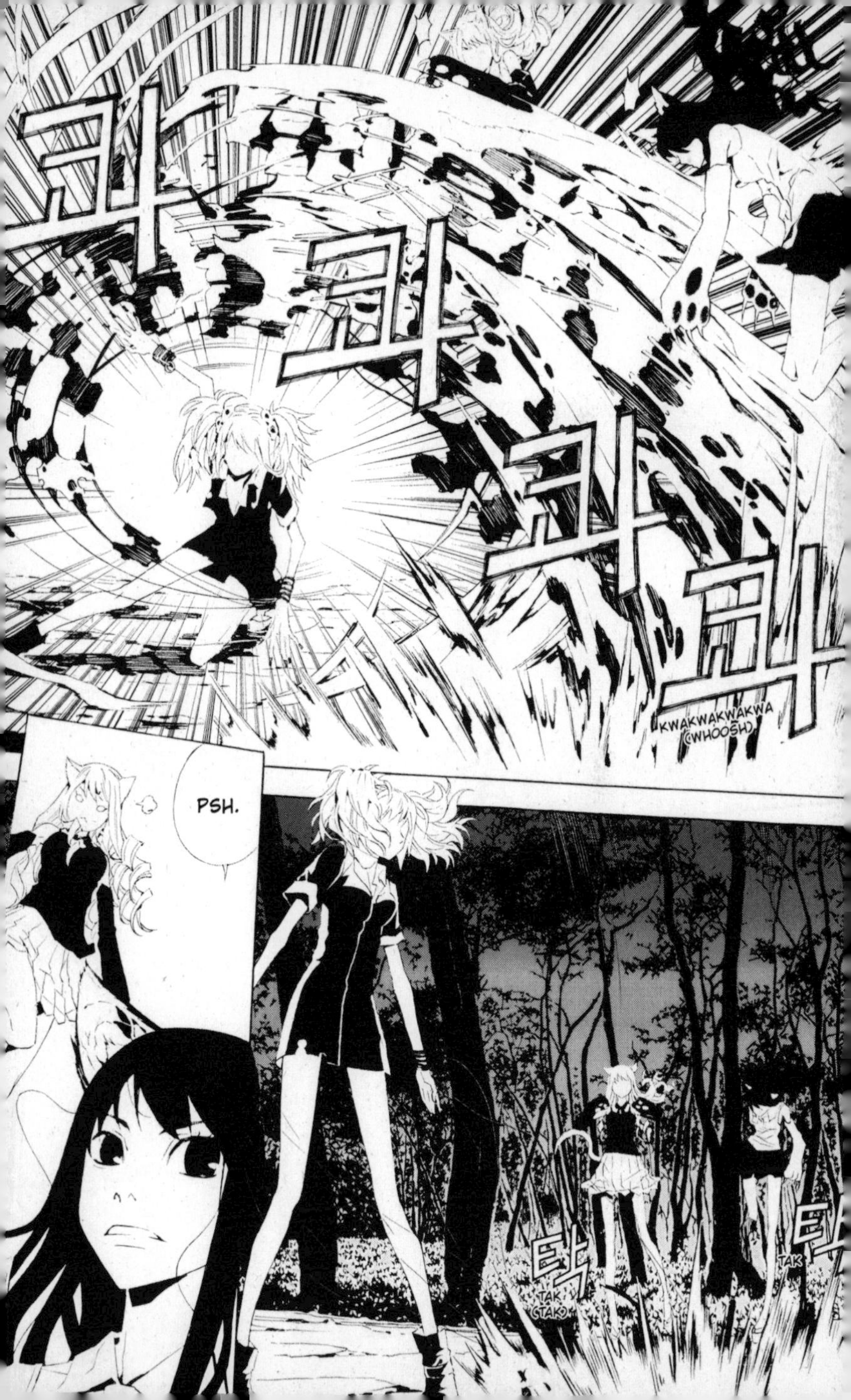
KWAKWAKWAKWA
(WHOOSH)
PSH.
TAK
(TAK)
TAK

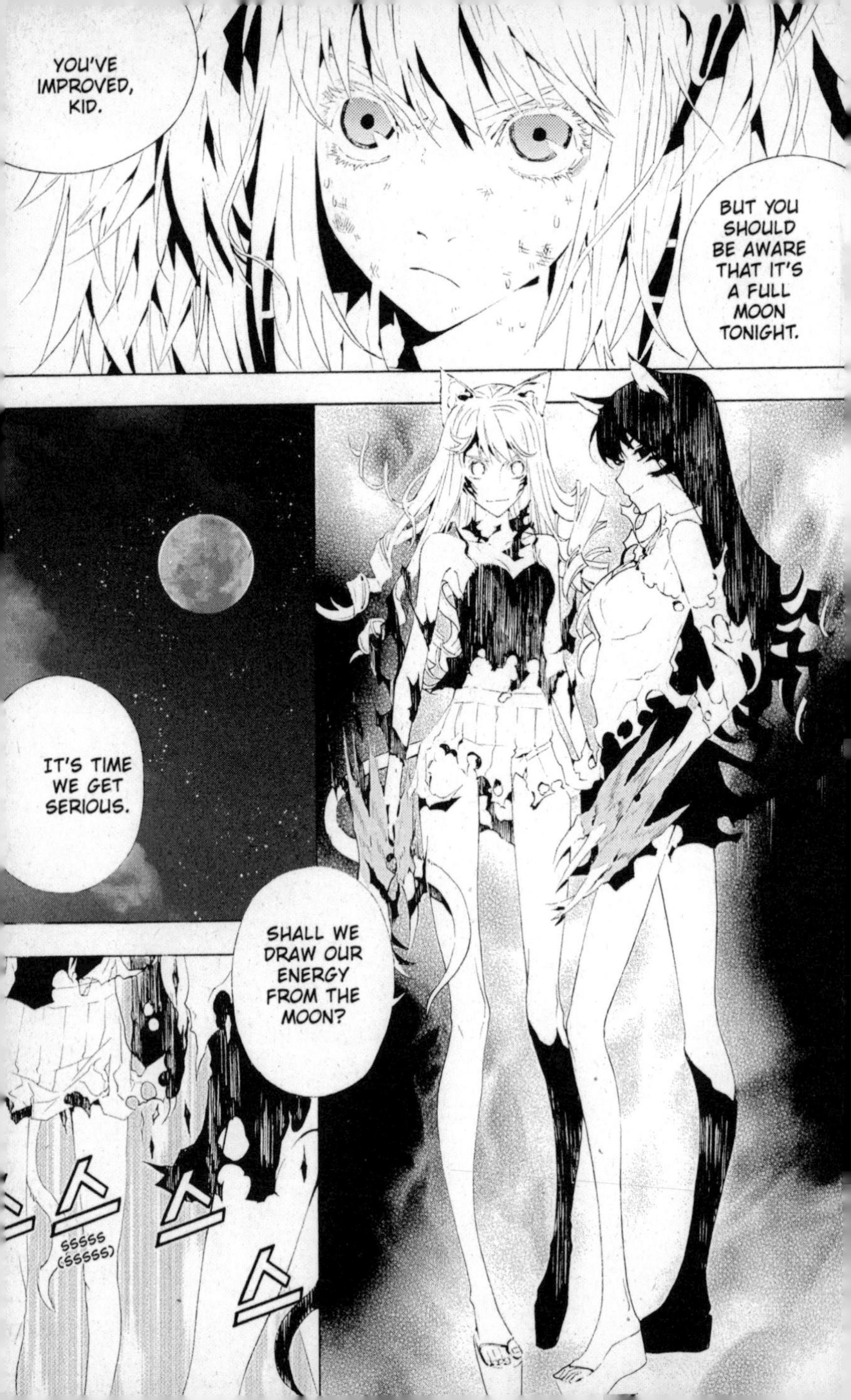
YOU'VE IMPROVED, KID.
BUT YOU SHOULD BE AWARE THAT IT'S A FULL MOON TONIGHT.
IT'S TIME WE GET SERIOUS.
SHALL WE DRAW OUR ENERGY FROM THE MOON?
SSSSS (SSSSS)

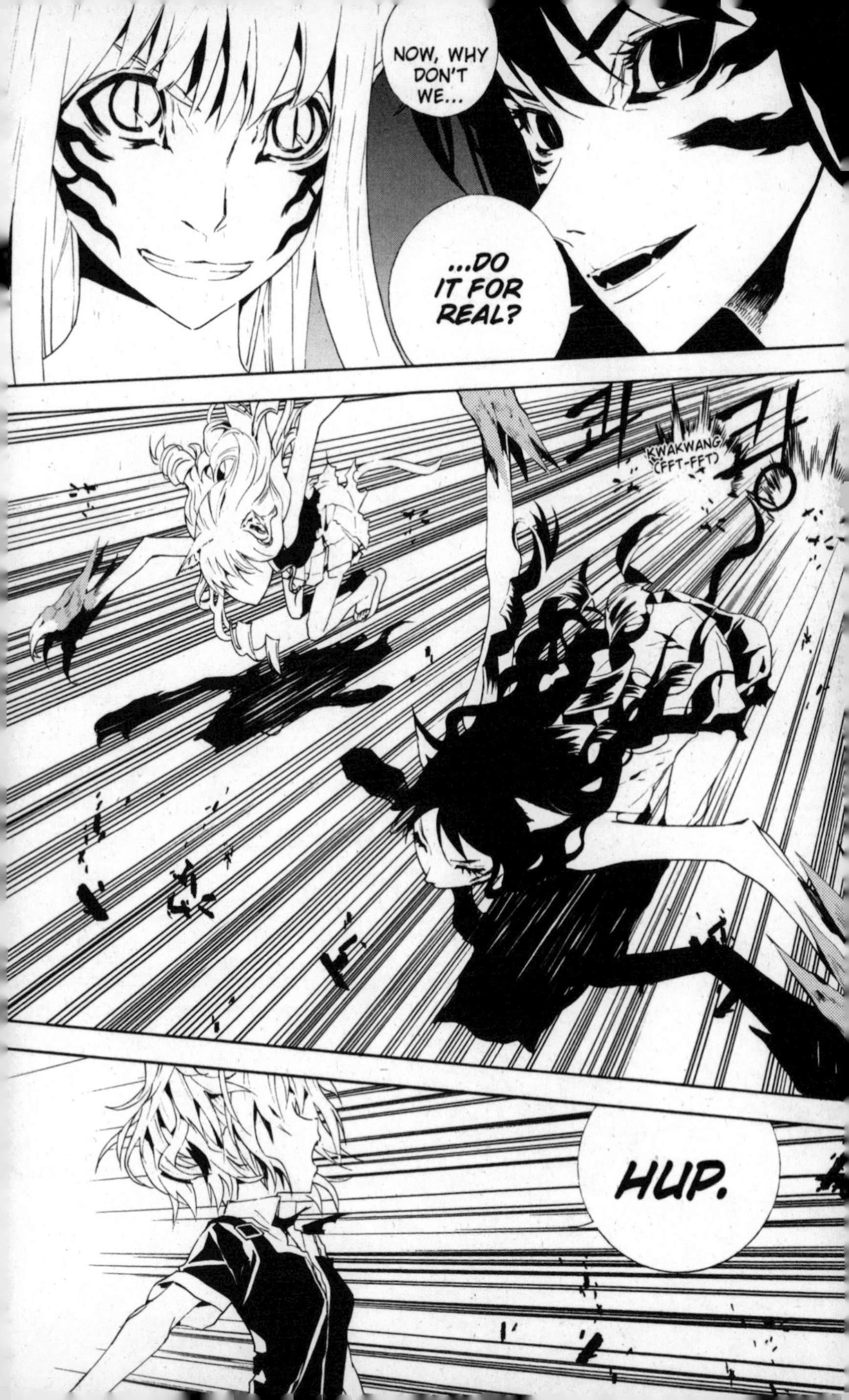
NOW, WHY DON'T WE...
...DO IT FOR REAL?
KWAKWANG (FFT-FFT)
HUP.

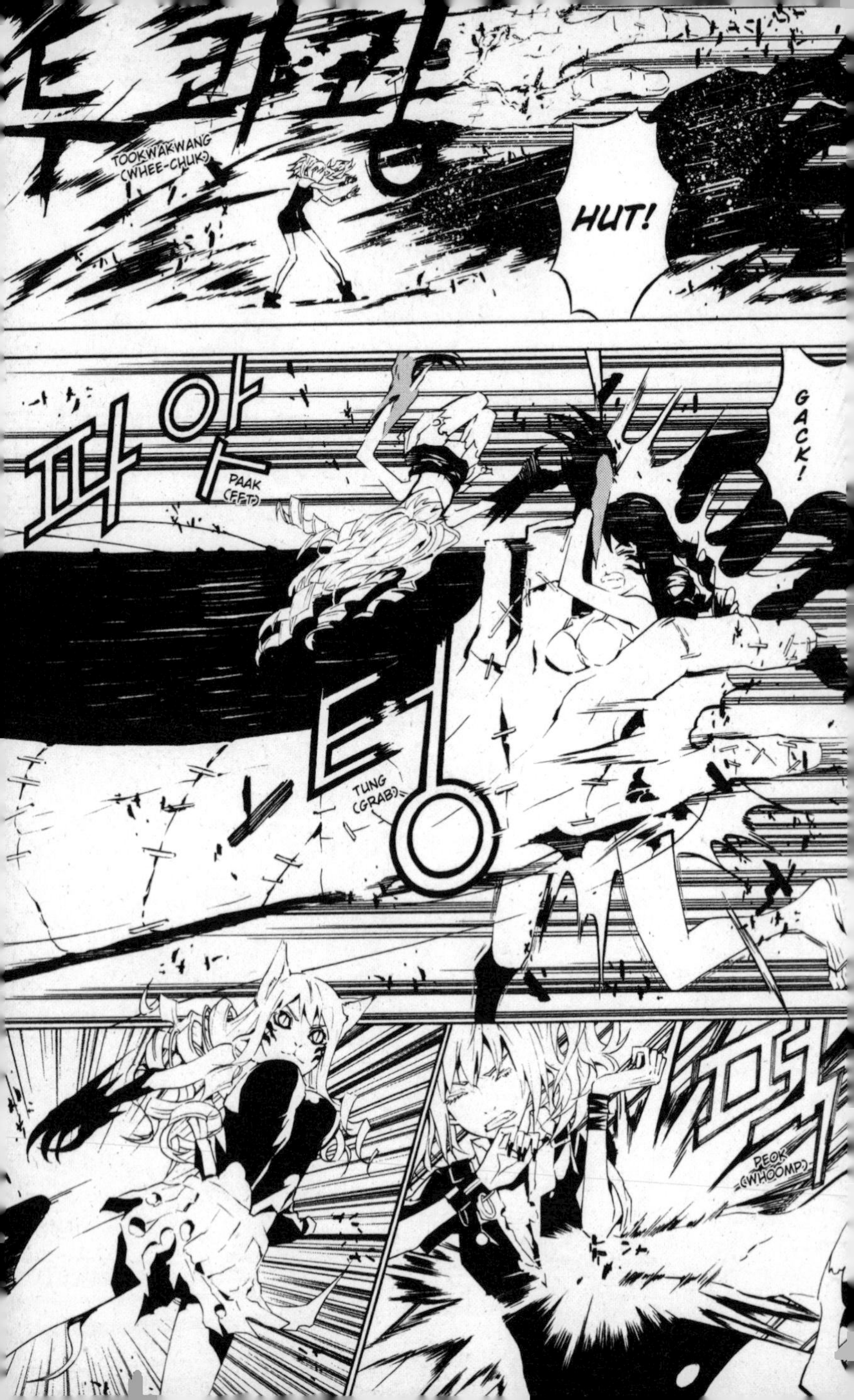

TOOKWAKWANG (WHEE-CHUK-)
HUT!
PAAK (FFT)
GACK!
TUNG (GRAB)
PEOK (WHOOMP)

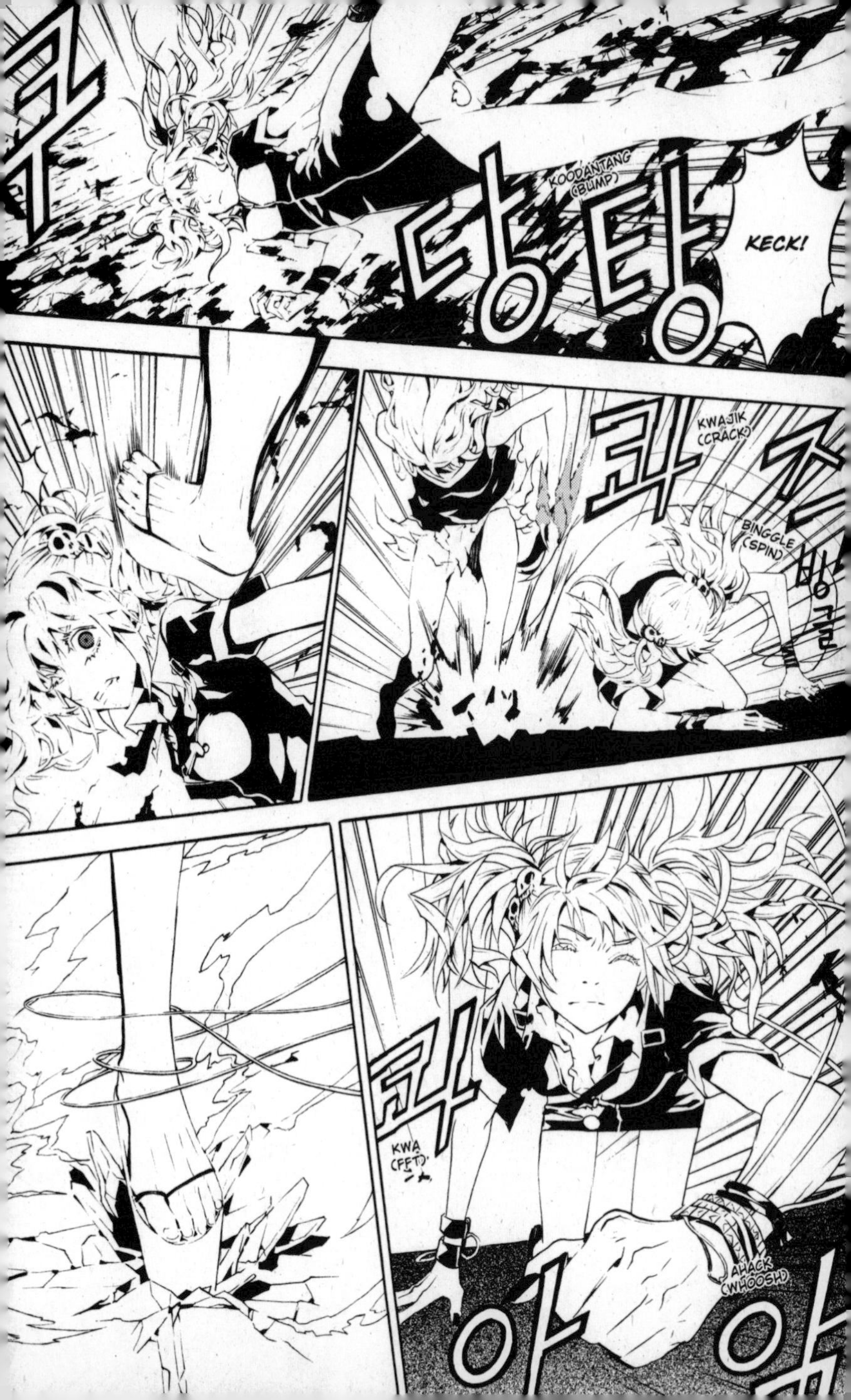
KOODANTANG (BUMP)
KECK!
KWAJIK (CRACK)
BINGGLE (SPIN)
KWA (FFT)
AHACK (WHOOSH)

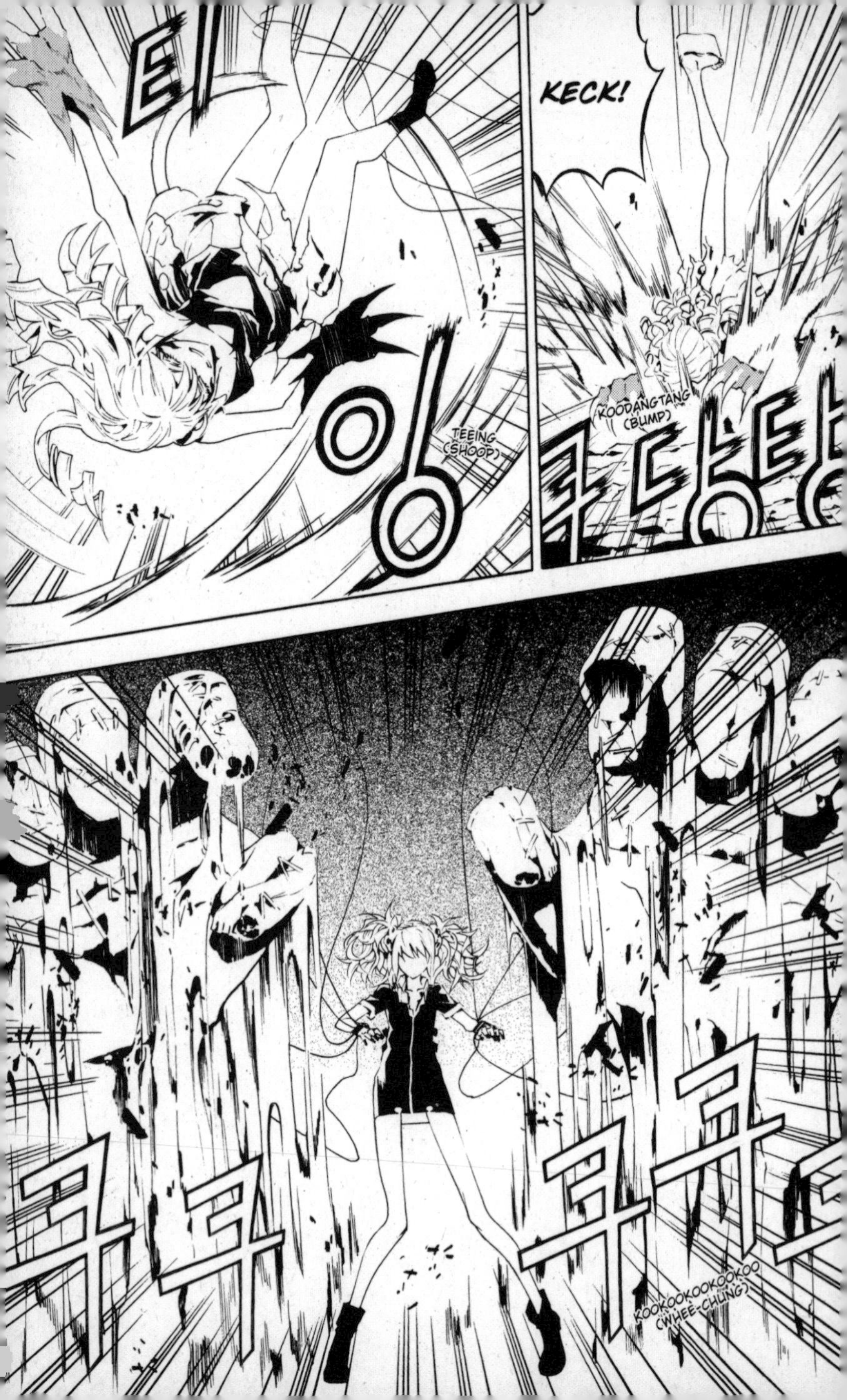
TEEING
(SHOOP)
KECK!
KOODANGTANG
(BUMP)
KOOKOOKOOKOOKOO
(WHEE-CHUNG)

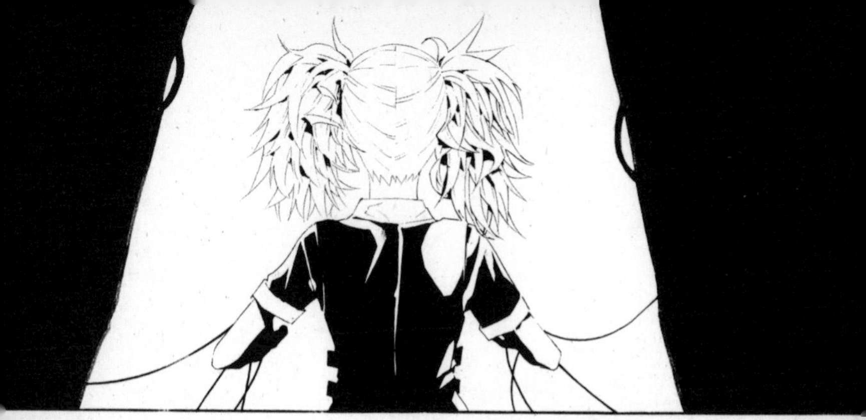
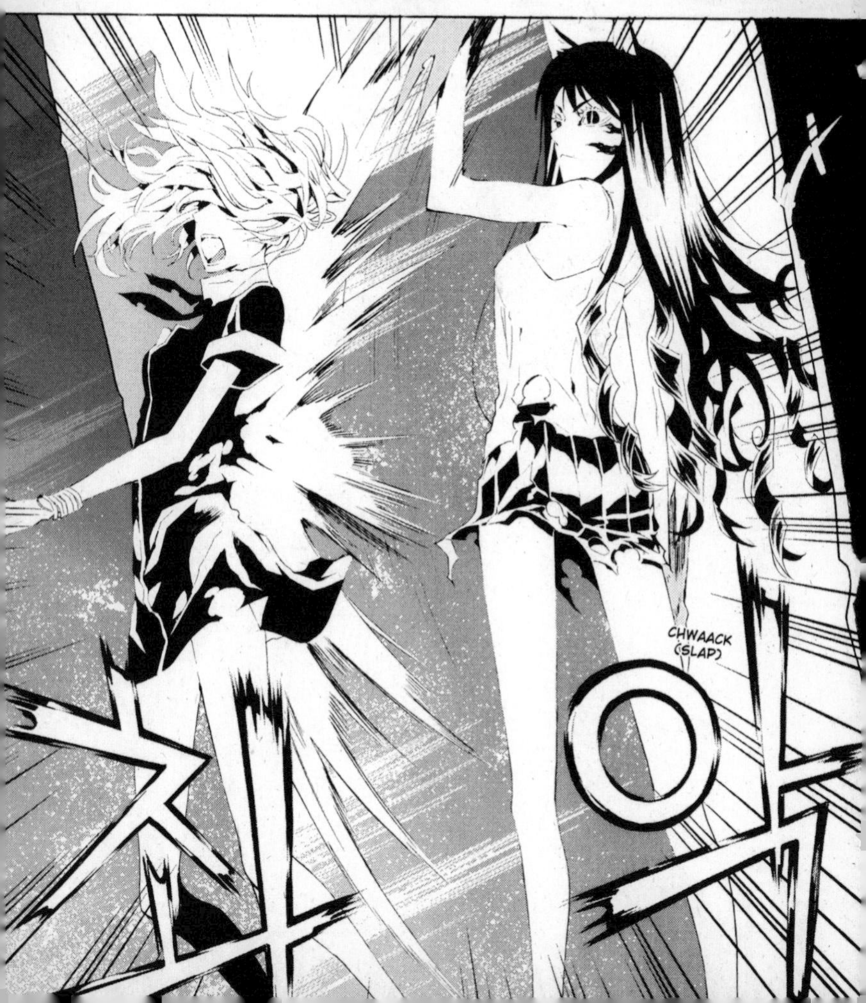
CHWAACK
(SLAP)

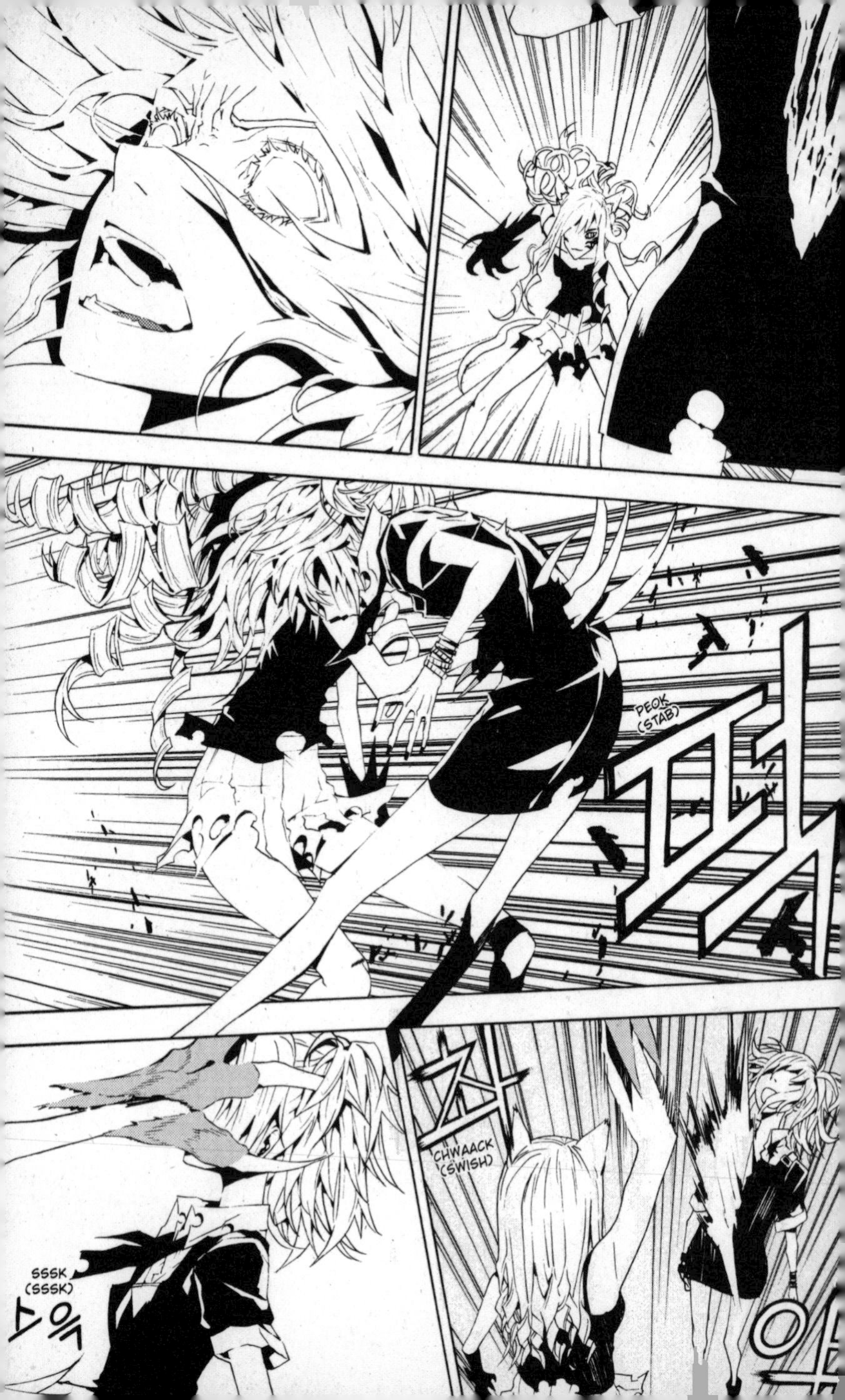
PEOK (STAB)
SSSK (SSSK)
CHWAACK (SWISH)

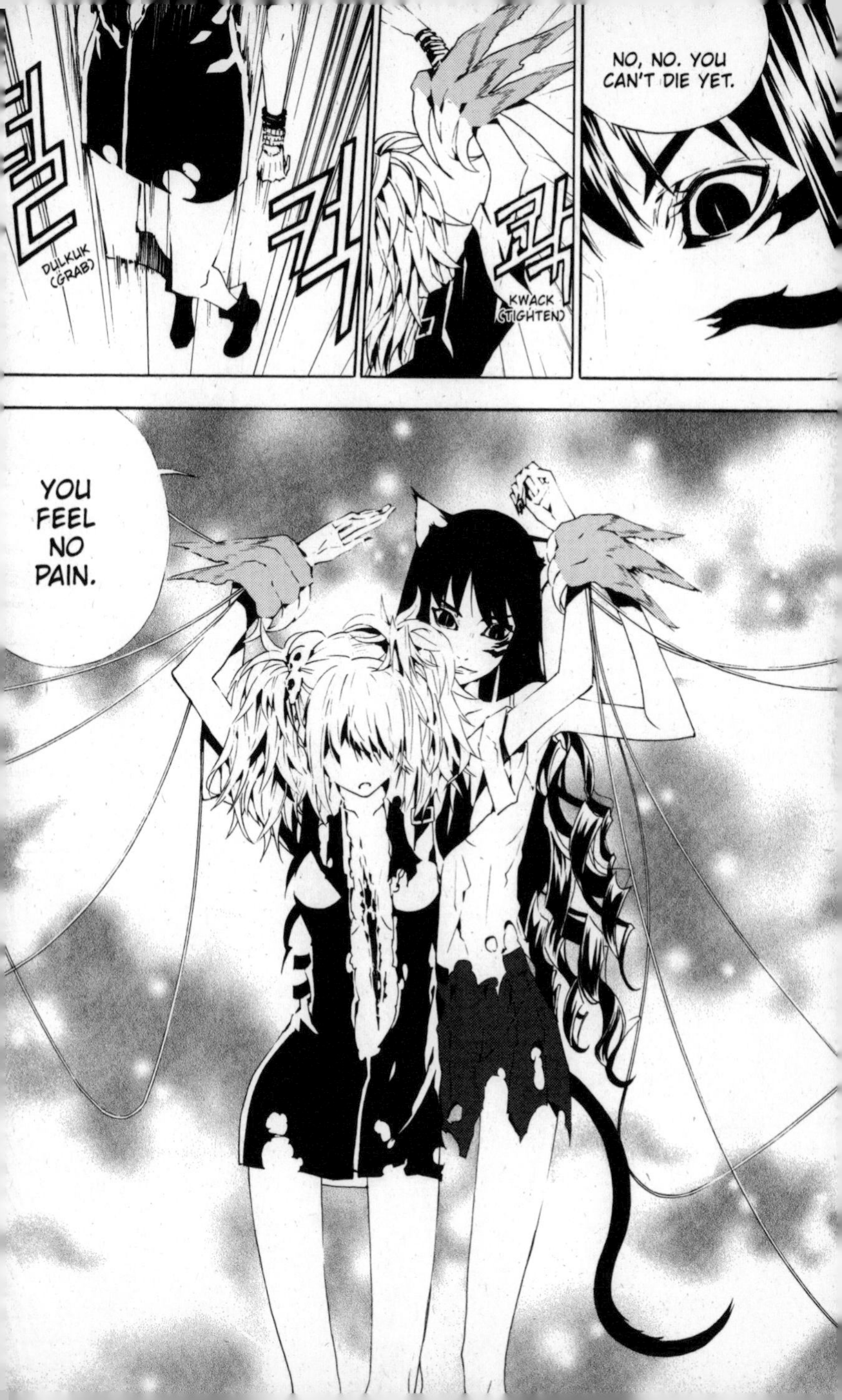
DULKUK (GRAB)
KWACK (TIGHTEN)
NO, NO. YOU CAN'T DIE YET.
YOU FEEL NO PAIN.

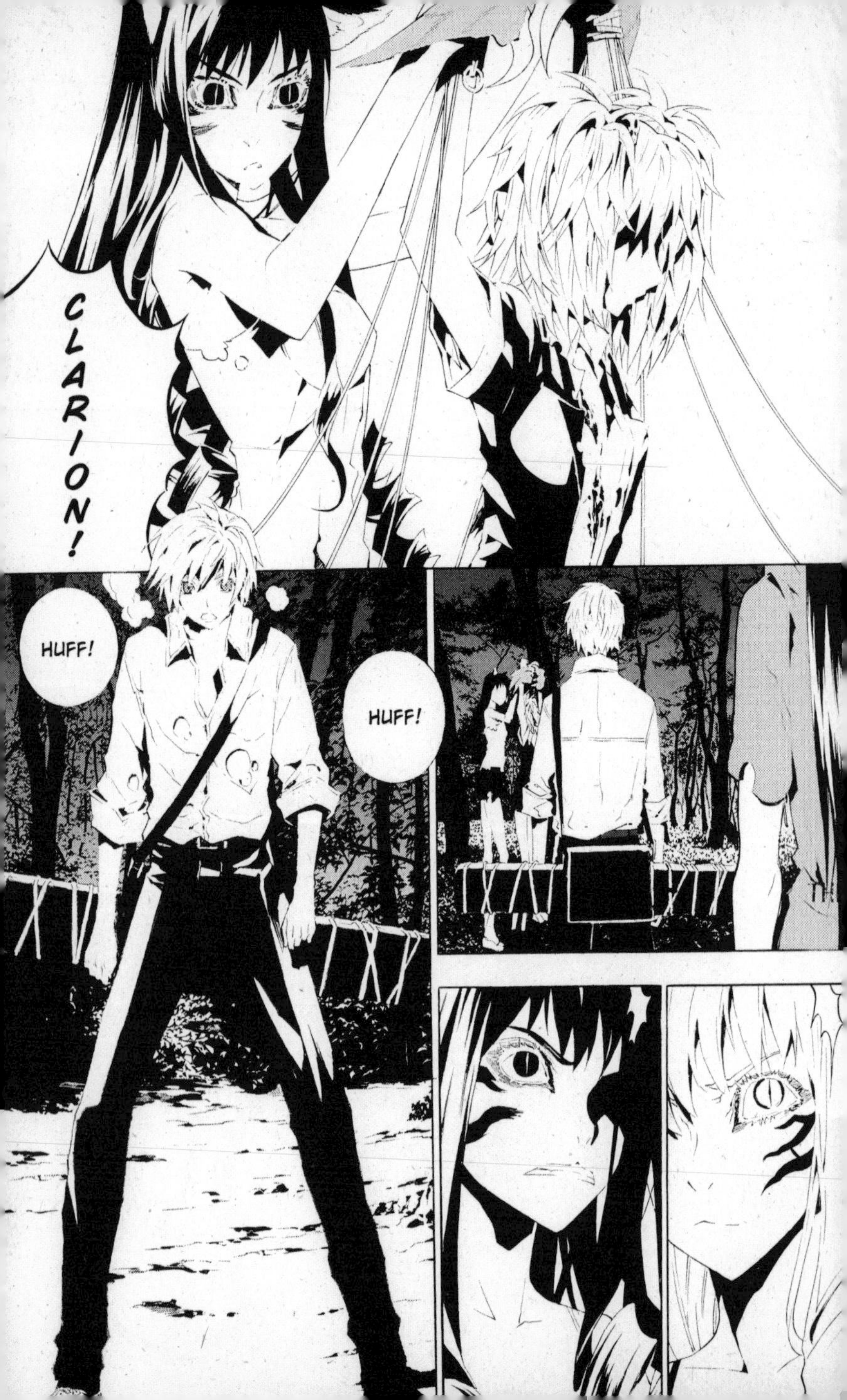
CLARION!
HUFF!
HUFF!

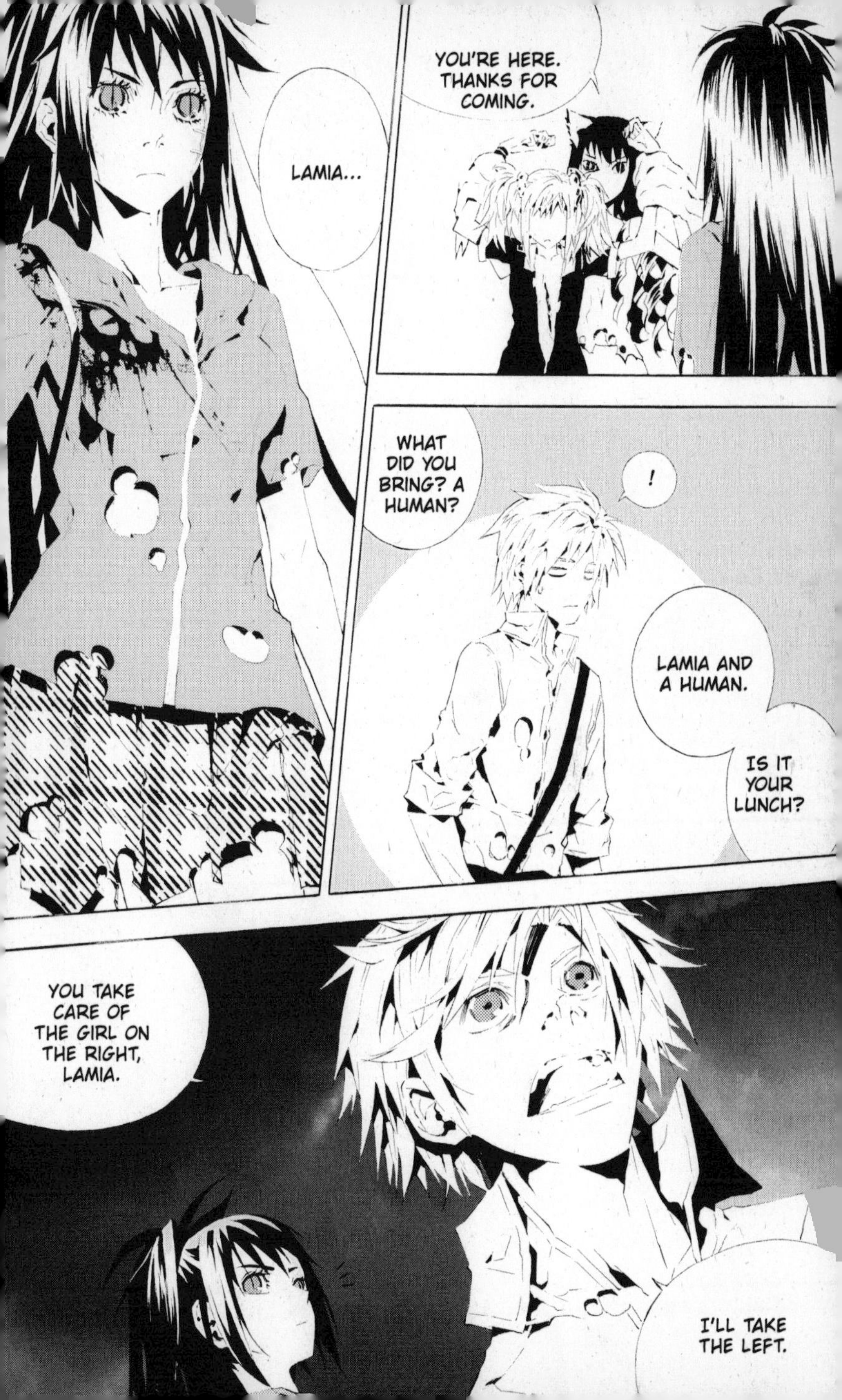
LAMIA...
YOU'RE HERE. THANKS FOR COMING.
WHAT DID YOU BRING? A HUMAN?
!
LAMIA AND A HUMAN.
IS IT YOUR LUNCH?
YOU TAKE CARE OF THE GIRL ON THE RIGHT, LAMIA.
I'LL TAKE THE LEFT.

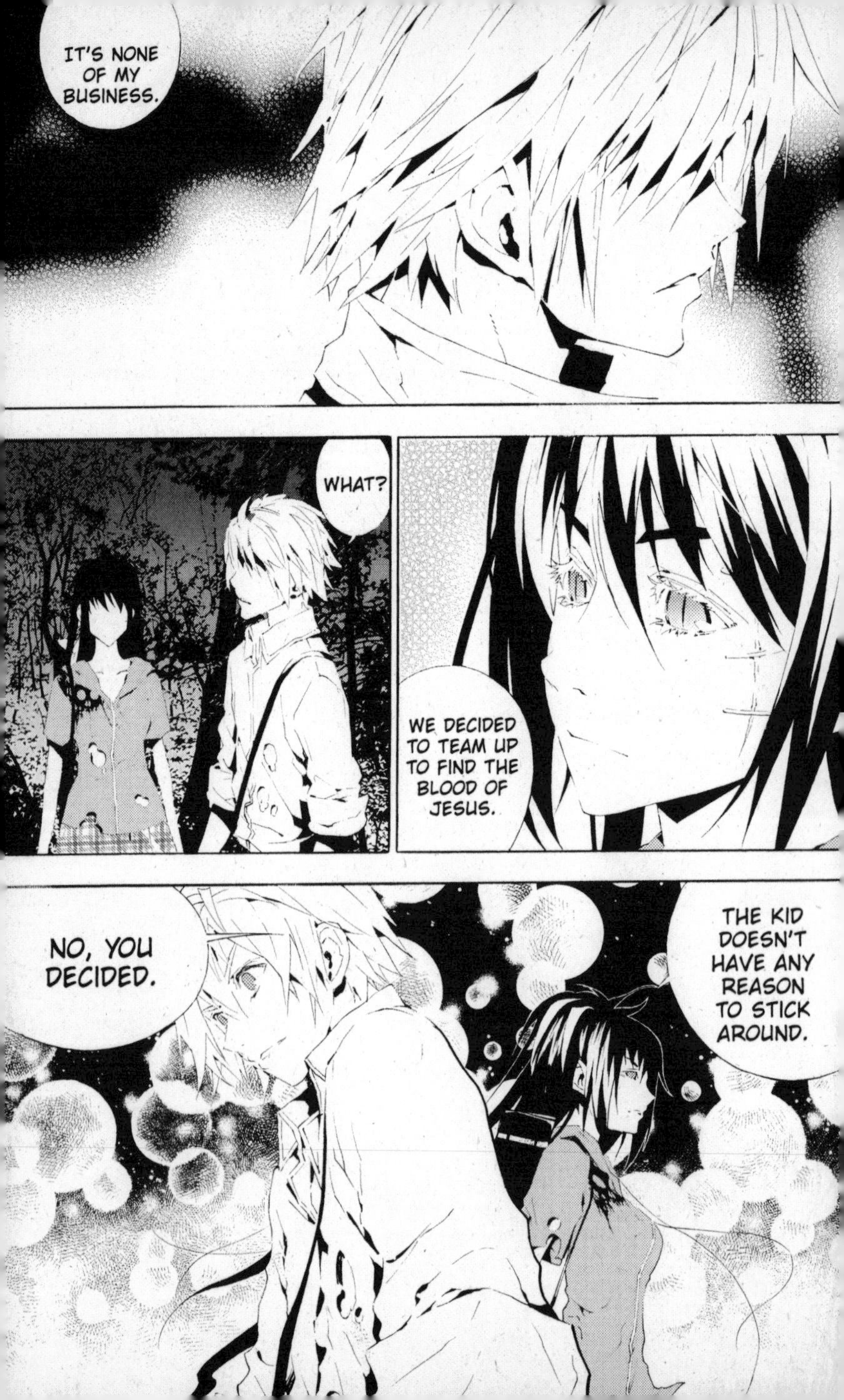
IT'S NONE OF MY BUSINESS.
WHAT?
WE DECIDED TO TEAM UP TO FIND THE BLOOD OF JESUS.
NO, YOU DECIDED.
THE KID DOESN'T HAVE ANY REASON TO STICK AROUND.

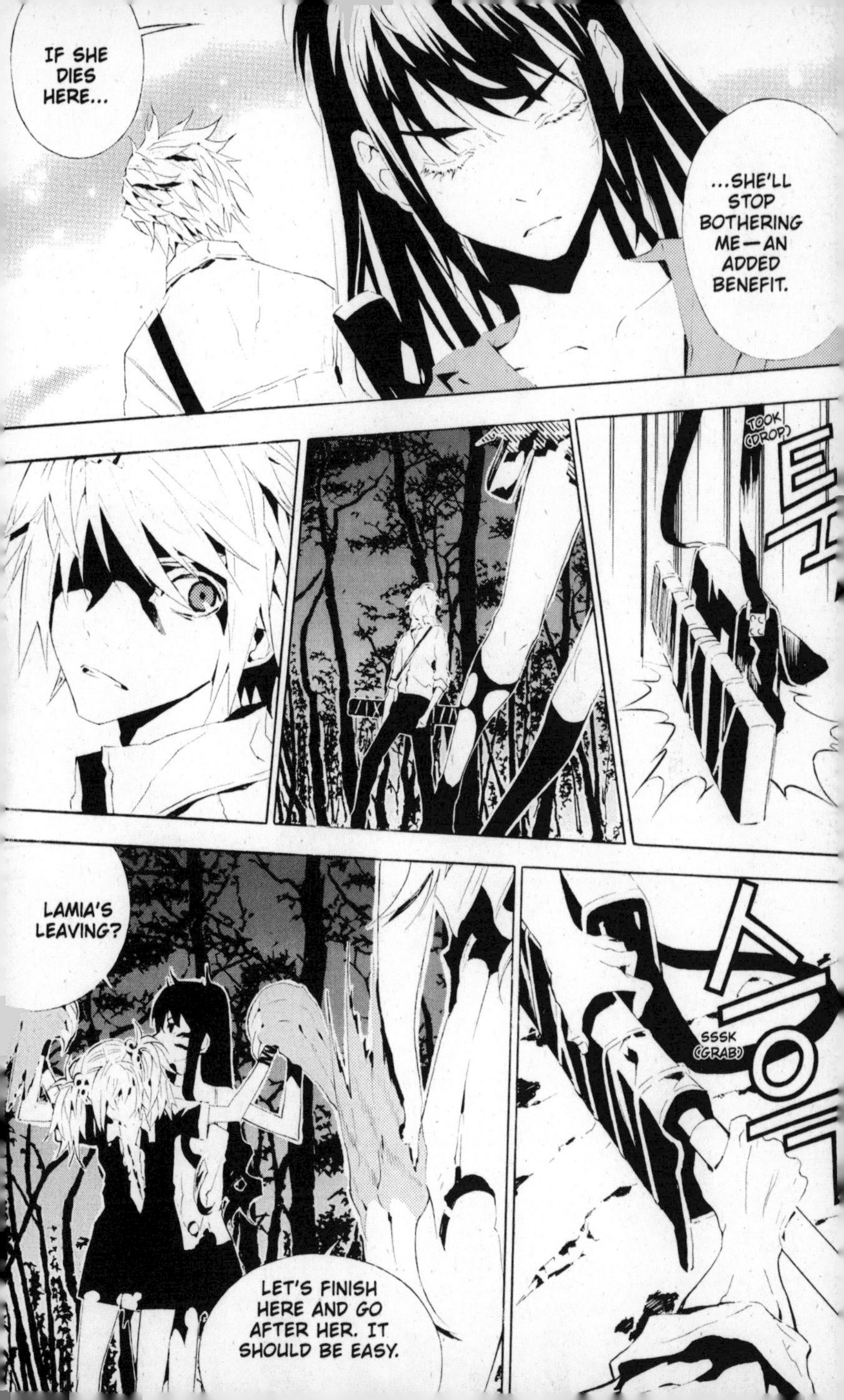
IF SHE DIES HERE...
...SHE'LL STOP BOTHERING ME—AN ADDED BENEFIT.
TOOK (DROP)
LAMIA'S LEAVING?
LET'S FINISH HERE AND GO AFTER HER. IT SHOULD BE EASY.
SSSK (GRAB)

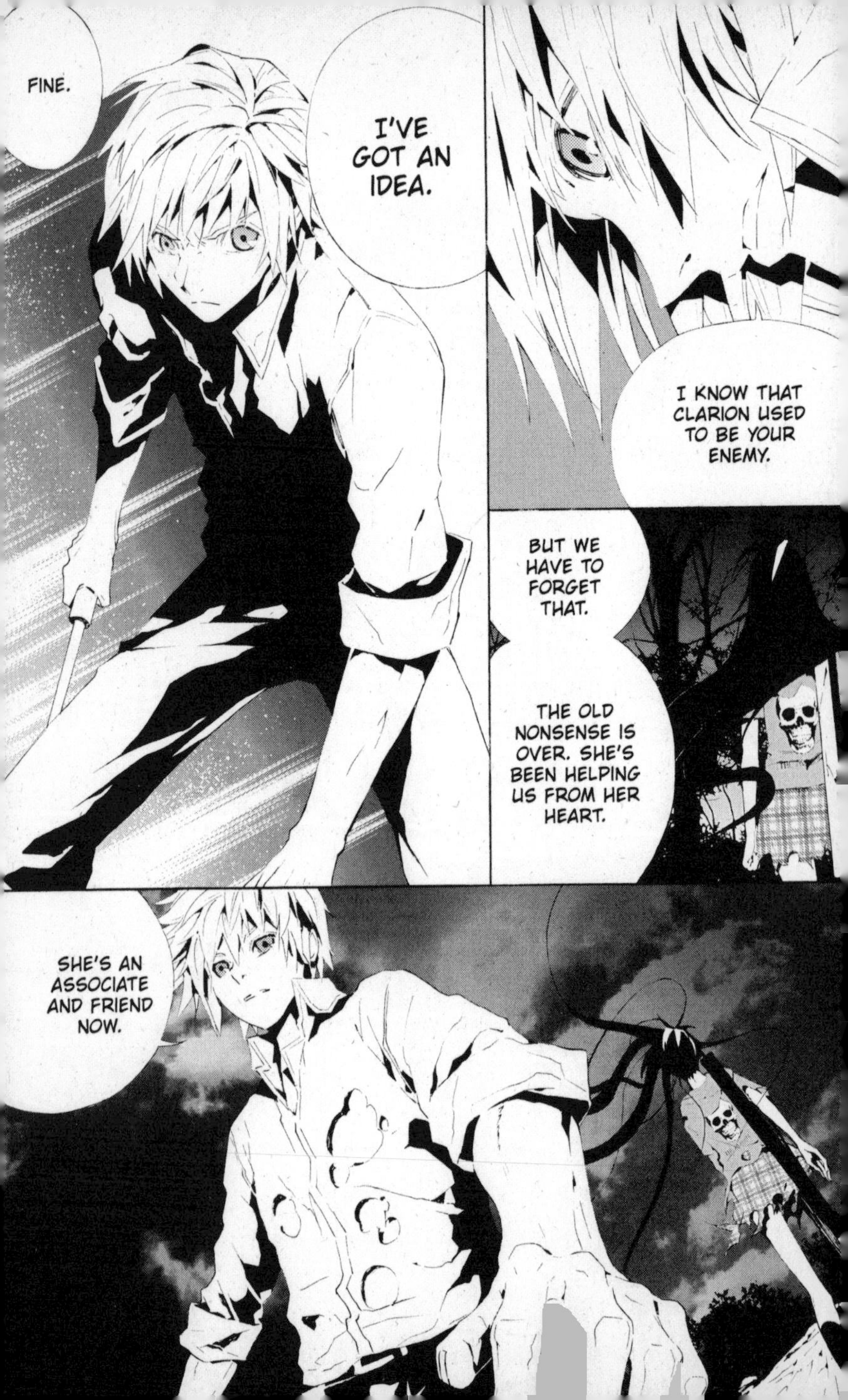
FINE.
I'VE GOT AN IDEA.
I KNOW THAT CLARION USED TO BE YOUR ENEMY.
BUT WE HAVE TO FORGET THAT.
THE OLD NONSENSE IS OVER. SHE'S BEEN HELPING US FROM HER HEART.
SHE'S AN ASSOCIATE AND FRIEND NOW.

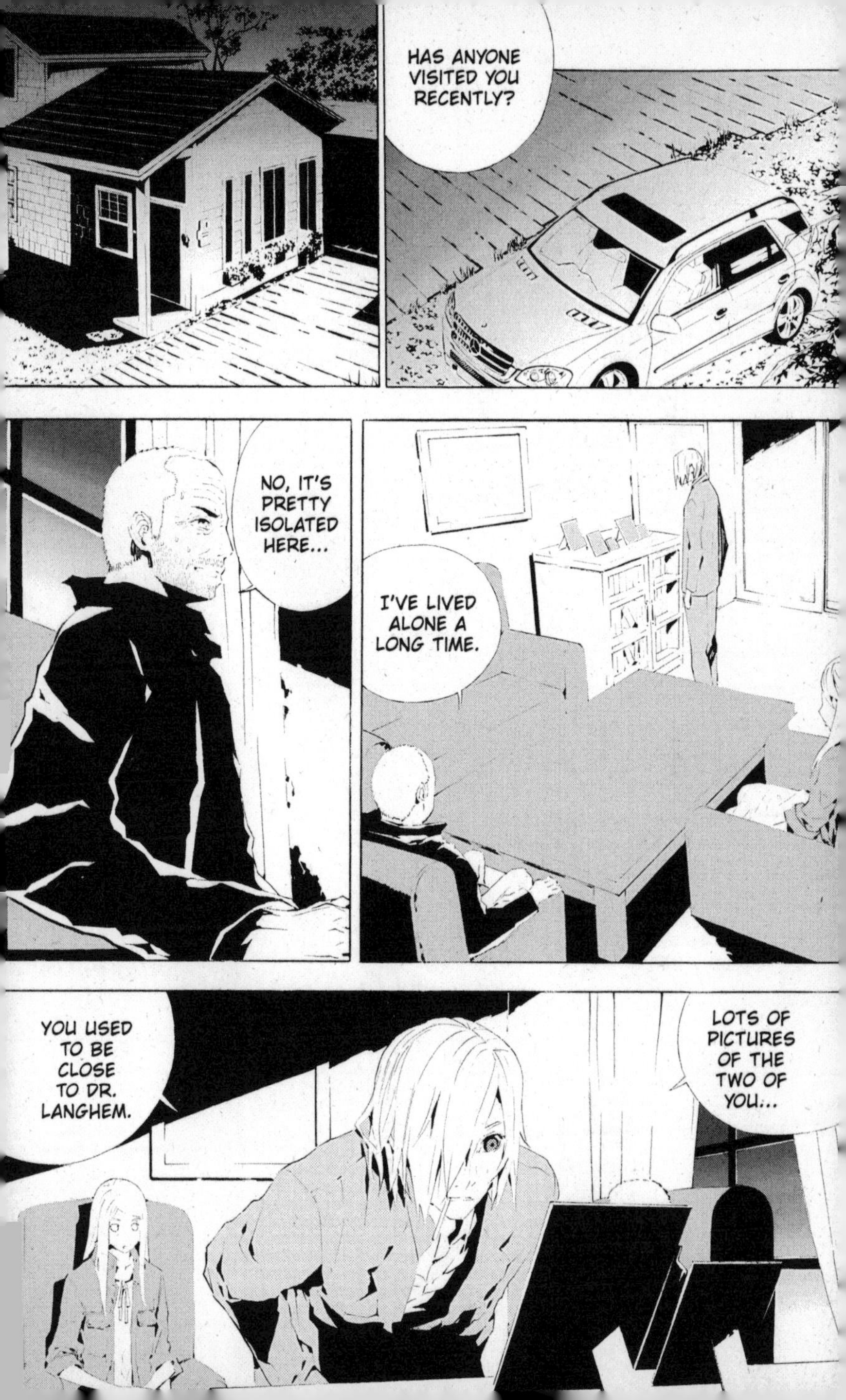
HAS ANYONE VISITED YOU RECENTLY?
NO, IT'S PRETTY ISOLATED HERE...
I'VE LIVED ALONE A LONG TIME.
YOU USED TO BE CLOSE TO DR. LANGHEM.
LOTS OF PICTURES OF THE TWO OF YOU...

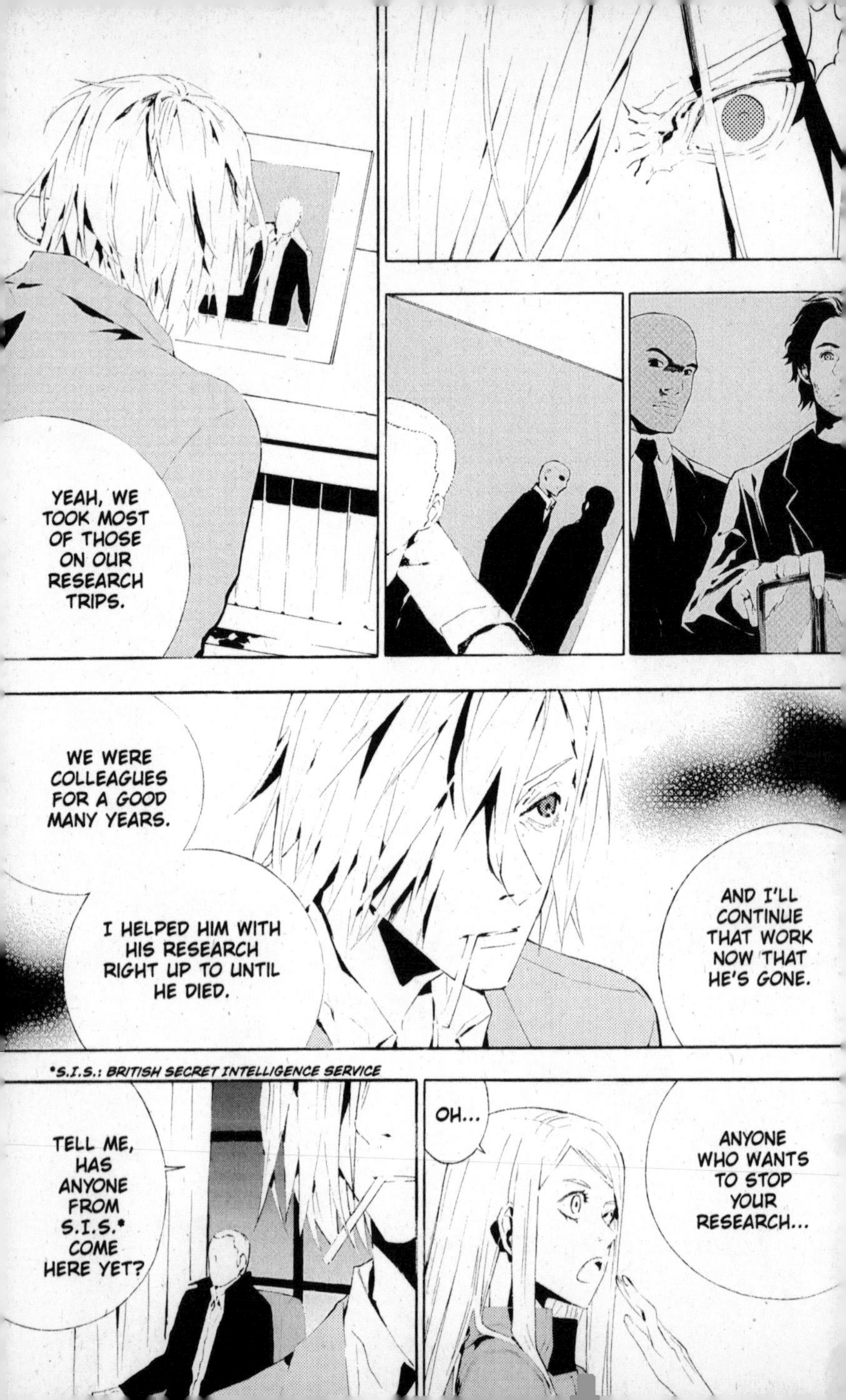
YEAH, WE TOOK MOST OF THOSE ON OUR RESEARCH TRIPS.
WE WERE COLLEAGUES FOR A GOOD MANY YEARS.
I HELPED HIM WITH HIS RESEARCH RIGHT UP TO UNTIL HE DIED.
AND I'LL CONTINUE THAT WORK NOW THAT HE'S GONE.
TELL ME, HAS ANYONE FROM S.I.S.* COME HERE YET?
OH...
ANYONE WHO WANTS TO STOP YOUR RESEARCH...
*S.I.S.: BRITISH SECRET INTELLIGENCE SERVICE

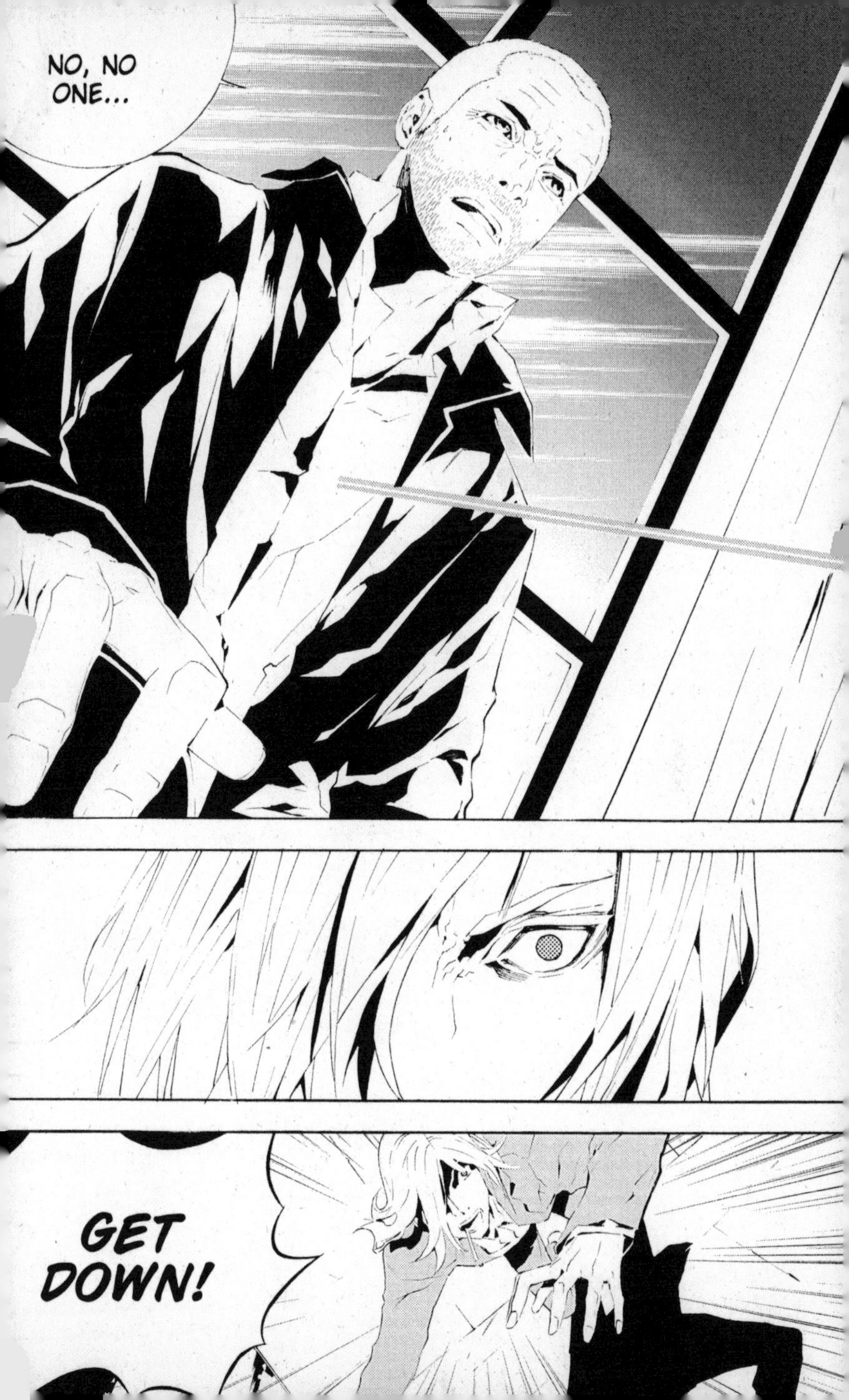
NO, NO ONE...
GET DOWN!

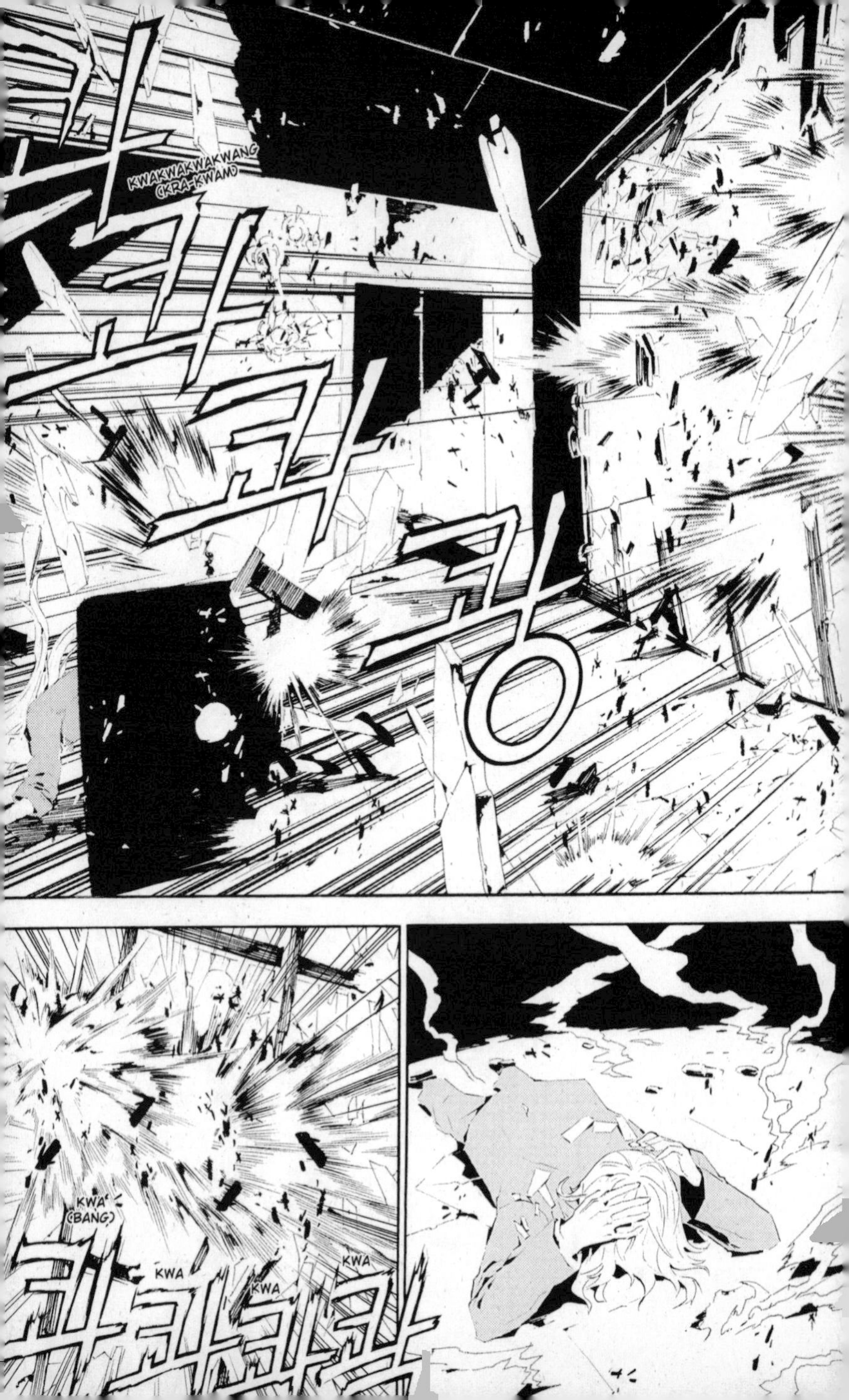
KWAKWAKWAKWANG
(KRA-KWAM)
KWA
(BANG)
KWA
KWA
KWA

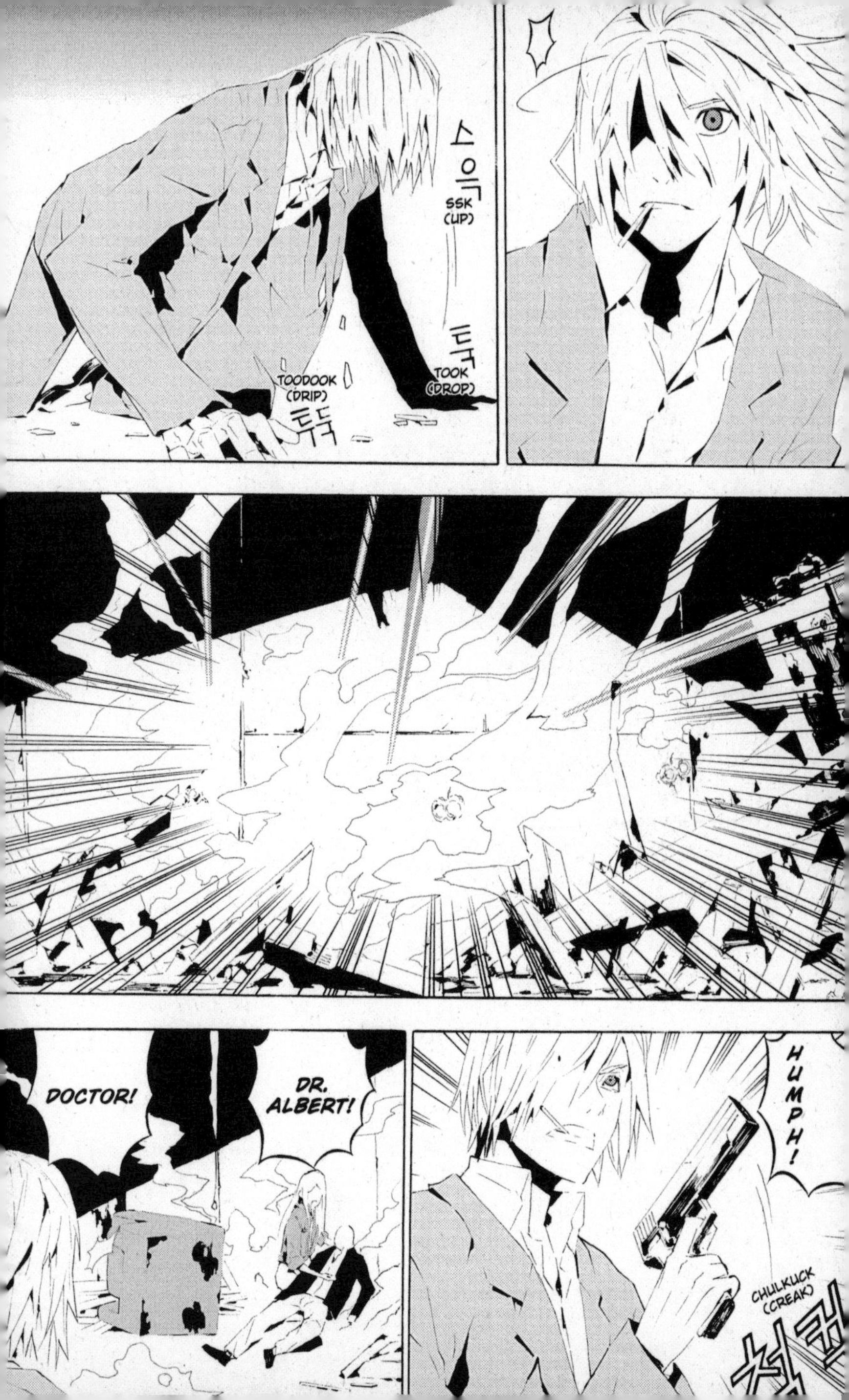
스윽
SSK (UP)
TOODOOK (DRIP)
투둑
툭
TOOK (DROP)
DOCTOR!
DR. ALBERT!
HUMPH!
CHULKUCK (CREAK)
철컥

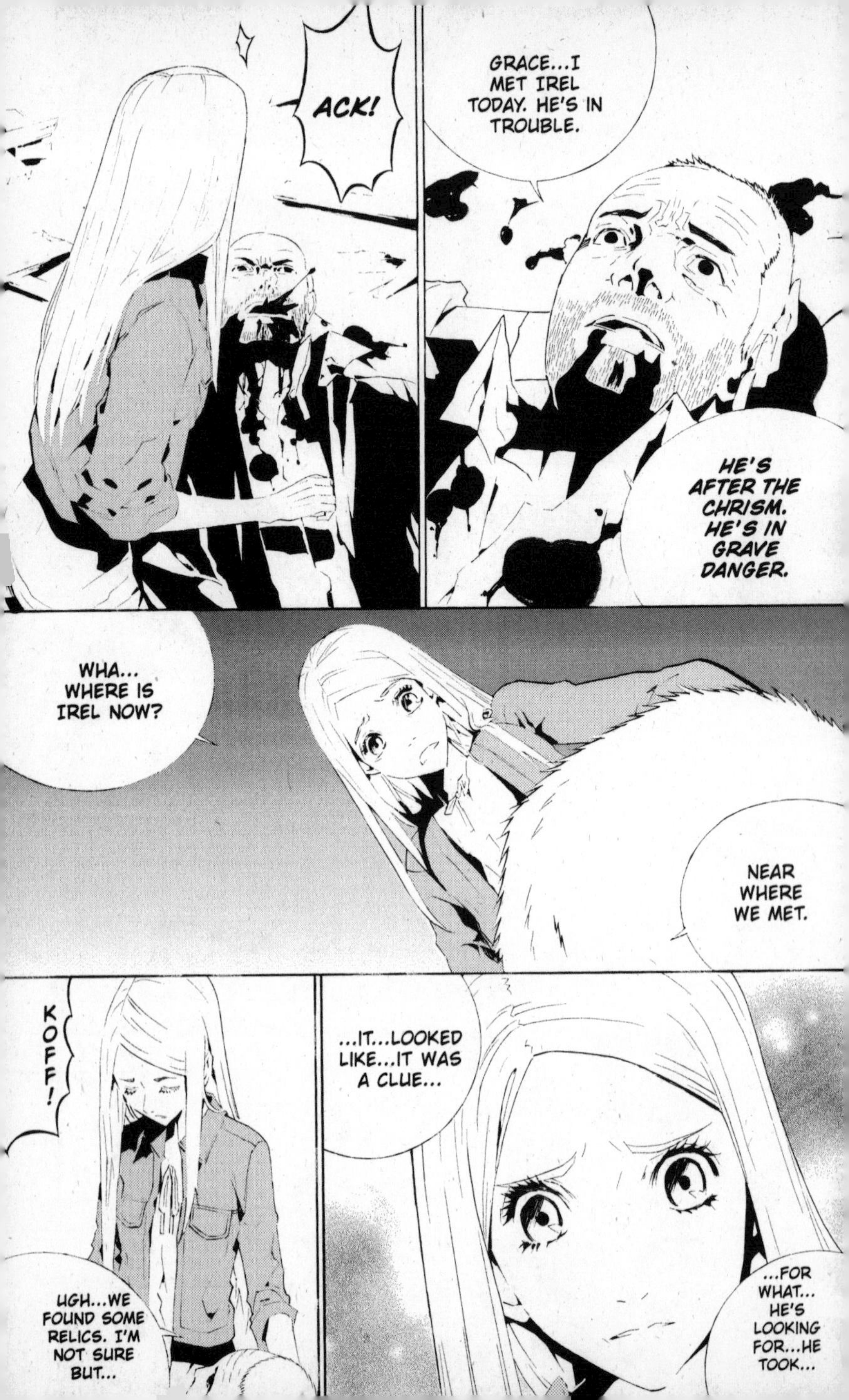
ACK!
GRACE...I MET IREL TODAY. HE'S IN TROUBLE.
HE'S AFTER THE CHRISM. HE'S IN GRAVE DANGER.
WHA... WHERE IS IREL NOW?
NEAR WHERE WE MET.
KOFF!
UGH...WE FOUND SOME RELICS. I'M NOT SURE BUT...
...IT...LOOKED LIKE...IT WAS A CLUE...
...FOR WHAT... HE'S LOOKING FOR...HE TOOK...

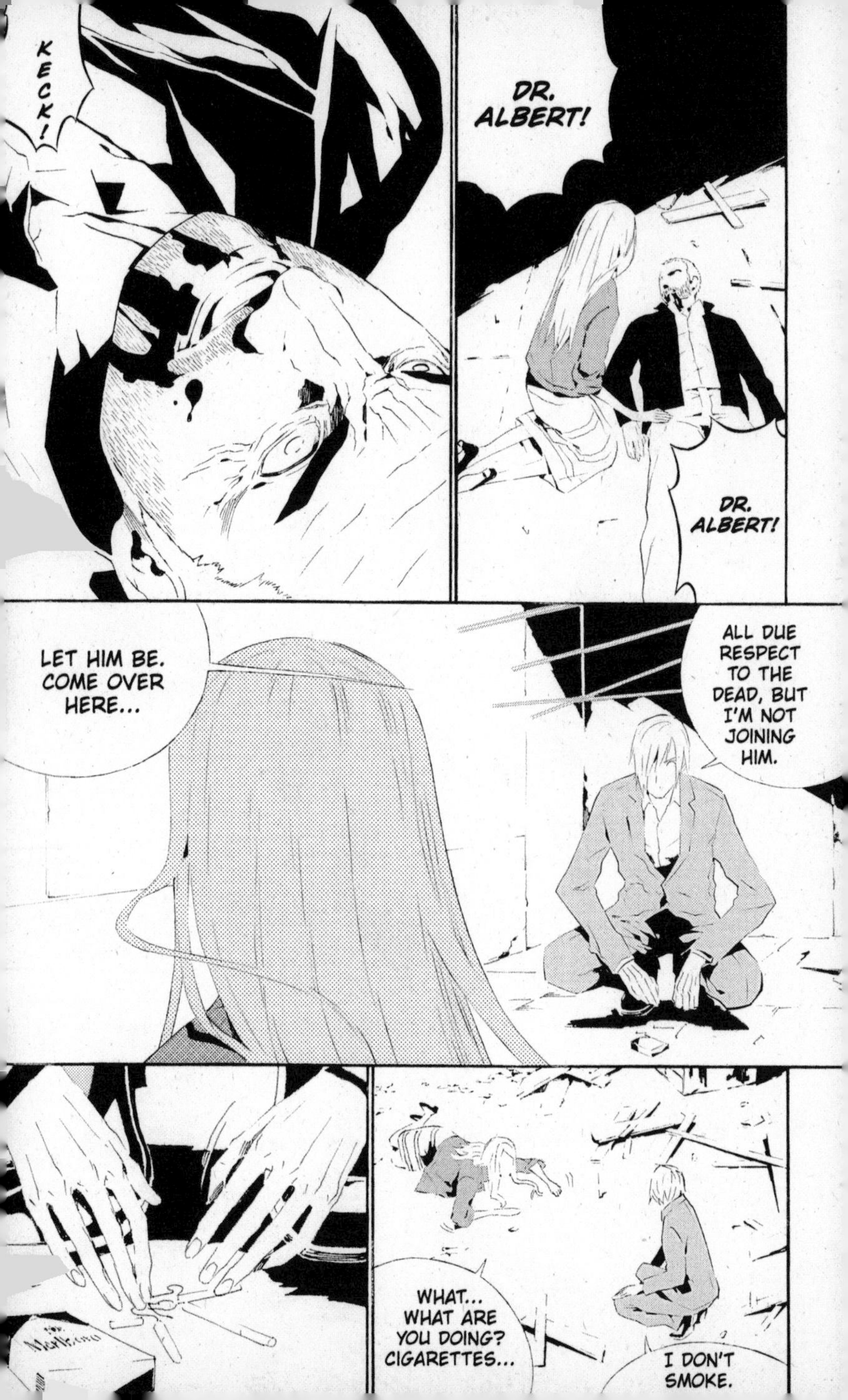
KECK!
DR. ALBERT!
DR. ALBERT!
LET HIM BE. COME OVER HERE...
ALL DUE RESPECT TO THE DEAD, BUT I'M NOT JOINING HIM.
WHAT... WHAT ARE YOU DOING? CIGARETTES...
I DON'T SMOKE.

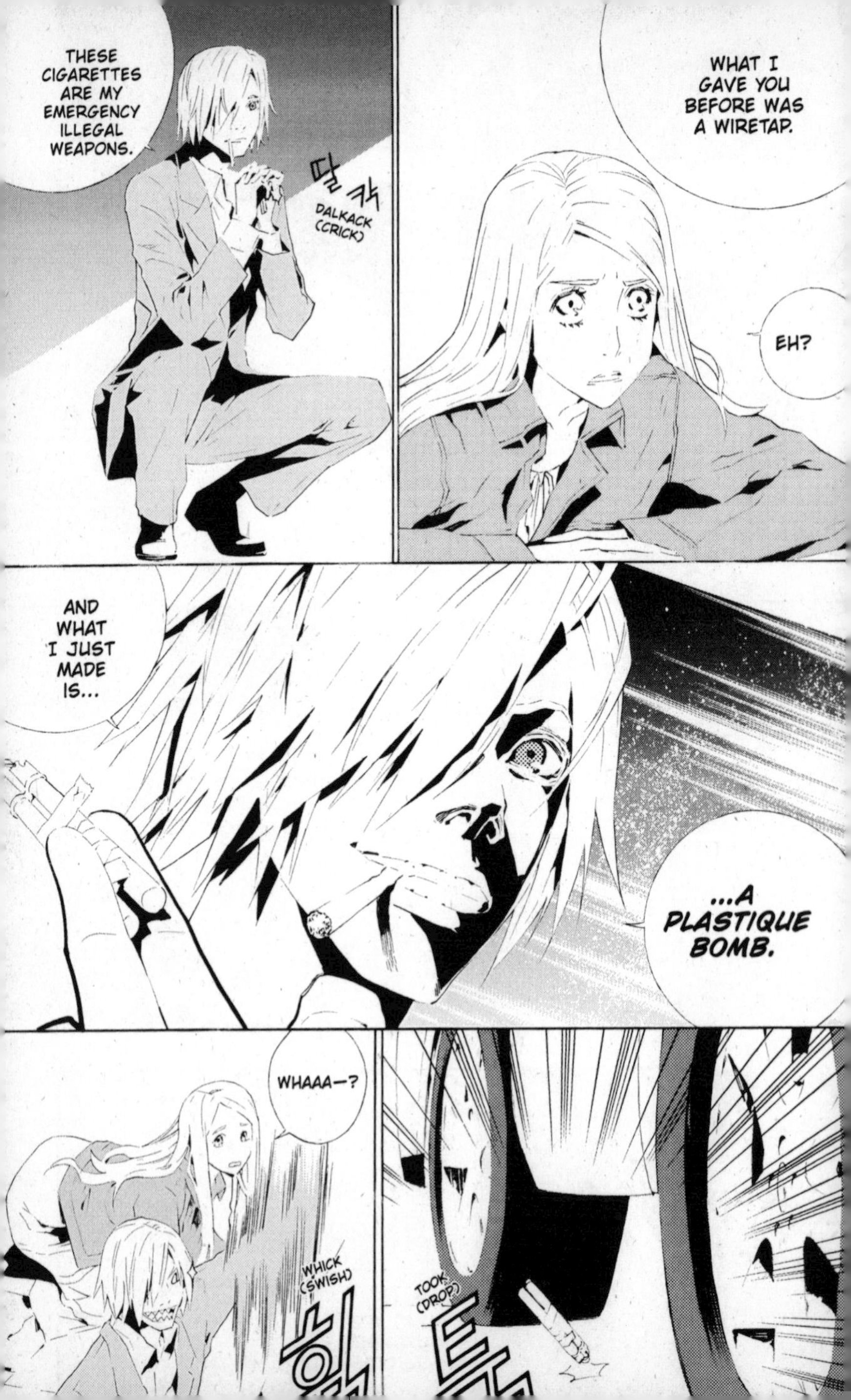
THESE CIGARETTES ARE MY EMERGENCY ILLEGAL WEAPONS.
딸칵
DALKACK (CRICK)
WHAT I GAVE YOU BEFORE WAS A WIRETAP.
EH?
AND WHAT I JUST MADE IS...
...A PLASTIQUE BOMB.
WHAAA—?
WHICK (SWISH)
TOOK (DROP)

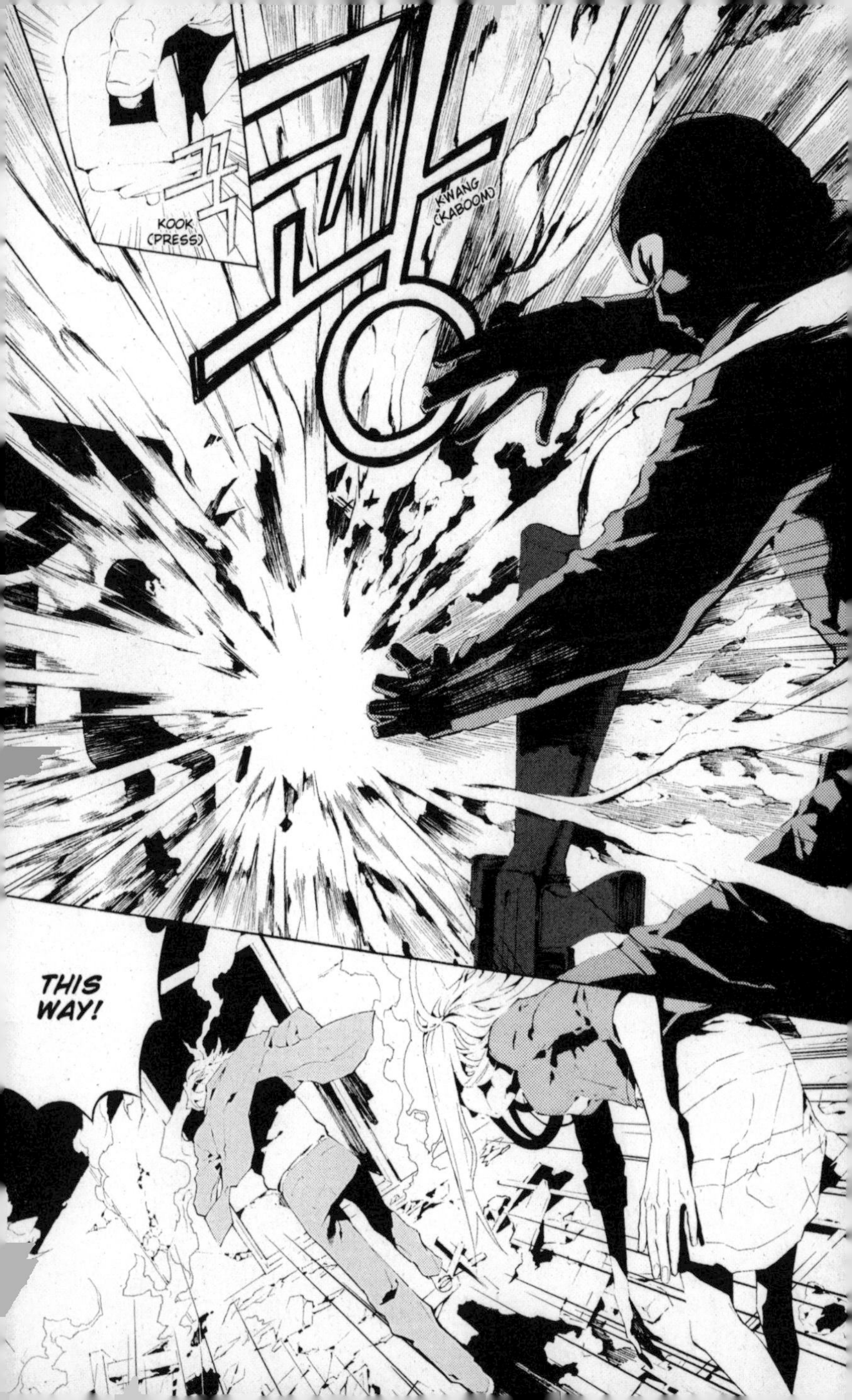
KOOK
(PRESS)
K'WANG
(KABOOM)
THIS
WAY!

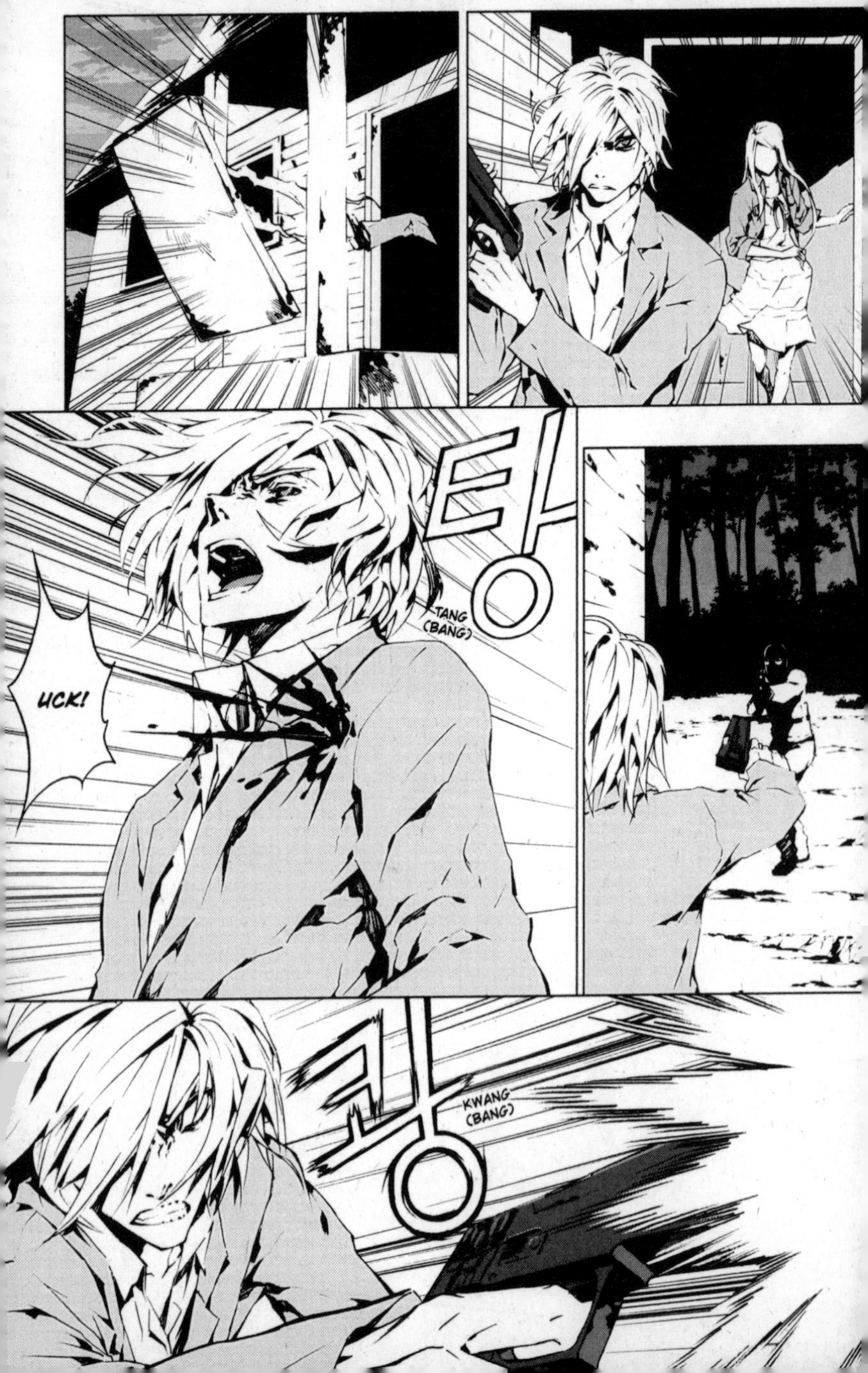
UCK!
TANG (BANG)
KWANG (BANG)

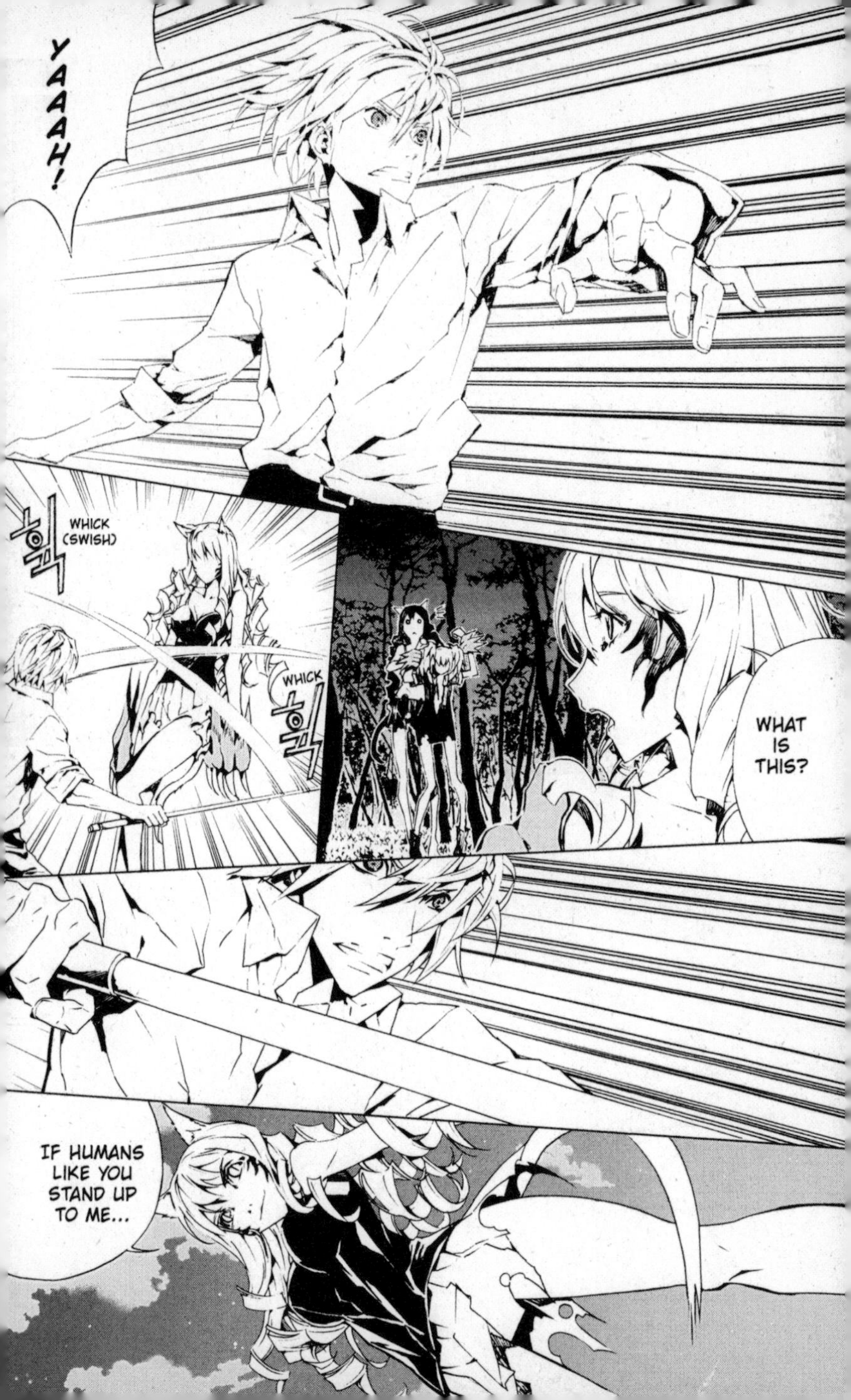
YAAAAH!
WHICK (SWISH)
WHICK
WHAT IS THIS?
IF HUMANS LIKE YOU STAND UP TO ME...

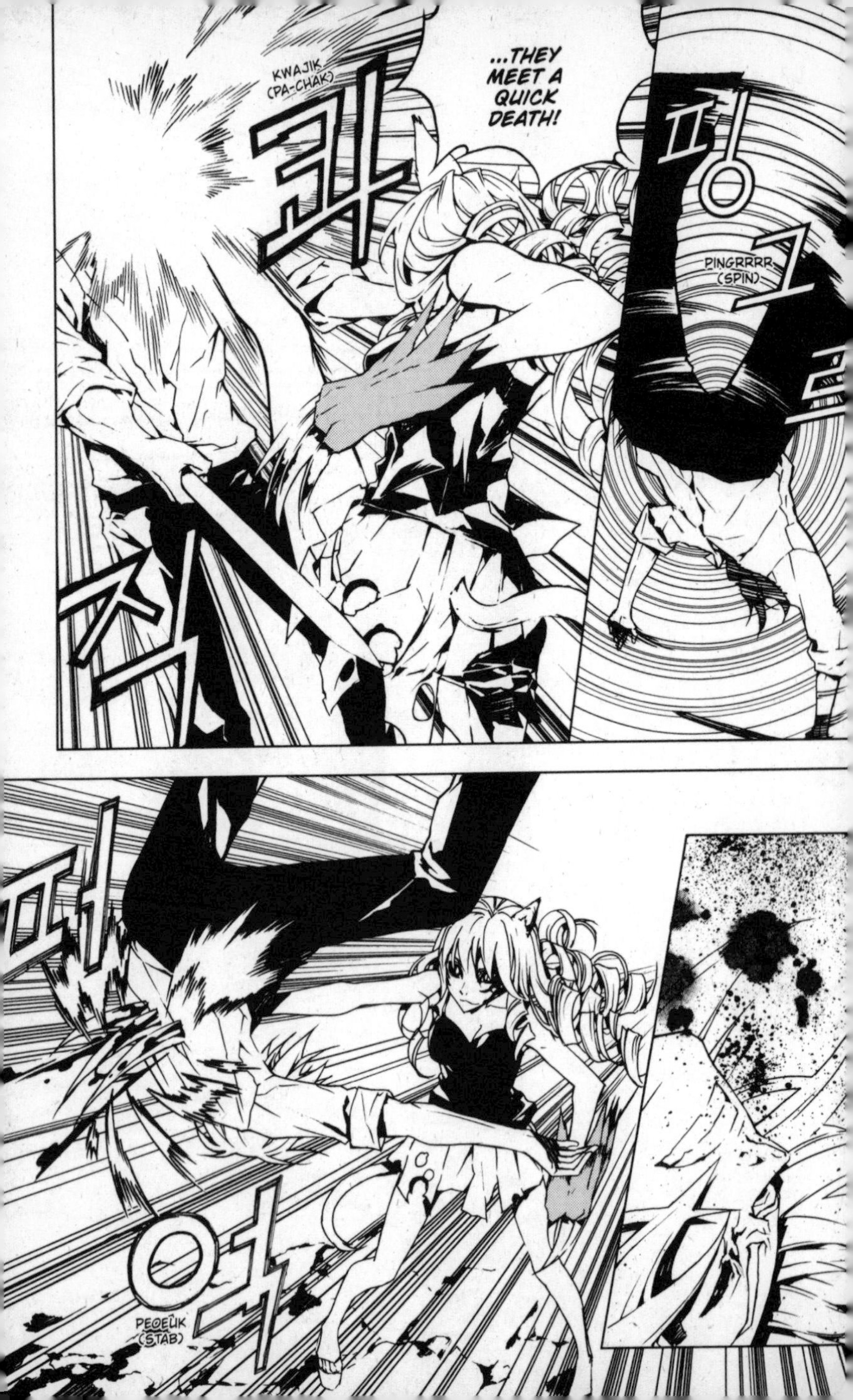

KWAJIK (PA-CHAK)
...THEY MEET A QUICK DEATH!
PINGRRRR (SPIN)
PEOEŬK (STAB)

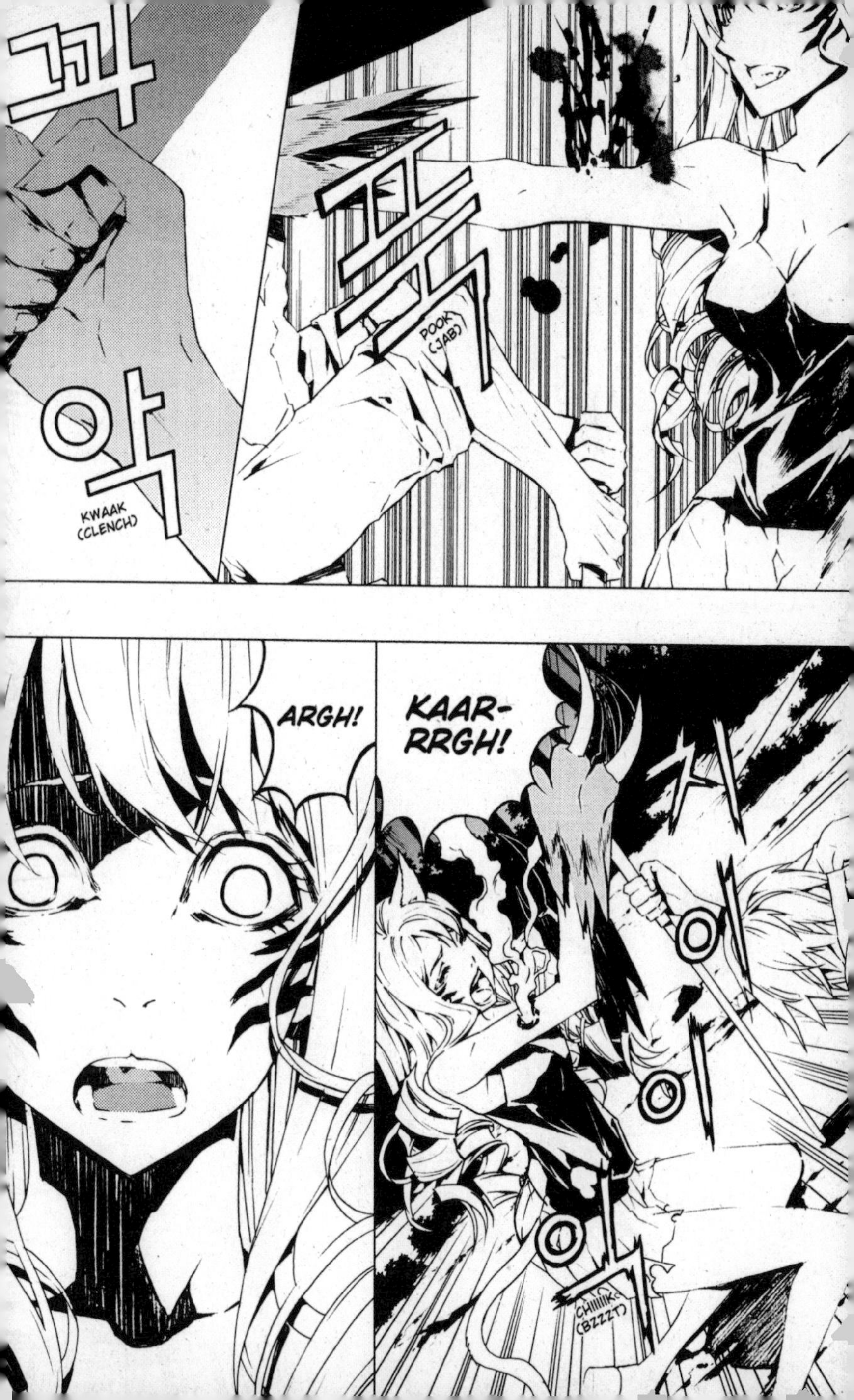
KWAAK (CLENCH)
POOK (JAB)
ARGH!
KAAR-RRGH!
CHIIIIIK (BZZZT)

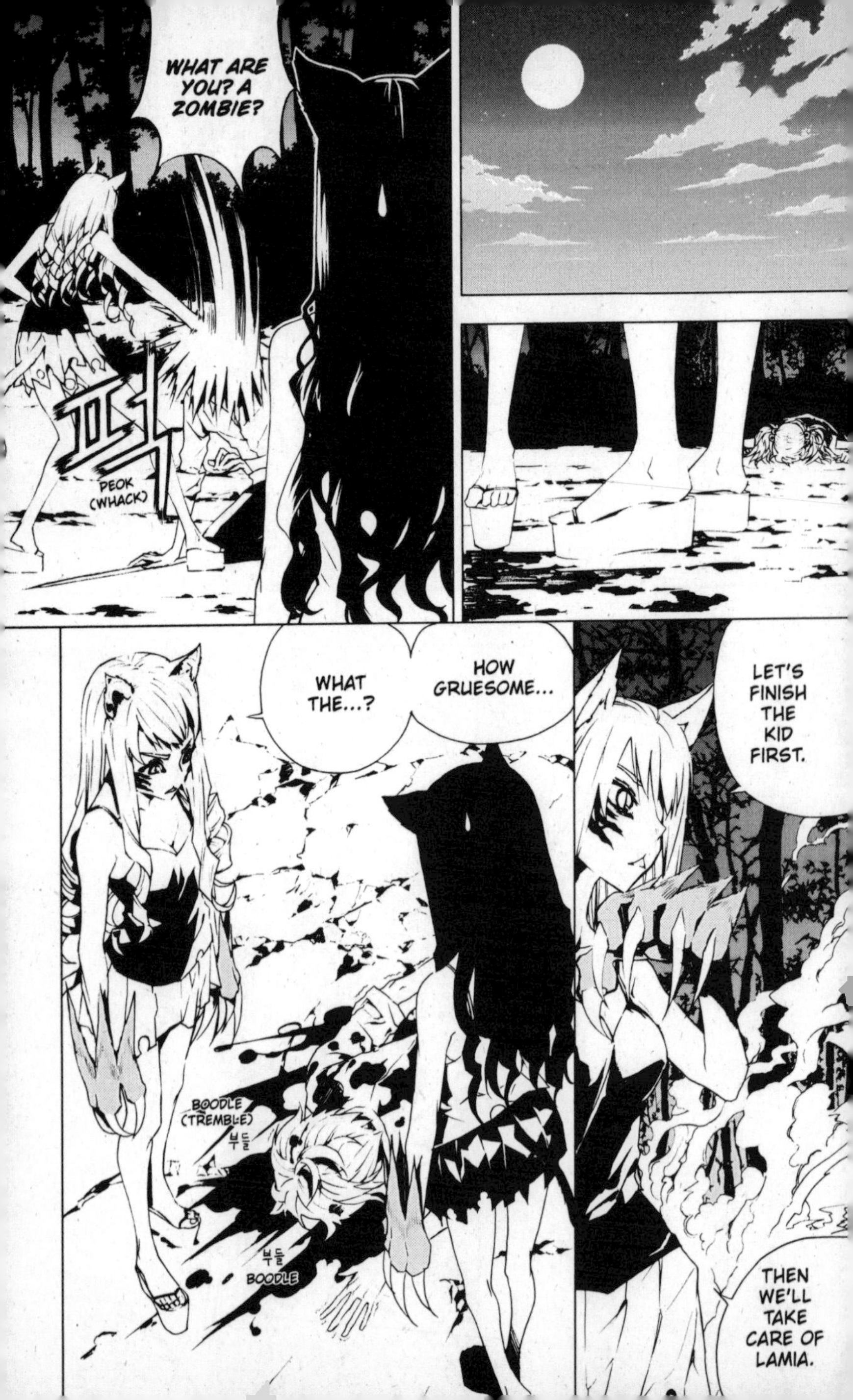
WHAT ARE YOU? A ZOMBIE?
PEOK (WHACK)
WHAT THE...?
HOW GRUESOME...
BOODLE (TREMBLE)
부들
부들
BOODLE
LET'S FINISH THE KID FIRST.
THEN WE'LL TAKE CARE OF LAMIA.

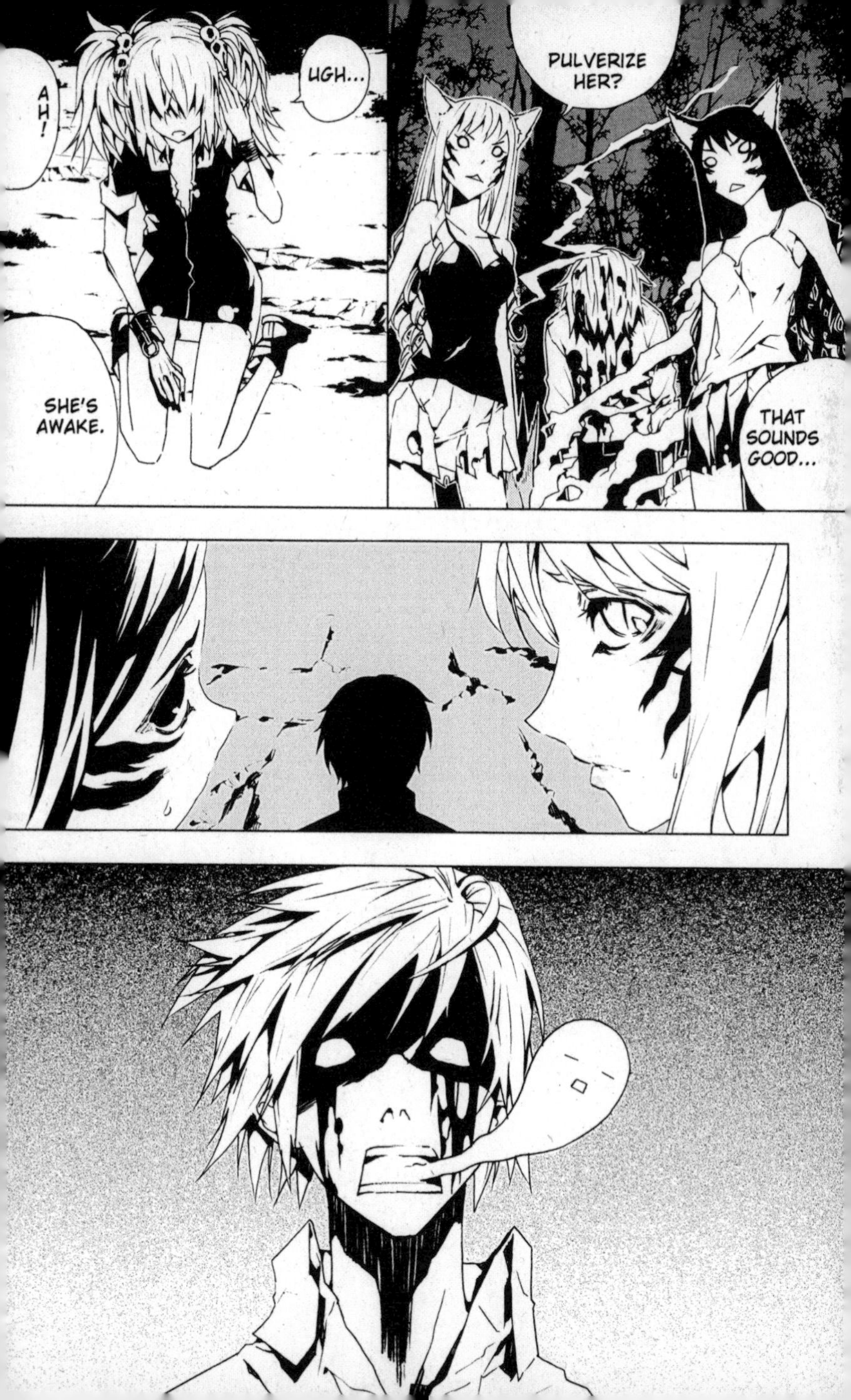
AH!
UGH...
SHE'S AWAKE.
PULVERIZE HER?
THAT SOUNDS GOOD...

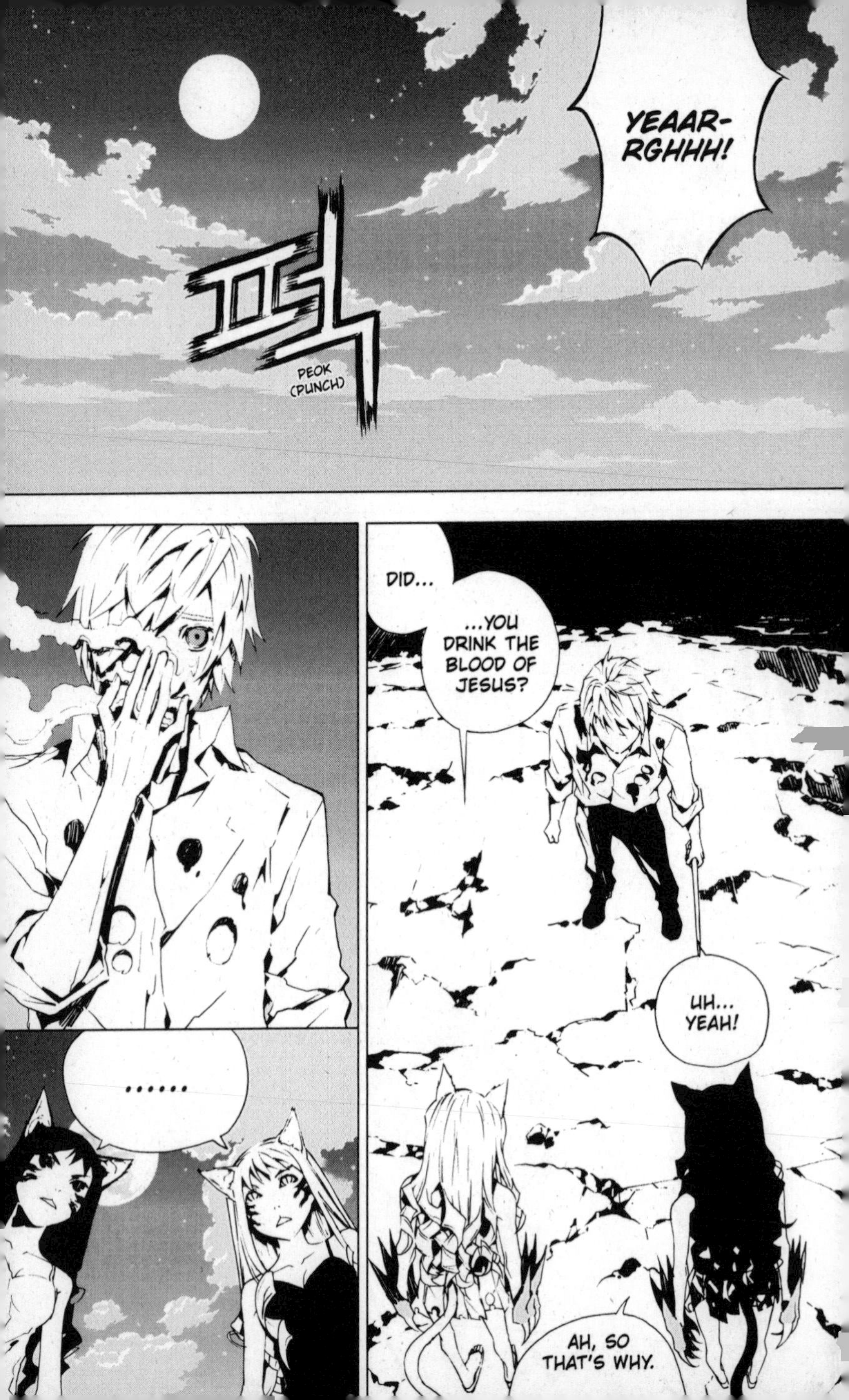
PEOK (PUNCH)
YEAAR-RGHHH!
......
DID...
...YOU DRINK THE BLOOD OF JESUS?
UH... YEAH!
AH, SO THAT'S WHY.

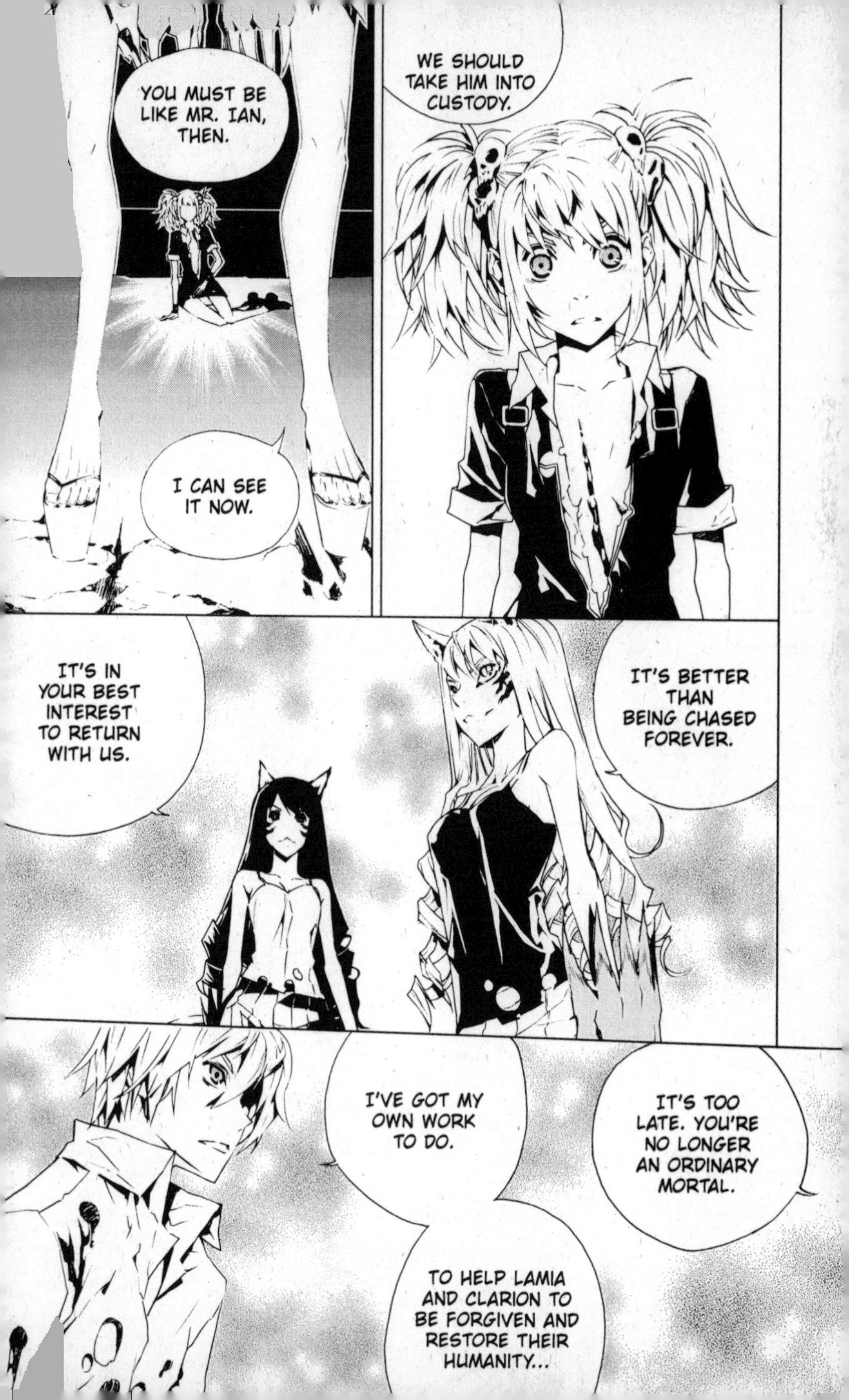
YOU MUST BE LIKE MR. IAN, THEN.
I CAN SEE IT NOW.
WE SHOULD TAKE HIM INTO CUSTODY.
IT'S IN YOUR BEST INTEREST TO RETURN WITH US.
IT'S BETTER THAN BEING CHASED FOREVER.
I'VE GOT MY OWN WORK TO DO.
TO HELP LAMIA AND CLARION TO BE FORGIVEN AND RESTORE THEIR HUMANITY...
IT'S TOO LATE. YOU'RE NO LONGER AN ORDINARY MORTAL.

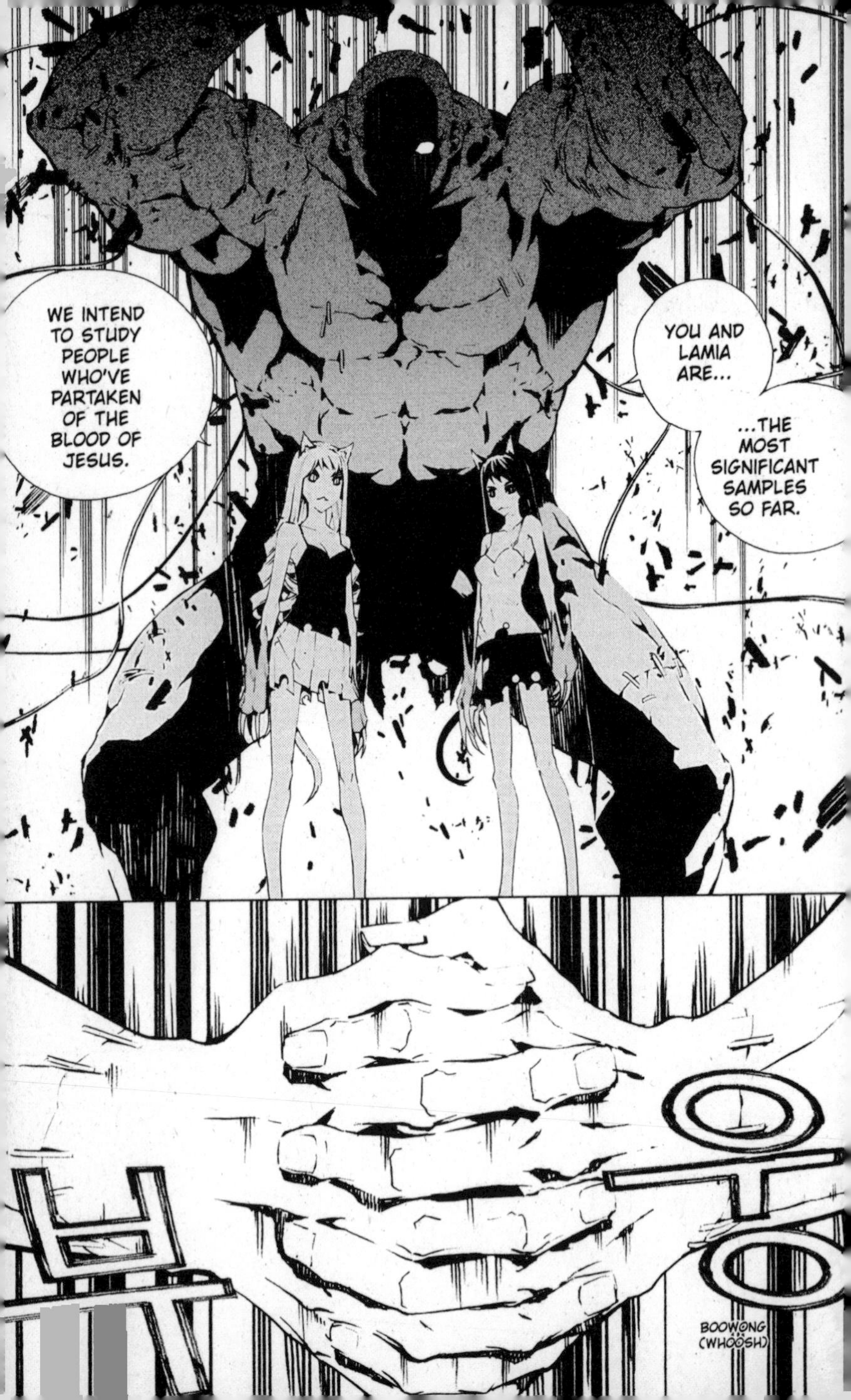
WE INTEND TO STUDY PEOPLE WHO'VE PARTAKEN OF THE BLOOD OF JESUS.
YOU AND LAMIA ARE...
...THE MOST SIGNIFICANT SAMPLES SO FAR.
BOOWONG (WHOOSH)

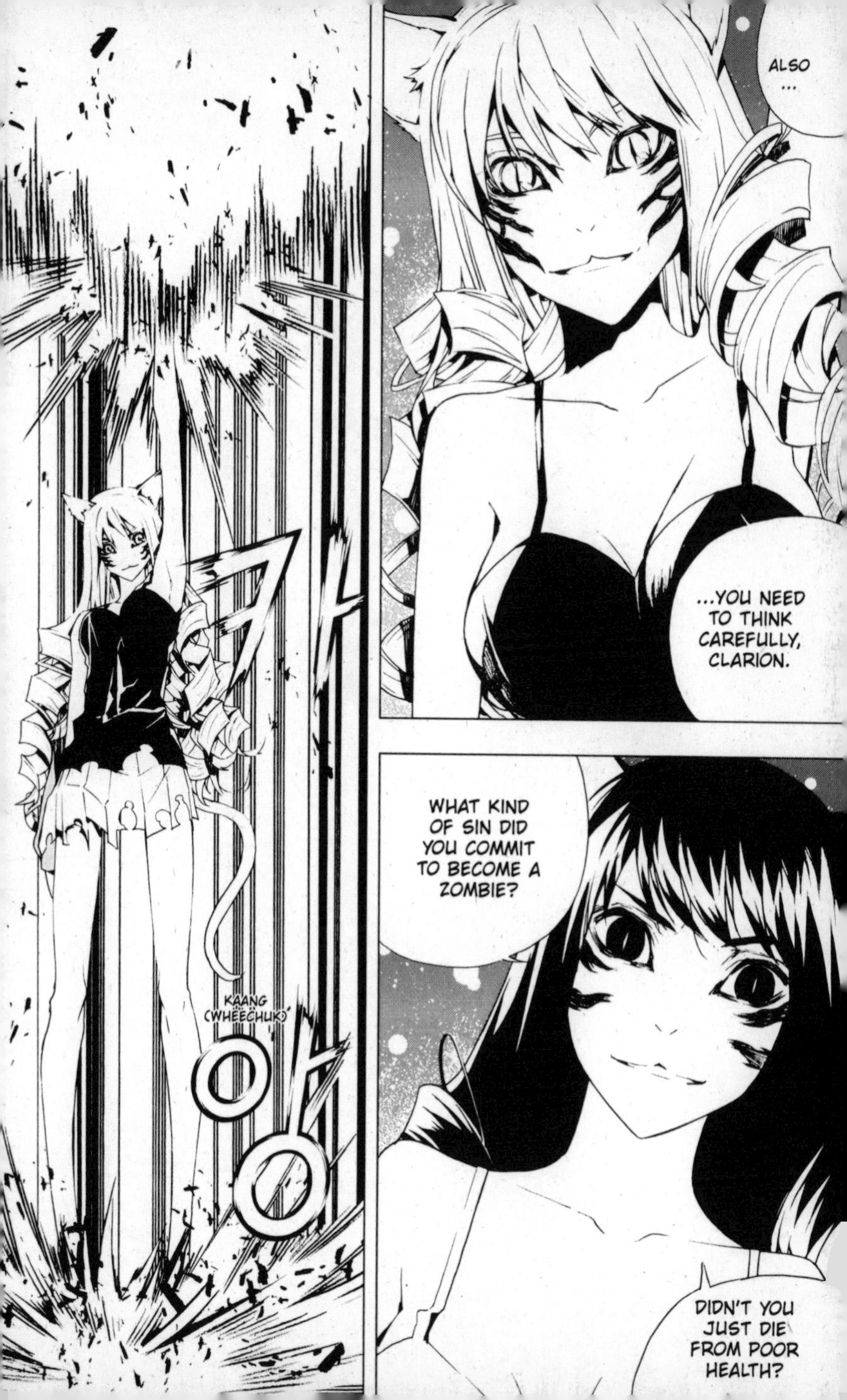
KAANG (WHEECHUK)
ALSO ...
...YOU NEED TO THINK CAREFULLY, CLARION.
WHAT KIND OF SIN DID YOU COMMIT TO BECOME A ZOMBIE?
DIDN'T YOU JUST DIE FROM POOR HEALTH?

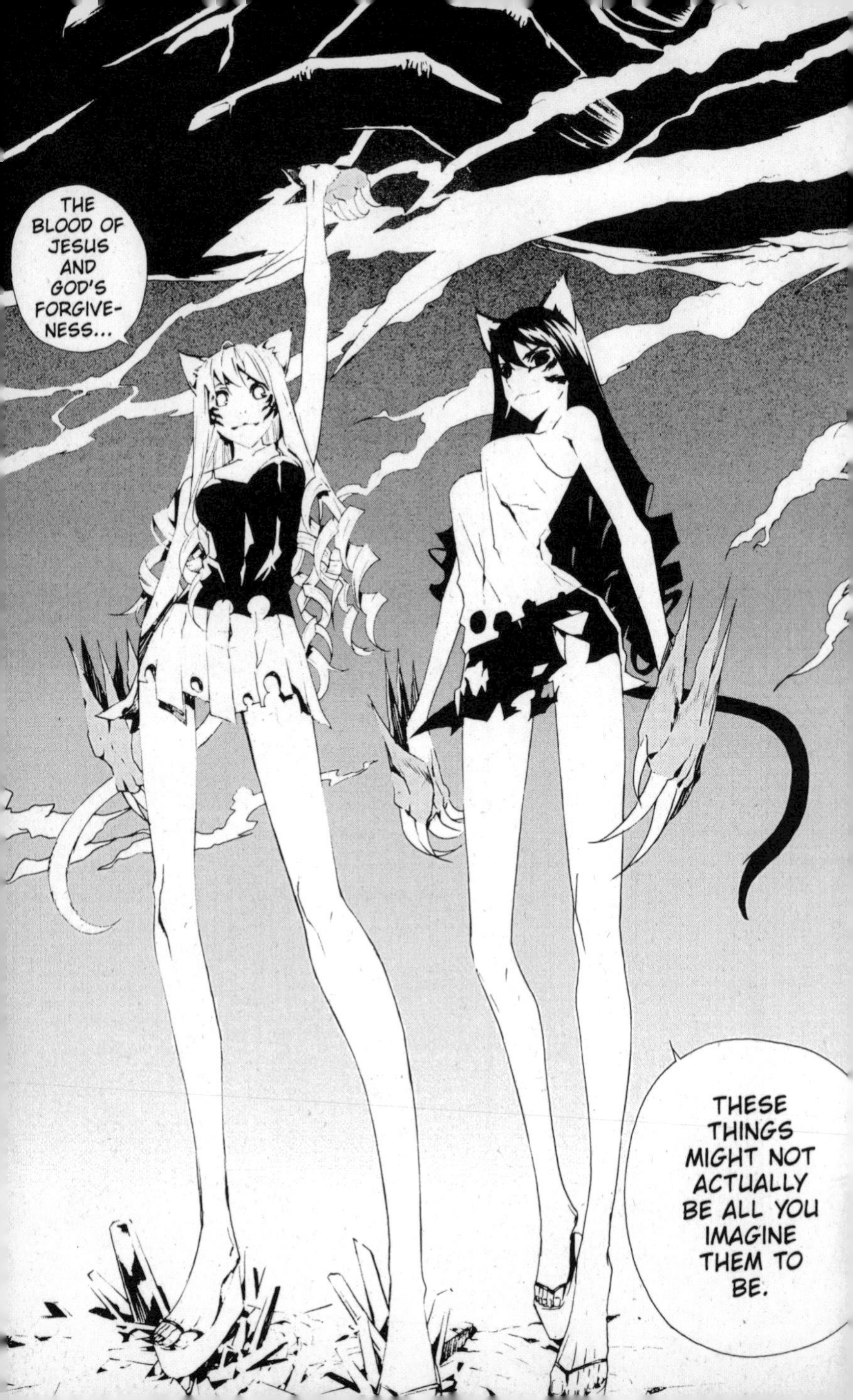
THE BLOOD OF JESUS AND GOD'S FORGIVE- NESS...
THESE THINGS MIGHT NOT ACTUALLY BE ALL YOU IMAGINE THEM TO BE.

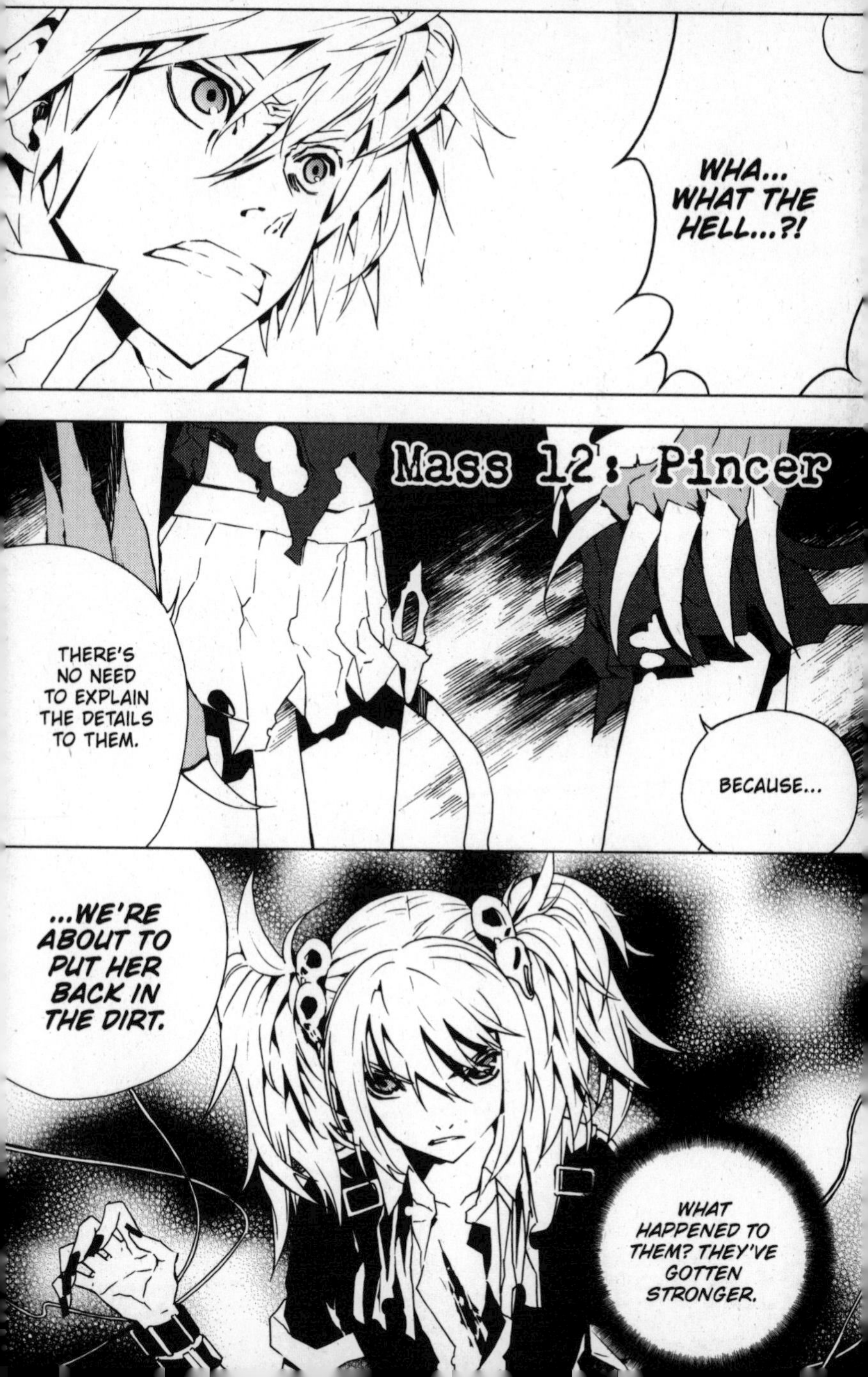
WHA... WHAT THE HELL...?!
Mass 12: Pincer
THERE'S NO NEED TO EXPLAIN THE DETAILS TO THEM.
BECAUSE...
...WE'RE ABOUT TO PUT HER BACK IN THE DIRT.
WHAT HAPPENED TO THEM? THEY'VE GOTTEN STRONGER.

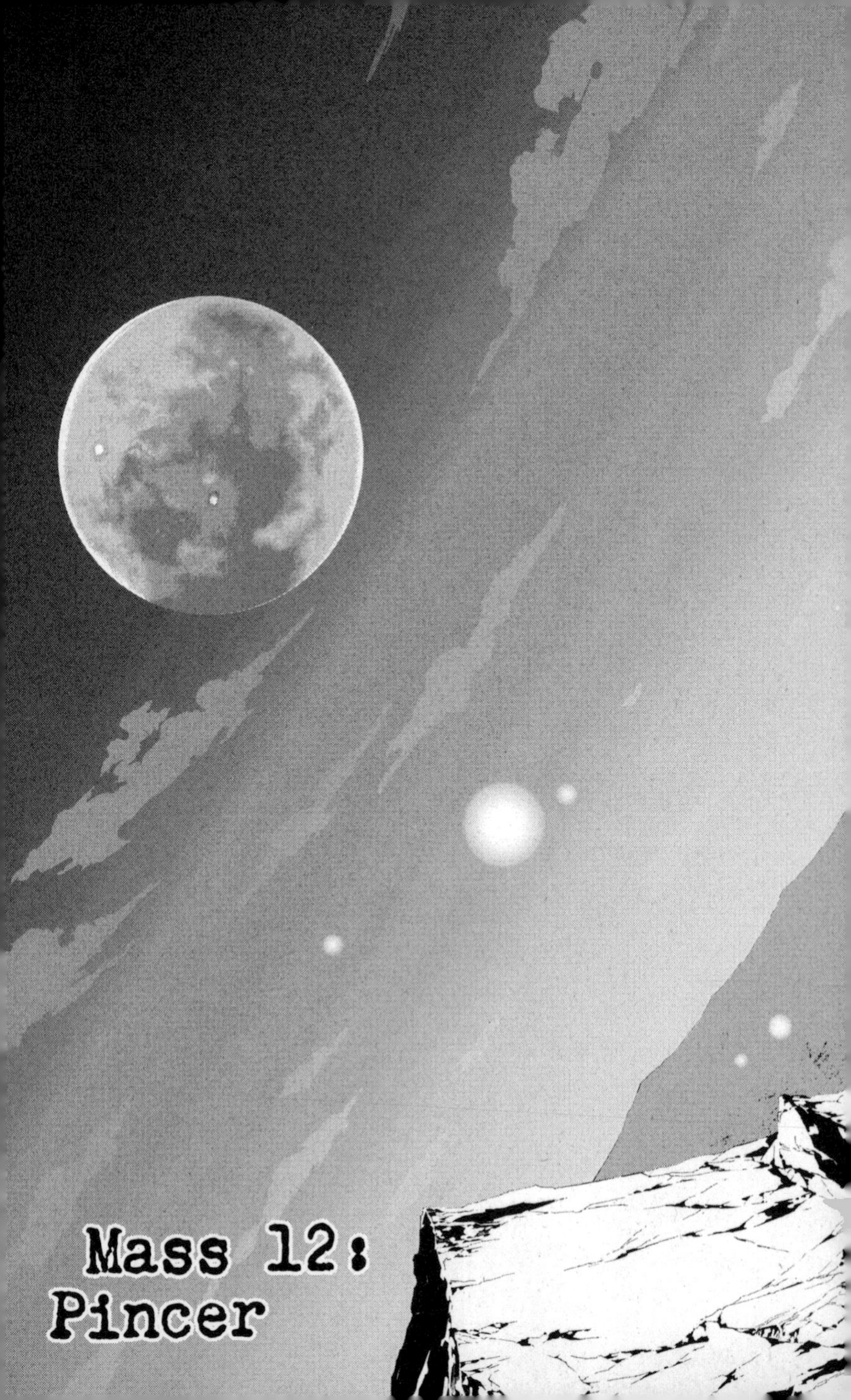
Mass 12:
Pincer

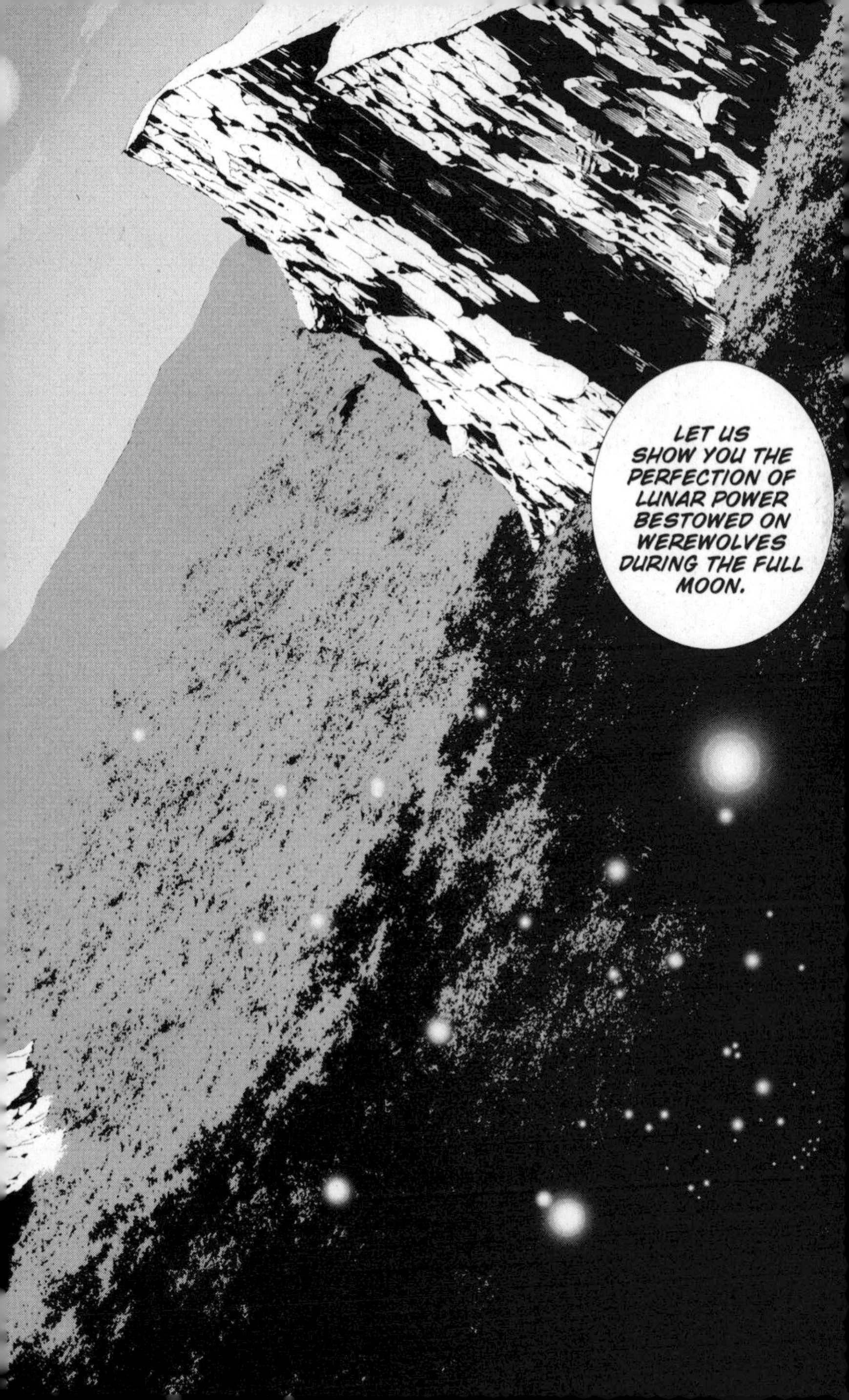
LET US SHOW YOU THE PERFECTION OF LUNAR POWER BESTOWED ON WEREWOLVES DURING THE FULL MOON.

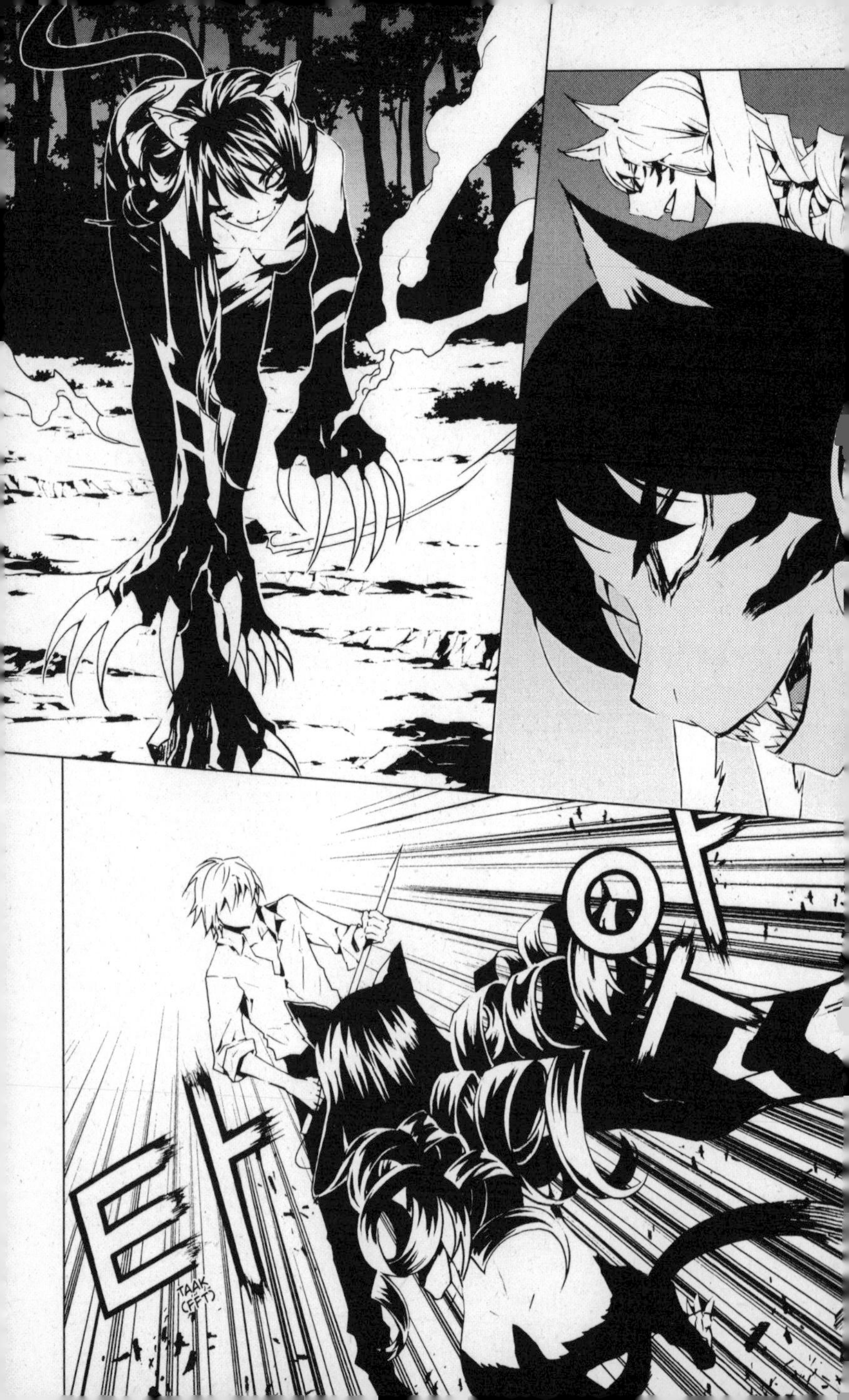
TAAK
(FFT)

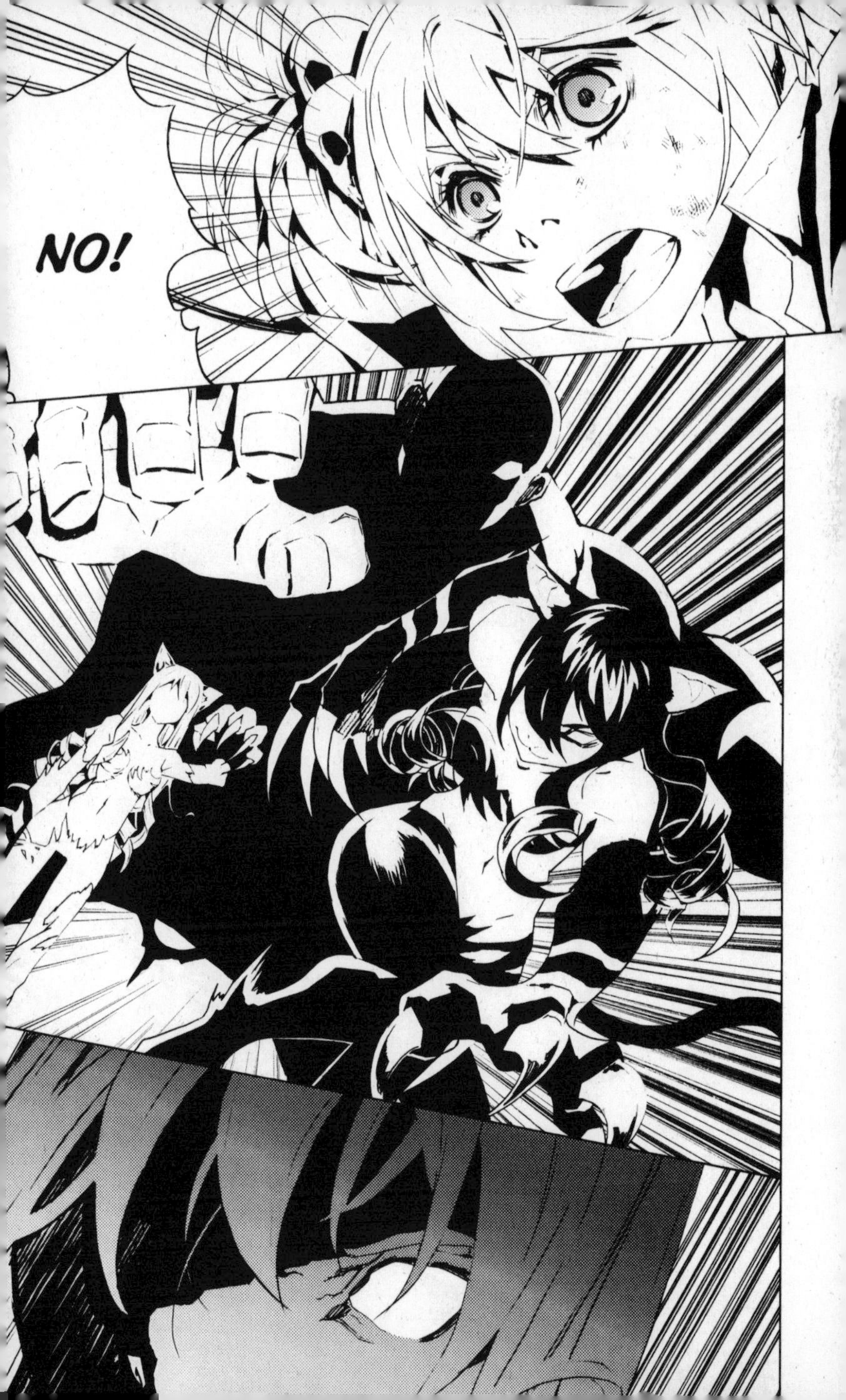
NO!

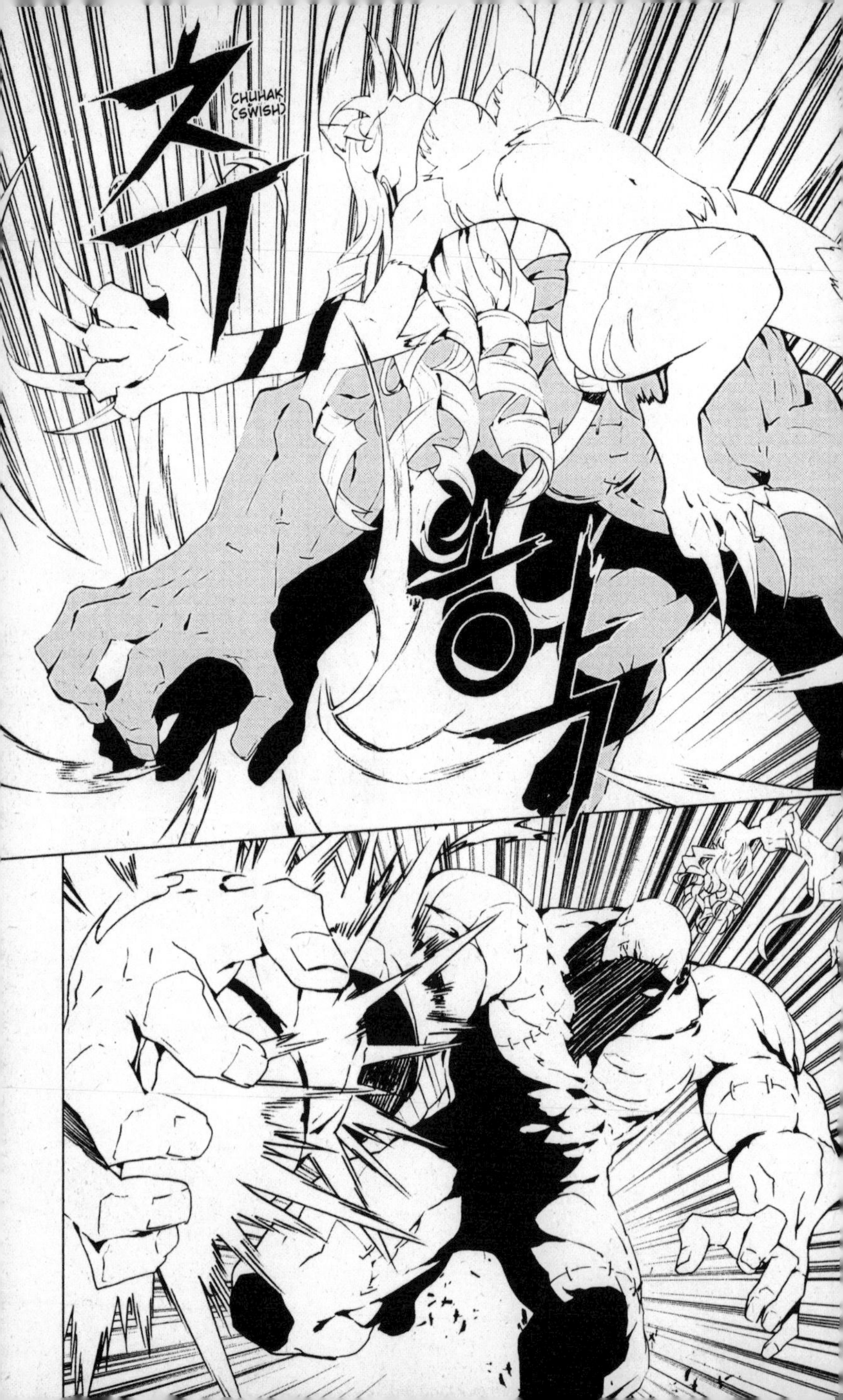
CHUHAK
(SWISH)

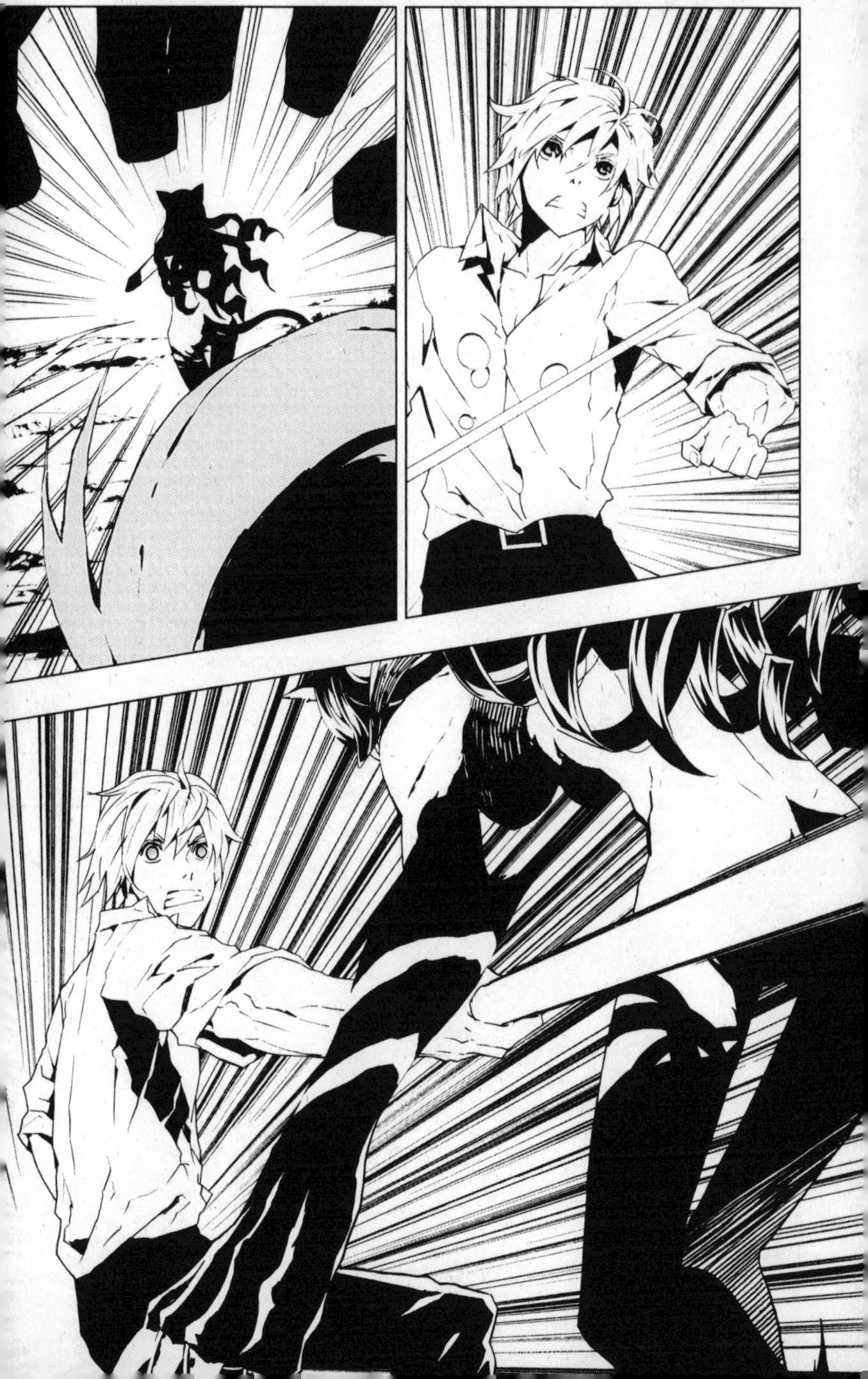

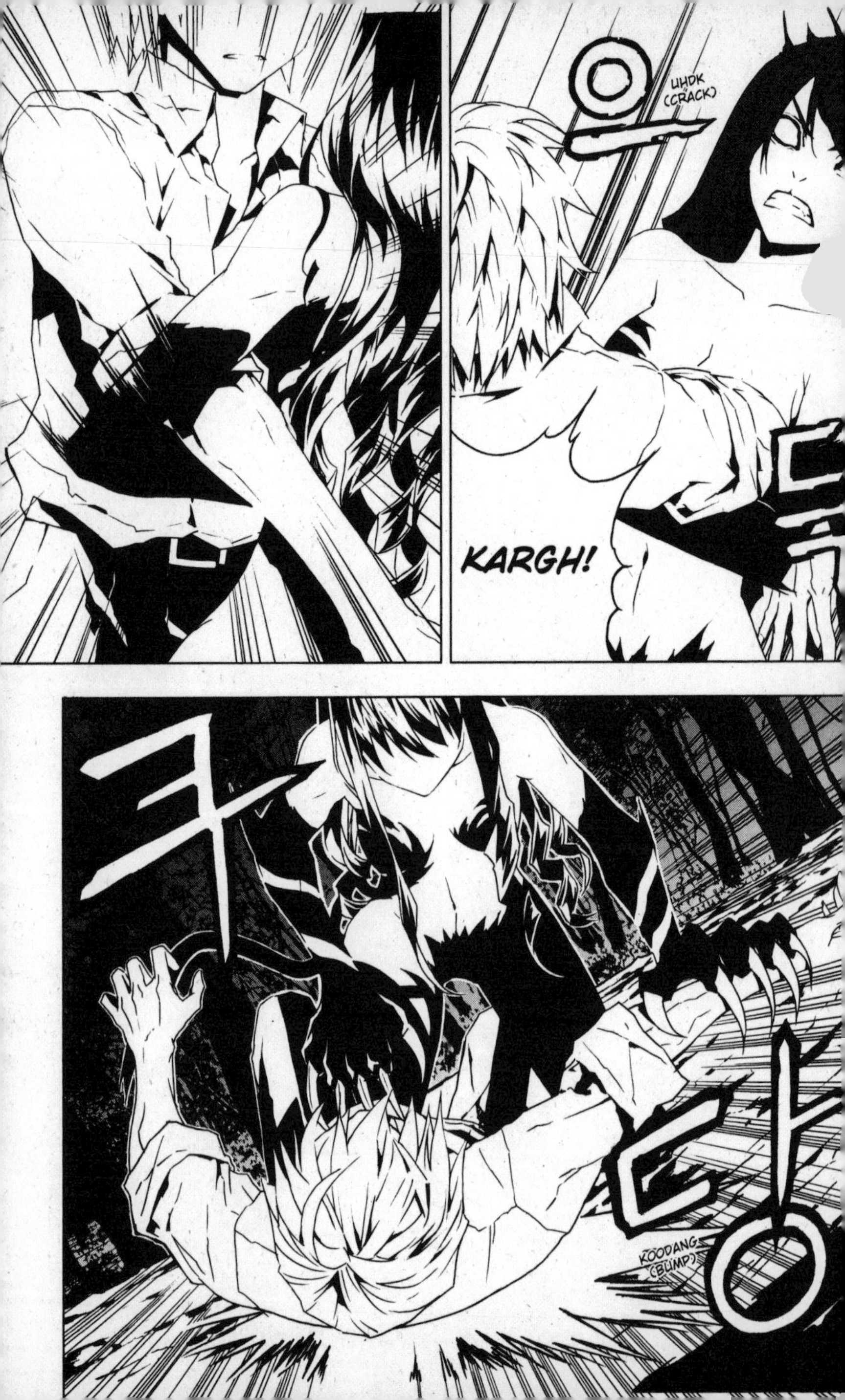
UHDK
(CRACK)
KARGH!
KOODANG
(BLUMP)

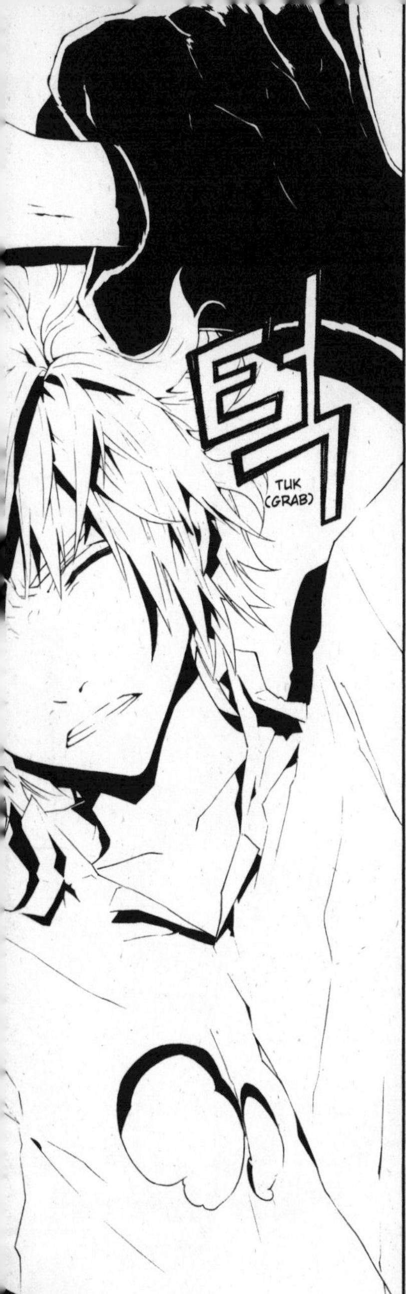
턱
TUK
(GRAB)

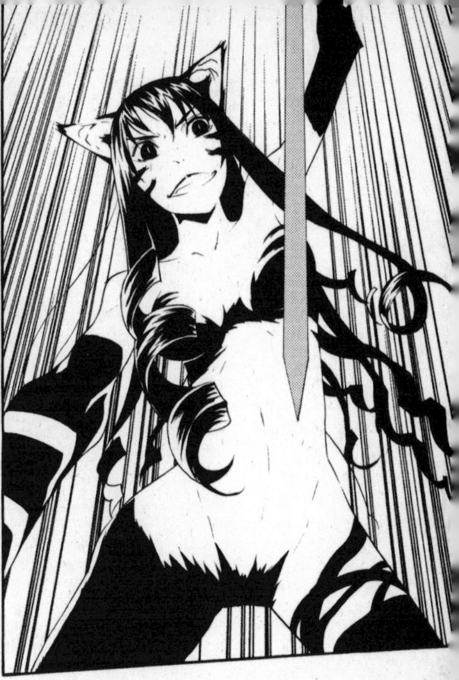

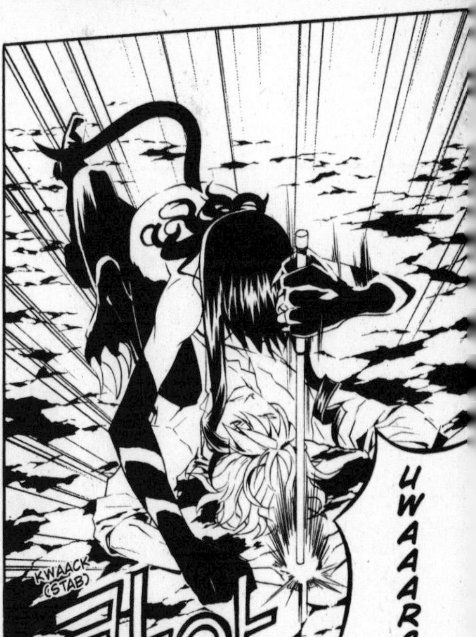
KWAACK
(STAB)
콰악
UWAAARGH!

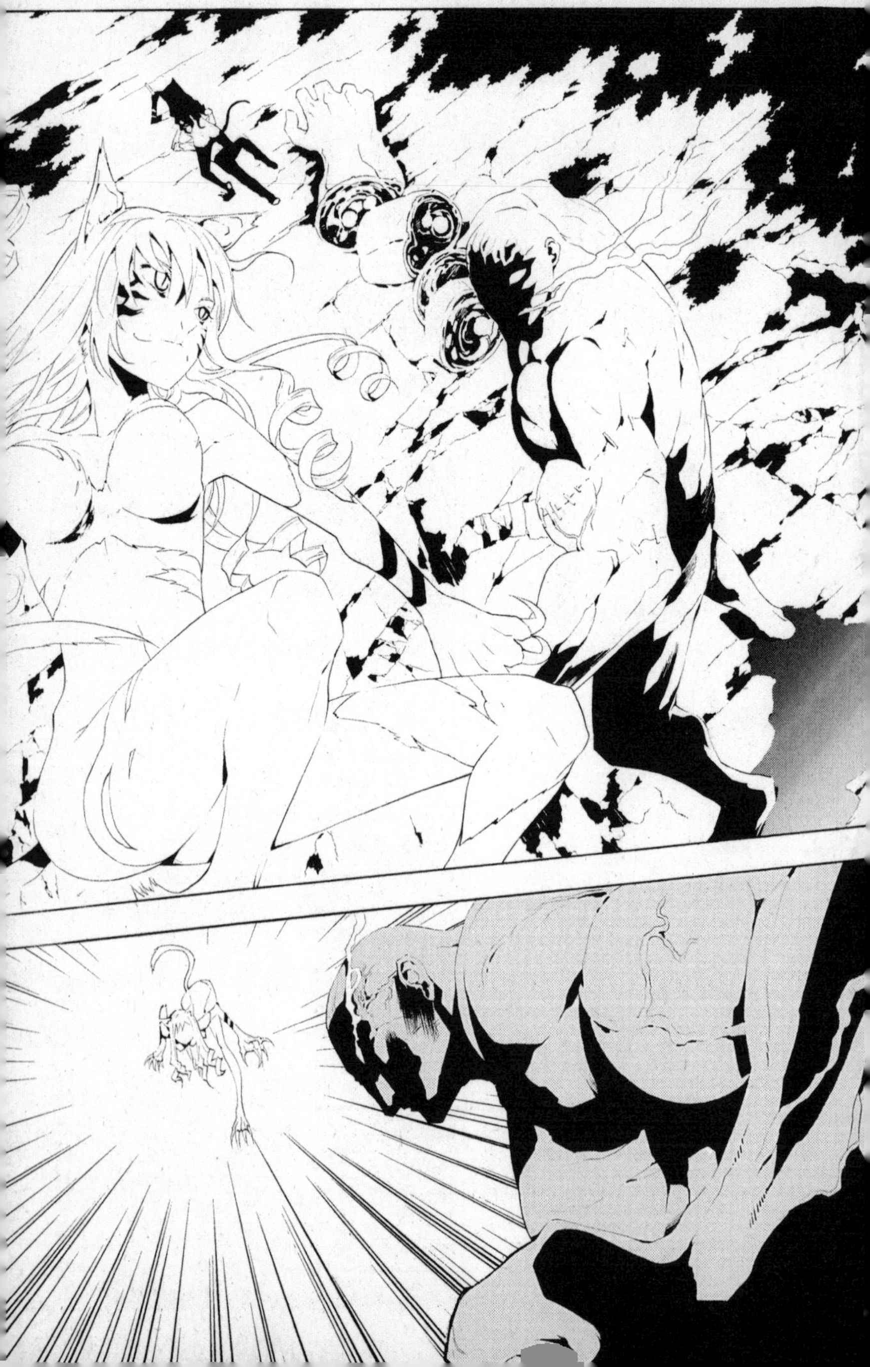

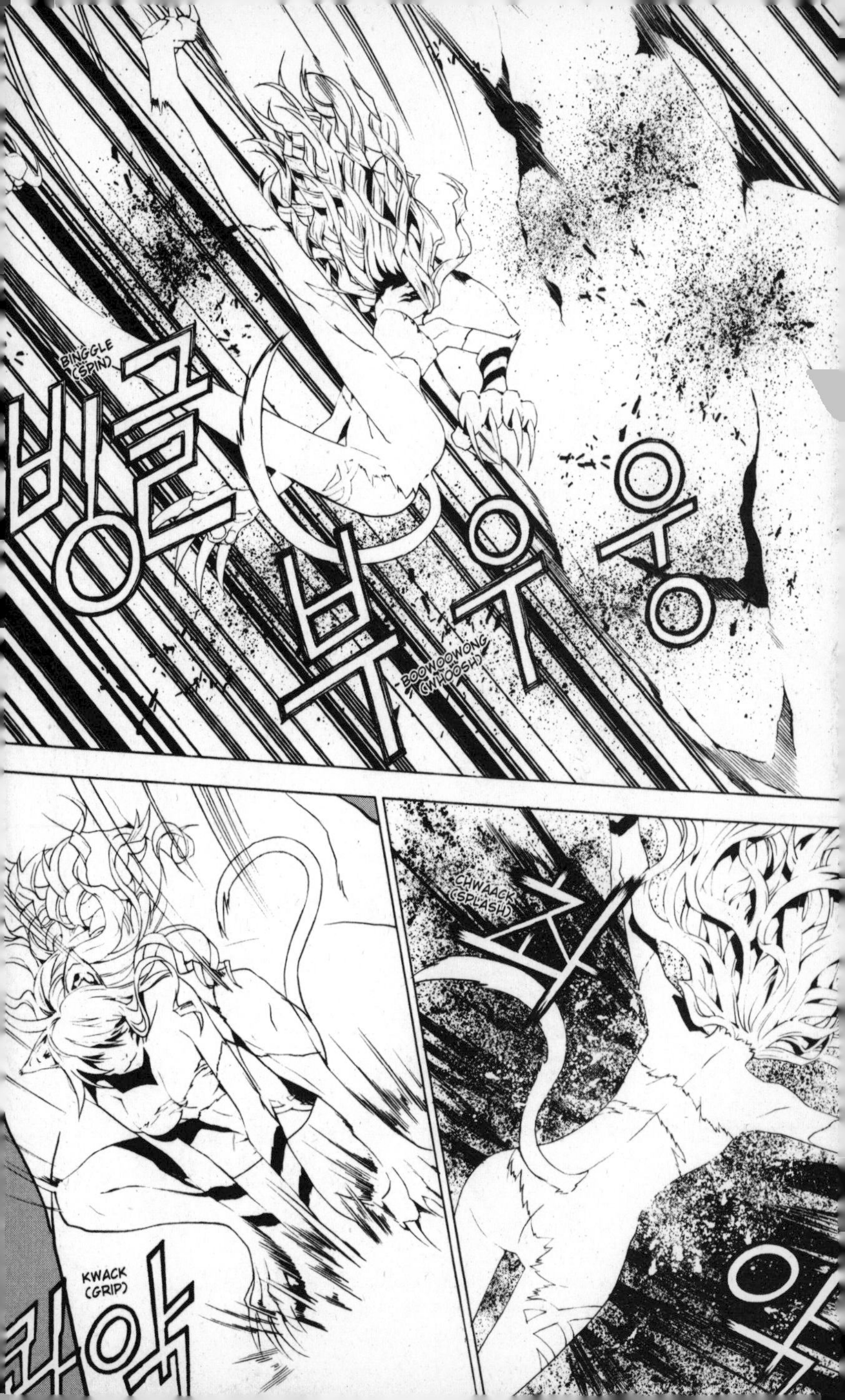
BINGGLE (SPIN)
BOOWOOWONG (WHOOSH)
KWACK (GRIP)
CHWAACK (SPLASH)

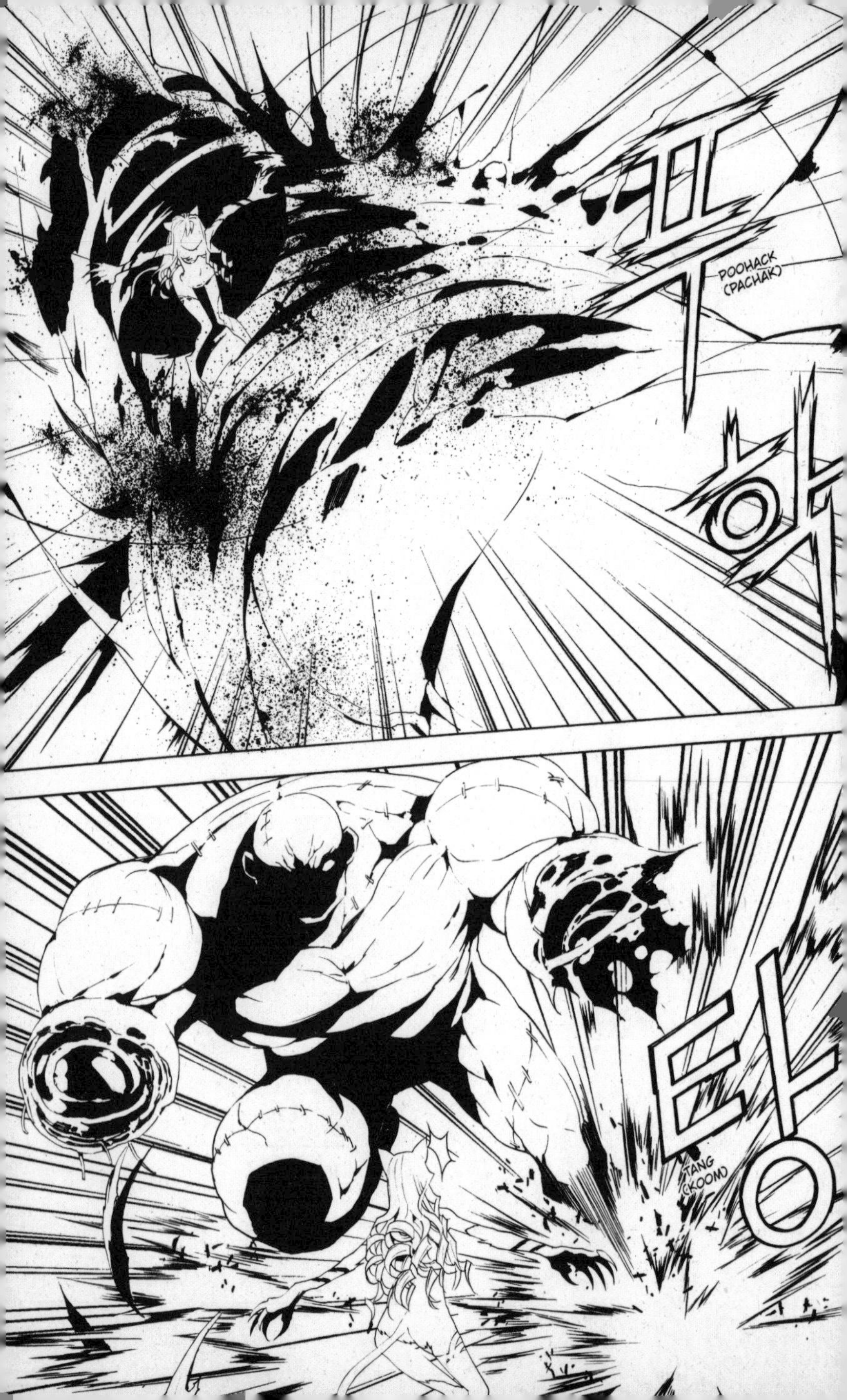
POOHACK (PACHAK)
TANG (KOOM)

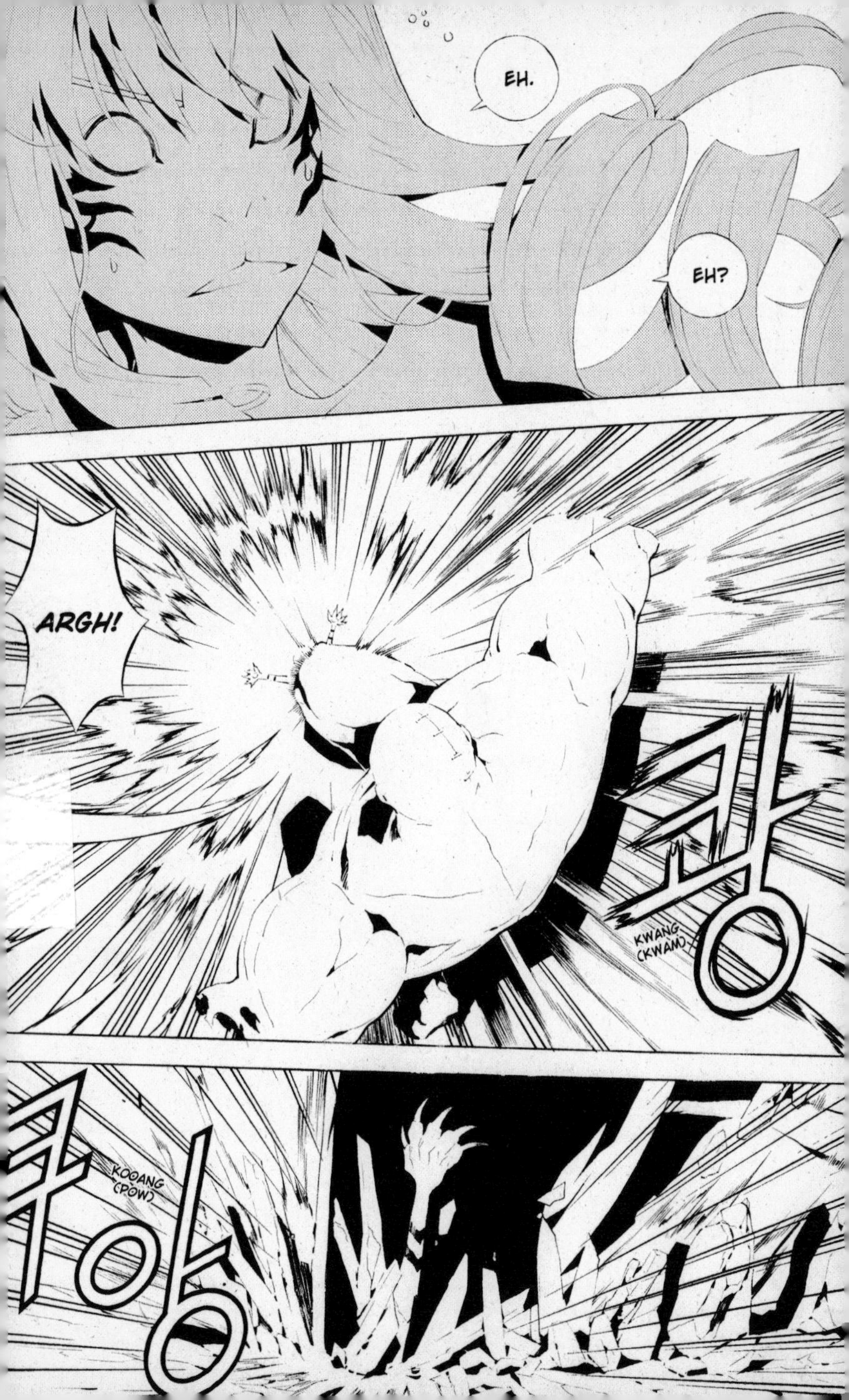
EH.
EH?
ARGH!
KWANG (KWAM)
KOOANG (POW)

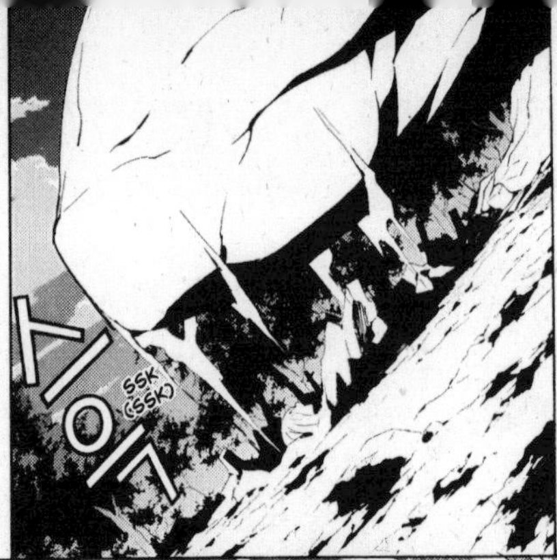
SSK
(SSK)
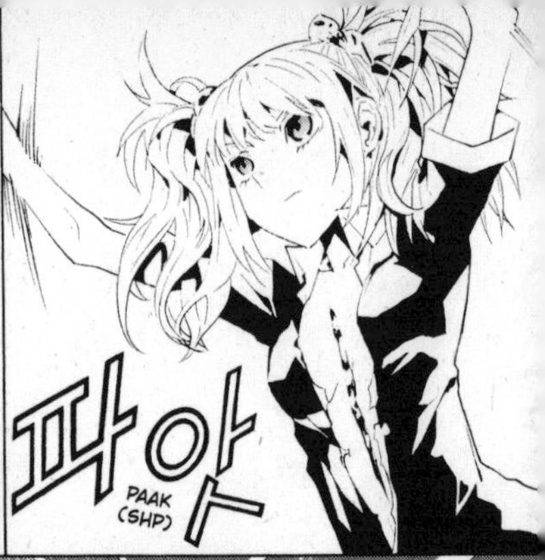
PAAK
(SHP)
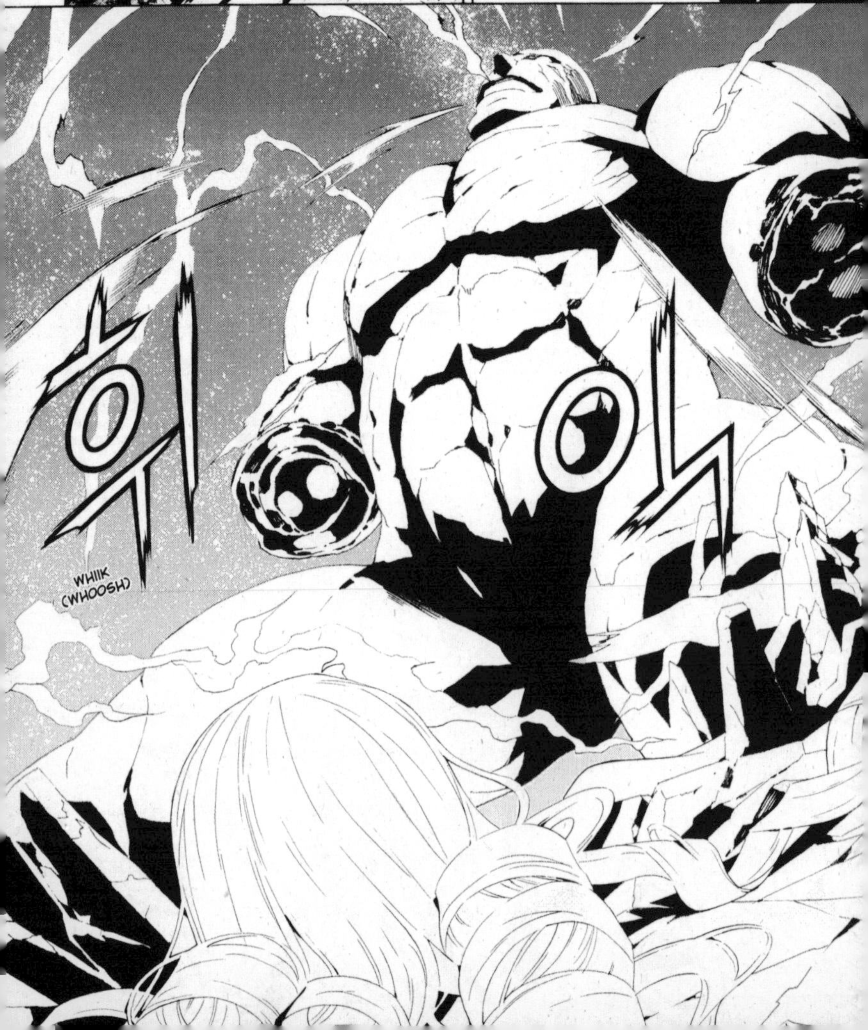
WHIIK
(WHOOSH)

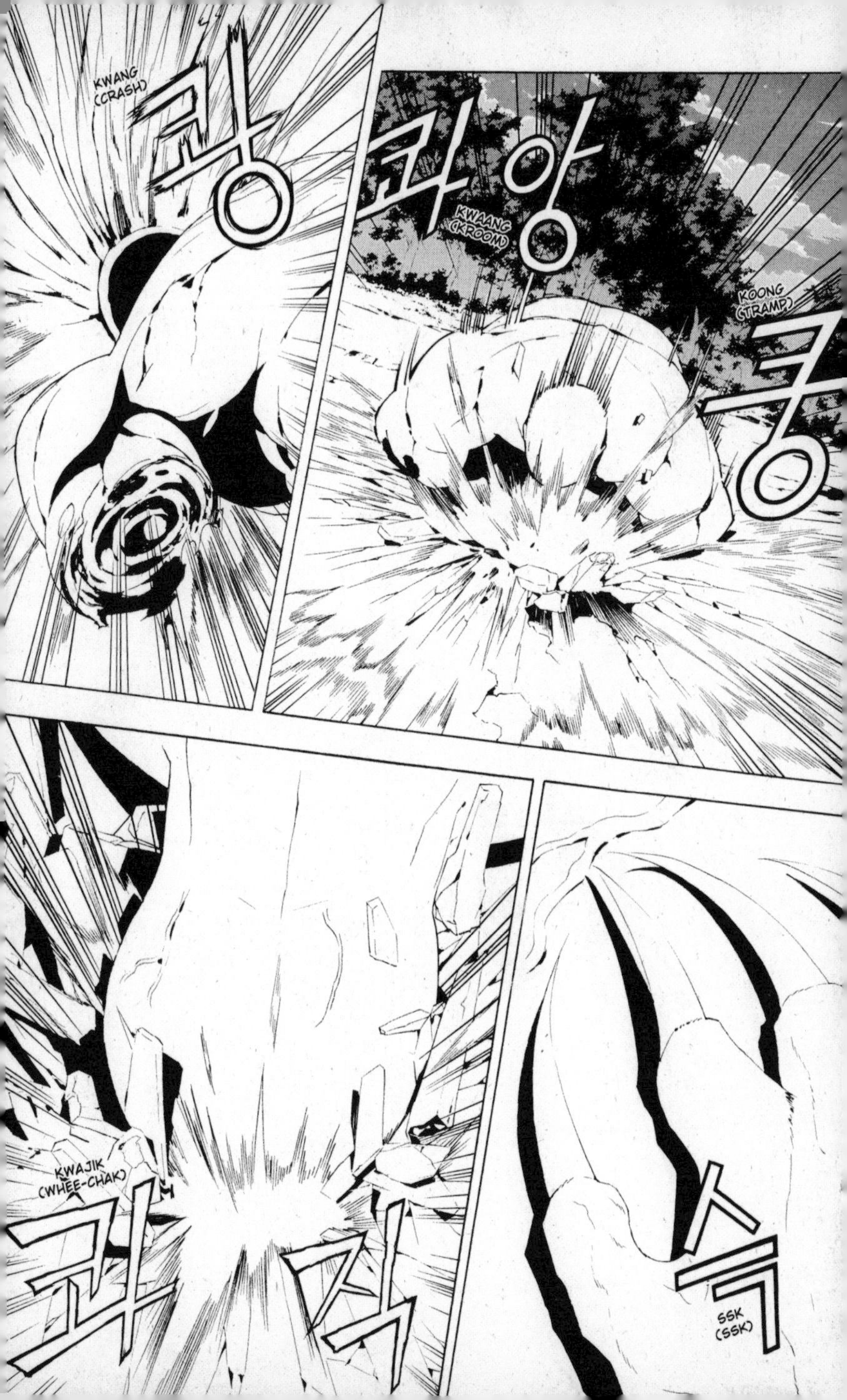
KWANG (CRASH)
광
콰앙
KWAANG (KROOM)
KOONG (STRAMP)
쿵
KWAJIK (WHEE-CHAK)
콰직
슥
SSK (SSK)

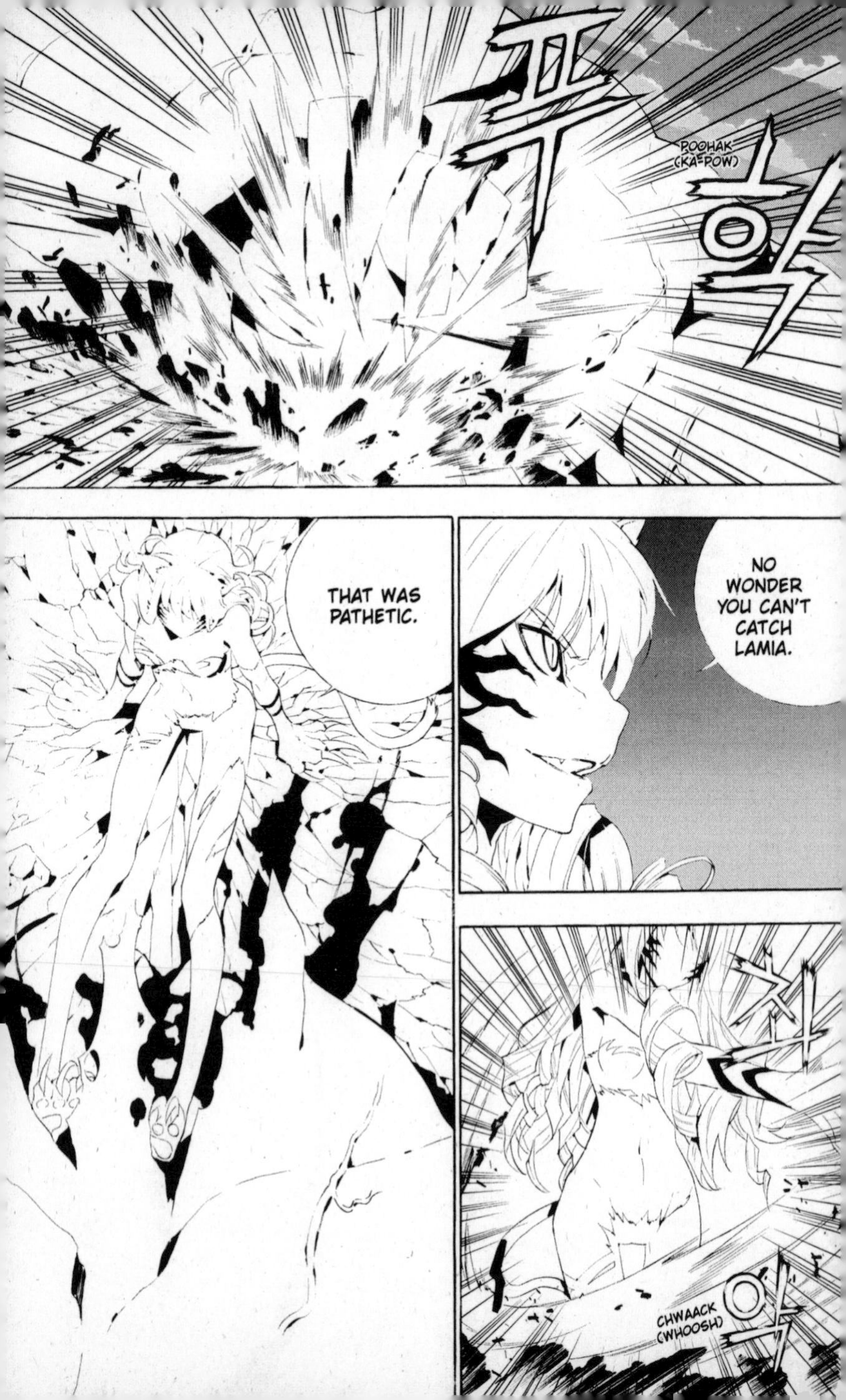
POOHAK
(KA-POW)
THAT WAS PATHETIC.
NO WONDER YOU CAN'T CATCH LAMIA.
CHWAACK
(WHOOSH)

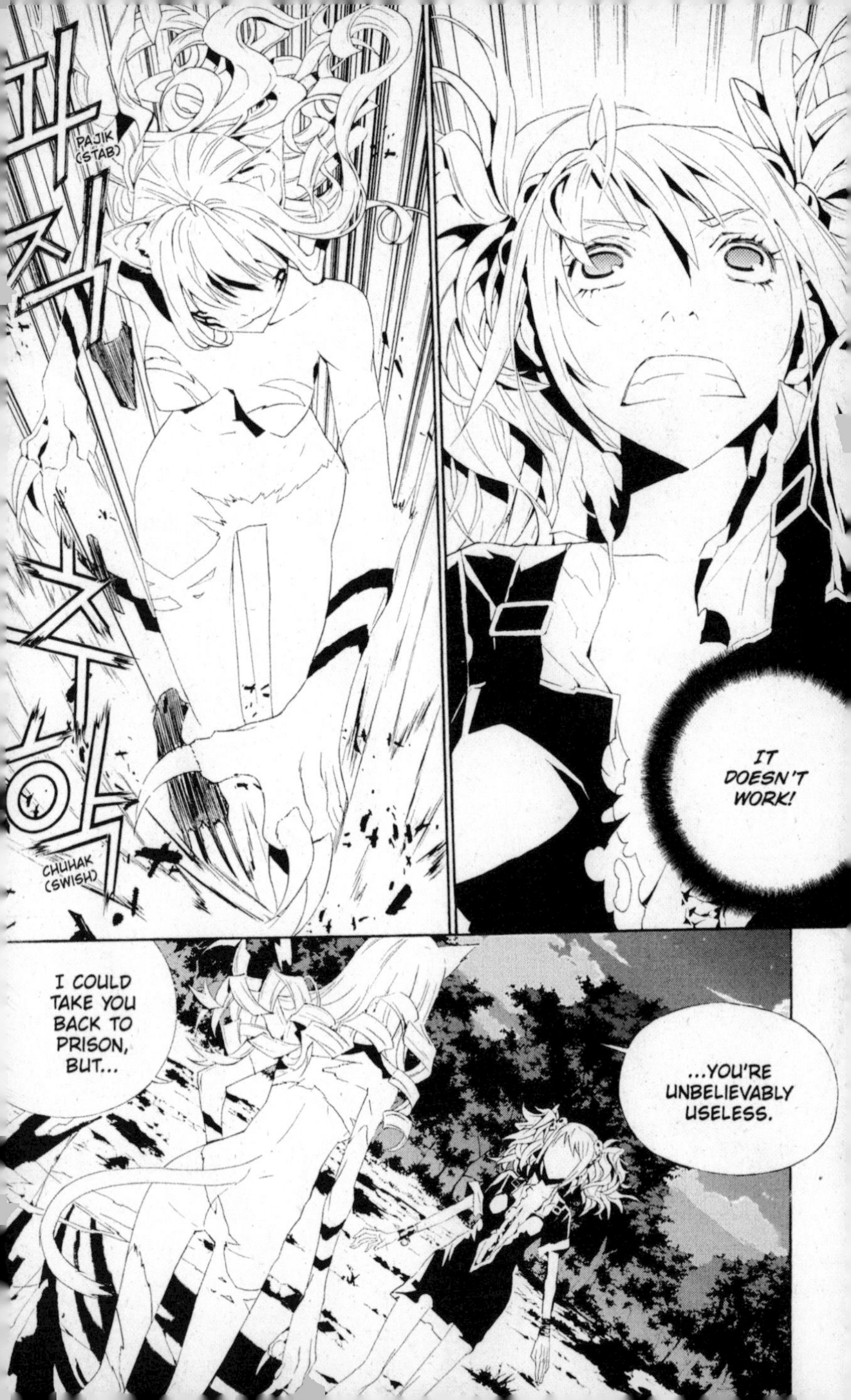
PAJIK (STAB)
CHUHAK (SWISH)
IT DOESN'T WORK!
I COULD TAKE YOU BACK TO PRISON, BUT...
...YOU'RE UNBELIEVABLY USELESS.

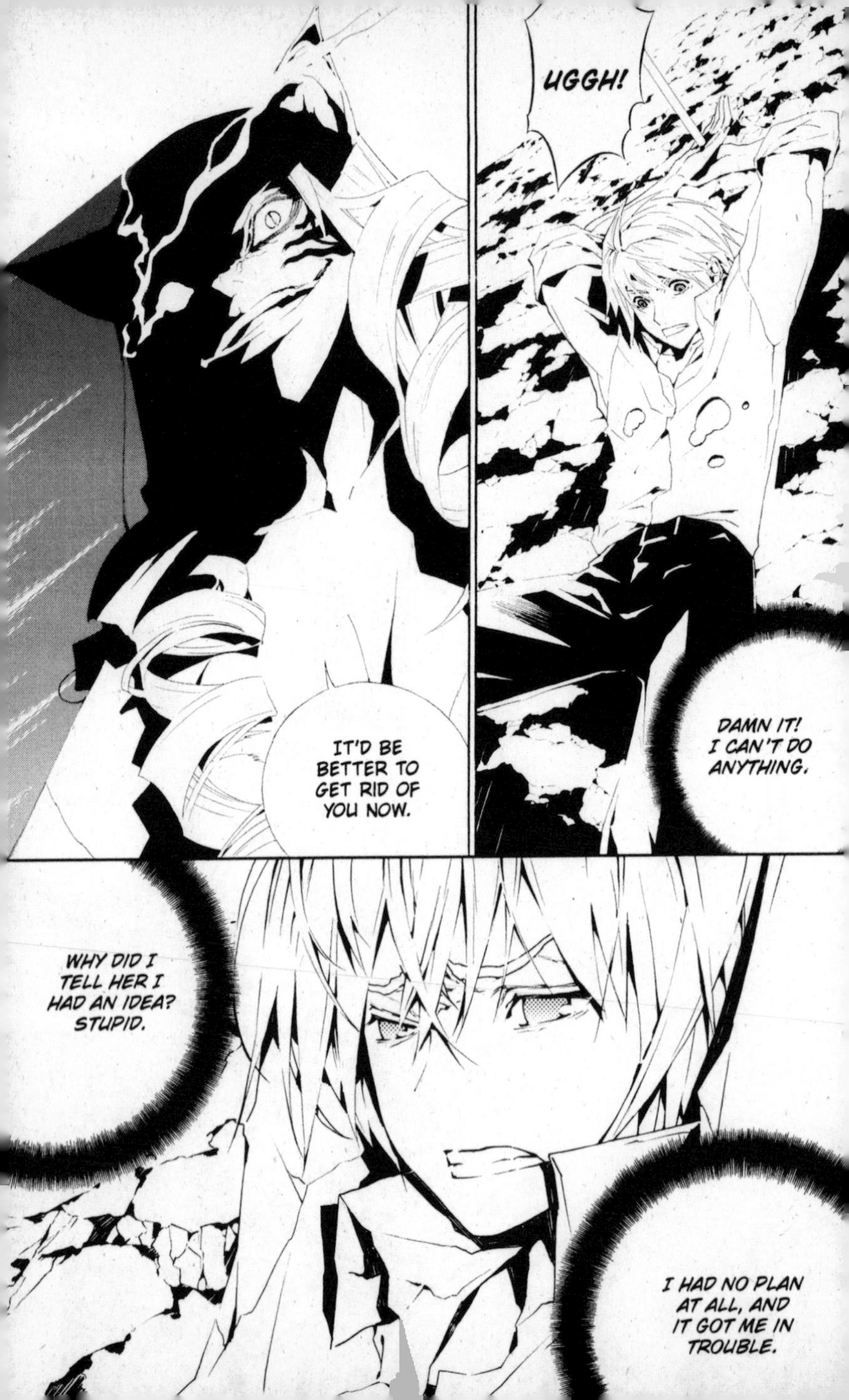
IT'D BE BETTER TO GET RID OF YOU NOW.
UGGH!
DAMN IT! I CAN'T DO ANYTHING.
WHY DID I TELL HER I HAD AN IDEA? STUPID.
I HAD NO PLAN AT ALL, AND IT GOT ME IN TROUBLE.

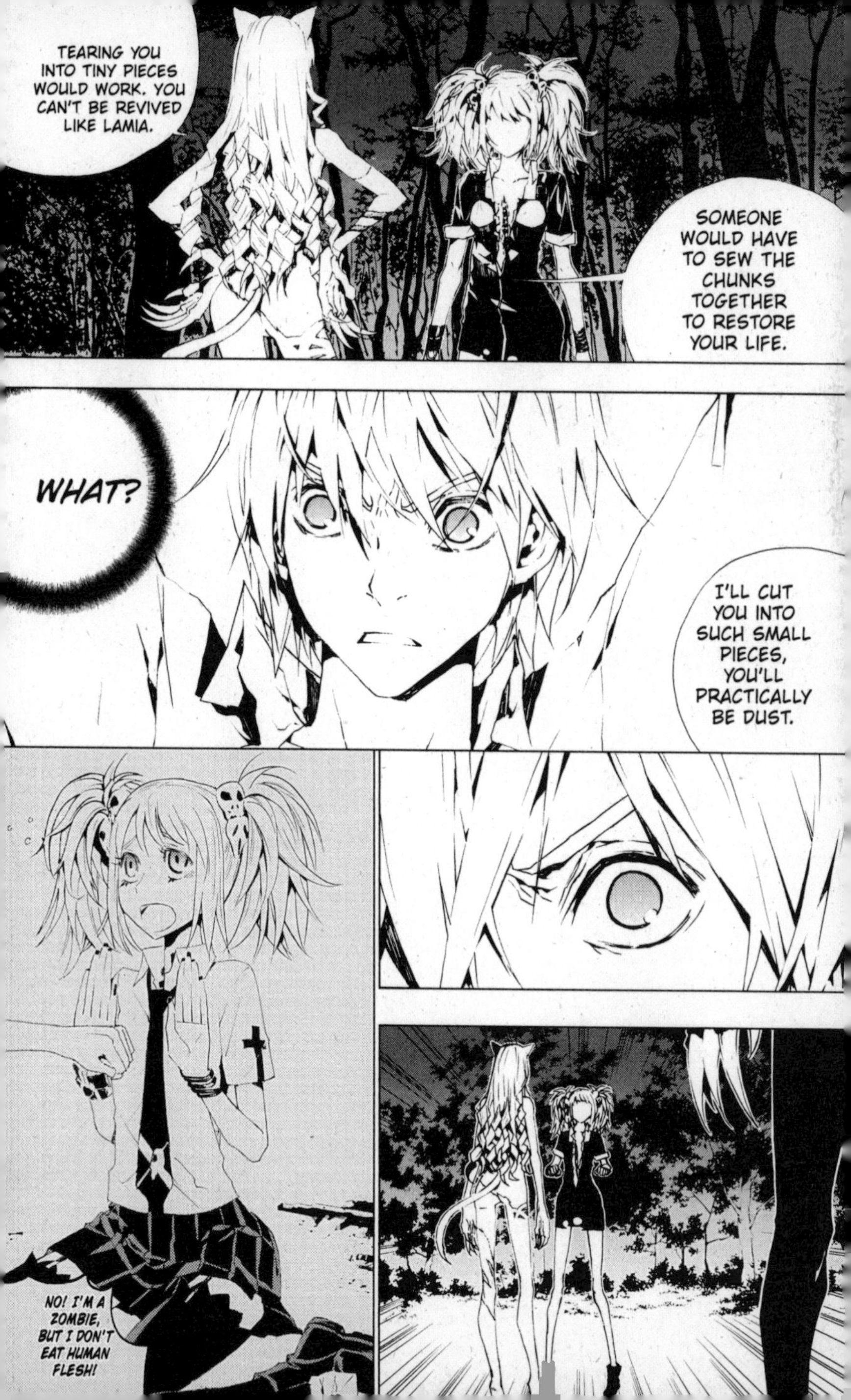
SOMEONE WOULD HAVE TO SEW THE CHUNKS TOGETHER TO RESTORE YOUR LIFE.
TEARING YOU INTO TINY PIECES WOULD WORK. YOU CAN'T BE REVIVED LIKE LAMIA.
I'LL CUT YOU INTO SUCH SMALL PIECES, YOU'LL PRACTICALLY BE DUST.
WHAT?
NO! I'M A ZOMBIE, BUT I DON'T EAT HUMAN FLESH!

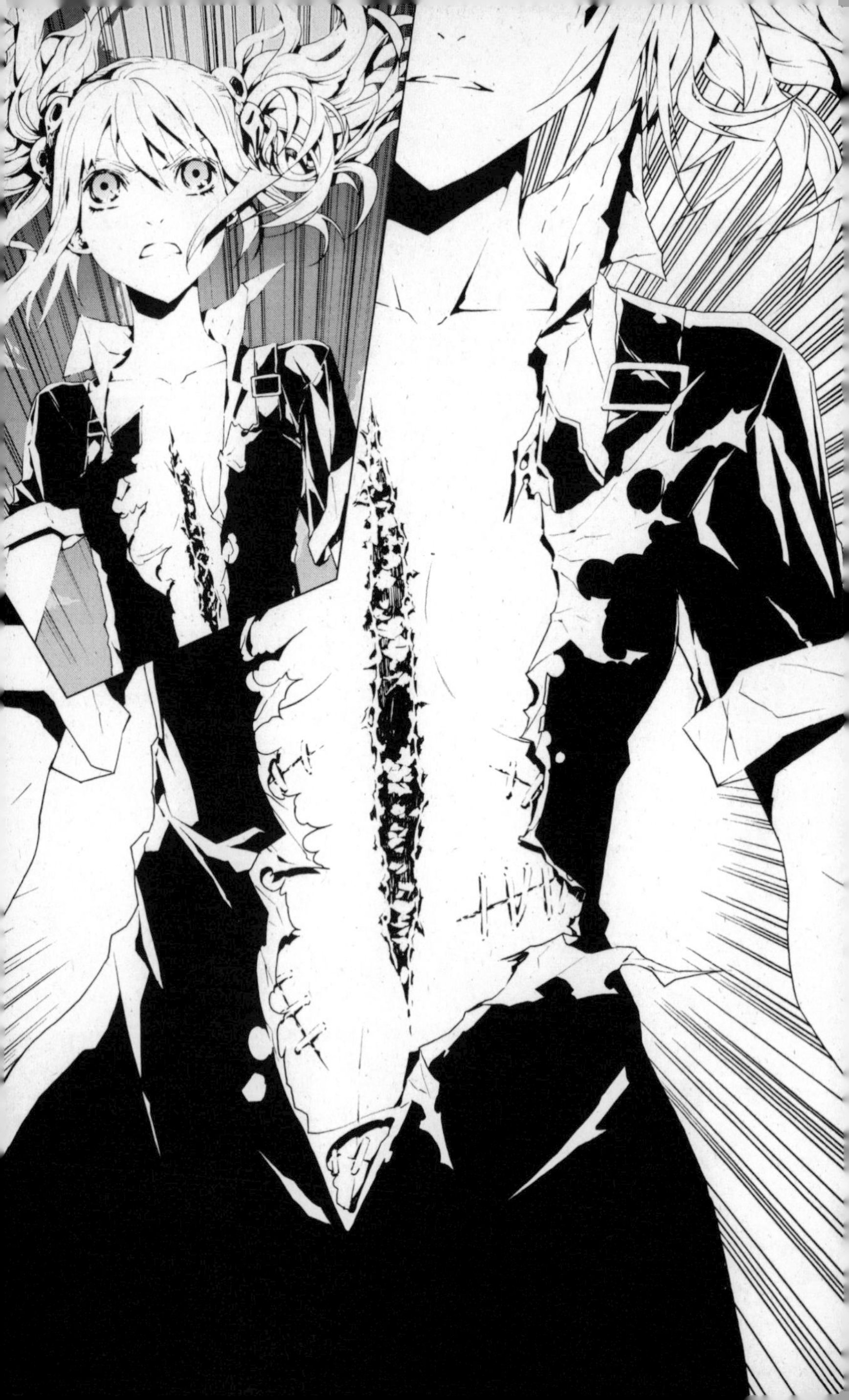

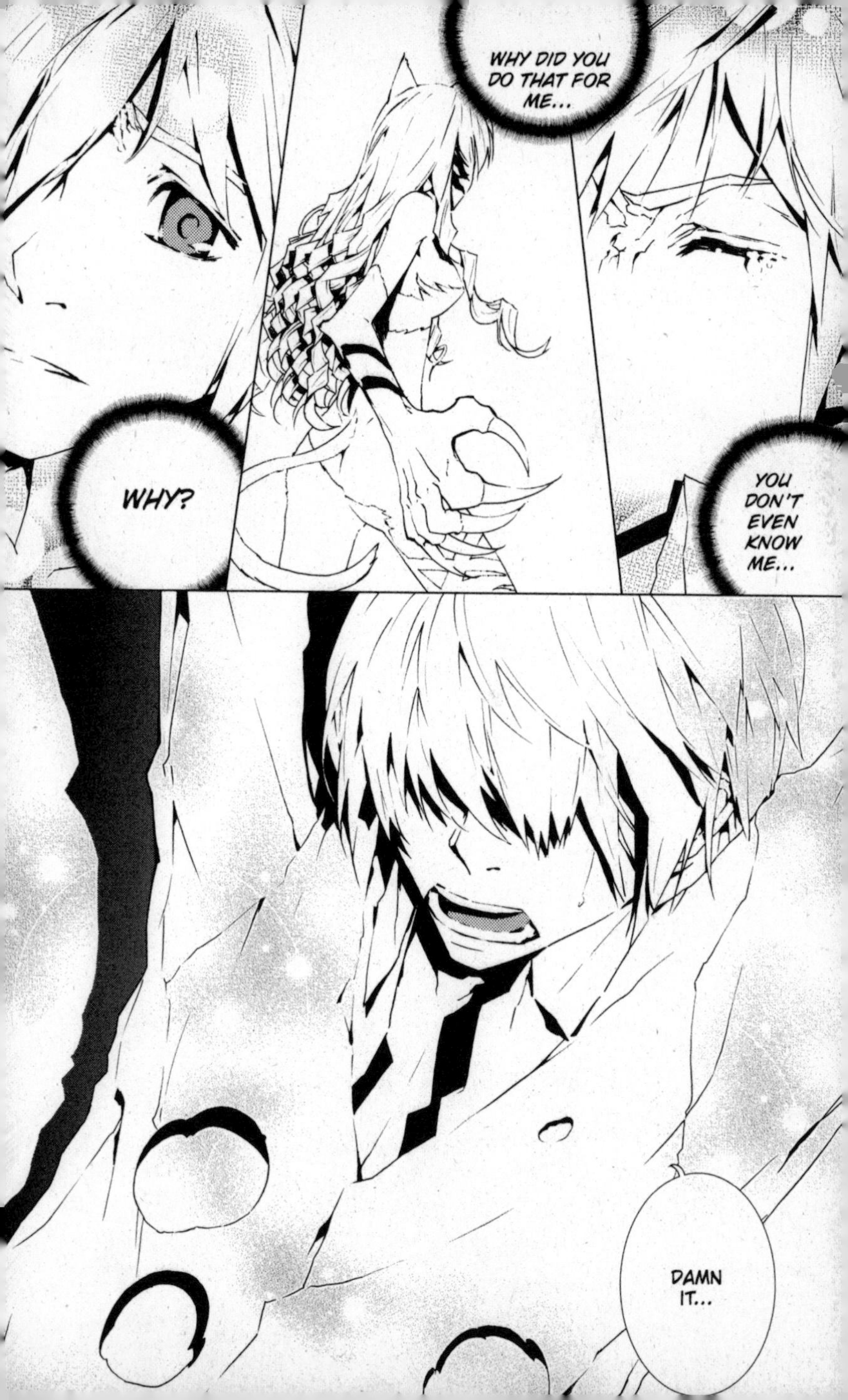
WHY?
WHY DID YOU DO THAT FOR ME...
YOU DON'T EVEN KNOW ME...
DAMN IT...

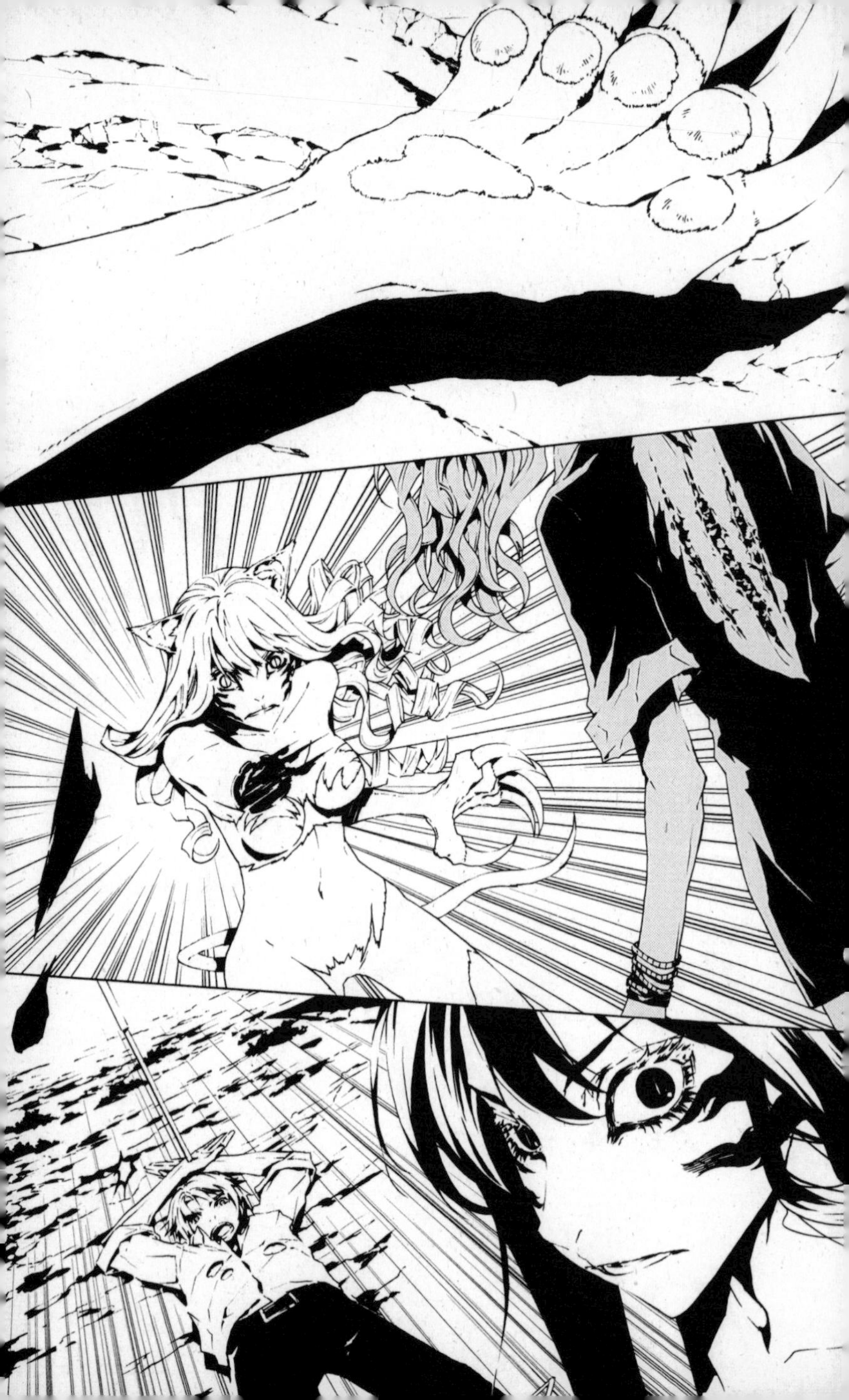

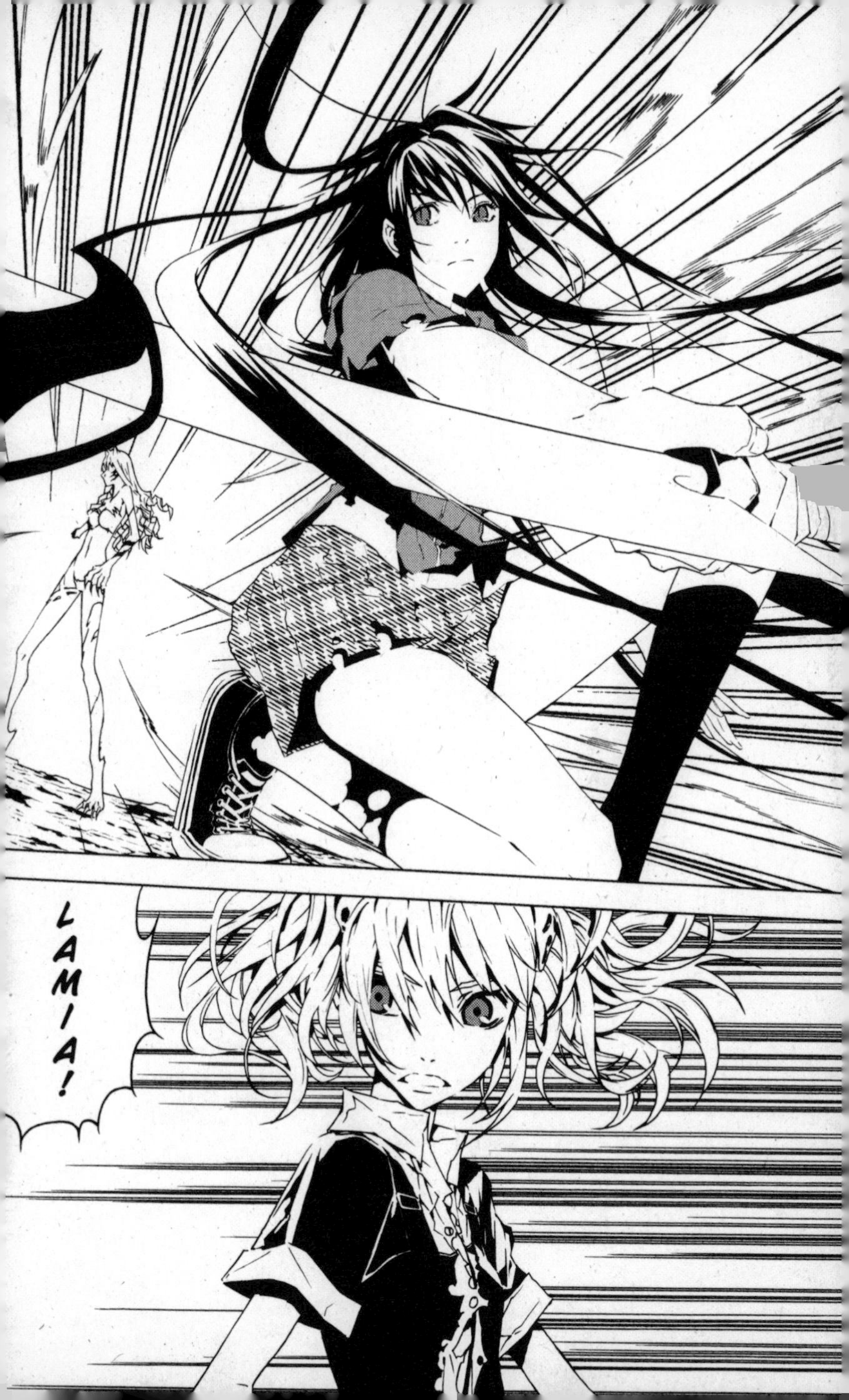
LAMIA!

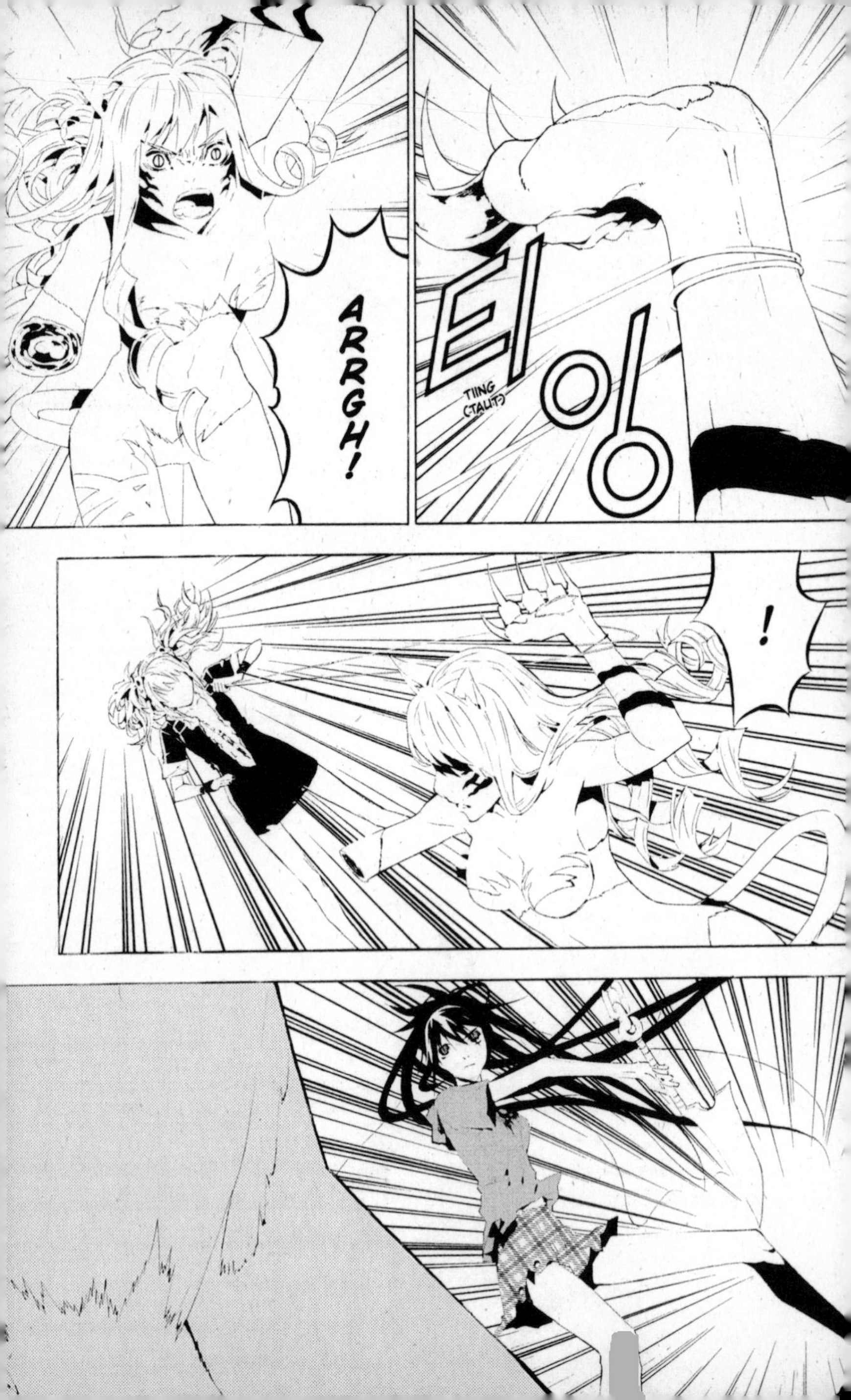
ARRGH!
EI
TIING
(TAUT)
!

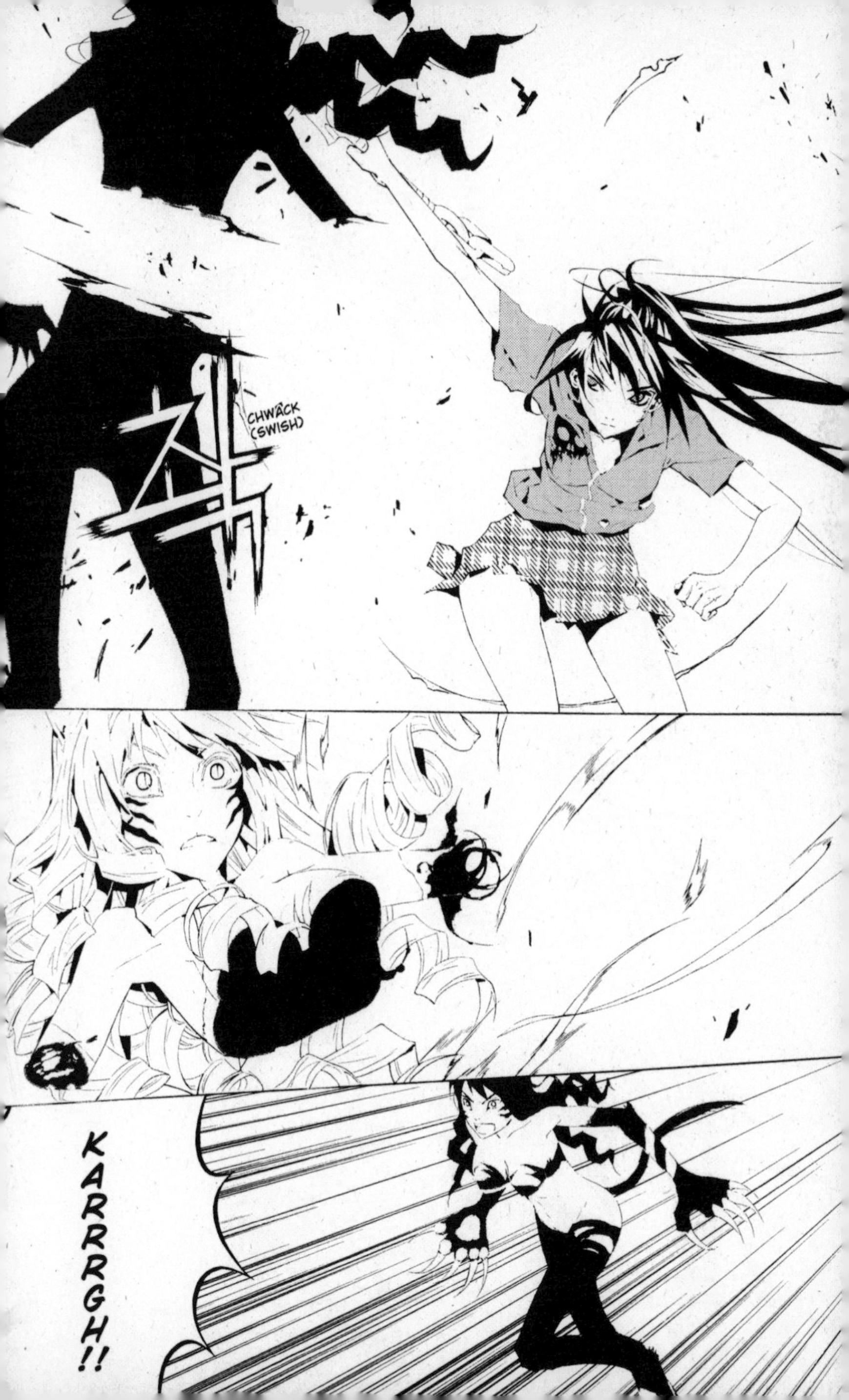
CHWACK
(SWISH)
KARRRGH!!

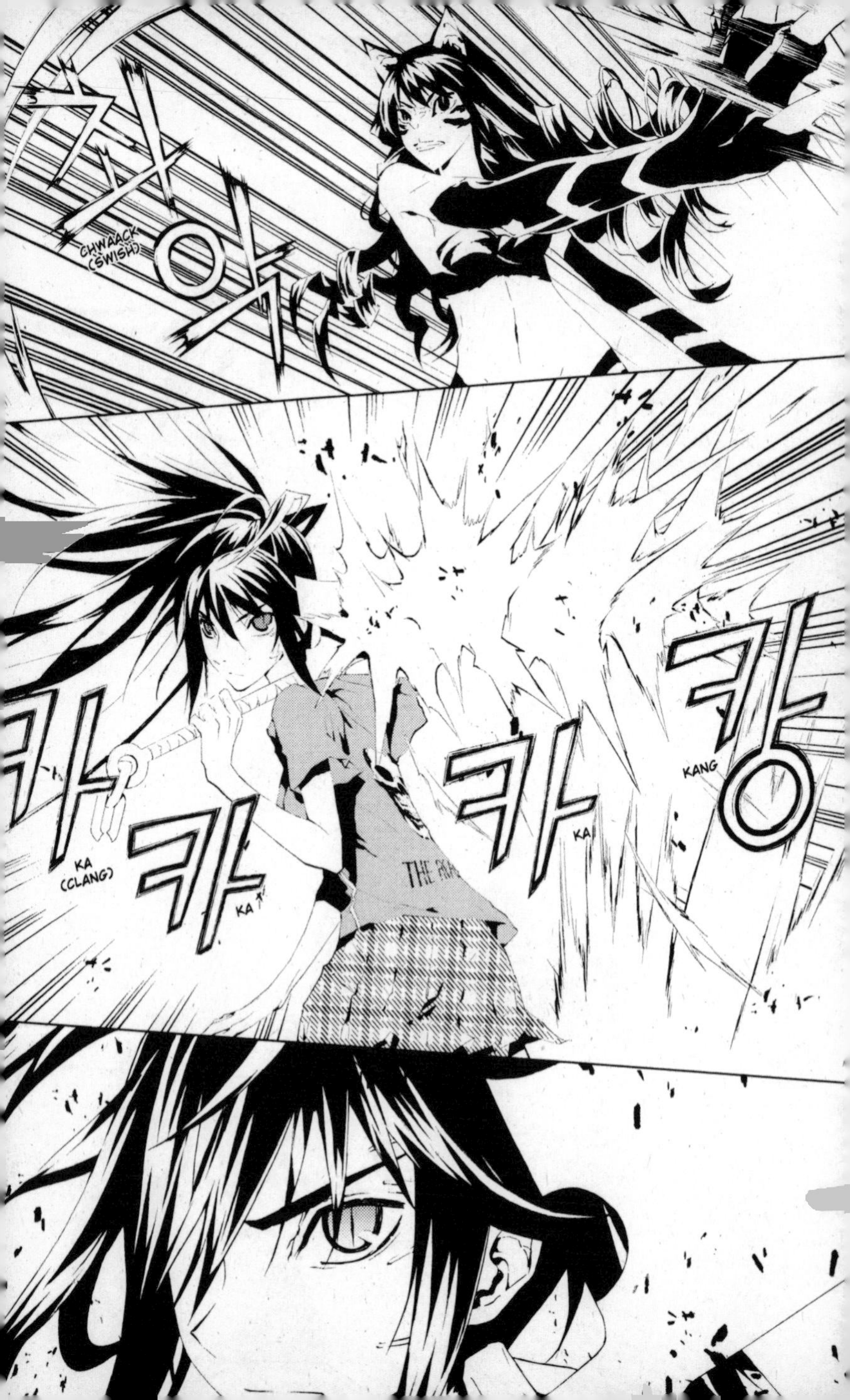
CHWAACK
(SWISH)
KA
(CLANG)
KA
KA
KANG

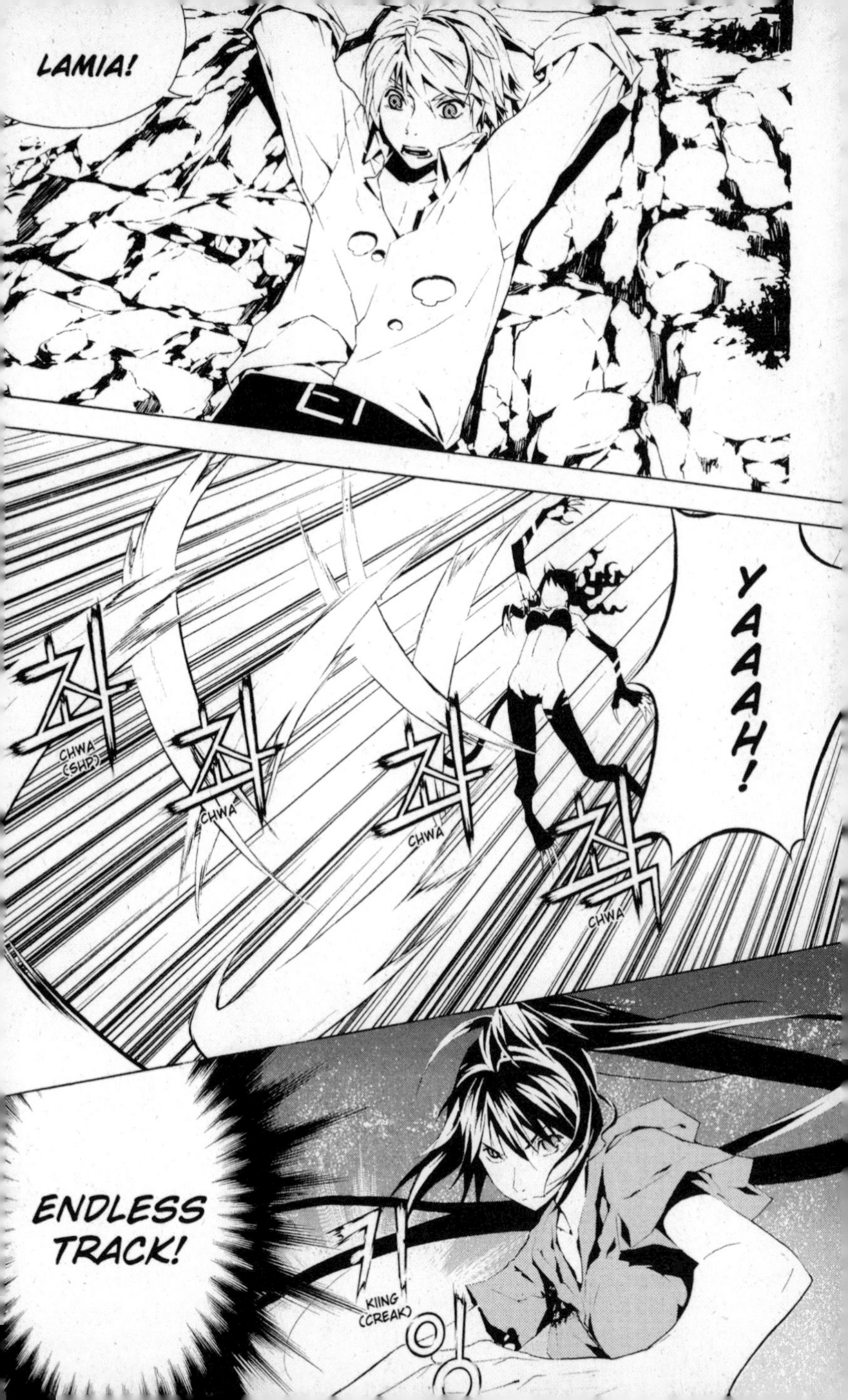
LAMIA!
CHWA (SHP)
CHWA
CHWA
CHWA
YAAAH!
ENDLESS TRACK!
KIING (CREAK)

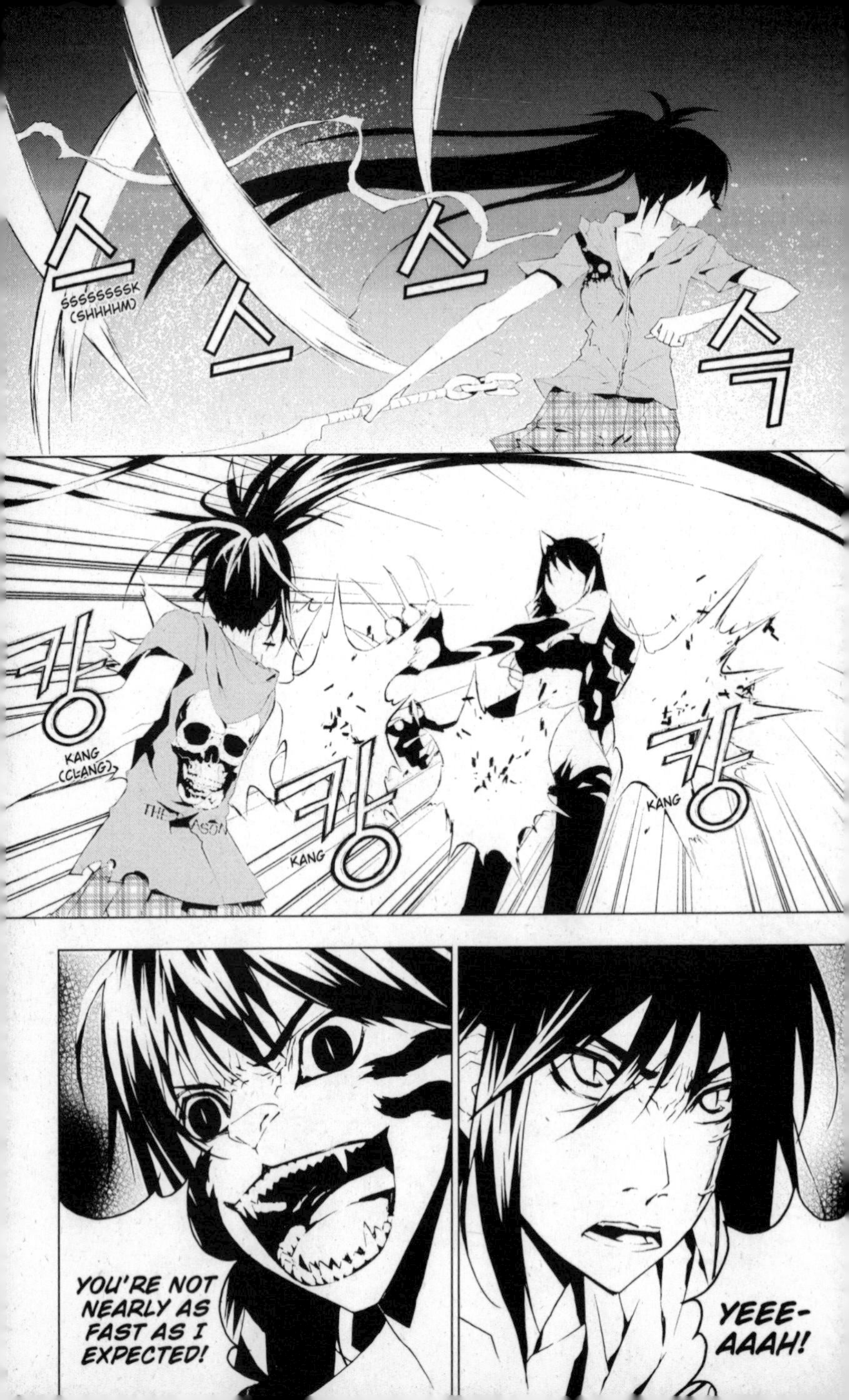
SSSSSSSSK (SHHHHM)
KANG (CLANG)
KANG
KANG
YOU'RE NOT NEARLY AS FAST AS I EXPECTED!
YEEE-AAAH!

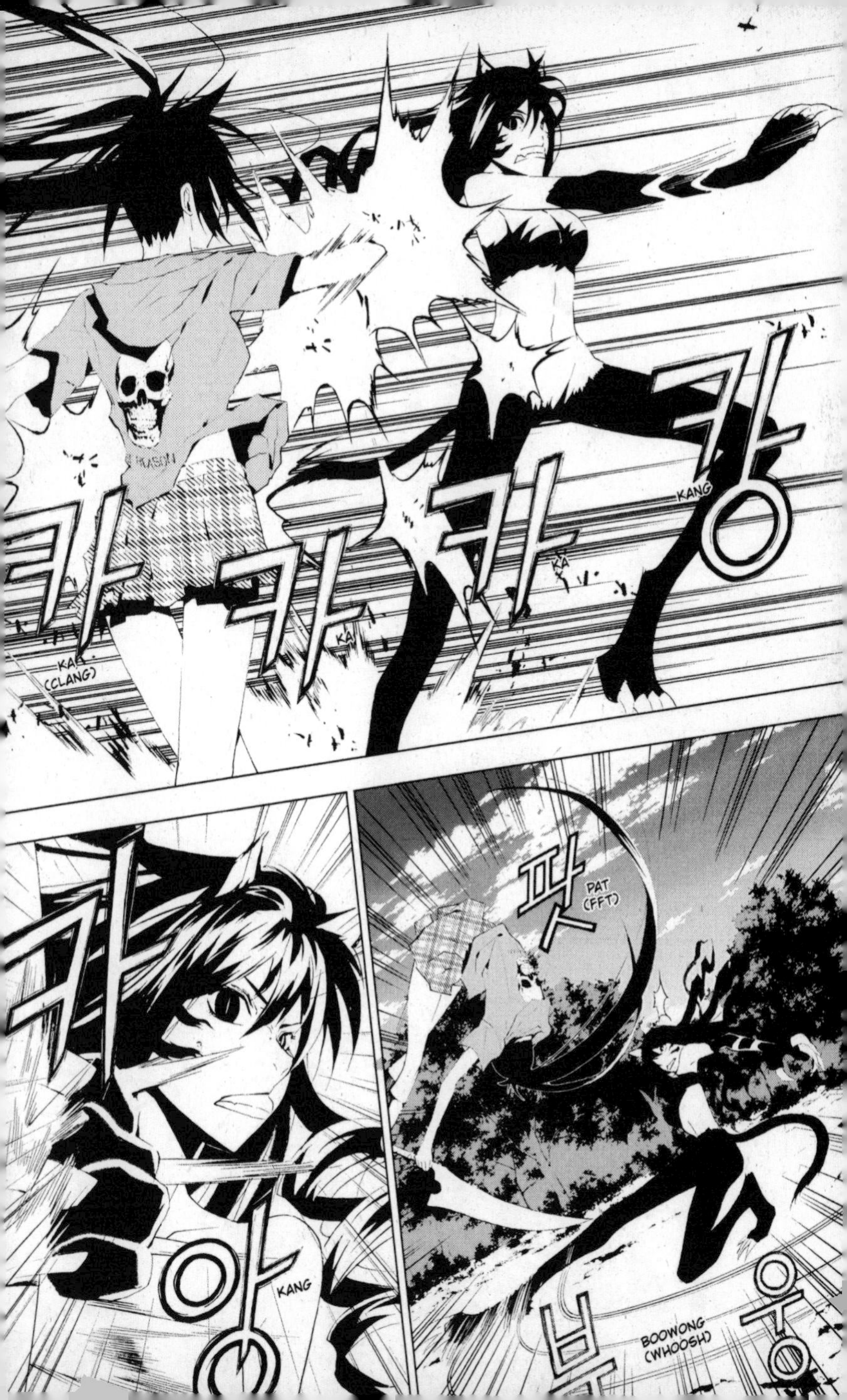

카
KA
(CLANG)
카
KA
카
KA
캉
KANG
캉
KANG
팟
PAT
(FFT)
부웅
BOOWONG
(WHOOSH)

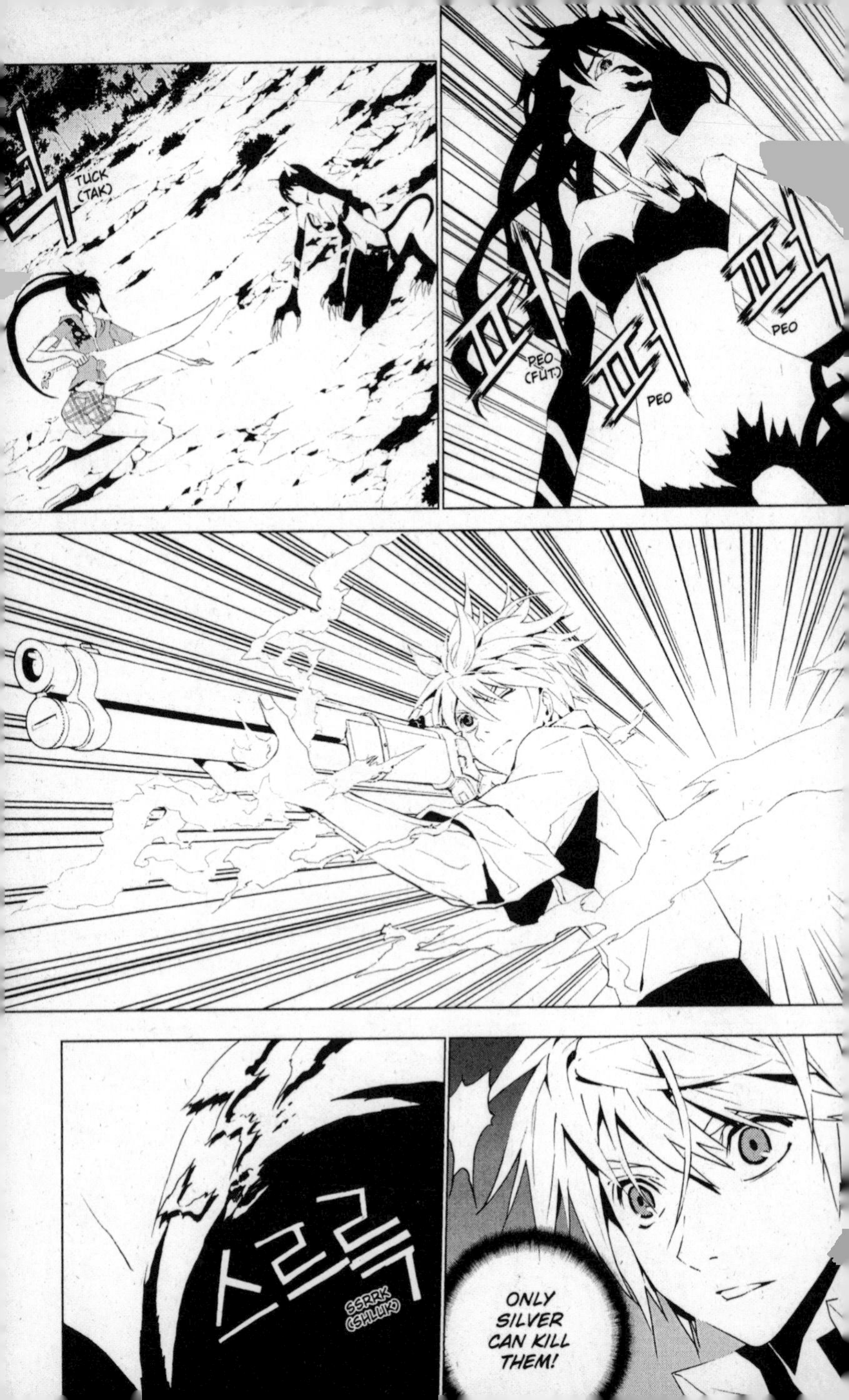
TUCK
(TAK)
PEO
(FUT)
PEO
PEO
SSRRK
(SHLUK)
ONLY SILVER CAN KILL THEM!

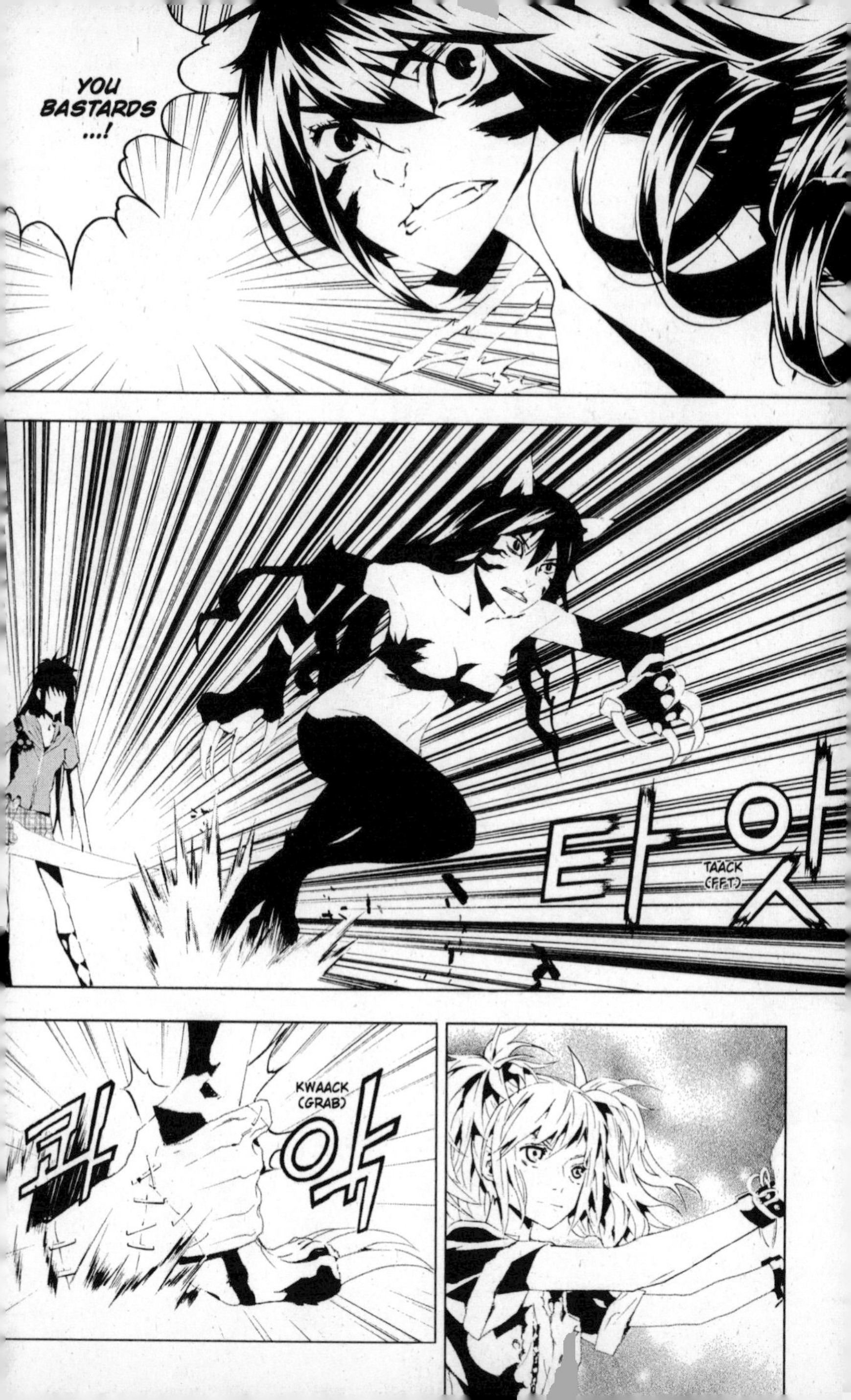
YOU BASTARDS ...!
타악
TAACK (FFT)
콱
KWAACK (GRAB)

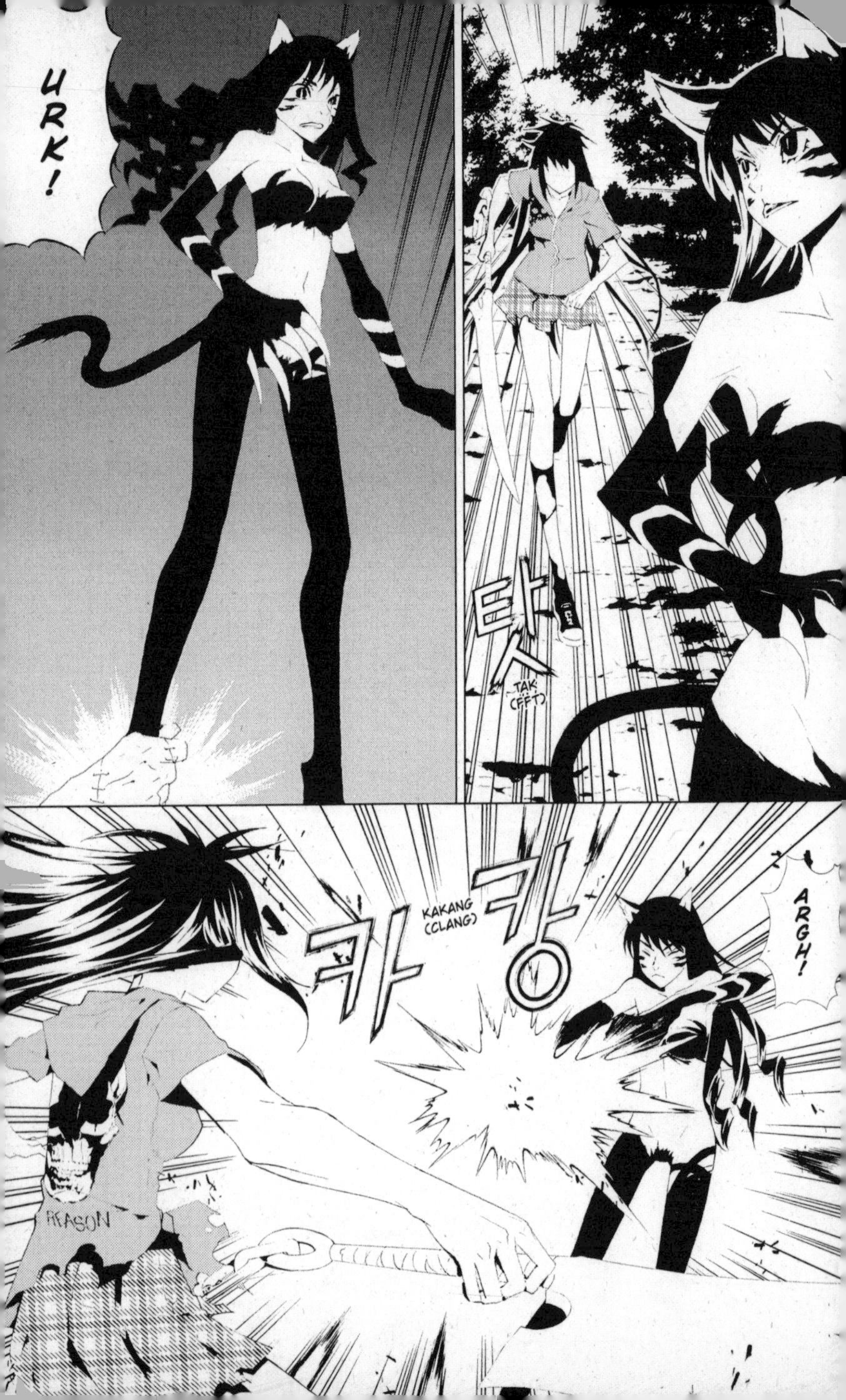
URK!
탁
TAK (FFT)
카캉
KAKANG (CLANG)
ARGH!
REASON

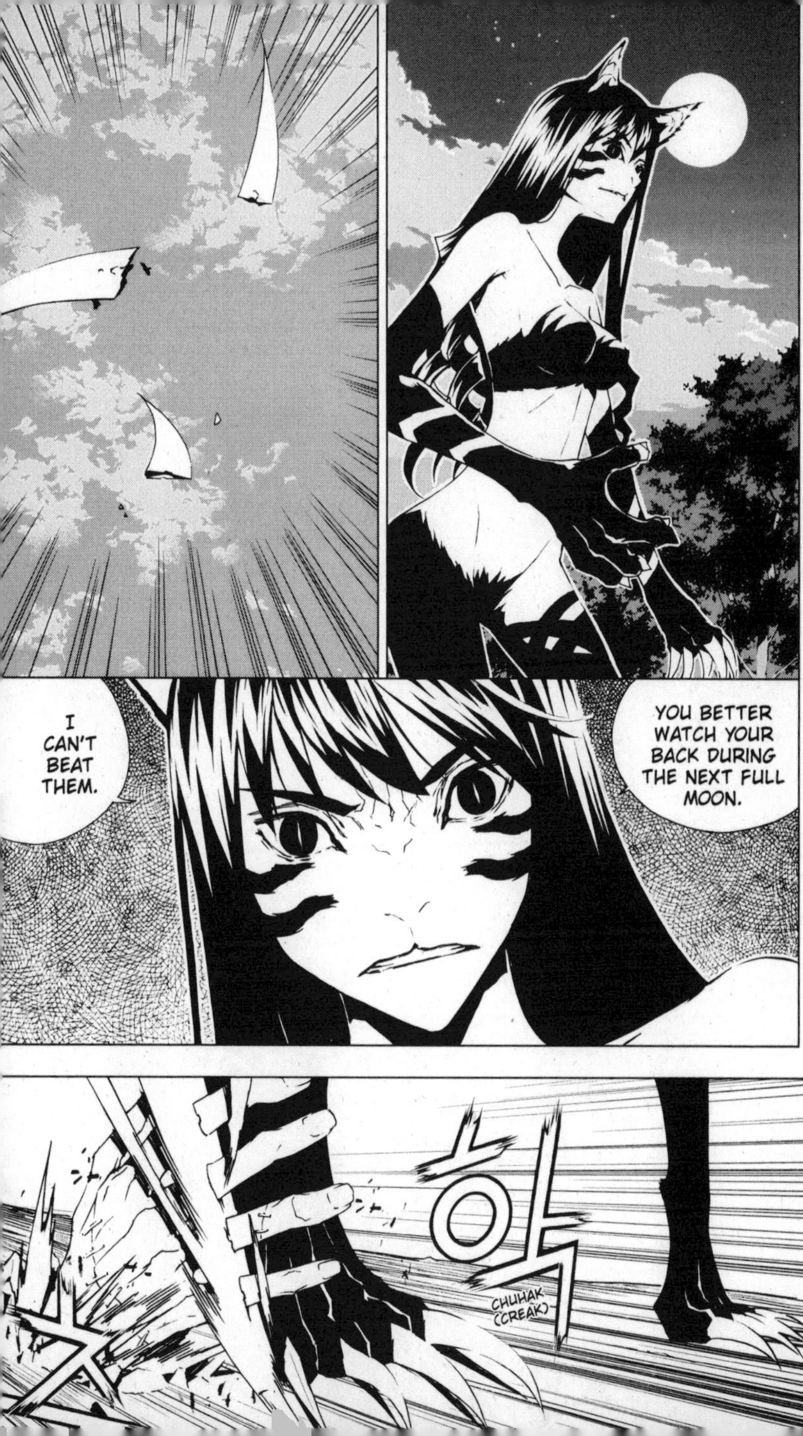
I CAN'T BEAT THEM.
YOU BETTER WATCH YOUR BACK DURING THE NEXT FULL MOON.
CHUHAK (CREAK)

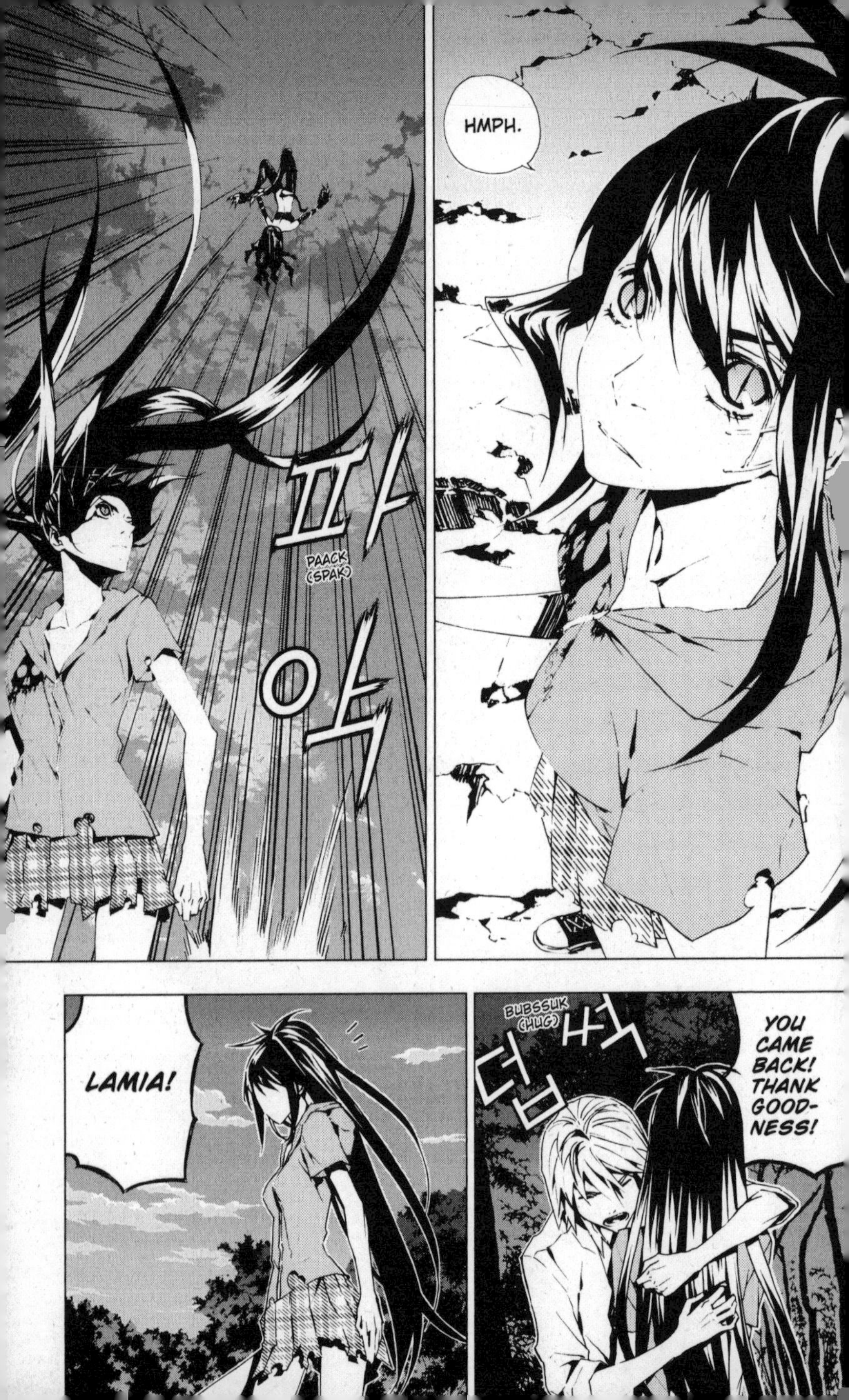
PAACK (SPAK)
HMPH.
LAMIA!
BUBSSUK (HUG)
YOU CAME BACK! THANK GOOD-NESS!

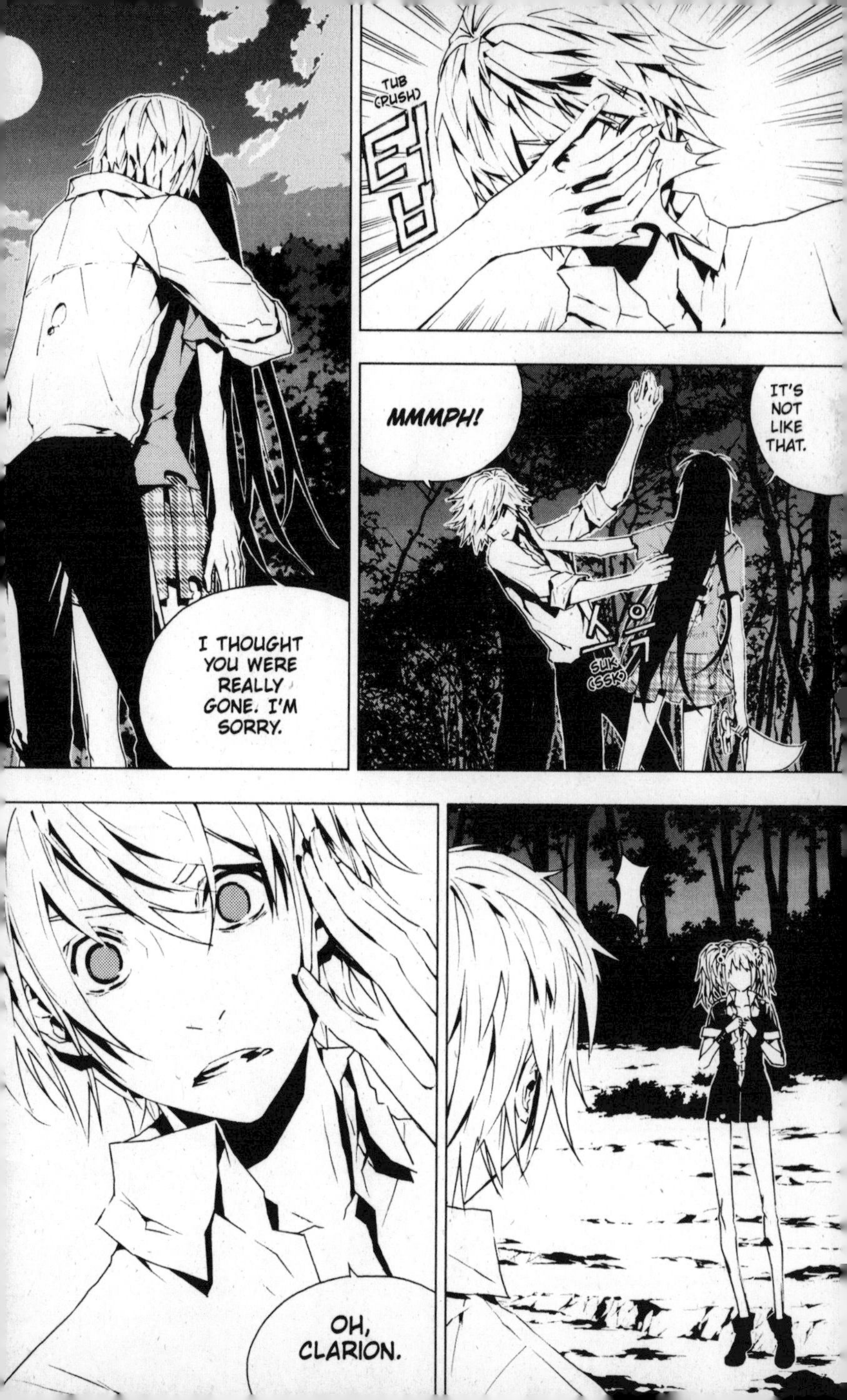
I THOUGHT YOU WERE REALLY GONE. I'M SORRY.
TUB (PUSH)
MMMPH!
IT'S NOT LIKE THAT.
SUK (SSK)
OH, CLARION.

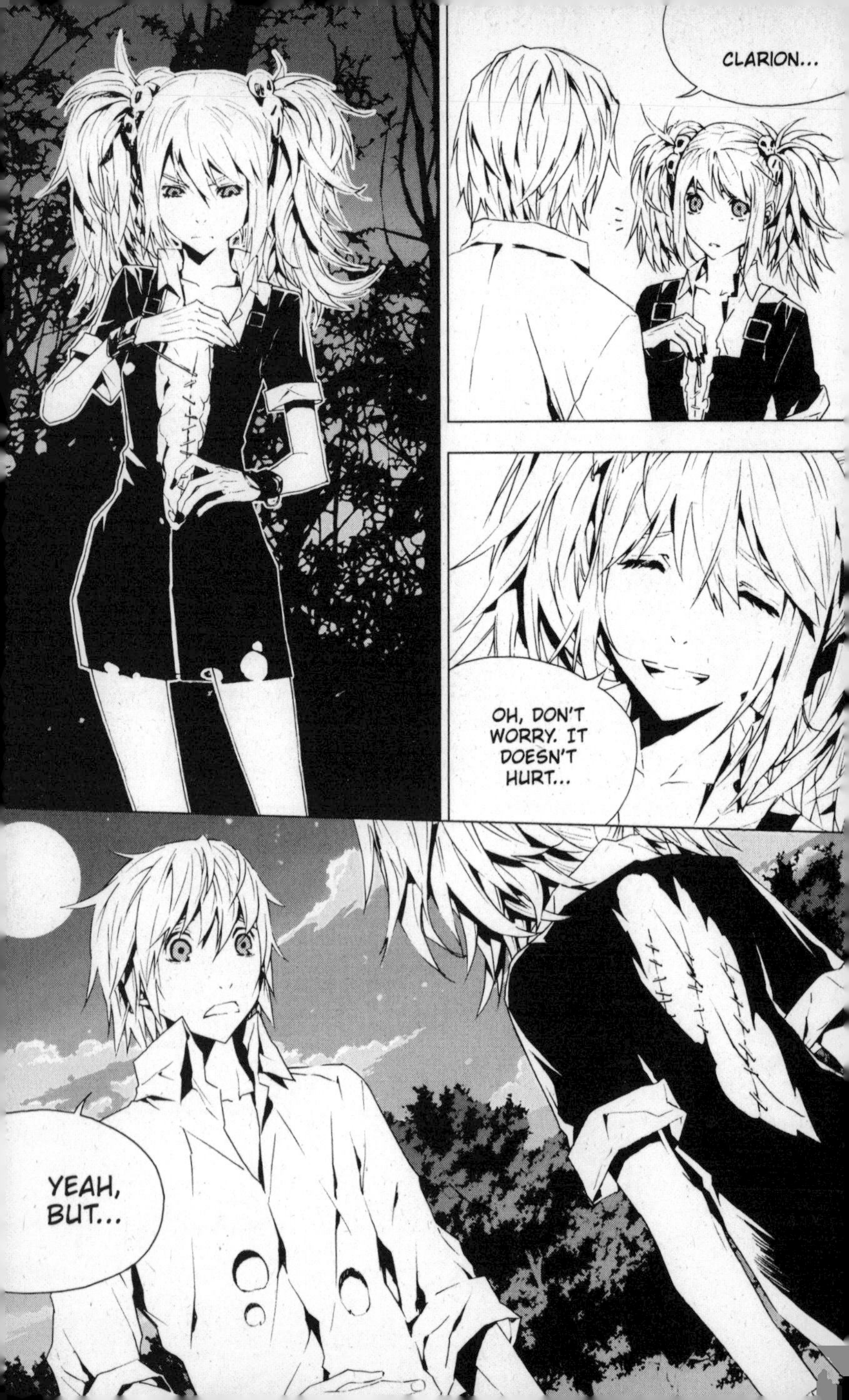
CLARION...
OH, DON'T WORRY. IT DOESN'T HURT...
YEAH, BUT...

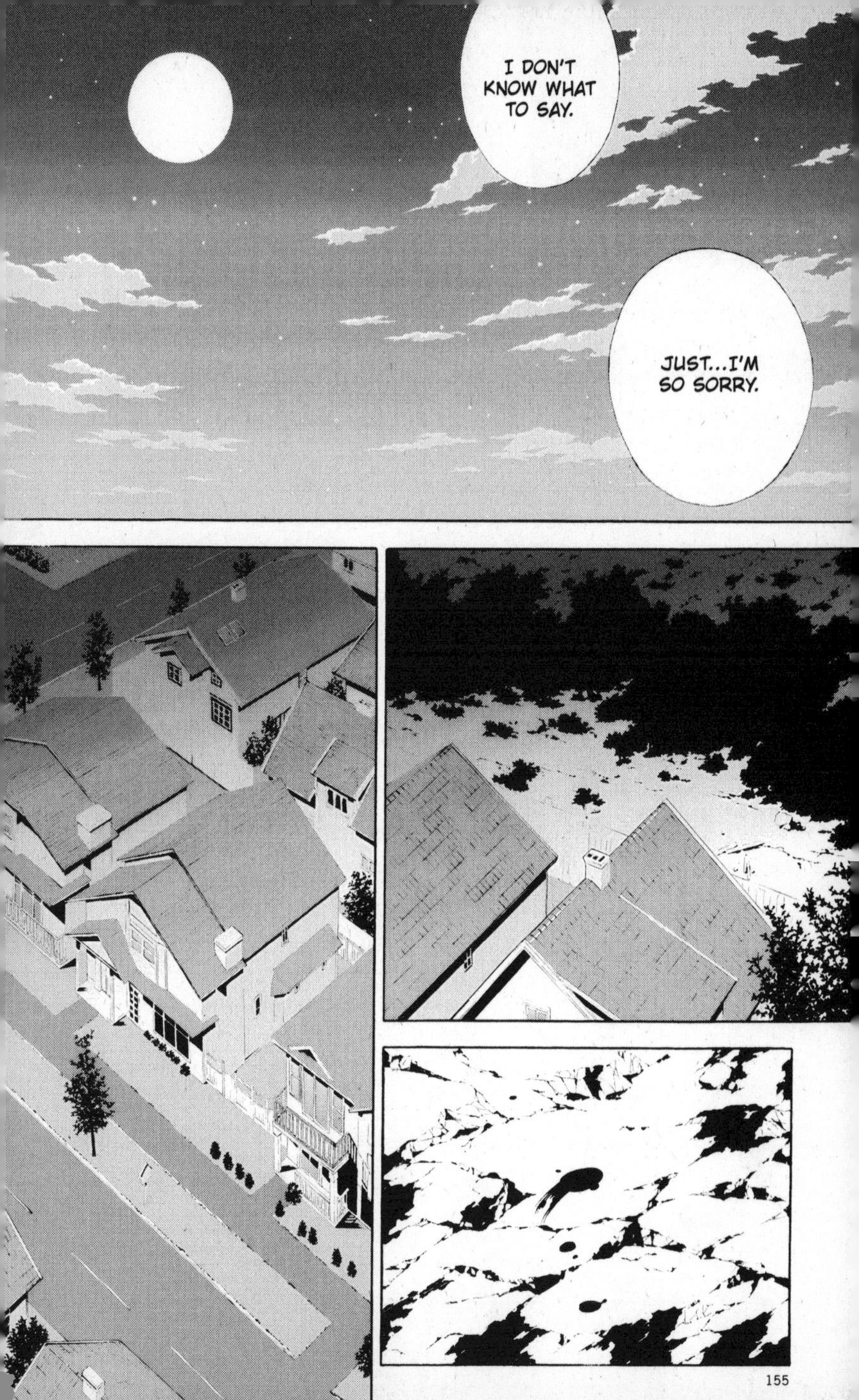
I DON'T KNOW WHAT TO SAY.
JUST...I'M SO SORRY.

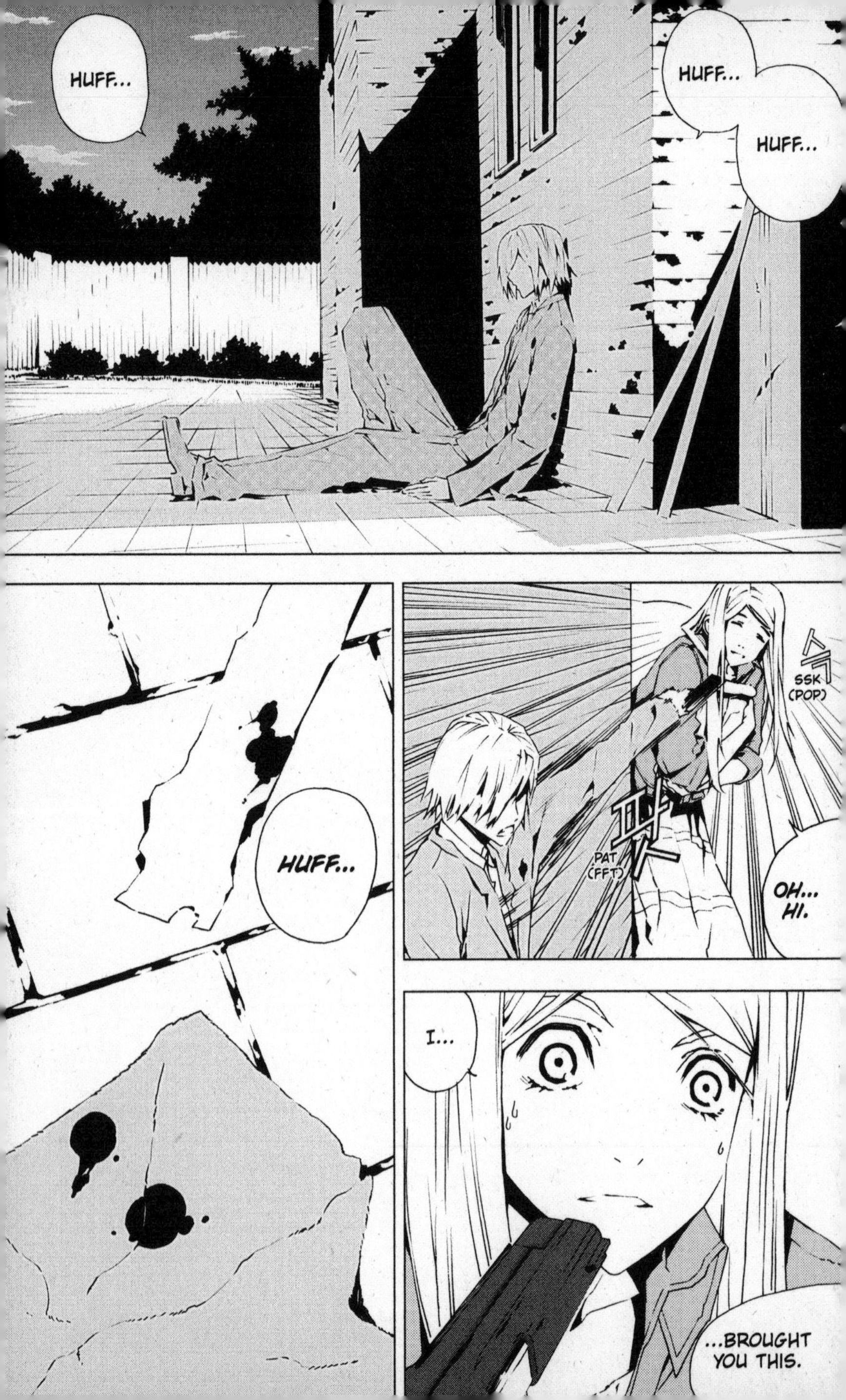
HUFF...
HUFF...
HUFF...
HUFF...
PAT (FFT)
SSK (POP)
OH... HI.
I...
...BROUGHT YOU THIS.

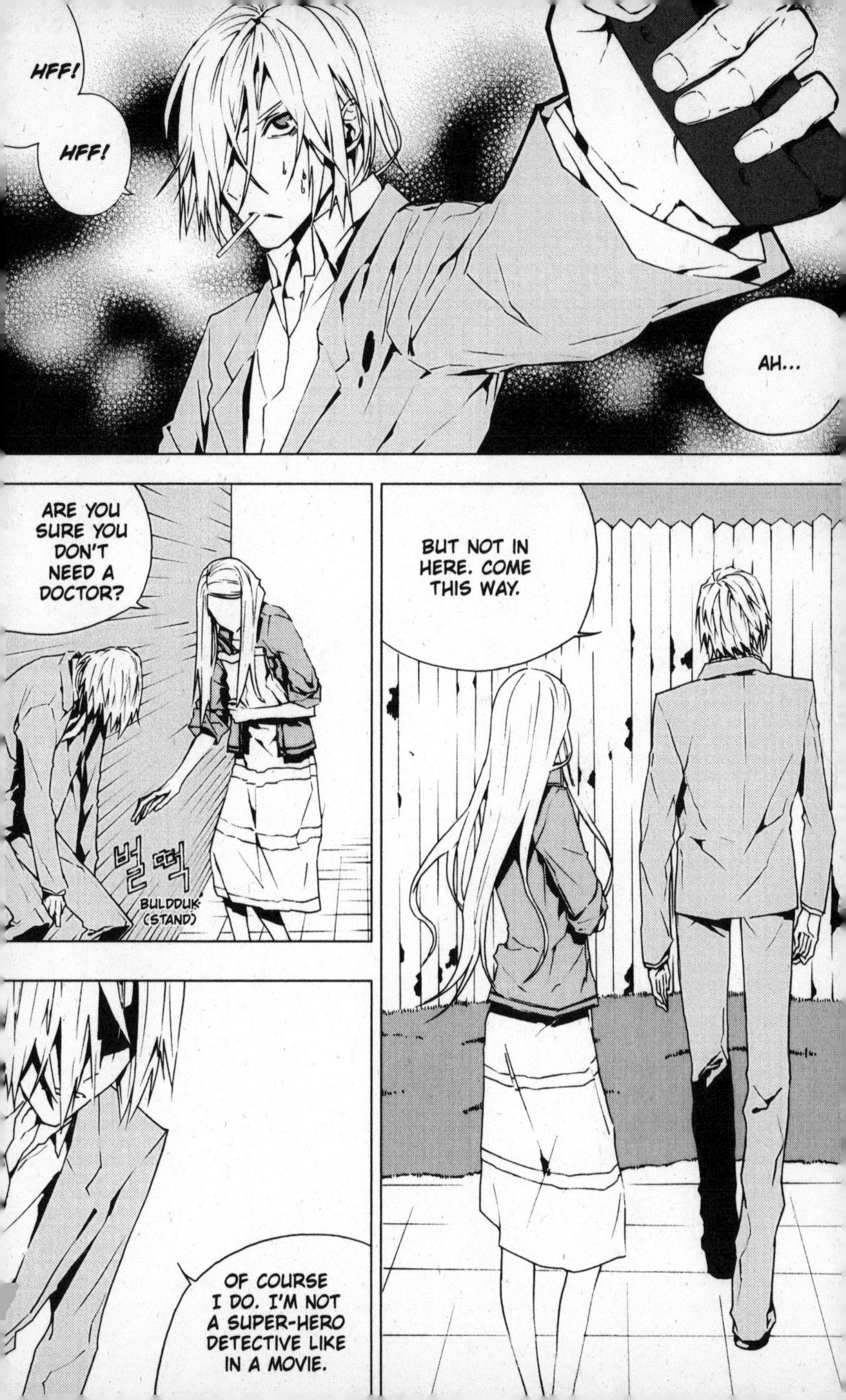
HFF!
HFF!
AH...
ARE YOU SURE YOU DON'T NEED A DOCTOR?
벌떡
BULDDUK (STAND)
OF COURSE I DO. I'M NOT A SUPER-HERO DETECTIVE LIKE IN A MOVIE.
BUT NOT IN HERE. COME THIS WAY.

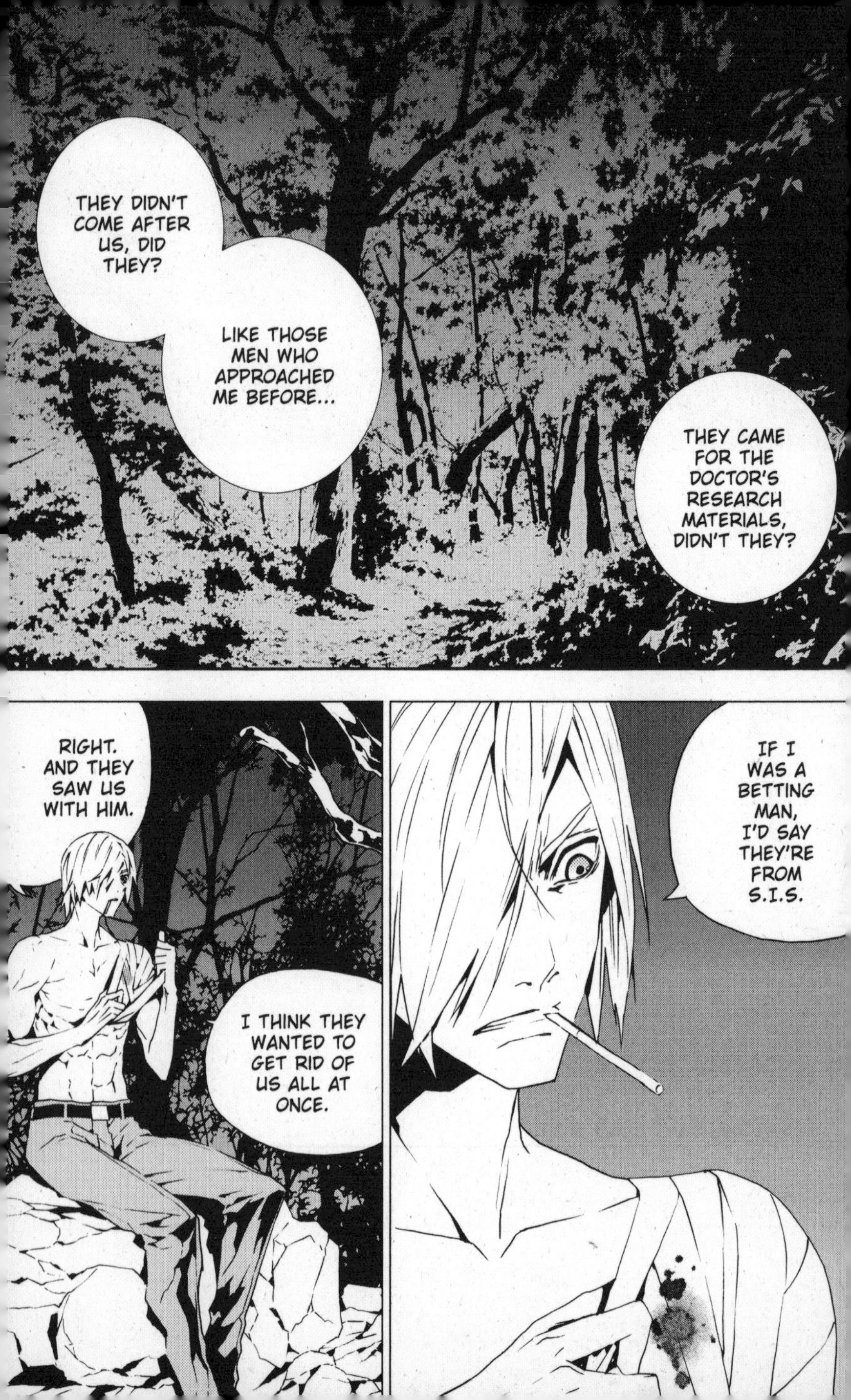
THEY DIDN'T COME AFTER US, DID THEY?
LIKE THOSE MEN WHO APPROACHED ME BEFORE...
THEY CAME FOR THE DOCTOR'S RESEARCH MATERIALS, DIDN'T THEY?
RIGHT. AND THEY SAW US WITH HIM.
I THINK THEY WANTED TO GET RID OF US ALL AT ONCE.
IF I WAS A BETTING MAN, I'D SAY THEY'RE FROM S.I.S.

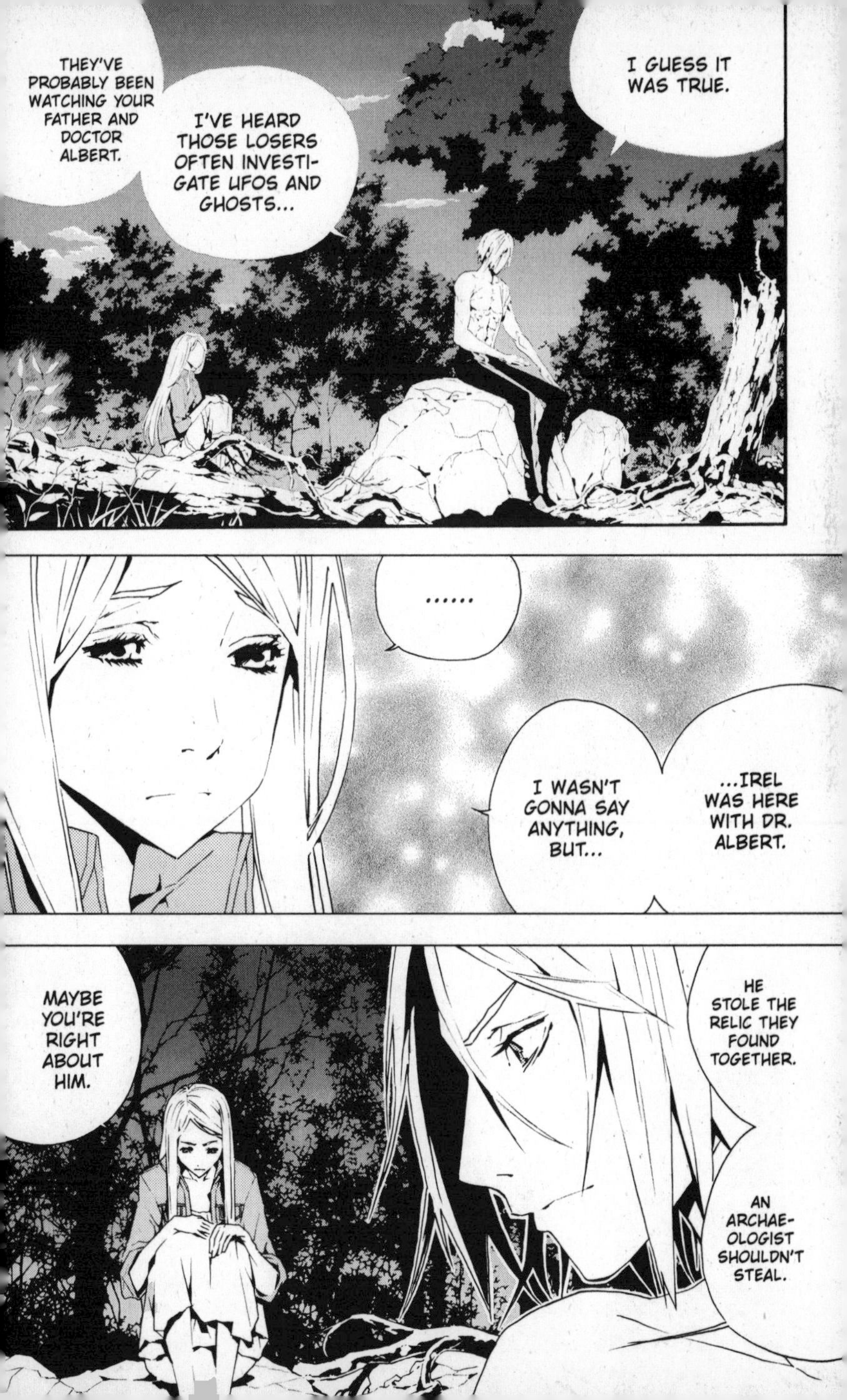
THEY'VE PROBABLY BEEN WATCHING YOUR FATHER AND DOCTOR ALBERT.
I'VE HEARD THOSE LOSERS OFTEN INVESTI-GATE UFOS AND GHOSTS...
I GUESS IT WAS TRUE.
......
I WASN'T GONNA SAY ANYTHING, BUT...
...IREL WAS HERE WITH DR. ALBERT.
MAYBE YOU'RE RIGHT ABOUT HIM.
HE STOLE THE RELIC THEY FOUND TOGETHER.
AN ARCHAE-OLOGIST SHOULDN'T STEAL.

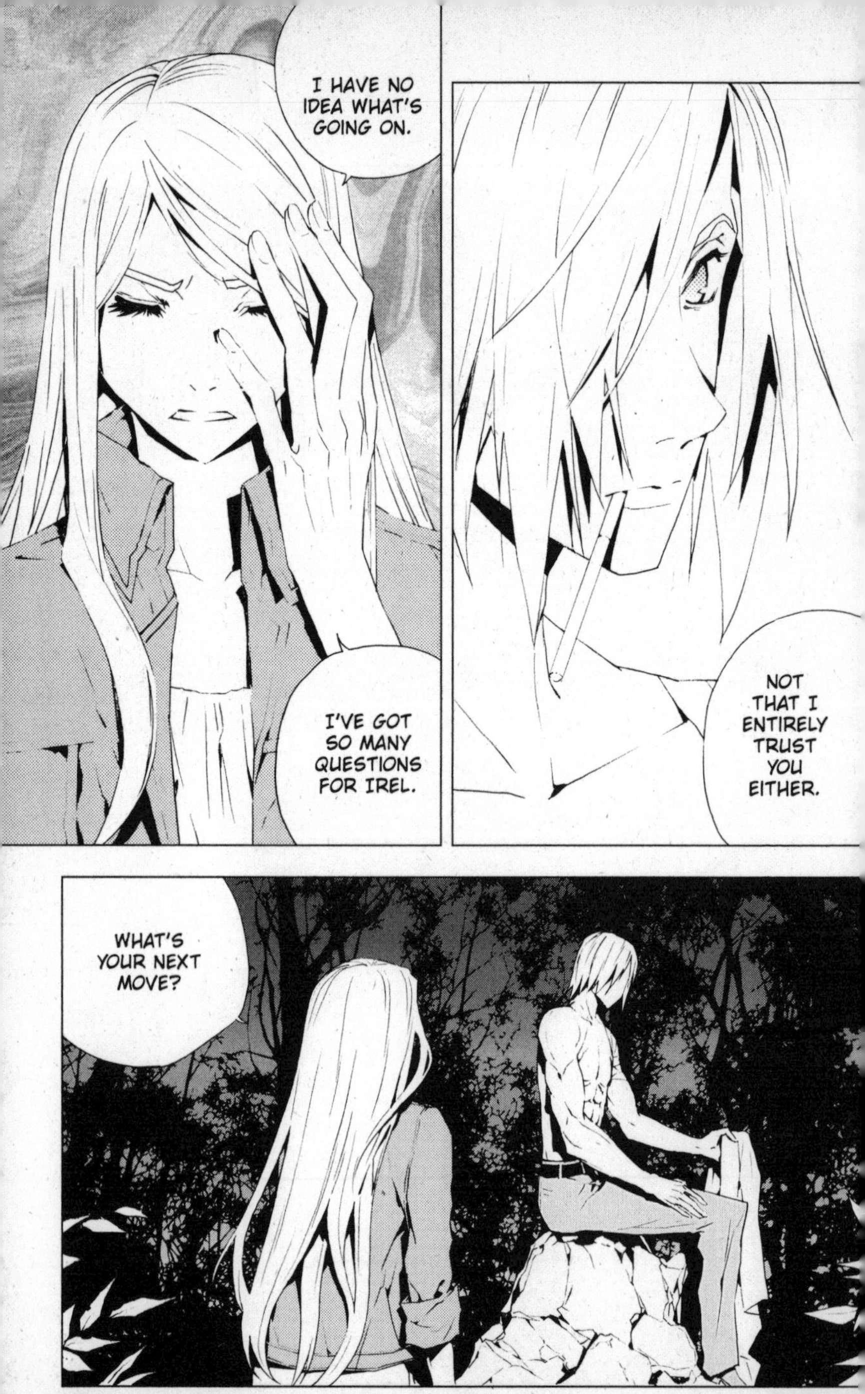
I HAVE NO IDEA WHAT'S GOING ON.
I'VE GOT SO MANY QUESTIONS FOR IREL.
NOT THAT I ENTIRELY TRUST YOU EITHER.
WHAT'S YOUR NEXT MOVE?

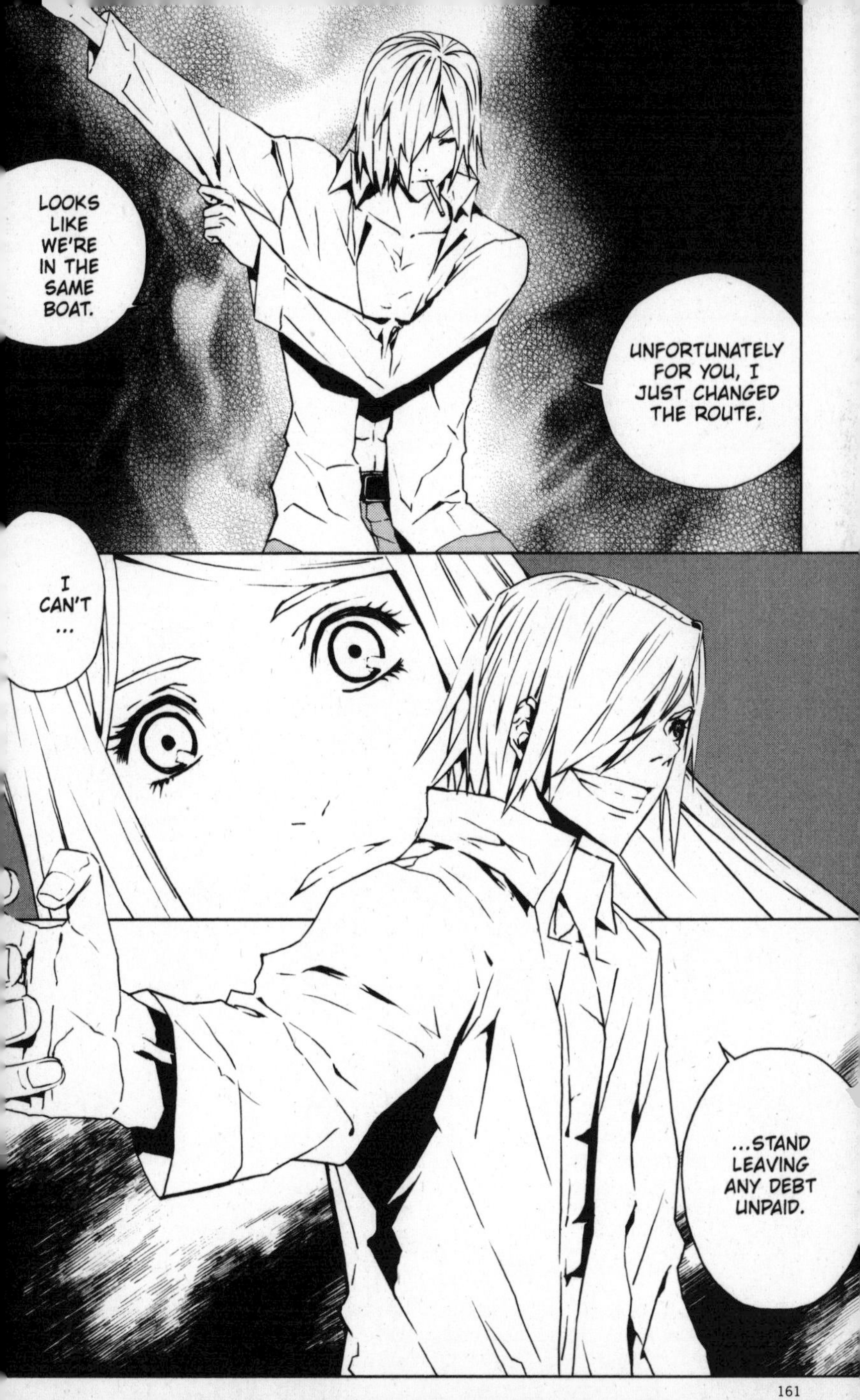
LOOKS LIKE WE'RE IN THE SAME BOAT.
UNFORTUNATELY FOR YOU, I JUST CHANGED THE ROUTE.
I CAN'T ...
...STAND LEAVING ANY DEBT UNPAID.

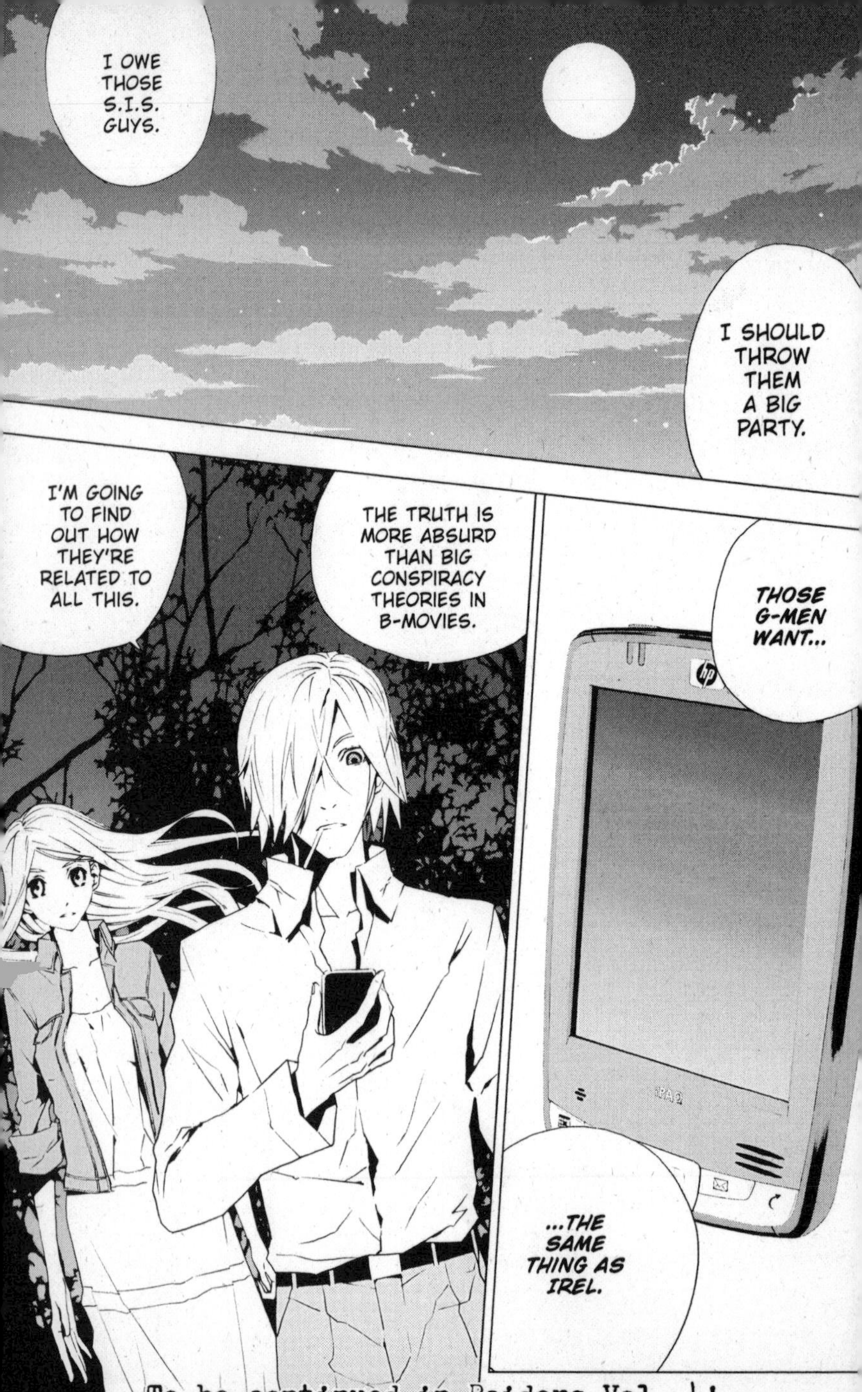
I OWE THOSE S.I.S. GUYS.
I SHOULD THROW THEM A BIG PARTY.
I'M GOING TO FIND OUT HOW THEY'RE RELATED TO ALL THIS.
THE TRUTH IS MORE ABSURD THAN BIG CONSPIRACY THEORIES IN B-MOVIES.
THOSE G-MEN WANT...
...THE SAME THING AS IREL.

To be continued in Raiders Vol. 4!

RAIDERS

To become the ultimate weapon, one boy must eat the souls of 99 humans...

...and one witch.

Maka is a scythe meister, working to perfect her demon scythe until it is good enough to become Death's Weapon—the weapon used by Shinigami-sama, the spirit of Death himself. And if that isn't strange enough, her scythe also has the power to change form—into a human-looking boy!

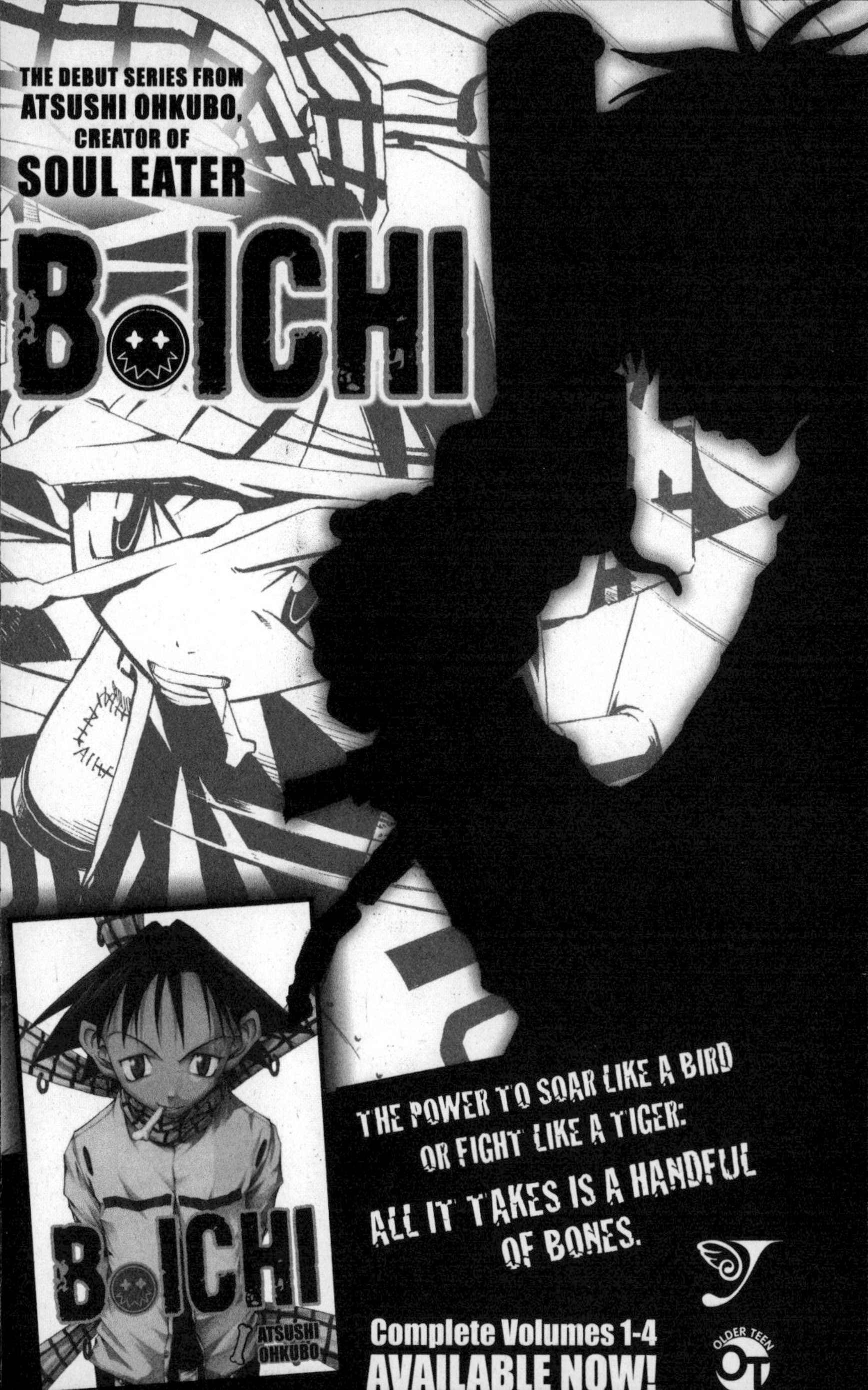
THE DEBUT SERIES FROM
ATSUSHI OHKUBO,
CREATOR OF
SOUL EATER
BOICHI
BOICHI
ATSUSHI OHKUBO
THE POWER TO SOAR LIKE A BIRD
OR FIGHT LIKE A TIGER:
ALL IT TAKES IS A HANDFUL
OF BONES.
Complete Volumes 1-4
AVAILABLE NOW!
OLDER TEEN
OT

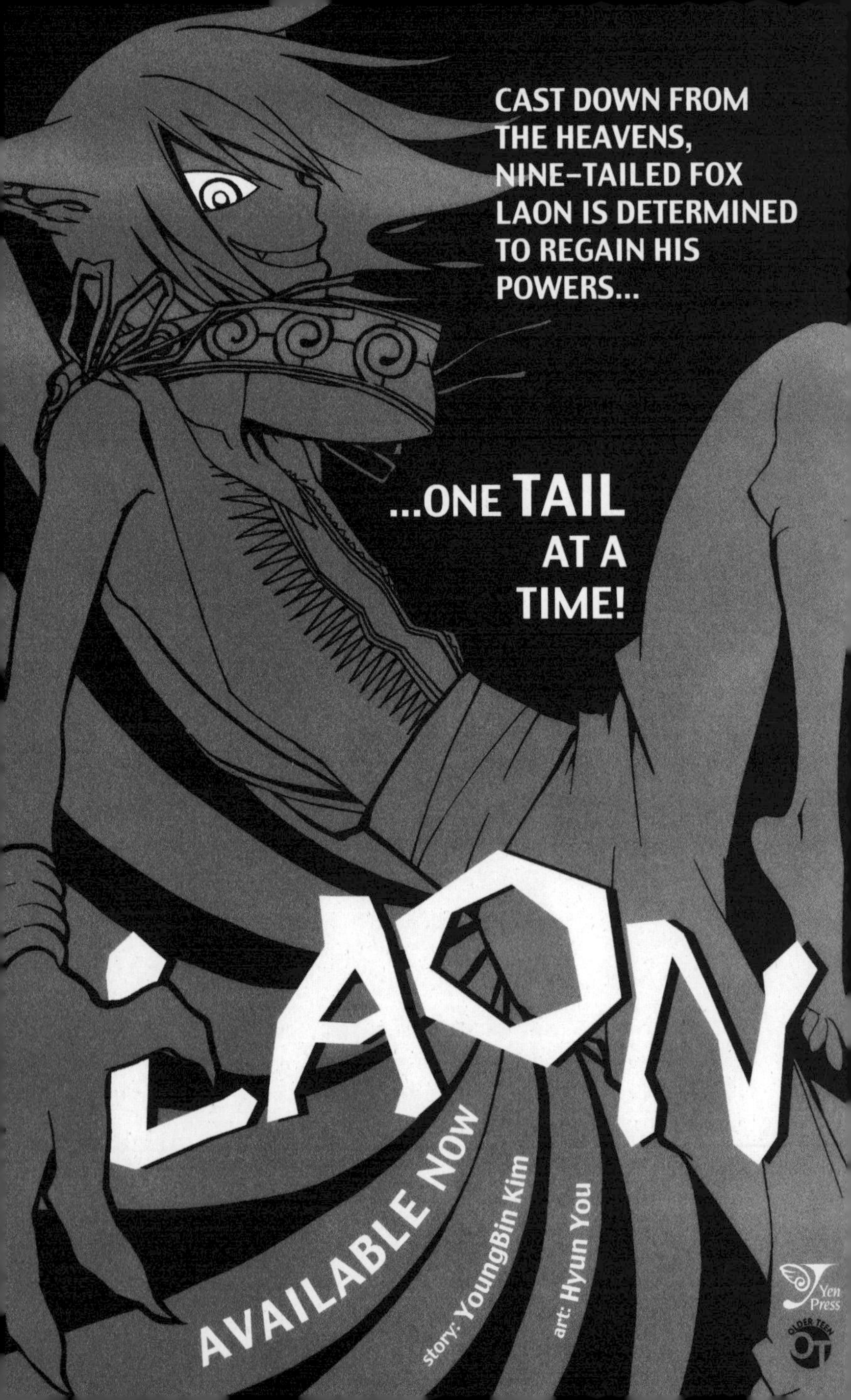

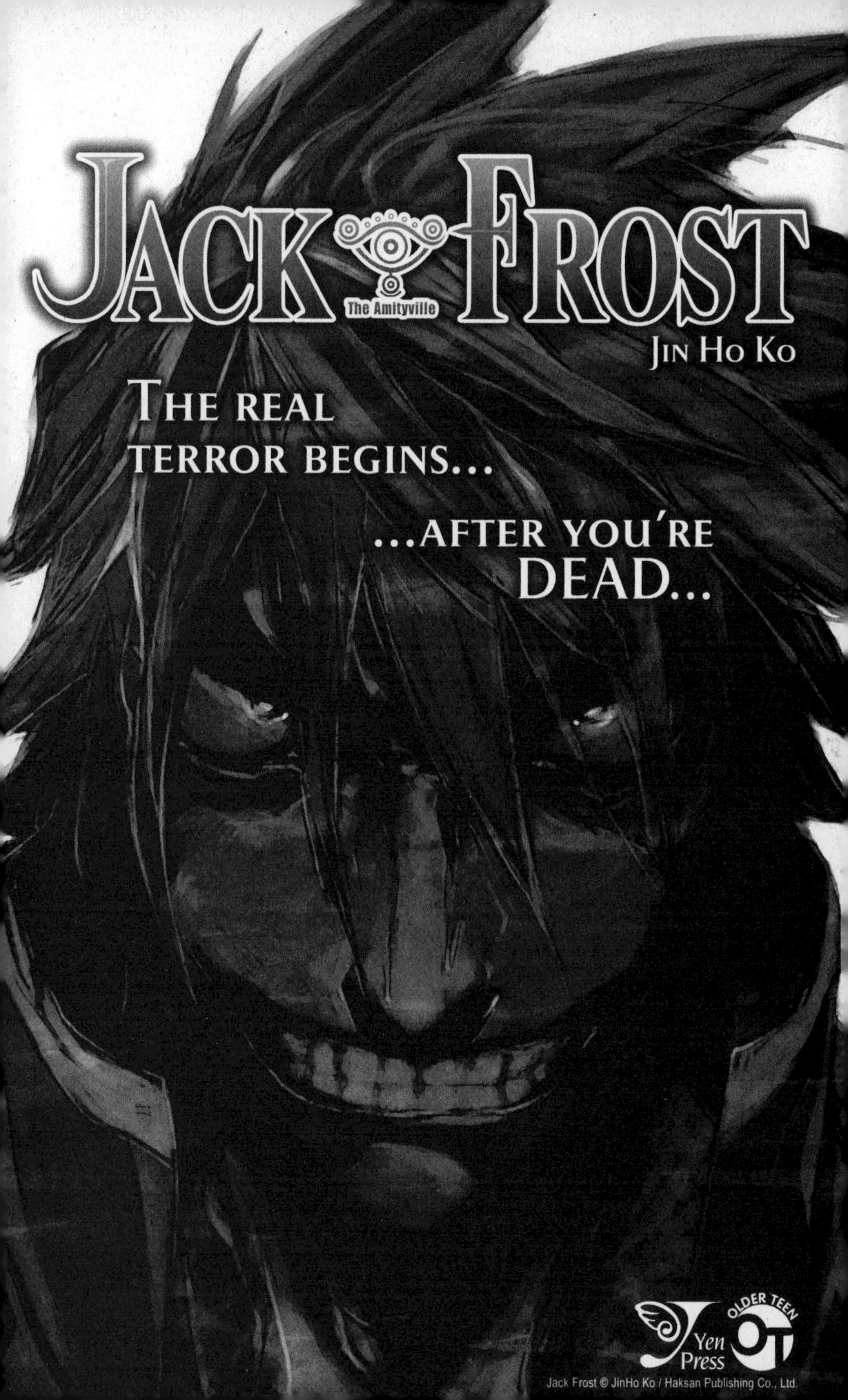
JACK FROST
The Amityville
JIN HO KO
THE REAL TERROR BEGINS...
...AFTER YOU'RE DEAD...
Yen Press
OLDER TEEN OT
Jack Frost © JinHo Ko / Haksan Publishing Co., Ltd.

Kieli sees ghosts.

Harvey cannot die.

He will throw her world into chaos...

...and become her one true friend.

STORY BY **Yukako Kabei**
ART BY **Shiori Teshirogi**

KIELI

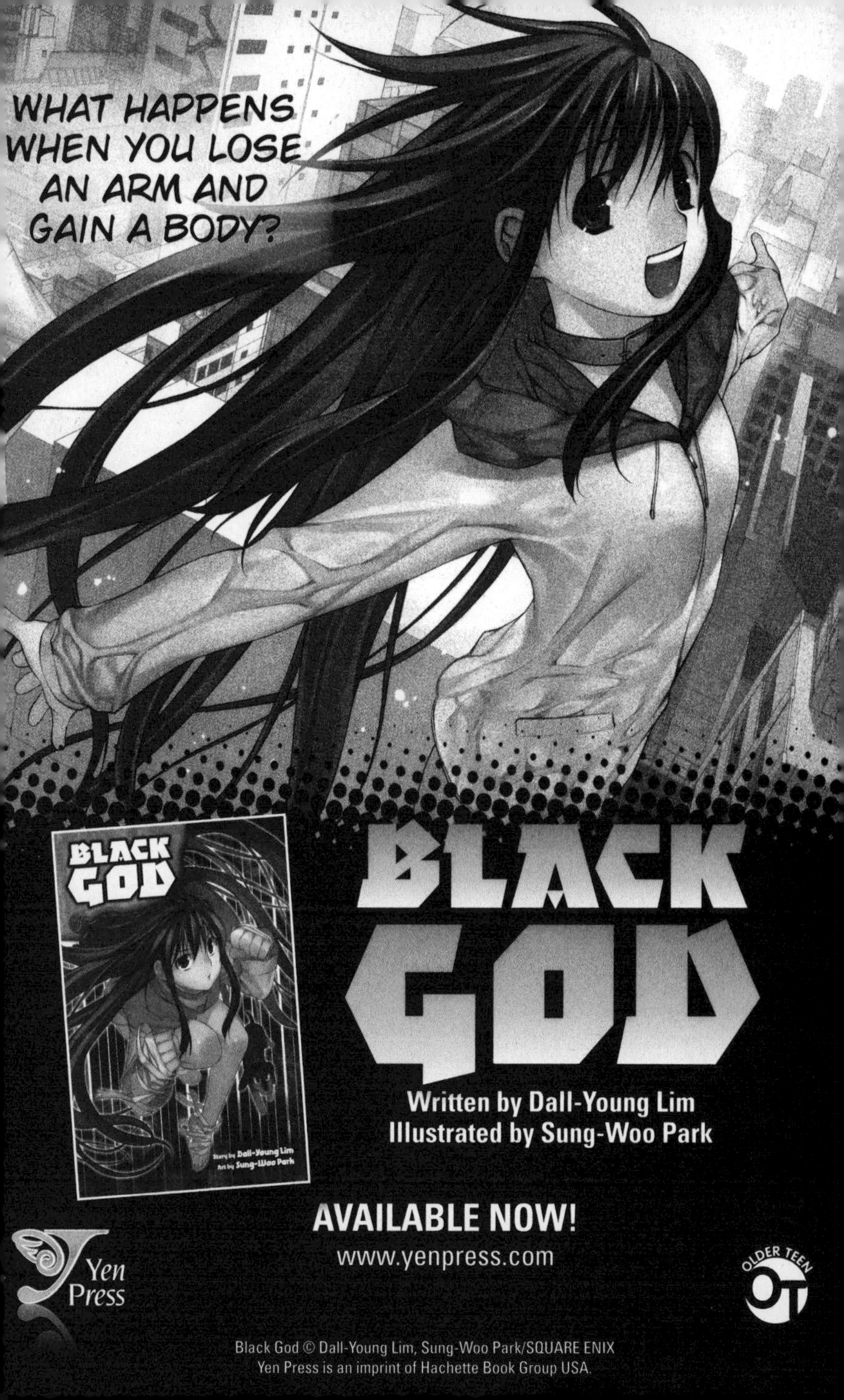
WHAT HAPPENS WHEN YOU LOSE AN ARM AND GAIN A BODY?
BLACK GOD
Story by Dall-Young Lim
Art by Sung-Woo Park
BLACK GOD
Written by Dall-Young Lim
Illustrated by Sung-Woo Park
AVAILABLE NOW!
www.yenpress.com
Yen Press
OLDER TEEN
OT
Black God © Dall-Young Lim, Sung-Woo Park/SQUARE ENIX
Yen Press is an imprint of Hachette Book Group USA.

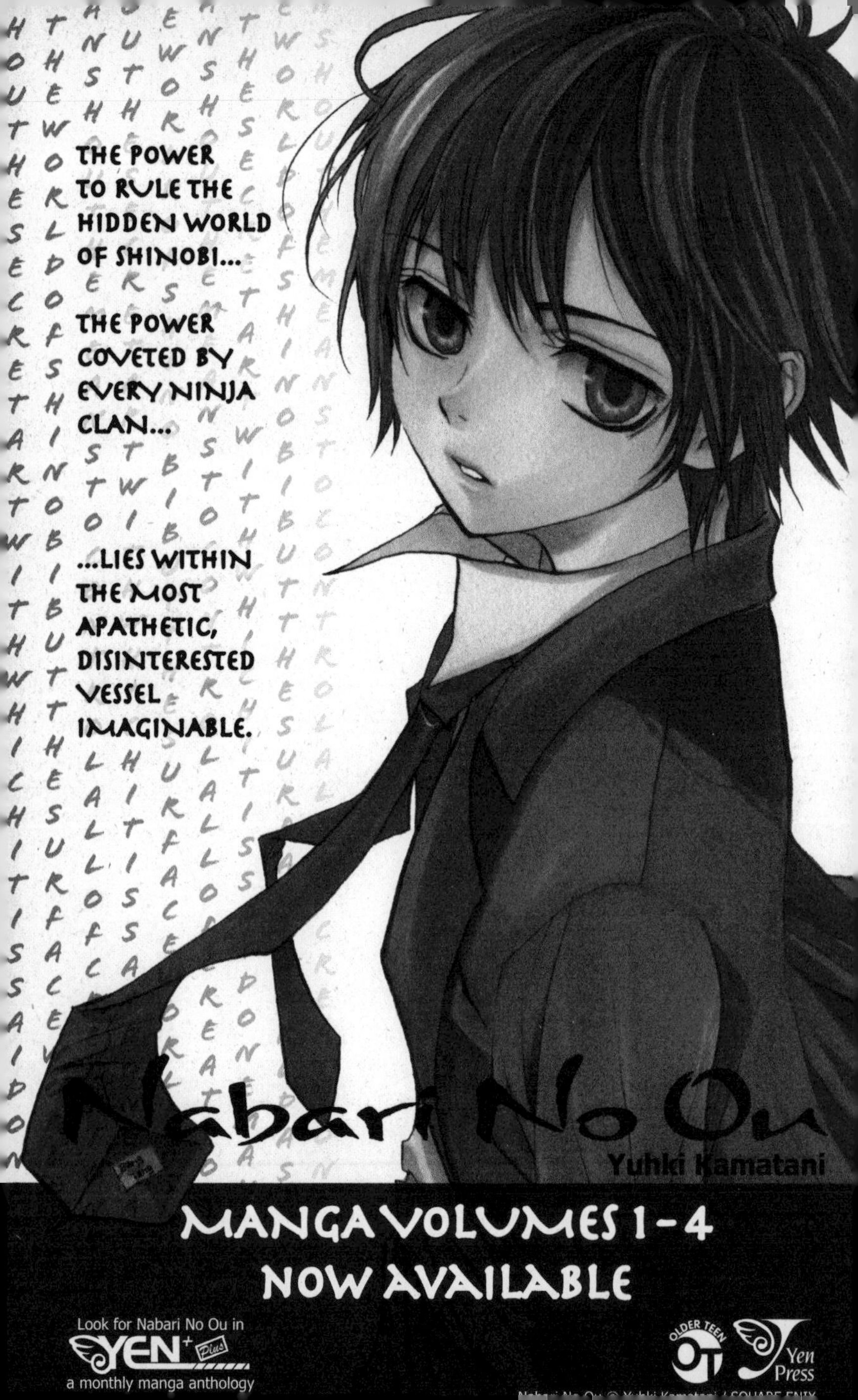
THE POWER TO RULE THE HIDDEN WORLD OF SHINOBI...
THE POWER COVETED BY EVERY NINJA CLAN...
...LIES WITHIN THE MOST APATHETIC, DISINTERESTED VESSEL IMAGINABLE.
Nabari No Ou
Yuhki Kamatani
MANGA VOLUMES 1-4 NOW AVAILABLE
Look for Nabari No Ou in
YEN+ Plus
a monthly manga anthology
OLDER TEEN OT
Yen Press

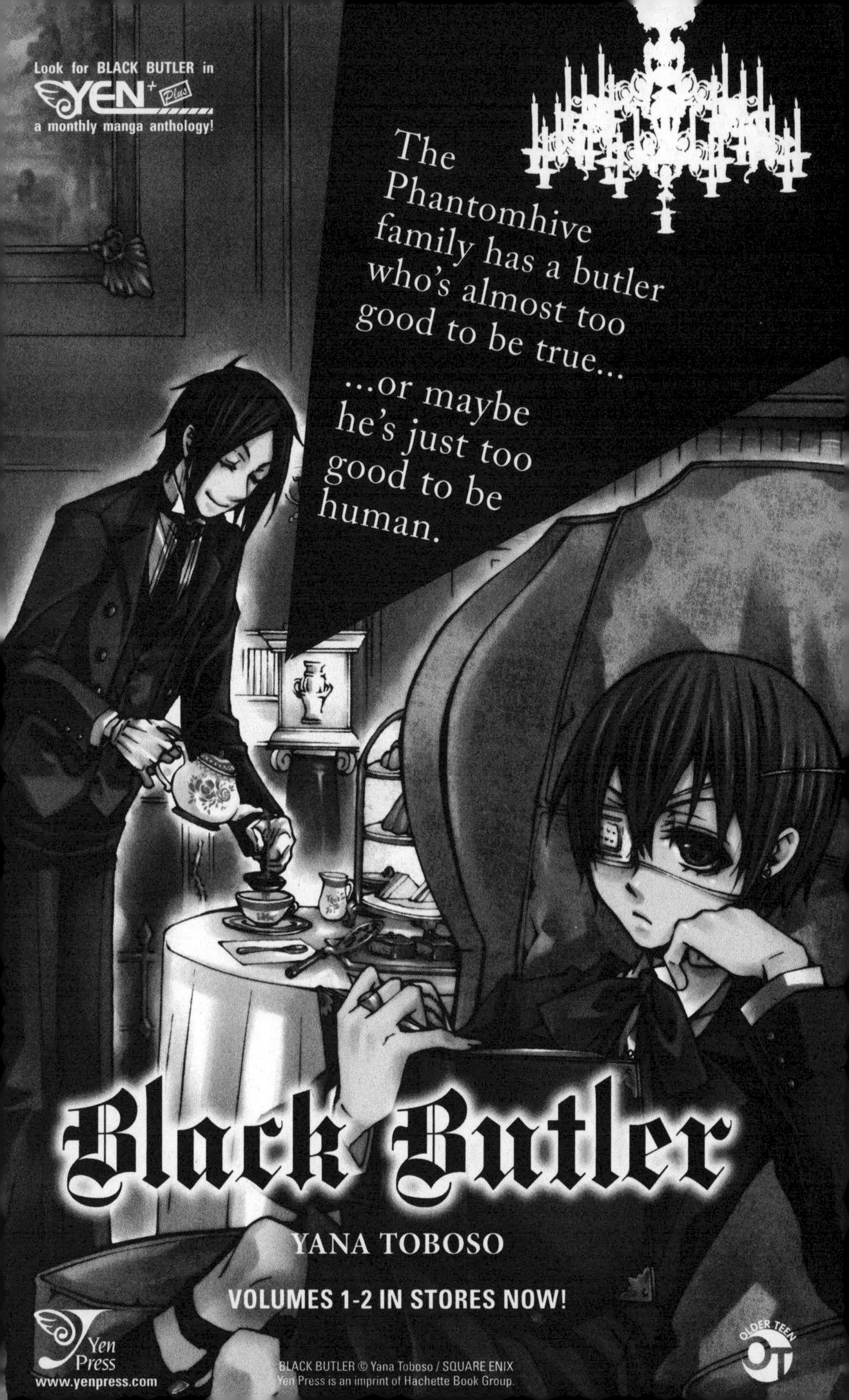
Look for BLACK BUTLER in
YEN+ Plus
a monthly manga anthology!
The Phantomhive family has a butler who's almost too good to be true...
...or maybe he's just too good to be human.
Black Butler
YANA TOBOSO
VOLUMES 1-2 IN STORES NOW!
Yen Press
www.yenpress.com
BLACK BUTLER © Yana Toboso / SQUARE ENIX
Yen Press is an imprint of Hachette Book Group.
OLDER TEEN
OT

CAT FIGHT ON CAMPUS...

Cat-lovers flock to Matabi Academy, where each student is allowed to bring their pet cat to the dorms.

Unfortunately, the grounds aren't just crawling with cats...

...an ancient evil lurks on campus, and only the combined efforts of student and feline can hold them at bay...

IN STORES NOW!

CAT
PARADISE

YUJI IWAHARA

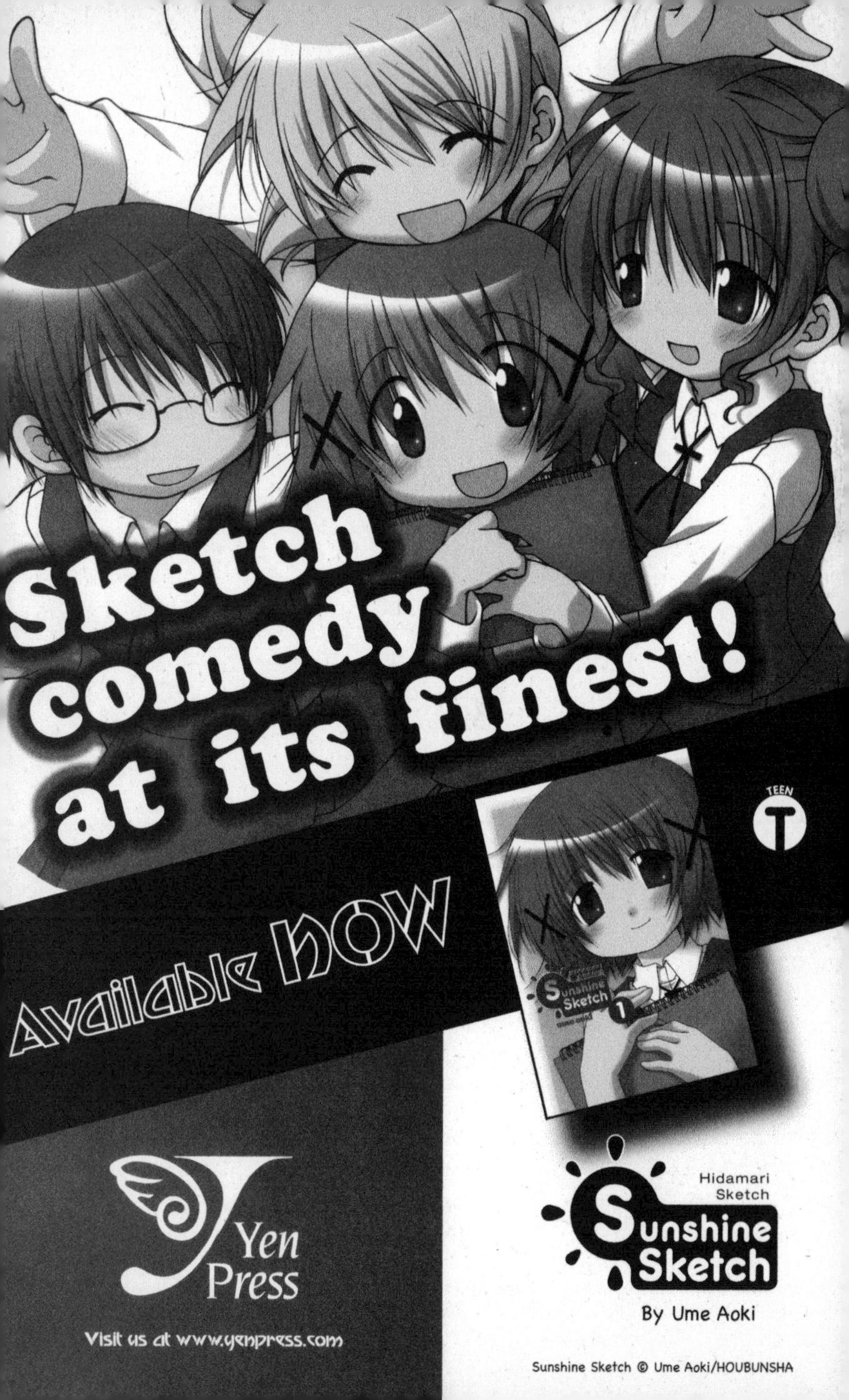

Sketch comedy at its finest!
TEEN
T
Sunshine Sketch 1
Available NOW
Yen Press
Visit us at www.yenpress.com
Hidamari Sketch
Sunshine Sketch
By Ume Aoki
Sunshine Sketch © Ume Aoki/HOUBUNSHA

Hello! This is YOTSUBA!

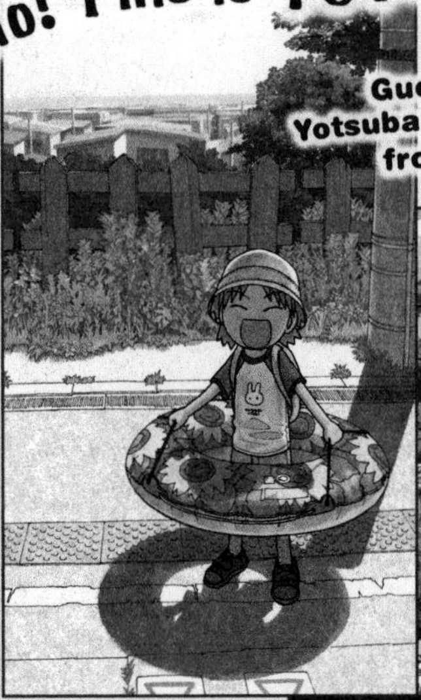

**Guess what? Guess what?
Yotsuba and Daddy just moved here
from waaaay over there!**

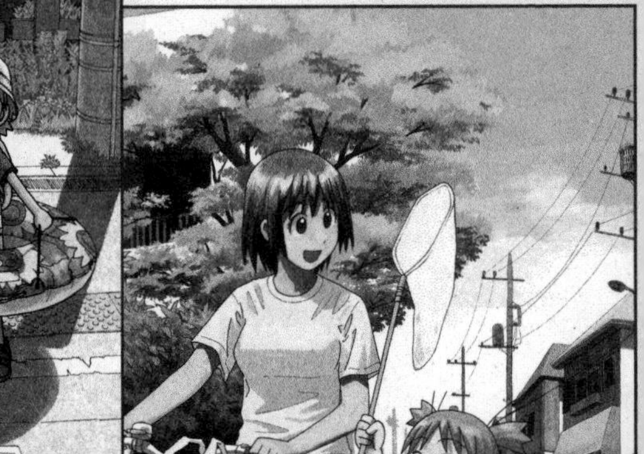

**And Yotsuba met these
nice people next door and made
new friends to play with!**

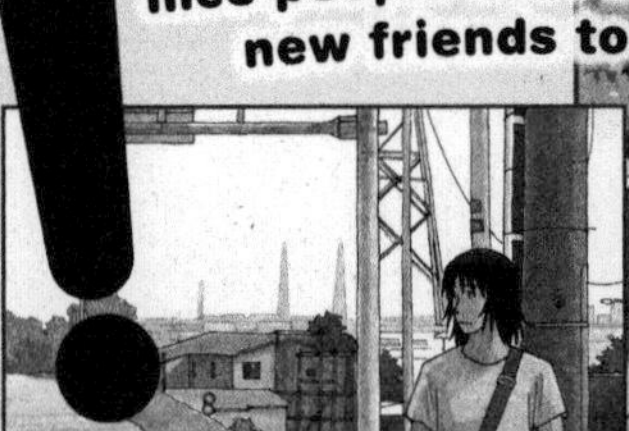

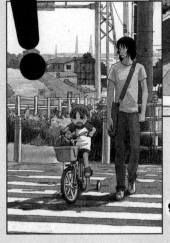

**The pretty one took
Yotsuba on a bike ride!**
(Whoooa! There was a big hill!)

And Ena's a good drawer!
(Almost as good as Yotsuba!)

**And their mom always
gives Yotsuba ice cream!**
(Yummy!)

**And...
And...
OHHHH!**

RAIDERS ❸

JINJUN PARK

Translation: JiEun Park • English Adaptation: Jamie S. Rich

Lettering: Chris Counasse

RAIDERS, vol. 3 © 2008 by PARK Jin-jun, DAEWON C.I. Inc. All rights reserved.
First published in Korea in 2008 by DAEWON C.I. Inc. English translation rights in
USA, Canada, UK and Commonwealth arranged by Daewon C.I. Inc. through TOPAZ
Agency Inc.

Translation © 2010 by Hachette Book Group, Inc.

Yen Press
Hachette Book Group
237 Park Avenue, New York, NY 10017

www.HachetteBookGroup.com
www.YenPress.com

Yen Press is an imprint of Hachette Book Group, Inc. The Yen Press name and logo
are trademarks of Hachette Book Group, Inc.

First Yen Press Edition: July 2010

ISBN: 978-0-7595-3051-5

10 9 8 7 6 5 4 3 2 1

BVG

Printed in the United States of America